A History of Children's Play and Play Environments

Children's play has historically been free, spontaneous, intertwined with work, and set in the playgrounds of the wilderness, fields, streams, and barnyards. Children in cities enjoyed similar forms of play but their playgrounds were the vacant lands, parks, and surrounding countryside or seashore. Today, children have become increasingly inactive, abandoning traditional outdoor play for sedentary, indoor cyber play, and diets of junk food. The consequences of play deprivation, the elimination and diminution of recess, and the abandonment of outdoor play are fundamental issues in a growing crisis that threatens the health, learning, and development of children.

This valuable book traces the history of children's play and play environments from their roots in ancient Greece and Rome to the present time in the high stakes testing environment. Distinguished scholar Dr. Joe Frost explores the evolving nature of children's play in both natural and built play environments, chronicles its benefits, and identifies impediments to play and playgrounds. Through this exploration, the author shows how this history informs where we are today and why we need to re-establish play as a priority. Ultimately, the author proposes active solutions to play deprivation—a much needed child-saving movement to preserve children's free, spontaneous outdoor play, recess, and natural and built play environments. This book is a must-read for scholars, researchers, and students in the fields of early childhood education and child development.

Joe L. Frost is the Parker Centennial Professor Emeritus, University of Texas.

D0322593

A History of Children's Play and Play Environments

Toward a Contemporary Child-Saving Movement

Joe L. Frost

Routledge
Taylor & Francis Group

NEW YORK AND LONDON

First published 2010
by Routledge
270 Madison Ave,
New York, NY 10016
Simultaneously published in the U.K.

by Routledge
2 Park Square,
Milton Park, Abingdon,
Oxon OX14 4RN

Routledge is an imprint of the Taylor & Francis Group, an informa business

© 2010 Taylor and Francis

Typeset in Minion Pro by Keyword Group Ltd.

Printed and bound in the United States of America on acid-free paper by Walsworth Publishing Company, Marceline, MO

Library of Congress Cataloging in Publication Data

Frost, Joe L.
A history of children's play and play environments : toward a contemporary child-saving movement/ Joe L. Frost.
p. cm.
Includes bibliographical references and index.
ISBN 978-0-415-80619-0 (hb : alk. paper) – ISBN 978-0-415-80620-6 (pb : alk. paper) –
ISBN 978-0-203-86865-2 (ebook) 1. Play. 2. Early childhood education. 3. Child development–
United States. I. Title.
LB1139.35.P55F765 2009
306.4′81–dc22   2009014942

British Library Cataloguing in Publication Data

A catalogue record for this book is available from the British Library

ISBN 10: 0-415-80619-4 (hbk)
ISBN 10: 0-415-80620-8 (pbk)
ISBN 10: 0-203-86865-X (ebk)
ISBN 13: 978-0-415-80619-0 (hbk)
ISBN 13: 978-0-415-80620-6 (pbk)
ISBN 13: 978-0-203-86865-2 (ebk)

Dedication

This book is dedicated to my family.
To my wonderful wife, Betty, who patiently accepts my
absence and freely gives her wise counsel.
To Nita and Tom, Terry and Bill, and Hailey and
Blake, who enrich our lives and the lives of their students,
friends, and colleagues.

Contents

List of Figures

List of Tables

Foreword

As I read Joe Frost's book, I find myself repeatedly asking and finding answers to major questions about human nature, culture, and the future of our species. These are fostered by the compelling evidence and historic landscapes of children's play so systematically organized, and through the loving output of evidences having been gleaned over the author's lifetime. They are presented in a rich menu of wonderful vignettes, facts, stories of heroic play pioneers, and the ebb and flow of how we see and have seen our children and what we have or have not done throughout the ages to and for them and in highly varied circumstances.

So some of the questions that come to mind while reading are: who are we humans, really, and what are we if the freedom for childhood play is lost or seriously deficient? It is clear between the lines and from the evidence presented that the destinies of our pluralistic society, the ability to pass on health and well-being, and perhaps the survival of the world itself require adherence to the solutions the author shows as being now mandatory in the realities of the twenty-first century. So this is more than a historic review. It speaks to the heart of what it is to be fully human, and to be so requires a legacy of play.

Here presented also is the weight of evidence for the multiple play-deficiency crises that now engulf our children and youth. These are different in our era than any other in history; they have accelerated rapidly and are more serious, more complex now than ever before. The context in which to put our current play-status has never been so vividly presented as in the pages that follow. Between the lines, again and again play can be seen as sowing the seeds of our competency. Its hijacking by the manifold themes of current cultural norms is ominous. Yet because play is so pervasive in our beings, and can be transformative, the overall messages of the last chapter are ones of extreme challenge, with practical solutions and collectively available hope—good and important themes for fostering idealism and vocational choices for the next generations.

My personal approaches to understanding play behavior have been to assess the clinical individual consequences of both its absence and its glowing presence and, through detailed review of animal and human play states, to place play behavior in an evolutionary, biological, and behavioral science framework. What Joe's comprehensive historic review has provided me personally is deep confirmation of its nature and importance over time collectively in the evolving real world. Whatever your orientation, you will find a play home and activist motivation within this book.

It takes the freedom to jump, chase, wrestle, imagine, build, joke, tease, watch the clouds form angels, talk to your dog, be safe to ask a dumb question of your teacher, and—if in rural Arkansas like Joe as a boy—dog-pile and catapult your friends skyward in a space that is your own. Play belongs, and you belong to play.

Stuart L. Brown, M.D.
Founder and President of the National Institute for Play
Carmel Valley, CA

Preface

This book is about children's play and play environments, two interdependent entities that have much to do with children's development and well-being. The intent here is to trace play and play environments across centuries to find clues for preserving and enhancing them for children. Given the crisis resulting from the diminution, modification, and/or disappearance of play and its traditional environments during the latter twentieth century, this is a worthy task. The focus of the book is on the importance of play, the consequences of not playing, and the prevention and remediation of those consequences. As in other historic events or crises threatening the welfare of many people, history offers insight into problems and solutions and provides perspective and a potential resolution for later generations.

Throughout the twentieth century scholars unsuccessfully wrestled with the formation of a clear definition of play, but to date none is clear or unequivocal. Across the century, proposed definitions reflected the academic roles of their developers, primarily behavioral scientists, resulting in a "crazy quilt" of theories about its meaning and purposes. Here is a sampling gleaned from various sources: play is broad, not narrow; play applies in humans, animals, adults, and children; play can be long or short; play involves leadership or domination (hegemony); play may involve social context; play is imaginary ('as if'ness); play involves frivolity; play involves peak experience and flow; play has biological underpinnings; play affects brain function; play is chaos—and the list continues. For each motive for play, one can construct a definition or at least a tenuous explanation, and, in circular fashion, for each explanation one can extract a motive. The motives include power (rivalry, recognition, and possession), acculturation (mastery, self-identification, and adaptation), and therapeutic (pleasure, arousal, and relaxation). This book will focus on the importance of play, the contexts of play, the consequences of not playing (play deprivation), and the proposed solutions for such deprivation. One of my several attempts at a definition was:

> Play is voluntary activity of ludic and imaginary quality that emerges from biological foundations through the child's initial solitary and social interactions with objects and people. Play is manifested and elaborated through games and amusements, and results in cognitive, social, motor, linguistic, and emotional growth and development. Play has therapeutic powers, yielding positions of cognitive clarity, power, and primacy to the player. (Frost, 2002, paper prepared for a conference address)

And in a more poetic mood: "Spontaneous play is the delicate dance of childhood that strengthens the mind and body, and nourishes the soul."

Play and play environments are inextricably interrelated. Both matter. The term "play environments" has broad meanings, encompasses many contexts, and is used interchangeably throughout this book with "playgrounds," "playscapes," "natural playscapes," "built playgrounds," and "grounds for play." "Playgrounds" is most frequently used to denote built places in schoolyards, parks, and backyards, but the term is also used to describe virtually all places where children gather to play, for example "cyber playgrounds" for playing indoors with video games, or elaborate "water playscapes" at theme parks; even places where adults go for entertainment may be called "playgrounds." Now, with the exploding interest in and action on getting children back to nature, labels such as "naturescapes" and "playscapes" are becoming more common. We cannot bring back to urbanbound children the expansive "wildscapes" for play enjoyed by most children for centuries, but we can bring back little pieces of them to complement their contemporary playthings and enrich their lives. Given the disappearance of nature and traditional children's play from children's lives, a "reemphasis on nature" is sorely needed, and a growing movement is addressing this need. Many skills attainable through playing with cyber toys and carefully selected play equipment are beneficial for child development, fitness, and success in a modern, technological, urban oriented age. It is balance children need in their play and in their grounds for play.

Joe L. Frost
March 24, 2009

Acknowledgments

I can never repay the generous people who influenced this book but wish to acknowledge the direct and indirect contributions of a few, while realizing that many who contributed indirectly remain anonymous.

To the University of Texas graduate students who created play environments in schools and neighborhoods and conducted on-site research, I am indebted and express regret for not having kept in closer touch; our world traveling "Johnny Appleseed," Jimi (James) Jolley (deceased), Sue and Marshal Wortham, Barry Klein, Marcia Guddemi, Eric Strickland, Marion Monroe (deceased), Libby Vernon, Ann Barbour, Mary Ruth Moore, Michael Henniger, Michael Bell, Sheila Campbell, John Alvarez, Lily Chiang, Joan Kissinger, Heeyeon Kim, Gloria Gamez, James Dempsey, Chiuchu Chuang, Sheila Deacon, Arturo Gutierrez, Steve Hoppes, Ronald Jackson, Jim Therrell, Paul Jacobs, Deborah Wisneski, Isabel Keesee, Stephan Jackson, Linda Jones, Dannette Littleton, Gloria Zamora, Sylvia Yang, Suzanne Winter, Wen-yueh Lu, Robert Maniss, Mary Dodge, Pauline Walker, Paula Matthews, Elizabeth Taylor, Cynthia Wade, Darryl Townsend, Rick Strot, Jill Thrift, Dongju Shin, Gwen Myers, Judy Blalock, Jackie Myers (deceased), Lem Railsback, Mauro Reyna, Elizabeth Keesee, Stephan Rozanski, Carole Schwartz, Betty Wagner, and Mavis Williams. Please know that I learned more from you than you learned from me. A special thanks to Pei-San Brown, John Sutterby, and Candra Thornton who collaborated in our recent research.

I am grateful to friends and colleagues and the children at Redeemer Lutheran School in Austin, Texas, who pitched in over three decades, renovating, improving, and maintaining play environments and supporting the many research related tasks, especially Norman Stuemke, school principal for forty-one years, Glen Kieschnick, principal, Pastors Dave Schroder and Kevin Westergren, and the entire faculty and staff who provided support and encouragement. I extend my gratitude to those who led the renovation work; O. T. Greer, John Saegert, Charlie Saegert, Jay Burks, Bill Ransom, Barry Samsel, Paul Burk, Steve Jahnke, Jay Jennings, Allen Moritz, Don Roy Hafner, Frank Jennings, and Woodie Arp. A special thanks to Danna Keyburn, teacher and naturalist, who transformed our limited naturescapes from small gardens, fruit trees, and shade trees into a virtual natural wonderland for children. Bob Farnsworth and Tom Norquist of PlayCore kept our research alive through their generous support for graduate students and research equipment.

In 2004, as the research and writing for this book was initiated, I joined with the University of the Incarnate Word (UIW) in San Antonio to establish a play and play environments research collection in the J. E. and L. E. Mabee Library. Thanks to friends and the World Wide Web, this collection grew rapidly, and virtually all the books and many of the reports cited in this book are in the collection or scheduled for inclusion and available for on-site use by students of play. This site was chosen because of faculty interest, the aura and devotion of a faith based institution, and the location of UIW in a marvelous complex of nearby play venues: the San Antonio Zoo, featuring an integrated built and natural play wonderland—"Tiny Tots Nature Spot," the San Antonio Botanical Gardens, the Witte Museum, Brackenridge Park, and the headwaters of the San Antonio River emerging from a crystal-clear spring and running through the campus, now being transformed into a nature site for people of all ages. I extend my appreciation to the faculty and students of UIW, especially Louis Agnese, Jr., President, Terry Diciano, Provost, Denise Staudt, Dean of the School of Education, Professor Mary Ruth Moore, Mendell Morgan, Dean Emeritus of Library Services, and to Michael Peters, Lisa Uribe, and Brandi Cross for their dedication to children's play, their cooperation in establishing the collection, their influence on this book, and their friendship. Thanks to the generous sponsorship of the International Playground Equipment Manufacturers' Association, Lakeshore Learning, Playcore, and other friends and colleagues, this collection continues to grow and serve as an enduring resource for play scholars.

I am also indebted to colleagues whose ideas and ideals influenced the content of this book: Stuart Brown, Founder of the National Institute for Play; Joan Almon, President of the Alliance for Play; Rollie Adams, CEO of the Strong Museum of Play, who reviewed early chapters; Sue Wortham and Stuart Reifel, partners in writing projects; Nancy Herron, Chair of the Texas Children and Nature Group; Elizabeth Goodenough, whose beautiful books about play enrich my imagination; Brian Sutton-Smith, who keeps the study of play lively and vital; Rich Louv, who is making dreams of play and nature become reality; European playworker friends, who convinced me many years ago that children often know best about their play environments.

The skillful assistance and unwaveringly positive approach of long-time friend and colleague Alita Zaepfel in preparing materials for press and assisting in securing and organizing photos was invaluable. She was instrumental in keeping the project on schedule and presenting well-organized materials to the publisher. The patience and skill of Heather Jarrow, New York Associate Editor for Education, Routledge/Taylor and Francis Group, Fintan Power, U.K. editor, and Alfred Symons, Production Editor, led us through the writing and editorial process. I extend my heartfelt thanks to them and the Routledge team.

Introduction

During the late Depression era and World War II, my childhood was filled with play and work in the hills and valley farms of Arkansas. During three summers, I worked and played alternately in a large Texas city, a remote share-cropper's farm in the Dust Bowl of West Texas, and in the California migrant stream. In all these places, we worked alongside adults but quickly discovered and established grounds for play and set about reveling in the many forms of play that only children seem to understand. Contrary to common contemporary thought, grounds for play or "playgrounds" are not just the commercial venues created by adults, but have also always been wherever the special places in the woods of the countryside and the vacant spaces of villages and cities can take children on magical flights of fantasy. This book is about all the grounds for play that children seek out and enjoy, the play they create, the benefits of their play, and the consequences of not playing. Further, it spans the centuries to illustrate how and where children play and the factors that influenced their play, and it seeks clues for resolving problems emerging from the disappearance of play in outdoor environments.

Memories of my wilderness and barnyard play and daily recesses at school remain strong and clear—mostly joyful times of building dams in the creek behind the school; choosing sides and playing war in the forest beyond the creek; playing shinny and baseball in the clearing; caring for the farm animals that served as pets, work stock, and some for food; tending gardens and eating raw vegetables directly from the plants; swimming and fishing in the clear, fast flowing river and creeks; playing rodeo with real animals in the barnyard; working in the fields with the "grown men" during the day and chasing "coon dogs" through the woods at night. Children's play throughout history was much like this, relatively free, intertwined with work, spontaneous, and set in the playgrounds of the wilderness, fields, streams, and barnyards. Children in cities enjoyed similar forms of play, but their playgrounds were the vacant lands, parks, and surrounding countryside or seashore. Except under insufferable conditions of poverty, abuse and disaster, play prevailed.

Now, during the short span of about a half-century, the centuries-old freedom to play evolved into a play and play environments crisis that threatens the health, fitness and welfare of children. Children in America have become less and less active, abandoning traditional outdoor play, work, and other physical activity for sedentary, indoor virtual play, technology play or cyber playgrounds, coupled with diets of junk food, fast food, and gorging at all-you-can-eat restaurants. As the Greatest Generation gave way to the technology revolution and excesses of growing affluence, children's play and play environments changed in remarkable ways. Adults' new-found concerns for children's safety and achievement led to abandonment of outdoor play in natural and child-created play spaces, and sedentary, indoor technology—cyber play—filled the void.

School systems across America joined the rush to over-parenting and over-management and reduced or deleted recess, restricted physical education, drilled children incessantly on standardized tests, and further interfered with their health and development with cafeteria diets of junk food and sugary drinks. Growing numbers of schools prohibit rough and tumble, chase, dodge ball, and other games allowing physical contact, and some prohibit running on the playground. Excessive safety standards replace adult oversight and many children grow progressively weak and fail to develop the physical and cognitive skills to protect themselves against injury. All this may prove to be only "the tip of the iceberg," as neuroscientists and other scholars continue to uncover the deleterious effects of play diminution on children's learning and cognitive, social, and emotional development.

The consequences of playing or not playing (play deprivation), the diminution of recess, and the abandonment of outdoor play in neighborhoods and natural areas are fundamental issues in a growing crisis resulting in serious health effects and potential diminishing life-span of the present generation. The "canaries in the coal mine," signaling this crisis, were the increases in obesity even before the turn of the present century, characterized by early signals of physiological and psychological disorders. Before the end of the first decade of the twenty-first century, rapid onset of childhood diabetes, circulatory diseases, rickets, and fatty liver disease had entered the scene, giving the health crisis the characteristics of a potential pandemic.

Many Americans have never appeared to understand that seemingly frivolous, inconsequential children's play is an innate, biological quality, and its expression is required for healthy development in both animals and humans. Play deprivation exacts serious consequences on children's development, health, and well-being. The play research of the past century provides a rich foundation for this conclusion but never fully entered the consciousness of those responsible for the care of children. As this is written, Americans are slowly awakening to the inept, corrupt fiscal management of the nation's financial resources because their own resources are dwindling and threatened in ways not seen since the Great Depression, all with ultimate consequences for the health and welfare of children.

Unlike the obscure, unacknowledged effects of play deprivation, the consequences of poor management of the nation's economy are readily observable and measurable and affect personal livelihoods. I recently attended an overflow crowd of officials and leaders of local, state, and national agencies and organizations working together to formulate plans for combating many factors underlying the present health and fitness crisis—neighborhoods unfriendly to children's play; loss of nature and outdoor play and work; regimented, test based schooling; fearful, hovering parents; diminution of school play, recess, and physical education; excessive safety standards and threats of playground injury lawsuits. Such gatherings are growing in frequency and Americans are beginning to see the effects of play deprivation in observable, measurable changes in natural and built environments and opportunities for children's play and learning. Americans eventually respond to and resolve major crises, but only after the consequences begin to threaten their pocketbooks, their security, and eventually their kids.

This book is about how we arrived at such a state of affairs, and how we can reverse the current state of things. Has outdoor play always been held in such low regard, and has children's access to traditional natural and built playgrounds always been so restricted? Historically, what did philosophers, educators, and prominent writers have to say about the value of play and its role in child development and the educative process? How did their advice impact later generations? What were the consequences of adult interference in children's play throughout America's history? What is the unique history of play and playgrounds in America from the early settlements to the present? How did we arrive at the present diminished state of children's play and what are the consequences? What are we doing about it and what additional steps should we be taking?

These are among the key issues to be addressed here, beginning with children's play and the great philosophers of ancient Greece and Rome—Plato, Aristotle, and Quintilian—and continuing with philosophers and educators of the Reformation and Renaissance—Luther, Comenius, and Locke—and prominent pre-modern thinkers—Rousseau, Pestalozzi, and Froebel. All these scholars recognized the multiple values of play and play environments for children's emotional and physical health and development, and recommended that play, both organized and free, be included in children's everyday lives. These pre-modern scholars were the first to successfully incorporate play into schools and set aside playgrounds for free, spontaneous play in nature and schoolyards, resulting in patterns of schooling that would influence the role of play in the development and philosophy of early American nursery schools and kindergartens.

The history of play in America began long before the early settlers set foot on the continent. Native American children enjoyed the finest of play environments—the unspoiled wilderness and plains—and play was supported by extended families who gave tutorial help and supported the integration of play and work roles, seemingly understanding that playing out the roles of elders in challenging environments honed the skills needed for future survival. Early settlers, primarily from Europe, brought with them their own games and toys and traditions of play in child rearing. Just as they had done in earlier centuries, children played, and their association with Native American children resulted in changes in both play and work patterns. Survival of the settlers was sometimes linked to the tutelage of Native Americans who had honed their own survival skills long before the arrival of the settlers.

No culture, then or now, seems to have perfected the art of play and work as fully as did the Native American. The children were strong, slender, graceful, woods wise, competent in both play and work. This was accomplished through extensive play, tutelage of extended family, and direct experience in planting and gathering food, preparing for war, hunting and fishing, and caring for the everyday needs of their people. Children of the early settlers, in contrast, were subject to some religious restrictions in their play, but even the Puritans were more deeply involved in play, games, merriment, and carousing than early historians revealed. Healthy children, even under duress, have always found ways and places to play, and until recently depended on their own creativity and ingenuity to create their toys and seek out their grounds for play.

Although children have always struggled to play, crises of one sort or another—extreme poverty, war, disease, natural and man-made disasters, and enforced child labor—diminished their free, spontaneous play. However, the values of play were revealed during such periods, demonstrating its therapeutic benefits and its powers to sustain and heal. Throughout the settlement of America, the expansion into the West, the homesteading of farms, and the development of cities, play and work endured and vestiges of original cultures survived, much as they existed in Europe and Asia before emigration to the new land. Play carried its cultural genes into America and had lasting effects on the lives of its people. One culture, forced from Africa and transported to America under the harshest and most devastating conditions, must have caused even the most cruel slave headmasters to marvel at their inner strength and resilience. No culture in America's history suffered such emotional and physical abuse as the Africans forced into servitude and abused as slaves. Yet their rich culture endured, their own cultural forms of play and merriment survived, and they prevailed to occupy positions of the highest status in many fields, and ultimately the presidency of the United States.

Yet another crisis was seen during the late nineteenth century and the early twentieth century. Immigrants were swarming into the crowded slums of large eastern cities, and families from failing farms were joining them in desperate efforts to improve their lives through the oft broken promises of jobs in industry. Disease, homelessness, hunger, and crime were rampant, orphans were everywhere, and thousands of abandoned children were surviving in the streets, shanties, and alleys while others endured long hours in factories. These same dangerous places were their play environments. Seeing the growing problems, New York City officials passed a law making it a crime to play in the streets, and hundreds of children were arrested. Avoiding arrest became a game in itself to resourceful children. Finally, charitable groups, government, concerned individuals, educators, and churches awakened to the plight of children and initiated a series of reforms to be called the "child-saving movement." One of the most successful programs for resolving the disaster of the cities was the Children's Aid Association, which shipped about 200,000 dispossessed children by "orphan trains" from the slums of cities to the Midwest and elsewhere to live with farm families. These "orphan train children" learned through play and work with intact families and grew up to enjoy fulfilling lives of work and leadership. Like the successful children of previous generations, the ingredients of outdoor play and work, regular schooling, and living among caring, resourceful families worked for these children.

Some of the reforms of the early child-saving movement were intertwined by reason of common contributors and leaders. This period saw the creation of the Playground Association of America (PAA), the American playground movement, and reforms or submovements to form children's museums, school gardens, nature study, botanical gardens, and summer camps. All these reforms have endured in some form to the present time and are now expanding and showing promise of contributing to the resolution of the present crisis in children's play, fitness, and health. Mandatory schooling and the expansion of schools helped prepare children for accelerating immigration, urbanization, and industrialization. The value of leadership and coordination of reform movements was evident throughout this era. President Theodore Roosevelt was instrumental in their success, serving as honorary president of the PAA and forming America's national parks, recreation areas, national forests, and many other natural American jewels. The PAA was instrumental in creating thousands of city parks and playgrounds, primarily focused on the German physical fitness movement. The child-saving movement phased into a child study movement during the early 1900s as leading educators and psychologists ushered in a "scientific era" that led to the eventual establishment of child research centers, research on play, and the formation of nursery schools and kindergartens based on principles of child development, including play and play environments designed to facilitate children's wide range of play forms. The emergence of professional organizations advocating that play be central in the educative process further strengthened the role of play in early childhood programs.

In 1928 the American economic system collapsed and the Great Depression changed the lives of people in both rural and urban areas. Standards of living plummeted, and homeless families hit the road in their jalopies in search of jobs and survival. Many small farmers continued to eke out a bare living from the land, and bread lines helped sustain families in the cities. Through it all, children continued to play while taking on any small jobs they could find to help support their families. This crisis, like others before it, eventually succumbed to the leadership of President Franklin D. Roosevelt and the New Deal program, a massive, coordinated program of work and relief for American laborers. World War II continued this revival by offering jobs and training to both men and women, leading to a series of events that initiated an unprecedented level of affluence and forever changed the culture of child rearing.

Following World War II, the technology revolution ushered in television, cyber toys, new forms of transportation, and parents intent on giving their children advantages they themselves had missed. Over time, the working, free-roaming child of previous eras would be replaced with a pampered child, created and sustained by hovering parents increasingly fearful for their children's safety and anxious about their achievements in school and vocation. Both parents went to work, leaving children to their cyber playgrounds and government-imposed, increasingly rigid, and illogical standards for schools. The X and Y generations gave way to the XXL generation, as outdoor play and play environments were abandoned, junk food became a major source of nutrition and sustenance, waist lines began to expand, and rare childhood diseases emerged and multiplied. Throughout this rapid transition, age-old traditions of play were short-circuited and the consequences for children's health and development were rapid and extensive. If the voluminous twentieth century research on the value of free, spontaneous outdoor play and physical activity had been heeded, and common sense nutrition had been followed, the crisis of obesity and related disease would have been over long ago. Among hundreds of research reports, I have never seen one concluding that play and school recess are of no value or damaging to children's development—physiological or psychological.

The effects of play deprivation are staggering in their scope and intensity and compounded by "balanced diets" of sugar drink in one hand and cookies in the other. Scientists who study both animal and human play no longer view it as nonessential but rather consider it as important for survival, adaptation, and well-being. Play and learning are mutually supportive and necessary for a healthy childhood and a competent adulthood. Play deprivation can be associated with physical and emotional illnesses, depression, violence, diminished impulse control, addictive predilections, low school achievement, and social abnormalities. The work of neuroscientists shows that play builds brains and play deprivation can change them in remarkable ways. Play deprivation contributes to obesity and, over time, the social and physical effects of obesity contribute, in circular fashion, to play deprivation. The research conclusions from studies of nature deprivation and play deprivation are similar in many respects, raising issues about the relative contributions of the *activity of play* and the *context or environments of play*—yet to be extensively explored. As the obese child grows progressively weak in relation to weight and dexterity, and coordination diminishes, he or she may withdraw from trying and wander aimlessly around the playground, avoiding strenuous activity during recess and physical education, and seek attention and status through bullying or helping smaller children.

In 2008 I moderated a three-day Internet symposium on obesity (enter "Common Good—New Talk" in an Internet search engine) involving fifteen prominent researchers and/or directors of professional organizations, U.S. government agencies, and university research centers. We were in apparent agreement that regular outdoor play, physical activity, and healthy diets are essential for physical and mental health, fitness, and learning, but Americans continue their headlong rush to regimented schooling and sedentary indoor entertainment in private cyber playgrounds. The dimensions of this multifaceted crisis are of such magnitude that a focus on single causative factors by one or a few groups working independently is unlikely to slow its progression. Many factors contribute to this state of events—poverty, lack of opportunity and access to places for physical activity, lack of motivation, lack of knowledge among both adults and children, and the appeal of leisure activity and entertainment over active lifestyles.

All this could be improved by creating natural spaces and activity-friendly neighborhoods, safe, challenging places to explore and play, using mass media to educate the public, focusing on relieving poverty, providing health and physical education classes in all schools, reinstating daily recess for elementary schools, and reducing significantly the time many children spend in cyber play. We can take lessons from solutions to past crises—slavery and emancipation struggles and successes; the plight of children in cities a century ago and the early child-saving movement; the Great Depression and the New Deal; World War II and the world alliance; the failed responses to hurricanes Katrina, Gustav, and Ike; the economic crisis exploding in 2008. The resolution to such crises requires public awareness of the severity of the consequences, shared leadership, and local, state, and national and/or international coordination.

The crisis most similar to the present one was the plight of children in the slums of early American cities a century ago, a depressed state receiving the attention of multiple agencies, resulting in hands-on help, growth, and resolution. Three brief decades of mounting physical inactivity created a modern crisis that will take years to resolve, and resolution will only happen if national, state, and local organizations and agencies come together to combine their resources to form a coordinated plan of action. Present efforts, though promising and expanding, lack coordination and the commitment needed to reverse the present conditions. Our current crisis is far more extensive and complex than the crisis of city slums a century ago, yet during this first decade of the twenty-first century a slowly growing force of parents, politicians, professional organizations, local, state, and national government agencies, and schools and park systems are joining forces to combat the debilitating consequences of play deprivation and the disappearance of natural environments for play. A much needed twenty-first century child-saving movement is emerging, and unprecedented energy is being directed toward saving children's free, spontaneous outdoor play, recess, and natural and built play environments.

Early Historical Views on Children's Play

What! Is it nothing to be happy, nothing to run and jump all day? He will never be so busy again all his life long. Plato, in his Republic, which is considered so stern, teaches the children only through festivals, games, songs, and amusements. It seems as if he had accomplished his purpose when he had taught them to be happy ... Do not be afraid, therefore, of this so-called idleness. (Rousseau, 2001, p. 84)

Records of children's play date back to antiquity, even earlier than classical Athens and Greece. Archaeological excavations of ancient China, Peru, and Egypt reveal drawings of various play scenes and play things such as tops, dolls, rattles, and other toys made of pottery and metal. Anthropological studies of primitive people among various cultures reveal evidence of acting, singing, storytelling, arts and crafts, dancing and rhythmic movement, and games and contests (Mitchell, 1937). Many games were of religious significance, dating back to ancient rites of divination. Plato expressed the idea that people were God's playthings and should spend their lives in the noblest of pastimes. He urged state legislation regarding children's games and offered practical advice to mothers on nursery play (Johnson, 1937). Plato was far from alone in his belief that play was valuable for children's development. Throughout recorded history, many of the most prominent philosophers/educators/thinkers appeared to understand that play was essential to the development of a full childhood and a happy and well-developed person.

Children's Play in Ancient Greece and Rome

During the time of Plato and Aristotle, about a half century before the birth of Christ, the classical Athenian attitude toward children saw them as simply cute, not to be taken too seriously, but to be loved and enjoyed. Plato divided children's development into levels or stages. During infancy (birth to 3 years) the child was to be protected and cared for, develop no fears, and experience little pain. The nursery stage (3 to 6 years) was for playing, and hearing mother goose stories and fairy tales. Punishment was to be infrequent and mild. During the elementary stage (6–13 years) boys and girls should be placed in separate living quarters and learn letters, mathematics, music, religion and morals. Boys were to receive some military training. The middle stage (13 to 16 years) was for advanced study of arithmetic, poetry, and music. From 16 to 20 years boys were to receive formal military and gymnastics training.

Up until the entry to formal education outside the home, children were to exercise through play under the watchful supervision of adults. They were allowed to play much as they pleased, but their play was seen as less serious and of lesser consequence than the play of adults. Indeed, the act of grown men entering into the games of children was viewed with contempt—a waste of time. Children's play was to be diverted into productive channels such as helping to identify aptitudes, and toys were to be used to prepare for future occupations as adults, such as building and teaching (Golden, 1990).

Plato's *Republic* (360 B.C.) is his chief treatise on education (Rusk, 1956). Jean-Jacques Rousseau later called this the greatest treatise on education ever written and said that those who wished to know the meaning of public education should read it. Education for Plato would begin early because of the importance of initial impressions. Tales and fables should be carefully selected to ensure that those first heard by the child should be models of virtue. Good (or virtue) and evil were considered of such importance as to be substituted for true and false, for God is the author of all things good and children must be taught to conform to His principles. Music and gymnastics, Plato believed, should also begin early, for musical training is the most potent of educational instruments and is the counterpart of gymnastics. "Education has two branches—one of gymnastics, which is concerned with the body, and the other of music, which is designed for the improvement of the soul" (Plato, 2000, p. 153). As accurately pointed out by Rusk (1956), we do not have to look to modern times, or to Herbart, Froebel, or Montessori, to find play as a guiding principle in education, for such was formulated by Plato.

Plato's proposed education would be a sort of amusement, allowing the teacher to better determine the natural bent of the child, and compulsion would not be used. In his *Laws*, Plato (2000) emphasized the positive significance of play, yet he admitted that there are both good and bad pleasures (Plato, 1952, p. 384), just as there are good and bad or right and wrong opinions (p. 623). Plato and other great thinkers to follow were concerned with children's play and with other fundamental factors in education. In defining the very nature and power of education, Plato inserts play into a central role.

> ... anyone who would be good at anything must practice that thing from his youth upwards, both in sport and earnest ... for example, he who is to be a good builder, should play at building children's houses; ... the future warrior should learn riding, or some other exercise ... The most important part of education is right training in the nursery. (Plato, 1952, p. 649)

Up to the age of six boys and girls were to play together, but after the age of six they were to be separated. "Let boys live with boys and girls in like manner

with girls" (Plato, 1952, p. 650). At the right times or ages, the appropriate training would be introduced: music, gymnastics, arithmetic, the alphabet, the mind
of nature existing in the stars. All children would have such knowledge as that
of a child learning the alphabet, but those who would be rulers of the state
would have additional studies to prepare for their future role.

The Greek educational games included games for the nursery, gymnastic
exercises for the school, and the social games of adults. In the nursery, both
boys and girls played with rattles, hoops, balls, swings and tops. Even then,
adults distinguished between boys and girls in their provision of toys. There
were stilts and carts for the boys and dolls for the girls, and children were
allowed to make their own toys. Plato did not countenance an excessive number
of toys but advocated play tools for carpentry and free play or natural modes of
amusement. Many Greek children's outdoor games are familiar even today;
Odd or Even, Slap in the Dark (guessing who boxed the ear), Hunt the Slipper,
Catch Ball, Hide and Seek, Heads or Tails, Tortoise, Blind Man's Buff, Kiss in the
Ring, Tag, and many others. A Greek boy was sent to the *palaestra* (ancient
Greek wrestling school) at age seven. Here, at the break of day for school he
engaged, along with his pedagogue, in early morning active play: racing, leaping,
wrestling, singing, and dancing until time for later morning rest and lunch.
Older boys were admitted to the gymnasia for participation in the pentathlon:
running, jumping, throwing the discus, boxing, and wrestling. Little wonder
that the world still marvels at the physical perfection of the ancient Greeks and
their influence on art, especially sculpture (Johnson, 1937).

Aristotle studied with Plato for twenty years, then traveled, tutored Alexander
the Great, and after twelve years returned to Athens and established the Lyceum,
a school located in a garden, where he taught until his death. He did not write
a book dedicated to education but discussed the topic in other works (Aristotle,
1925, 1943). He proposed that training (Aristotle, 1943) should fall into stages
according to children's developmental stages: early home education, grammar
school, and training in rhetoric from five to seven years of age. The curriculum
included reading and writing for utility, gymnastics for health and strength,
and music for character formation, enjoyment, and education. The curricula
were expanded for older children. For health and proper habits, the young child
should be given milk, allowed to move her body, and exposed to cold. Up until
the age of five there should be no demands for study or labor lest growth be
impeded, but there should be sufficient motion to prevent the limbs from being
inactive. The home rearing should allow much play and physical exercise. This
could be achieved through amusements, which were for the most part imita-
tions of future occupations. The rattle was given to infants because it was suited
to the infant mind but education was a rattle or toy suited for older children.

Aristotle, like Plato, believed that until children are five years old they should
be taught nothing lest it hinder growth. Children should be as active as possible, even in their play, to avoid an indolent habit of body. Such activity could be

acquired through play, which should not be too hard or too easy—children who played slowly or without spirit would not develop an aptitude for any branch of science. During the first few years of a child's life toys were seen as useful and even later, when the child was being taught to read, Aristotle would give him ivory figures or letters to play with.

According to Aristotle, the branches of education to be entered after age seven were reading and writing, gymnastic exercises, and music, but "the first principle of all action is leisure" (Quintilian, 1965, p. 322). Both leisure and occupation were required, but leisure was better. Amusement was needed during pursuit of occupations more than at other times ... amusement gives relaxation, whereas occupation is always accompanied with exertion and effort. Pleasure springs from the noblest sources; therefore music, drawing, and gymnastics are introduced at the proper times. Parents should train their sons not simply because education is necessary or useful but because it is liberal or noble.

During the first century of the Roman Empire, education was left in the hands of the pater familias (highest ranking male in a familia) and, being a matter of private rather than public interest, lagged far behind education in Greece. The Greek Plato elucidated the education of the philosopher with the end being that of the speculative life. In contrast, the Roman Quintilian (35–97 A.D.) detailed the education of the orator, aimed at the practical life. From infancy, even when cared for by nurses, children's minds should be imbued with excellent instruction and should be a pleasure to them. Quintilian did not "disapprove" of items or toys, or whatever could be invented for stimulating children to learn. He emphasized that, during play time, memory, which is so important to an orator and strengthened by exercise, can profit from the sayings of eminent men and poets.

Quintilian would have education begin early, provided that no burden or requirement be too exacting. The first instruction was to be in the form of play, for one who cannot yet love studies should not learn to hate all learning. Perhaps the idea of the kindergarten is thus foreshadowed (Smail, 1938). Quintilian condemned corporal punishment as degrading, unnecessary, and ineffective given proper instruction, and he insisted that teachers must recognize differences in temperament and intellectual gifts among pupils. Not unlike later great reformers, he emphasized the value of observing children and recognizing their individuality—strong premonitions indeed given contemporary educational practice. He recognized that the main purpose of education was to foster mental activity but games had their place in his educational scheme: "nor should I be displeased by a love of play in my pupils, for this too is a sign of alertness; only let there be moderation ... so that ... refusal to allow them may not breed hatred of studies" (Smail, 1938, p. xxv).

Threads of Quintilian's thought pervade the philosophies of the great humanists of the Renaissance. Martin Luther stated that he preferred Quintilian to almost all other authorities on education for he gives a model of eloquence and teaches by the happiest combination of theory and practice. John Stuart Mill called his work an encyclopedia about the thoughts of the ancients and on the whole field of education (Colson, 1924; Smail, 1938).

The Play of Medieval Children

During the latter period of the twentieth century historians explored and extensively documented the life of children during the medieval period. Aries (1962), French historian of the family and childhood, studied the metamorphosis of childhood through paintings and diaries across four centuries and described the medieval child as a little adult and childhood as being undiscovered until the end of the Middle Ages. Since he did not discover pre-twelfth century art portraying childhood, he concluded that there was no place for childhood in previous periods. Aristocratic children played with toys during infancy, were taught to play musical instruments, dance, and sing as early as age two and participated in festivals by age three. While he still played with dolls, the child of four or five practiced archery, played cards, chess, and adult games, and by age six was playing parlor games and pantomime games commonly played by adults. By age seven there was riding, hunting and fencing, and starting school or work.

Such variety in play, common among aristocratic children, did not apply equally to the children of the poor. Many died young and others were sent away to school or to serve in other people's homes. Aries argued that childhood was not a distinct cultural phenomenon until the Renaissance or the sixteenth or seventeenth centuries.

> In medieval society the idea of childhood did not exist ... as soon as the child could live without the constant solicitude of his mother, his nanny or his cradle-rocker, he belonged to adult society ... The absence of definition extended to every sort of social activity: games, crafts, arms. (Aries, 1962, p. 128)

Aries found no example of a collective picture of medieval times in which children were not seen in the presence or service of adults. In a rich anthology prepared by ten historians, DeMause (1974, p. 1) summarized his major conclusions, seemingly echoing Aries' findings:

> The history of childhood is a nightmare from which we have only recently begun to awaken. The further back in history one goes, the lower the level of child care, and the more likely children are to be killed, abandoned, beaten, terrorized, and sexually abused. (DeMause, 1974, p. 1)

DeMause went on to point out that a favorite medieval doctrine was "Work is worship" and everyone, even the littlest children, had work to do. There was no separate world of childhood; children lived their lives with adults, never apart, sharing the same games, toys, and fairy stories (Tucker, 1974, p. 229). Bruegels' famous paintings of festivals, and other works of art, were commonly used as evidence for this view of childhood by Aries, DeMause, and other historians. The searching of documents, records, and original papers by later historians painted a more complete and somewhat different portrait of medieval childhood.

Aries' research focused primarily on France and, to a lesser degree, England. His sources were essentially limited to paintings, sculpture, and diaries, and the bulk of his writing was about the Renaissance or the 14th through 16th centuries. The research of Orme (2001), Shahar (1990), Crawford (2000), and other contemporary historians on medieval childhood stands in contrast to that of Aries; all rebut some of his major conclusions and examine the previously unexplored richness of evidence, including translated sources, writings, art, records, and archeology, demonstrating that medieval adults considered childhood a distinct period, treated children with affection and care, and allowed them their own possessions and play activities.

> Adults provided culture for children by means of toys, games, and literature, but children created their own toys and games as well. They spent time by themselves, talking and playing away from their elders, sometimes against their elders' conventions and wishes. (Orme, 2001, p. 6)

Also relying primarily on depictions of childhood in works of art, Schorsch's (1979) conclusions about childhood during the medieval and Renaissance periods were similar to those of Aries in some respects, but his descriptions of play were more liberal:

> The reality is that until fairly modern times most children were either abandoned by their mothers or farmed out to other women shortly after birth and that, in fact, both the family and the family house as we know them today did not even exist until well into the 17th century. (Schorsch, 1979, p. 12)

Acknowledging exceptions to the rule, Schorsch maintained that medieval adults dealt with children much as they dealt with their animals—both shared the dirt, worms, and every manner of disease that being a child or an animal implied. Such degraded living, characteristic of the most destitute and poor throughout history, has not applied to the rich and not necessarily to those falling in between these extremes.

Despite such dire descriptions of the state of the child, Schorsch devotes a chapter to children playing vigorously with their friends yet finding this painful to the conscience, even producing guilt at feelings of delight. Fathers and clergymen set about restraining play and thus destroying evil, yet the medieval community engaged in play, sports, and games as amusement and enjoyed festivals, holidays, and celebrations as "a natural part of life itself" (Schorsch, 1979, p. 77). "Each medieval man, unlike the generations that followed, gave his child as much access to entertainment as to the work of the day" (p. 78).

Hanawalt's (1993) extensively documented history of childhood in medieval London, utilizing court records, coroners' rolls, literary sources, and books of advice, as does the work of Orme, weaves a more complete description of childhood during that period. These writers demonstrate through rich data that medieval adults recognized and paid close attention to the various stages of childhood, though the meanings of these stages were not dissimilar to those described for other periods. Play, they demonstrated, was common to both children and adults. Playing, pimping, carousing, soliciting, and working were common in street life though the streets were often little more than sewers, helping to explain the stories of dirt and filth in some accounts. Extreme contrasts of luxury and poverty lent further insight into conflicting accounts of life during this period, with drunken immorality, cruelty, and crime existing side by side with the large gardens and grandeur of the rich.

As far back as the twelfth century adults in London knew that children would and should play. Hanawalt (1993) describes their play life in some detail, noting that on Shrove Tuesday children brought fighting cocks to their schoolmasters and watched cockfights. They also played ball in London fields, competing with students from other schools. At various times, they played tag, ball games, ran races, rolled hoops and imitated adult ceremonies copied from marriages, festivals, pageants, and church masses. By the late fourteenth century many guilds required that apprentices achieve functional literacy before enrolling. Some students went on to enroll at university and a few were sent abroad for university study. Some girls may have attended grammar school with boys and yet others received separate schooling. Schorsch (1979) found that girls, being considered inferior in temperament and condition, were not admitted to fifteenth century choir schools or sixteenth century grammar schools. They were taught literacy and religion at home or in the petty schools that later became the dame or academy schools of the 18th and 19th centuries. Encouraging girls' training in music and dance was considered to be a sign of the devil at work.

The school day and the play of twelfth century eight-year-old Richard in London was described by Hanawalt (1993, p. 81). Richard's day began at 6 a.m., with washing and getting ready for school. He made his own bed, greeted his parents and said prayers with them. His parents were illiterate but held schooling in high regard. Richard looked at the shops and ran to make it to school on time. He was reverent toward his schoolmaster in order to avoid a whipping but today everyone behaved so no one felt the sting of the willow twigs. He was tired from the Latin exercises when he walked home for his midday dinner. After dinner, while his elders were busy with guests, he was free to play and on this fateful day he joined his friends for street games. Today's game was to hang from a beam protruding from London Bridge. Richard was feeling brave from the wine given him at lunchtime but his hands slipped, resulting in a fatal plunge into the river. Accidents, some fatal, were the fate of many children playing unsupervised in the streets and byways of medieval London.

Throughout recorded history, as now, children played games appropriate to their stages of development. During the medieval and Renaissance period they played with small objects such as marbles and balls and even dice and chess made from various materials. Jumping, swinging, and balancing devices and "totters" or "merry totters" were used, probably referring to swings, seesaws, or spring boards (Orme, 2001, p. 179). The deeper one looks into the depth and variety of children's play during earlier centuries, the more similarities with the play of modern children become visible. The types of toys and the nature of games change with children's age and development and reflect the beliefs, occupations, pleasures, and state of technology of the time and culture, but the basic nature of play across centuries, countries, and cultures is remarkably similar.

During the medieval period, children played games of chase and competition, games depicting elders and heroes, games reflecting vivid imaginations, and games of war. Children's observation of and participation at adult festivals, athletic events, and musical and dramatic productions or public plays are historic sources that influence and provide substance for play. No historic age or culture appears to have been devoid of children singing simple songs and rhymes and making crude musical instruments. War and other disasters were common throughout history. Children's games emerged from direct experiences of and through hearing about war from the conversations of adults. There are indications that the natural therapeutic qualities of play stimulate children to engage in war games and games related to the traumatic consequences of other man-made and natural disasters (Frost, 2005b).

Girls were expected to be more demure, modest, or proper, to attend to household tasks, and to be reserved about entering into boys' games, but, then as now, they did so from time to time. There are elements of truth in the point of view that play helps prepare children for adult roles. Girls learned household tasks such as cooking, tending house, sewing, and gathering food and practiced their skills in play. Similarly, boys worked with adult men in rural and urban trades such as carpentry, farming, and tending animals, and practiced and extended their skills through play. Even war games helped equip boys to use bows and arrows and other weapons. Girls' toys included dolls and household items they used for make-believe play, as do modern children. Only recently have girls entered extensively into many of the physically challenging ball games and athletic contests traditionally played by boys.

Marked differences have always existed in the play of the poor and the rich. Poor children made some of their own toys, assigning to them their own names, yet they played many active organized games similar to those of rich children and probably equaled or surpassed them in certain physical abilities. Such games as chess, tennis, and others requiring special equipment were more common among the rich. In cities children played in the streets, vacant areas, and surrounding fields, and in the country children played in the barnyards, fields, and forests, a pattern that exists today but is diluted by the growing interest in indoor technology play.

Toys are children's first treasures. At first they give pleasure, stimulate interest, amuse, comfort, even teach. For centuries babies and young children were given rattles and toys to handle, chew, shake, and spin. As children developed physical and mental skills, tops and balls were time-proven toys, and dolls and small vessels were favorites for pretend play. With advancing skill and age, children engaged in play with puppets and model figures of soldiers and animals. Both poor and rich children made their own toys using sand, rags, string, sticks, and whatever scrap material was at hand.

Irrational Play, Child Abuse, and Accidents in Medieval Times

This book is written from a child development/education perspective and emphasizes those forms of play commonly seen in families, schools, and other supervised places. Other forms of child activity, which may be described as illogical or "irrational play", were also common across the ages—bullying, abusing animals, violent fighting, gambling, gang play of various sorts, and sexual play. Fights were likely during school and after school involving bullies and groups or gangs. Such violence continued into early American schools, and, perhaps in lesser degree, into contemporary schools. Outdoor play places at school or in the neighborhood were typically lacking in adult supervision and likely places for arguing, bullying, and fighting. Although fields for organized games were common across the centuries, the present writer found no evidence that organized, equipped places like school playgrounds with adult supervisors and periods called "recess" existed during the medieval period.

Many children in the medieval period were abused by adults, both at home and at school. For this the law offered little relief. Families, friends, neighbors, and clergy sometimes came to the rescue of children who were abused, whether by family members, schoolmasters, or employers of child laborers. For example:

> Henry Machyn, the London chronicler of the mid sixteenth century, reported how in 1563, a man named Penred, who had a child to teach, beat him so severely with a buckled belt that the affair came to public notice. The master was set on the pillory, whipped till the blood ran down, and the boy's injuries were exhibited, the "pitiest sight to see at any time." (Orme, 2001, p. 101)

Accidental injuries to children were common during the medieval period. This topic, related to children's play and play environments, will enter into discussions of the modern period when play environments are discussed in Chapter 7. The marvelously thorough, scholarly research of Orme (2001) gives perhaps the best available insight into this issue. First, he says, there were miracle stories of parents taking their injured children to saints or shrines, with beneficial results. More boys than girls were discussed in records of both rich and poor, perhaps because boys were more active than girls or even because their survival was of greater interest. The stories of miracles and coroners' reports revealed that the accidents then were quite similar to those of today and they had similar causes. Infants were caught in cords or straps, burned in fires, crushed by falling objects, or eaten by pigs entering houses through open doors. With growing mobility, additional hazards were introduced: crawling into hearths to be burned by fire or scalded by liquid in cooking pots, falling into vessels of liquids or pools of water, swallowing various small objects, putting objects in the ears and nose, being cut or punctured by tools, and falling from open windows. Not unlike today, many injuries resulted from the absence or distraction of parents or the carelessness of one too young to monitor wisely. Unlike today, parents were rarely held accountable for children's injuries.

History leaves no doubt that children played, and played extensively, during the medieval period, although many among their elders disapproved, believing that playing led to truancy, indolence, vandalism, and inattention to school work and church activities. Some believed that certain types of play and games were acceptable while others were bad, such as games of dice which were equivalent to gambling, and ball games that could destroy property—even doll play by girls was criticized by some as image worship. The effects of play and frivolity on education were wrapped in the cloak of their presumed destructive effects on discipline, character, morals, and attentiveness. Despite the criticism, disapproval and censuring of their play, medieval children played extensively and enthusiastically.

With a child's experience and advancing development, play becomes more physical for running and jumping, more dexterous for building and creating, more social for developing friendships and engaging in games. Little in this respect has changed since the Middle Ages. Play, it seems, has innate qualities and transcends ages and cultures. All healthy children play. Play was recognized for centuries by many great philosophers as being essential for children's development, yet as far back as the ancient Greeks some adults tried to control it, and some attempted to abolish it in favor of other activities (Orme, 2001, p. 165). Given its history and the extent of scholarly research demonstrating the developmental values of play, one can only stand amazed that many contemporary school administrators, politicians, and parents favor the reduction or dissolution of play, recess, and playgrounds.

Reformation and Renaissance Philosophers/Educators on Play

Though not generally recognized, Martin Luther (1483–1546) brought about a reformation in education as well as in religion. His influence on religion, called by some the most important event in history since the birth of Christ and a singular event for the German people, is seen worldwide through the activities of the Lutheran Church. His was a powerful influence in changing the repressive, cruel discipline extant in many places during the Middle Ages and fostering attractive schoolrooms and pleasant studies—even music and physical education—in the schools. In the words of Luther: "Our schools are no longer a hell and purgatory, in which children are tortured over cases and tenses, and in which with much flogging, trembling, anguish, and wretchedness, they learn nothing" (Painter, 1889, p. 67).

Despite his great intellect and extraordinary scholarship and writing, Luther was sensitive to aesthetics, a lover of nature, a skillful musician, and a poet—all playful activities. To him the right training of children was a divine requirement and parents were to spare no diligence, time, or cost in educating them. Children's education should be liberal and pleasant and adults should adapt themselves to children's ways, prattle with them, enter into their activities, and train them in a childlike way in the midst of their play (Painter, 1889).

Not the least of Luther's contributions to education was his anticipation of modern pedagogy. He was a careful observer of children and proposed that methods of instruction be adapted to their nature, a precursor of modern views about individual differences and developmentally appropriate practice. Indeed, in his *Letter to the Mayors and Aldermen*, he noted that children have a natural desire for being active, such as running and jumping, and they should not be restrained from such activity—since we preach to children we must also prattle with them. "Let no one think himself too wise, and disdain such child's play" (Painter, 1889, pp. 154–5). Luther's liberal education would include time in school, work at home, learning a trade but also playing ball, running, and tumbling. He proposed universal, compulsory education and state support of schools and censured monks and schoolmasters who prohibited children from playing at the proper time, thus making them "mere logs and sticks."

A century after Luther, John Amos Comenius, a Czech theologian, reinforced Luther's educational ideas, proposing an educational ladder for all children, both boys and girls, beginning with the mother school for children up to 6 years and progressing through to university. Like Luther, he emphasized instruction in "useful knowledge," morality, and religion. Many of the great educational reformers were commonly steeped in church doctrine, believing that God operates in everything, and they made religion a central component of their proposed schools. Like Luther, Comenius proposed easier, more humane methods of instruction than those seen in most schools of his period.

Instead of developing an antipathy towards learning, children should be "enticed by irresistible attractions, so that they should gain no less pleasure from study as from playing and amusing themselves" (Comenius, 1910, p. 77).

The remarkable likenesses in philosophical thought carried over into educational ideas and principles are perhaps nowhere better illustrated than in the views of Comenius. "Almost every educational idea of Comenius can be found in some other great thinker; in Plato and Aristotle; in Cicero, Plutarch, and Quintilian ... and in Erasmus of Rotterdam, not to mention Francis Bacon" (Ulich, 1945, p. 188). Such similarity in thought, susceptible to foreign influence, is attributable by Ulich to an equally strong faculty of systematic integration, which is fundamentally different from mere imitation, enriching itself through others' ideas but not springing from them. For the benefit of all those great educators-thinkers to follow him, Comenius' profound intuition into human growth allowed him to formulate the classical laws of teaching.

Comenius pre-dated John Dewey through his focus on learning through active, firsthand experience with the subjects or skills to be learned. His emphasis on things over words and doing over passive study was later to be seen in the philosophies of Rousseau, Pestalozzi, Froebel, Montessori, and Piaget. He broke with the harsh educational methods of his era and focused on play as a vehicle for promoting healthy development, calling for humor and lightness in every lesson. Contemporary schools can learn lessons about recess and playgrounds from his words:

> In the playground, boys are urged to run, to jump, and to play games with balls, since it is necessary to put the body in motion and allow the mind to rest. Forbidden pastimes are games played with dice, wrestling, boxing, and swimming, since these are either useless or dangerous. (Comenius, 1910, p. 6)

Comenius' educational method was formulated to ensure that the art of intellectual discipline was so firmly established that "sure and certain progress" could be made. All the subjects to be learned should suit the age of the students and nothing beyond their comprehension would be presented to them for learning and the cycles of learning would be laid out much as the seasons. The reader may immediately think of Froebel when seeing the reliance on nature that Comenius later illustrated in his curriculum. For example, he compared his methods for instructing children to the stages in the development of a tree. The very young are tenderly cared for by parents, much as they would care for tree shoots carefully planted that take root and put forth buds. Later the child's education is compared to caring for a tree with branches and buds that are not yet developed. Eventually, the student will resemble a tree covered with fruit waiting to be plucked and used.

Such reflection about the natural cycle of animals and plants led to basic educational principles: beginning early, proceeding from the general to the particular and from easy to difficult, avoiding overburdening students, proceeding according to what the intellect is prepared to receive, teaching through the senses, and making education pleasant (Comenius, 1910, p. 127). The reader will later see the contrast between such views and contemporary practices that reflect industrial models of education that focus on the important components of literacy and scientific knowledge yet withhold instruction in the age-old benefits of play, arts, spiritual understanding, politeness, charity, ethics, patience, and manners as espoused by Comenius and other great reformers before and after his time.

Writing in the seventeenth century, John Locke influenced a number of eighteenth century, prominent historical figures in philosophy. In the field of education these included Rousseau, Basedow, Pestalozzi, Herbart, and others. Locke's aims for education revolved around several themes: virtue derived from proper religious training, wisdom in practical matters, breeding or good manners in accordance with English standards, and learning or knowledge based on practical judgment. Learning was not to be forced or achieved through compulsion lest children learn to dislike learning.

> I have always had a fancy, that Learning might be made a Play and Recreation to children; and they might be brought to desire to be taught, if it were propos'd to them as a thing of Honour, Credit, Delight and Recreation, or as a Reward for doing something else; and if they were never chid or corrected for the neglect of it. (Locke, 1989, p. 208)

In *How to Bring up Your Children*, Locke (1902) explained that children should have playthings or toys of different sorts, but should be allowed to play with only one at a time. This would teach them not to lose or spoil their playthings and help prevent them from being wanton and careless or from becoming squanderers and wasters (p. 100). He believed that such restrictions, to be managed by the tutor or parent, are seemingly unimportant, but nothing that can form young children's minds and introduces good habits should be overlooked. Whatever the child does leaves an impression during that tender age and can influence tendencies to do good or evil. Nothing that exerts such influence should be neglected.

People of condition (wealthy) who shower their little ones with many toys do the child great harm, teaching them pride, vanity, and covetousness even before they can speak. Such children, Locke observed, grew so accustomed to abundance that they never thought they had enough, always asking, "What more? What new thing shall I have?" Locke responds to this dilemma by maintaining that playthings should not be bought for children except when they are older and in need of certain toys such as tops and items that are required for exercise.

Even then children should continue to make toys for themselves, sometimes delighting in having an adult help with a difficult problem. The young child can secure playthings from nature, sticks, pebbles, sand, and from items such as pieces of paper and keys already available in the home.

Locke's training in medicine was a probable cause for his interest in child health. Though a healthy body was a necessary condition for education, having a sound mind was more important, and exercise of the senses was essential for developing the mind. Apparently some critics overlooked Locke's treatment of the development of the young in such works as *How to Bring up Your Children*, and he was criticized for emphasizing some mental faculties at the expense of others (Locke, 1902, p. 36). In his work, Locke speaks of observing children at play, leading him to advise against suppressing play but replacing it with educative play. This perhaps influenced later scholars who suggested a play curriculum for young children in many schools and child development centers. Locke's "play-way" meant that learning should be made as much a recreation to children's play as play is to learning and the task of learning should begin at the right moment, when the child is ready (Rusk, 1956).

Though Locke had little access to the psychology of learning extant today, he made a beginning by entering into the world of the child to learn and discover features of growth and development useful in the formulation of his educational philosophy. We now know that observing children in their natural play environments leads to understanding of their stages of development and gives insight into their abilities or capacities at different stages. Such understanding appears to have been extant among the great reformers discussed here. A fundamental outcome of carefully observing children is comprehending the profound differences in their developmental abilities, capacities, and needs, and understanding, valuing, and responding to their individual differences.

Pre-modern Philosophers on Play

During the eighteenth century, Jean-Jacques Rousseau (1712–72) was a giant among philosophers. His book *Emile* made a strong case for beginning a child's education early, which was initially to center in the family and be conducted in harmony with the nature of the child and guided by its dictates. He reacted against the harsh child-rearing practices of his time, such as binding children in swaddling clothes to avoid having to care for them and to ensure they caused no trouble. (Since about 4000 B.C., some children were wrapped snugly in blankets or similar materials to restrict their movement.) The heart of his education for the young child was family life involving both mother and father, an emphasis that is echoed by contemporary psychologists. Like Luther and Comenius, he identified developmental stages in childhood and believed that education should address individual differences in children, natural learning, and a curriculum that grew out of natural interests and curiosity. Memory work should be abandoned in favor of activities that foster judgment, and reasoning and play should be central components of children's everyday lives. During the first five years of life children were to learn totally from their own direct experiences, their exploration of the environment, and a curriculum guided by the development of the child. To Rousseau, the most important and most useful rule in education was "not to gain time, but to lose it." Despite his genius, Rousseau's *Emile* attracted criticism from religious leaders who objected to his "atheism," or postponing religious education until adolescence, from educational leaders who believed his system fraught with practical impossibilities, and even from those who denounced him as a plagiarist. "Certainly not every pioneer in education after Rousseau, beginning with Pestalozzi, is merely a disciple of Rousseau. Thinking men may have much in common and still be original" (Ulich, 1945, p. 218).

In his classic *Emile*, Rousseau (2001) made his case for play, leisure, and the development of strong, healthy bodies. "A feeble body makes a feeble mind ... The weaker the body, the more imperious its demands; the stronger it is, the better it obeys" (Rousseau, 2001, p. 24). Nature, he believed, must be given time to work. He rejected the common perception of adults that play was essentially doing nothing, and favored children's natural running, jumping and engaging in festivals, games, singing, and amusements.

Rousseau wished to train all the senses and saw a connection between development and efficient use of the senses and the child's playful activities, letting the child perform every exercise that encourages agility: jumping and leaping, climbing trees and walls, and letting the child run barefoot indoors and in the garden. Because children are always moving freely, it is easy, he believed, to engage them in learning through natural activities. Will the plank be long enough to reach the other side? Will two fathoms of cord be enough to hang a swing from a tree? Here are two villages. Which one can we get to first? When a child flies a kite or whips a top, he is training eye and hand and increasing his strength. He argued that children should be given the same games as men: football, archery, tennis, billiards, and musical instruments. They can only learn to master their limbs and strengthen them by using them; otherwise they may grow up to be clumsy as are many men. Children can be seen at carnivals and comedy houses swinging, dancing, and walking on their hands with great skill. With proper training and practice children can engage in acrobatics, playing musical instruments, as well as reading and writing. The supposed incapacity of the young for adult games is imaginary and the lack of success is for want of practice.

> We must never forget that all this should be play, the easy and voluntary control of the movements which nature demands of them, the art of varying their games to make them pleasanter, without the least bit of

constraint to transform them into work; for what games do they play in which I cannot find material for instruction for them? (Rousseau, 2001, p. 133)

For Rousseau, work and play were all one to the child, his games are his work, and he does not know the difference. In play and games the child brings everything: the cheerful interest, the charm of freedom, the bent of his mind, the extent of his knowledge. He contrasts his carefully educated child with the child of a tutor who makes a point of wasting no time and "loads his mind with a pack of rubbish." The many questions of the tutor are pedantic and useless. The child quickly stops listening to the everlasting questions. Such a teaching or testing method, not unlike the contemporary American-style high stakes testing, is pedantic and useless; a question by a skillful teacher would reveal the child's intelligence and academic ability much more quickly and thoroughly. The central point here is that one needs good judgment if one is to estimate the judgment of a child.

Rousseau relates the story of a Lord Hyde who, anxious to test the progress of his child, took a walk with the child and his tutor where schoolboys were flying kites. He asked his son, "Where is the kite that casts this shadow?" Without hesitation and without looking upward the child responded, "Over the high road." And he was correct. The high road was between the kite and the sun. Lord Hyde kissed his child and later gave the tutor an annuity in addition to his salary. This practical method in a real-life context contrasted sharply with the pedantic, endless questioning of tutors that Rousseau rebelled against, illustrating how turning the child from trivial details to observing, judging, and reasoning was far more effective.

Johann Pestalozzi (1746–1827) was greatly influenced by Rousseau's ideas about the nature of the child and implemented them a generation later. Among the great educational reformers, Pestalozzi was the first to establish a school for children, personally teach them, and apply the ideas of earlier reformers, representing a new era in education. He was successful in changing many long-standing educational views and practices. He deplored and initiated reform in three particular practices: the exclusion of children of the poor from schooling, rote learning, and cruel punishment. Kindness ruled in his school, as he abolished flogging and posited love as the foundation of his work and regarded it as essential to the child's physical and intellectual abilities. Like Rousseau, he believed in individual differences in children's interests, needs, and rates of learning. He originated the concept of readiness, and substituted time and experience for rote learning. His idea that objects and events must be seen, felt, and observed in their concrete form would later influence the writing of Dewey, Montessori, and Piaget (Frost and Kissinger, 1976).

Pestalozzi's (1977) educational principles revolved around his desire to improve the indescribable conditions of the poor, perhaps evolving from his personal experience of poverty. His lessons to contemporary educators included his tenet that the children of the poor required greater refinement of instruction than the children of the rich. He believed that reform should begin with the individual instead of society and was dependent upon helping the individual help himself. Like Rousseau, he held that education was essentially a process of establishing healthy conditions for the natural unfolding of the child and, like Comenius before him and Froebel and the humanists to follow, he believed that schools should protect and nurture the children's self-esteem. His views on education focused on the "organic whole," including the intellectual, the physical, and moral and religious relationships with others and with God. Instruction would proceed from object lessons, from the known to the unknown, and from concrete to abstract. The child was not to be forced but should be guided to make his own judgments rather than rely upon those of others. The environment would follow the plan of nature to stimulate full development of the child, much as a good gardener would do for his plants. A chief principle was "learning by doing," a theme later to be made popular by John Dewey. (See Pestalozzi, 1892, 1977; Ulich, 1945; Rusk, 1956.)

Pestalozzi emphasized in the higher exercises of the mind the Comenius principle that "things should be learned by doing." Faith is cultivated by believing, not by reasoning; love by loving, not by talking about love; thought by thinking, not by appropriating the thoughts of others; and knowledge by personal investigation, not by endless talk about art and science (Painter, 1889). In *How Gertrude Teaches Her Children*, first published in 1801, Pestalozzi's (1977) most important treatise on education, he explained his method of instruction as implemented by Gertrude, the ideal teacher. He described the methods of his ideal teacher as more playful and practical than didactic. Rather than using the tone of an instructor who would say, "Child, this is your head, your nose, your hand," she would say gently: "Come here, child, I will wash your little hands," "I will comb your hair," "I will cut your fingernails." Such was taught so thoroughly that the child could in turn teach the younger children. In this classic work, Pestalozzi (1977, pp. 139–40) reduced all instruction to three branches: sense impression as the absolute foundation of all knowledge, the nature of teaching, and his prototype wherein nature itself determines the instruction. He argued that these branches, though unpopular, were historically correct and psychologically inevitable.

Pestalozzi focused on sense impressions or training the senses as the point of beginning of all instruction; yet his focus on instruction belies his emphasis on play as an educational tool. To him, instruction was by necessity easy, pleasant, and delightful, to the contemporary reader characteristics of play or playfulness.

> From the moment that a mother takes a child upon her lap, she teaches him. She brings nearer to his senses what nature has scattered afar off

over large areas and in confusion, and makes the action of receiving sense-impressions and the knowledge derived from them, easy, pleasant, and delightful to him … in her pure simplicity, she follows the high course of Nature without knowing what Nature does through her; and Nature does very much through her. (Pestalozzi, 1977, p. 145)

In *How Gertrude Teaches Her Children* (1977) and *Leonard and Gertrude* (1892), Pestalozzi summarizes his most important educational principles. Fundamental to these principles was the point that play is a natural gift, propensity, or inclination of children, and following its dictates would result in a free-play approach to delightful or playful activities.

The richness of its charm and the variety of its free play cause the results of physical necessity to bear the impress of freedom and independence. Here, too, the Art must imitate the course of Nature, and by the richness of its charm and variety of its free play, try to make its results bear the impress of freedom and independence. (Pestalozzi, 1977, p. 202)

The word "play" rarely occurs in the works of Pestalozzi, yet he had a profound influence on one of his pupils and disciples, Friedrich Froebel, who studied with him, learned from him, took exception to certain of his methods but employed many of his ideas in his school, including the integration of play into his curriculum. Froebel developed his own school for children and overshadowed the other great philosopher-educators of the Middle Ages and the reformation in his depth of understanding about play and its implementation into educational methods for children.

Friedrich Froebel: The Architect of the Kindergarten or "Garden for Children"

Froebel (1782–1852), the son of a Lutheran minister, followed most of the great philosopher-educators discussed here by placing great importance on faith and God in all aspects of his educational program. Arguably, his work was more influential in promoting play and natural play environments for schoolchildren than that of any other historical figure. His early surroundings brought him daily into contact with nature and he learned to love being alone in the woods with the streams, the plants, and the animals, all of which became the objects of contemplative thought for him and were to exercise a prominent influence on his children's program. He later became a forester's apprentice, enlarged his knowledge of nature, and, while living for a period entirely among plants, changed his religion into a "religious life in nature" (Painter, 1889, pp. 280–1). His higher education at the University of Jena extended his vast knowledge of nature and science, including lectures on botany, architecture, natural history, physics, chemistry, finance, and forest matters—he later found himself in prison for nine weeks for being unable to pay his debt at the university.

Figure 1.1 Friedrich Froebel, father of the "kindergarten" (garden for children).
Source: First published by C. W. Bardeen, c.1897, Syracuse, NY. Courtesy of the Library of Congress.

The turning point of Froebel's life came when a school principal offered him a job as a teacher, interrupting his short-term work with an architect. In this new role he felt for the first time that he had found his place in life, that the "fish was in the water." He was soon to become one of many scholars to study in Pestalozzi's school. During his first visit, he experienced a variety of emotions— arousal, elevation, depression, and bewilderment. He felt that in Pestalozzi's methods there was no organized connection between the subjects of education (Froebel, 1908). He was sympathetic toward the goals of the school but felt that the methods ranged from lacking to successful. He believed that the nature of the child should be emphasized in both method and subject matter. After spending two years at Pestalozzi's school and intensive intellectual reflection, he opened the first kindergarten in 1837 in Blankenburg, Germany.

Froebel's philosophy of education was religious in nature. He believed that in all things there lives an eternal law based on an all-pervading, eternal unity. A quietly observant mind and clear human intellect would never fail to recognize this unity that is God, the source of all things. Froebel's education was rooted in nature and subject to its laws; harmony in thinking, feeling, willing, and doing; subordination of self to the common good; and leading man to an inner harmony and unity with God. Like Rousseau he envisioned several stages in the development of the individual—childhood, boyhood, and man. From Froebel, Rousseau, and Pestalozzi there springs the modern emphasis on "child centered" education and individual differences in child development. These concepts will be revisited when later discussing the effects of the contemporary standardization of school curricula, and the nature and effects of the high stakes testing movement on children's play and play environments.

Froebel's curriculum was based upon the child's inner unfolding much as a young plant unfolds, requiring tender care and nourishment rather than force and restraint. Education was to grow out of the natural interests of the child and, hence, from life itself. His vehicle of instruction was play, which was to be instructive and enjoyable, unlike the rigid instruction and dull, passive tasks prevalent during his day. The physical body is developed through callisthenic exercises, the social instincts by association with companions in play and work; the senses are cultivated by means of playthings; and the mind is exercised by imitative or inventive uses of Froebel's "gifts" and "occupations." He designed his own materials, the "gifts," consisting of such objects as blocks, cubes, balls, and cylinders which were to be handled, examined, counted, and so on. These were to be played with and manipulated alone until all possible meanings had been explored. Then they were used in combination with other gifts for further development of ideas or concepts aimed at understanding the environment. The "occupations," including such things and activities as paper cutting, weaving, drawing, painting, threading, and stringing, invite transforming and creating activities. The gifts were intended to lead to discovery and the occupations to inventiveness (Froebel, 1887; Ulich, 1945; Frost and Kissinger, 1976). The idea that young children learn best from actively manipulating and exploring concrete materials was further supported in the twentieth century by Dewey, Montessori, and Piaget.

Froebel credited the children themselves for teaching him how to teach them. Considering their ways, he saw their delight in movement, their powers of observation, their use of senses, their ability to invent and construct, and he turned this to the interest of children. This was an "ah ha" moment, for he saw, perhaps more clearly than any of his predecessors, the power of play in the education and development of children. He could, and did, convert children's energies, activities, amusements, occupations, all that goes by the name of play, into educational instruments and therefore transformed work, even manual labor, into play (see Froebel, 1887; Painter, 1889). Froebel exhibited deep insight into children's play and his respect for its profound significance in their development.

> Play is the purest, most spiritual activity of man at this stage, and, at the same time, typical of human life as a whole—of the inner hidden natural life in man and all things. It gives, therefore, joy, freedom, contentment,

inner and outer rest, peace with the world. It holds the source of all that is good ... Play at this time is of deep significance ... the germinal leaves of all later life. (Froebel, 1887, p. 55)

The earliest stage of development for Froebel's child, the period of childhood, was life for the sake of living. The second period, that of boyhood, was the period of learning, and the period in which training predominates either at home, as taught by members of the family, or at school by a teacher. The child was a "school-boy" who had grown from a period of making the internal external to one of making the external internal through the conscious communication of knowledge for a definite purpose. What the child formerly did for the sake of the activity (play), he now did for the sake of the result (work). In childhood he imitated domestic life, in boyhood he shared the work of the family in the field, forest, meadow and garden, and in the trade of the father. All this was accompanied by the daring adventures of childhood: exploring caves and ravines, climbing trees and mountains, and roaming the forests.

From such explorations the child brought to light exciting new stones, plants, and animals, with questions to be answered and further discoveries to be made. He constructed his huts and fortresses with rocks, boards, and branches, learning to use tools and eventually to assess heights and take in views of a beautiful whole. The child would need an external point, self-chosen—a box, closet, grotto, hut, or garden—on which he could center his activity. Brooks or streams also entered into the child's play and required the building of bridges, canals, dams, and mills. Froebel (1887, p. 111) believed that boys who played in these ways made good pupils and would become efficient men. Particularly helpful during boyhood was the cultivation of gardens, for here the child could see his work bearing fruit, subject to the inner laws of natural development, and depending upon the quality of his work. Even if the child could not have his own garden, he should at least have boxes and pots in which to grow a few plants. All this was to be incorporated into Froebel's kindergarten and extensively incorporated into early American kindergartens.

Throughout the history of children's play from antiquity, the great philosopher-educators gave only limited attention to the nature of play consisting simply of activity as such, but emphasized its definite, conscious purpose or the thing or outcome to be represented, for example the free, organized games of running, boxing, ball games, wrestling, and games of hunting or war. Many of the activities were mere practice and exercise of strength. Froebel recognized that such activities were increasingly seen among boys as they advanced in age, and he waxed lyrical about the values of such play, just as he had done about the values of play of a different sort that were characteristic of early childhood.

It is by no means, however, only the physical power that is fed and strengthened in these games; intellectual and moral power, too, is definitely and steadily gained and brought under control ... Whoever would inhale a fresh, quickening breath of life should visit the *playgrounds* of such boys ... Would that all who, in the education of boys, barely tolerate playgrounds, might consider these things! ... Every town should have its own playground. (Froebel, 1887, pp. 113–14, italics added)

Here, in his classic *Education of Man*, the term "playground" is introduced by Froebel. His writings are the first to provide an extensive description of the characteristics and functions of children's school playgrounds as prepared, organized, and supervised by adults. Although his were by no means the first play environments designed and developed by adults for or with children, they appear to be the first to be called "playgrounds." If this is accurate, and contrary to modern thought, the term "playground" did not arise with the onset of manufactured play equipment. Froebel's playgrounds were nature and gardens established on schoolyards and it was there in nature that children played. These playgrounds were in many ways little different from the country surroundings and farms where most children lived, but they were established at Froebel's school where the children spent their days and had their daily times for play—their recesses—and were also rich places for learning.

For Froebel, outdoor life for children should encompass far more than providing times and spaces for children's play. Outdoor life in open nature is particularly valuable because it develops, strengthens, ennobles, and lends a higher significance to all things. His short educational walks or excursions with his pupils became a valuable means of education, even for the younger schoolchildren. During these walks, he would have children forget their hurrying and search for the details in nature, thus helping them to see the whole of the area in which they lived and to learn that they were a part of it. Careful inspection should reveal to children the mutual relations of mountains, valleys, and rivers, the natural abodes of animals; the interrelationships and mutual dependence of living things; the inner constancy and unity of all things and phenomena in nature. On such excursions, children should also see man and his unity with nature, in his occupation's social circumstances, actions, manners, customs, and language. The learning resulting from such experiences during the first stage of childhood conditioned the child for later subjects of instruction, but not before the above subjects, on which all others depended, had been fully presented. Being in the forest and wilderness, common among boys, was not the same as living there, learning its essential properties, and becoming intimate with nature.

Froebel's influence on the role of play, nature, and the outdoors in American education, especially kindergartens and child development centers, is perhaps unsurpassed. His influence, not so widely known, reached to the American child study movement of the early twentieth century. The great American educator William T. Harris, writing in the introduction to Froebel's *Pedagogics of the Kindergarten* (1909, p. vii), identifies him as the great pioneer and founder of child study (see Chapter 4) and of the pedagogic theory of intellectual values. Harris also credits G. Stanley Hall for his labors in the movement.

Joachim Liebschner (1992), a trustee of the National Froebel Foundation, reviewed a rich collection of Froebel's original writings found in Berlin's Deutsche Akademie der Wissenschaften to glean deep and personal insights into the man, his philosophy, and his influence. He concluded that: "No philosopher, no educator before Froebel had seen the importance of play for educational purposes with such clarity" (p. 62). Froebel had little to say about play during his first fifty years of life, devoting but a few pages in his *Education of Man* to the importance of play in education and never attempting to develop a coherent theory of play. He did propose three types of play: symbolic play or representations of ordinary life, creative play, where the material being played with is the only limiting factor, and imitative play or re-creating what is learned in school.

Over time, a shift in focus was gradually seen in Froebel's papers as he began to turn his attention to play in early childhood, and in 1837, when he was fifty-five, play became central in his thinking as a means for educating children. During the next several years he founded the kindergarten, the gifts and occupations, and the movement games, and he wrote his *Mother Song Book* (Blow, 1908; Froebel, 1887, 1909; Liebschner, 1992). In his kindergarten, play was the central instrument for learning but he was ambivalent about the degree of freedom needed; early on he emphasized letting children play with blocks and build what they like, but later he provided a blueprint on how and what to build with bricks or gifts. Play to Froebel was more than a mere tool for the educator; it was also valuable for its intellectual, social, and emotional benefits. He was quite modern in this belief and, like Huizinga, in his view that, "play was essentially a manifestation of the cultural advancement of a society" (Liebschner, 1992, p. 56).

Linking the Contributions of Early Scholars

Lacking the advantages of first-hand experience, historians depend upon original documents and the work of other historians in formulating histories of earlier people, cultures, and eras. The earliest prominent writers about children's play made their original contributions through observation, reflection, and direct experience. The great philosophers that followed were avid students of such early writings, which enriched their existing perspectives and influenced their theories and practices. Beginning in ancient Greece and Rome, the sages or great thinkers discussed here understood and recommended that children should be treated with kindness, that corporal punishment should be banned, that there were developmental stages in childhood, and that children should receive early education within the family but not be introduced to formal education until they were about five years of age. Further, children should be allowed to play at home and at school, for play supports health and physical development and helps prepare children for roles later in life. Indeed, they argued that education should be an amusement, learning should be pleasant, a wide variety of games and amusements should be encouraged, and work should have playful qualities.

The "Renaissance" is aptly named, signifying as it does the revival or flowering of the arts, literature, and vigorous intellectual activity. The works of the great Reformation, Renaissance and pre-modern thinkers in Europe are of great importance in tracing the history of play, for their work, building upon that of their predecessors, was characterized and applied in ever deeper conceptualizations and in broader contexts. In certain respects they revived play-related themes and conclusions much like those noted for Greek and Roman scholars, yet they also reached new, emerging themes and conclusions. Consequently, over time, the nature of play and its importance in child development gradually occupied the growing attention of scholars and resulted in ever-deeper theoretical perspectives and broader practical applications.

Historians have only recently put to rest the common view that children's play and amusements during the medieval period were universally restricted or prohibited. Many religious leaders and parents considered play as the work of the devil and subscribed to such prohibitions, but, despite this, most children were given playthings or toys, many made their own toys, and virtually all played their games much as children have done throughout recorded history. The records show that poverty versus affluence has always been a primary factor influencing the availability of children's time, toys, places, and supervision for play, but, excepting the most extreme conditions of child labor, abuse, war, and natural disasters, children are remarkably skillful in creating such basic play conditions for themselves.

Leading scholars of the Renaissance and the Reformation refined and broadened the perspectives on play set forth by such figures as Plato, Aristotle, and Quintilian. They proposed that education should be reformed, harsh discipline banned, and schooling pleasant. Children should be taught according to stages of development, individual differences should be addressed, both boys and girls should be educated, and children should learn through doing. The pre-modern scholars discussed here became avid students of children at play, helping to enrich existing views or theories, adding substance to knowledge of play, and leaving a rich body of knowledge for later scholars. For example, "learning by doing," a theme developed by Comenius, Pestallozi, and Froebel, was later to become a basic principle espoused by Dewey, Piaget, and Montessori. All understood, as did the ancient Greeks and Romans, that play was essential for health and development. Comenius was influenced by Plato, Aristotle, Cicero, Plutarch, Quintilian, Erasmus, and Bacon (Ulich, 1945).

With time and experience, Renaissance writers began to describe the play and games of children in greater detail, pointing out that children engaged in various forms of play, both illogical and logical and both helpful and harmful. They also gradually applied such knowledge in schools, expanding the curricula to include play and recreation, nature study, and work and play in natural settings and gardens. Education was to be liberal, focusing on play and instruction to strengthen physical, moral, artistic, and intellectual powers. By the time of Froebel, many philosopher/educators saw play as essential for children's physical, intellectual, social, and aesthetic development. There are certain common threads among the philosophies and work of many of the world's most prominent philosophers and scholars of earlier historical eras, and the more recent research of leading scholars across the behavioral sciences. Despite the passage of centuries, many of the lessons drawn out here are still widely ignored in American schools and in American playgrounds—specifically, the lessons that individual differences in children are universal, that there are stages in childhood that should be recognized, that adults can learn much about child rearing and education by observing children, that all the senses should be trained, that direct experience should play an important role in child rearing and education, that work and learning should be playful, that kindness should rule over punishment, that objects and events must be seen, felt, and observed in concrete form, that schools should be child centered, and that play and exercise are essential for the health and development of children. These are lessons forgotten or yet to be learned by those responsible for contemporary actions to reduce recess, playgrounds, and free, spontaneous outdoor play. The chapters that follow will add meaning and substance to these conclusions.

2
Play and Play Environments in Early America

One day after Sunday School a bunch of us children decided to play church. I was the preacher. We all pitched in and cleared off a place on top of a little hill, over in the woods. It was just as nice, all covered with them slick brown pine needles that smell so good when the sun shines on them. We dragged in some logs to use for pews. They called it, "Charley's Church." My pulpit was beside a big pine tree. (White and Holland, 1969, p. 3, as told by Reverend C. C. White, an elderly African American minister who grew up in east Texas and spent his adult years in charitable work with needy people of all races)

In 1620 a small sailing ship, the *Mayflower*, completed its three-month stormy voyage across the Atlantic from Plymouth, England, to the "New World" with 100 emigrants (including 30 children) intent on forming their own government, establishing their own churches, and living their own way. The *Log of the Mayflower*, written by William Bradford, later governor of the colony, is a careful account of the voyage and of the early experiences in their new home, and is held in the Boston Library. The welfare of their children was one of the reasons for the pilgrims' perilous voyage, for they wished them to be free of association with worldly companions and the temptations of city streets (MacElroy, 1929). Little did they realize how monumental would be the obstacles they were to face in the New World.

Many children of the early settlers died in the harsh climate, some shortly after birth, and many survivors were stricken with sore throats, fever, and smallpox. Fortunately for historians, the making of diaries was common among both adults and children. MacElroy quotes from the diary of Judge Sewell of Boston: "A very extraordinary storm by reason of the falling and driving of snow. Few women could get to meeting. A child named Alexander was baptized in the afternoon." Sewell tells of his own baby, four days old, shrinking from the icy water, but not crying. A physician gave his prescription for rickets, a disease previously unknown to the pilgrims:

Dip the child in cold water, naked in the morning, head foremost in cold water, don't dress it Immediately but let it be made warm in ye cradle &

sweat at least half an hour. Do this 3 mornings going & if one or both feet are cold while other parts sweat, Let a little blood be taken out of ye feet ye 2d morning, and it will cause them to sweat afterward. (MacElroy, 1929, p. 16)

Families were large, contributing to the preservation of the colony, with up to 26 children in one family. Just as the settlers had experienced in England, children were expected to work in both the home and out-of-doors, but they were allowed to play after the work was done. The natural dangers of the wilderness and the presence of Native Americans or "savages" kept them under the surveillance of adults, who admonished them not to wander far from home. Later, the settlers made friends with the Native Americans, who taught them improved means of planting crops and building homes. Many early American children played and learned with Native American children. Perhaps no culture integrated play into daily life, culture, and work more richly than that of the Native Americans prior to the arrival of the settlers. Both groups played and worked in a never-ending cycle, with the activities at times being almost indistinguishable one from the other. Playing out the roles of adults and the work requirements of children prepared them to provide sustenance for the family, and hunting, fishing, planting, harvesting, and related skills were developed through make-believe play and games.

Play and Play Environments of Native American and Early Settlers' Children

When America belonged to the Native Americans, they spent a great deal of time in amusements and athletics. Native American braves and married women joined in the athletics of the tribe and the elderly took part in quieter games in the shade and around the winter fires. Like children everywhere, the young children engaged in the most trifling play and the older children and young adults engaged in inter-tribal athletics with as many as several hundred players taking the field. When a challenge was received, the athletes went into training by dieting, bathing, and practicing, and the glory of winning went not to the individual but fell on the whole tribe. Several types of football were played, differing across geographical regions and tribes, some so far scattered they were not likely to have been learned from each other. The many games included, apart from football, shinny, quoits, hoop and spear, bounce-on-the-rock, kicking the stick, tossing games, the Indian and the rabbits, snow snake and numerous games suited to the seasons. The younger children had their own special circle games, singing games, imitating animal games, and chasing games (Stow, 1924).

When the early settlers arrived, they met both friendly and hostile Native Americans, the former assisting them in accommodating themselves to the unfamiliar environment and the latter terrorizing them beyond their wildest imaginations. Native Americans taught the pilgrims how to hunt, fish, and plant and fertilize corn, which became a common food staple in the colonies. Foods made from corn included a variety of cereals: samp, hominy, suppawn, pone, and succotash, all Native American foods cooked in Native American ways (Earle, 1899). The pilgrims also copied the homes of Native Americans, building cave dwellings and houses made from natural resources, such as earth, sod, grass, deerskins, tree boughs, and other natural materials, as they moved south (Earle, 1899). Many books have been written about the early settlers and the Native Americans who greeted them, and the extensive record continues to the present day. Knowing about Native American children's play in the New World assists in understanding the origins and the mutual influences of play across cultures and across historical eras.

A French traveler to the colonies in the seventeenth century described a favorite game of children—football. "It is a leather ball about as big as one's head, filled with wind. This is kicked about from one to the other in the streets by him that can get it, and that is all the art of it." In his book *The Anatomie of Abuses*, Philip Stubbes wrote in 1583 regarding the game of football:

> For as concerning football playing I proteste unto you that it may rather be called a friendlie kind of fighte than a playe or recreation—a bloody and murderin practice than a sport or pastime. (MacElroy, 1929, pp. 29–30)

Earle (1953) also quoted Stubbes on football:

> So that by this means sometimes their necks are broken, sometimes their backs, sometimes their legs, sometimes their armes, sometimes their noses gush out with blood, sometimes their eyes start out, and sometimes hurte in one place, sometimes in another. (Earle, 1953, p. 356)

Whether in imitation of the settlers or as their own game, Native Americans played football. A traveler in New England after Boston had been established for a half century described one game that he observed Native Americans play:

> There was that day a great game of football to be played. There was another town played against them as is common in England; but they played with their bare feet which I thought very odd; but it was upon a broad sandy shoar free from stones which made it easie. Neither were they so apt to trip up one another's heels and quarrel as I have seen in England. (MacElroy, 1929, pp. 30–1)

Schools in the New England colonies were small and uncomfortable with few furnishings and books. Many teachers were poorly prepared and most were intense disciplinarians, dealing out harsh punishment for infractions. The first country schoolhouses in Pennsylvania and New York were made with logs, some with dirt floors and log benches. Families and colony leaders were intent on securing an education for their children, requiring the building of a school in each town where there were sufficient children and teachers. Education for boys was eventually provided in all the colonies but education for girls was considered less important than learning household duties, although some learned to read, write, and cipher, and others were tutored at home. In 1636 the General Court of Massachusetts earmarked more than half of the annual income of the entire colony to establish the school which two years later became Harvard College (Earle, 1899). This marked the first time that any body of people in any country gave money through their representatives to establish a place of education.

Early colonial children had the finest of "play-grounds" (their hyphenated designation) with acres of fields, meadows, streams, and woodlands, and they invented games learned from experiences in this new land—building and defending forts, making bows and arrows, Native American surprises, and playing soldiers (MacElroy, 1929). In common with children through history, they played games of tag, ball games, hiding games, leap frog, and various others learned by their elders while in England and Holland and taught to their children. In about 1867 Mary Holbrook MacElroy, a teacher at the State Normal School in Oswego, New York, wrote (p. 28) that she learned on a public school playground some of the singing games that children had played hundreds of years before. These included "Green gravel, green gravel, the grass is so green"; "Oats, peas, beans, and barley grows"; "Ring around a rosy"; "Here I brew, here I bake, here I make my wedding cake." In some respects, though perhaps not so refined, colonial children, especially those who lived in the countryside, assumed work roles similar to those assumed by Native American children—boys taking responsibility for hunting, fishing, and planting and girls for tasks related to food preparation, housekeeping, gardening, and securing wild fruit from the woodlands.

The colonists, both children and adults, played numerous games, many brought from their homelands. These included singing games, finger-string games, flying kites, dancing around maypoles, marbles, fishing, blind man's buff, baseball, swimming, tops, thread the needle, boys and girls come out to play, leap frog, hop-scotch, riding, cards, dice, and cockfighting. Seasons tended to influence the types of games chosen. In winter, coasting or sledding down hills on improvised sleds was popular. Some games were frowned upon and prohibited in certain places, including cards, dice, quoits, ninepins, bowls, cockfighting, and cock throwing. The prohibitions were similar to those imposed in England, with exceptions. For example, cockfighting was allowed in English classrooms and at holiday celebrations. Manufactured toys were limited in number but children, sometimes with the help of adults, fabricated their toys themselves from scrap material. No toys were manufactured in seventeenth century New England (Daniels, 1995, p. 187). However, early settlers brought with them a wide assortment of toys that still exist today, but most of their toys were made from scrap and materials found in the natural outdoor environments that served as their play-grounds.

Girls and boys were allowed to have their respective toys and games, many gender based. Girls played with paper dolls, doll-houses, and cradles. Boys played with kites, toy boats, and animal pets, collected items such as rocks and birds' eggs, and played at being Native Americans (Mintz, 2004). Their work was gender focused. As early as age three, children were assigned work roles, but there was little supervision and adults trusted them early with responsibilities "that would horrify a modern parent" (Hawke, 1988, p. 67). However, such work roles for young children were not unique to the early colonists but were a part of struggling, poverty-ridden societies for centuries, including the children of the Great Depression. Play survived through it all.

The Changing Picture of Early Colonists' Play

Daniels (1995) paints a more positive picture of the play and leisure of the colonists than is depicted in the works of earlier writers. Contrary to the popular view of the lives of Puritans and other early settlers as joyless, boring, and dull, modern historians, beginning in the 1960s, began to replace the "gloomy, religious Puritan fanatic with a relaxed moderate," asserting, for example, that they enjoyed sex, beer, and time off work. Daniels (1995, pp. xii–xiii) explains this ambivalence about the Puritans not as their failure to live up to ideals, but as the failure to agree upon ideals and ways of translating them into practice. He studied this ambivalence by developing "thick descriptions" of what the Puritans said and what they did during the 17th and eighteenth centuries, or, more specifically, by examining the intersection of belief, practice, and social milieu. Chudacoff's rich history of play in America also paints a more relaxed portrait of early colonists' expectations for their children: "different groups of early Americans ... tolerated youthful indulgences, and virtually all groups, including the Puritans, lavished affection on their children, disciplined them gently, and rationally tried to shield them from the adult world's corruptions" (Chudacoff, 2007, pp. 19–20).

Daniels showed that pleasure had a useful role in Puritan life in music, sex, celebrations, parties, courtship, taverns, reading, and sports and games—all these were acceptable, even among many ministers, if practiced in moderation. Contrary to earlier thought, most Puritans never believed that their behavior was sinful simply because it was enjoyable; in fact they held that such pleasures helped prevent one from practicing such sins as gluttony, idleness, and lust. They maintained that these and other sins were subject to punishment and must be abandoned. Miller's influential book *The New England Mind in the Seventeenth Century* (1939) argued that Puritans, even the ministerial elite, sought and experienced pleasure in their lives. His work influenced a new generation of historians. Puritan children engaged in their self-chosen play, considered "idleness" and sinful by some adults, yet many, including John Cotton, did not consider it idleness for young children to spend much time in play (Morgan, 1966, p. 66).

Revolutionary New England owed a great deal to the Puritans. Their commitment to literacy and education and their belief in hard work contributed to their legacy of literature, a public school system, success in industry, and elegant churches. The Puritans also had a long-lasting influence on play and leisure and on a strict code of Christian morality, which became relaxed over time, yet they shared this influence with other Christian religions. Christians all over the world are uncomfortable with immoderate or indecent behaviors, yet they are often also uncomfortable with prevailing ideas about their meanings.

> Beyond this general sense of Christian morality, decency, and restraint ...
> it is difficult to attribute specific thoughts or practices concerning leisure
> and recreation to any leftovers from Puritan culture. We should stop look-
> ing for the ghosts of John Winthrop and Cotton Mather every time we see
> a prude or fanatic on the American landscape. (Daniels, 1995, p. 221)

Life in England during the seventeenth and eighteenth centuries ranged from extravagant for the nobility, wretched for the peasantry, to bleak and monotonous for the middle class. By this time, life in the American colonies was better in many ways. Children were economic assets and increasingly valued themselves as contributing members of the family and community. Both boys and girls living on farms worked long hours in the fields, allowing large families to raise crops and improve the family's economic position. When slaves were introduced, their children assumed many of the work roles of the plantation owners' families.

Girls at Play in Nineteenth Century New England

In the colonial period in America, just as in Renaissance Europe, little girls had their dolls, some brought by ship from Europe and differing according to the resources of the family—the very poor making their own rag dolls and the wealthy purchasing sweet-faced dolls wearing fabulous, expensive clothing. These dolls, whatever their appearance, were alternately treated by their child owners as their own babies, as symbolic representations of heroes and heroines, as props for house play and soldier play, and were used for many other roles too numerous to mention. Dolls of ivory and wood with jointed legs and arms have been found in excavations dating back to ancient Greece. In seventeenth century England, dolls were sold at fairs and were used by milliners and dressmakers to display their fashions during the eighteenth century. In about 1620 Ward, an English poet, wrote:

> Ladies d'y want fine Toys
> For Misses or for Boys
> Of all sorts I have choice

And pretty things to tease ye.
I want a little babye
As pretty a one as may be
With head dress made of feathers

> (MacElroy, 1929, p. 37)

This desire to play with dolls and the natural tendency to create playthings are reflected in modern times. A day before this page was written, I observed third grade girls playing in a sand pile on a school playground. They found an abandoned clear plastic sack, long and narrow, about six inches wide. They filled it with sand, tied a string around it to designate the waist, tied a knot in the sack to retain the sand and represent the neck, and shaped the excess sack material to represent the head, then gently cradled the doll in their arms and proudly carried it to me for my approval.

In 1889 Lucy Larcom published her autobiography, *A New England Girlhood*, in which she recorded her experiences as a girl at play and work near the sea in Salem, Massachusetts, a time when old ways of doing things had not wholly been abandoned. Her home was primitive yet comfortable, with oil lamps, an open fireplace for roasting, and an oven for baking. Cooking stoves were just coming into fashion. Her aunt's well close to their door contained the coldest and clearest water she ever drank and supplied the entire neighborhood. Beyond the wall were the buttercups and lady's slipper waiting to be gathered. The hill and space beyond was the playground, with miniature precipices, neighbor's gardens, and ledges shaped into rock-stairs, carpeted with lovely mosses. These were the ways to her "castle-towers" with breakfast rooms among the landings where she and her friends set tables for their guests using pieces of broken china and tucked their rag children in to sleep while they climbed to the turret to watch for ships arriving from the sea. The barking of dogs in the distance made the place all the more mysterious.

Larcom described how the children were always free to go down the lane to yet another lane or cow path, bordered with corn fields and orchards, then on into a wider cart road and there was the river! A neighbor boy was sometimes there to row them down the river in his boat—a fearful and forbidden delight. As they rowed into the open sea, stories were told of children drifting away and drowning, leading the boy to row swiftly back to the tumbledown wharf. By the time Larcom wrote her story as an adult, the lanes had become a broad thoroughfare, and the hill with all its charm and irregularities had been buried under houses. The riverside playground station had become a noisy train station and the joyful shouts of boys and girls at play were no longer there. The special play places of children in the cities had already begun to disappear and their interests were beginning to shift to less natural spaces in streets and vacant lots.

A neighbor everyone called "Aunt Hannah" kept Larcom's school. The students were all the little ones, no matter how young, and up a flight of stairs to the second floor of a house was the schoolroom. Then down another flight was the garden with its spearmint, tansy, southernwood, wormwood, and an abundance of old fashioned flowers. The regular afternoon opening of the "four o'clocks" just at the close of school was "a daily wonder to us babies" (Larcom, 1889, p. 39). Larcom's father had a shop downstairs from the school and Aunt Hannah often allowed her to go there for a half-hour's recreation while the older children continued their school work. She was allowed to spend much time there playing around the candy counter, marveling at the rich colors and listening to the stories of the visitors to the shop. She thought of both school and shop as places of entertainment for little children.

Going "huckleberrying" with her brother, through Cat Swamp to Burnt Hills and Beaver Pond, allowed Larcom to sense the enchantment of the pine trees whispering to each other while her brother thrashed through the woods picking berries. Such stories, common in the autobiographies of writers who played and worked in natural settings, are reminiscent of Alice McLerran's (1991) delightful little book *Roxaboxen*, written a century later about her childhood playground, a magical village lovingly created with stones, sticks, and old boards and bottles on a rocky hillside among the *ocotillo* bushes in Arizona. Such stories and places, no doubt common across the centuries, are testimonials to the active imagination and creative genius of children who are free to play with simple objects in natural habitats.

There were plenty of children for Larcom to play with in both city and surrounding countryside. She joined her cousins on the farm to watch the cows being milked and the chickens being fed. She preferred the quieter games typically played by girls to those of her brother and his male friends. His boyish sports of walking on stilts, riding in wheelbarrows, coasting down hills, and ball games did not appeal to her because she considered herself a rather clumsy child. Perhaps the apparent lack of opportunity for girls to engage in such active games contributed to her feelings. Girls were seldom allowed to play with boys other than their brothers, but sometimes they did enter into their games and all played together in "delightful unconsciousness" (Larcom, 1889, p. 109).

When her father died, leaving her mother with eight children to support and no property except the roof over their heads and a small strip of land, Larcom at first sang hymns to her mother to cheer her:

For strangers into life we come,
And dying is but going home.
(Larcom, 1889, p. 140)

Her mother soon realized that even after her older siblings had found occupations, more had to be done. They moved to Lowell, a mill town, in 1835 and

Larcom entered her first grammar school for both boys and girls and was taught by her first male teacher. She helped her family run a small boarding house for mill girls and later took a job in the mill at one dollar a week, maintaining all the while that there was plenty of play in between. Larcom later entered Monticello Seminary in Mississippi and was to become a successful writer. She closed her book thus:

> let me say to you, dear girls, that the meaning of life is education; not through book knowledge alone, sometimes entirely without it ... Humility, Sympathy, Helpfulness, and Faith are the best teachers in this great university, and none of us are well educated who do not accept their training. (Larcom, 1889, p. 273)

Boys at Play in Nineteenth Century New England

The literature about children's play in New England is greatly enriched by Edward Everett Hale's book *A New England Boyhood* (1908), which chronicled the social life and customs of his childhood in Boston at a time when the population was 40,000 and cows were still pastured on the Common. Hale was to become one of America's great, most widely loved writers. He enjoyed his Latin School but hated Harvard, due at least in part to the drunkenness and devilry among the students—behavior contrary to that of the "pious believers" of his time. James Russell Lowell was his associate and companion, Longfellow was his teacher at Harvard, and his contemporaries included many of America's great writers. He personally heard Emerson read from his own notes his poetic description of Boston on the same day that this poem was born:

> The rocky nook, with hill-tops three,
> Looked eastward from the farms,
> And twice each day the flowing sea
> Took Boston in its arms.
>
> The wild rose and the barberry thorn
> Hung out their summer pride,
> Where now on heated pavements worn
> The feet of millions stride.

> (Hale, 1908, p. xix)

Notwithstanding Hale's contention that he would not attempt anything so ambitious as an autobiography, his rich, incisive accounts of school and social life while growing up in New England Boston and his eye-witness accounts of the introduction of organized playgrounds in an American city make his *New England Boyhood* a valued reference for play scholars.

In brief, here is Hale's story of his early schooling and his play, the only eye-witness account found by the present writer of the creation and use of one of the earliest organized playgrounds or "outdoor gymnasiums" erected in America. He was born in 1822 and died in 1909, becoming along the way the most famous preacher in Boston by 1866. His great grandfather was Captain Nathan Hale of Revolutionary history. He was born on Tremont Street, a location that allowed him later to have quick access to the "outdoor gymnasia" erected on that street. For present purposes, it is noteworthy that he was the last survivor of a group of boys who protested to a British general about his soldier's interfering with coasting down Beacon and School streets on home-made carts past the Latin School. Hale (1908, p. xvii) and Horace Scudder, editor of the *Atlantic Monthly*, were much attracted to Lucy Larcom's "charming book", *A New England Girlhood*, published in 1889 and set in Salem and Lowell, Massachusetts. They decided that Hale should write about his own boyhood in Boston, leading to the publication of his *A New England Boyhood*.

In 1824, at age two, Hale started school on the second floor of an old fashioned wood house. Since the floor was sanded with clean sand twice a week, the children were able to make sand pies with their feet. He mentioned this detail as a contrast with later schools where carpets on the kindergarten floors did not allow sand for playing, so that teachers had to provide clay for modeling and heaps of sand in backyards. The fact that the teacher, Miss Whitney, allowed Hale, a two-year-old, into her class led him to believe later that she conducted the school exercises or lessons on an "individual basis" (p. 14). In the winter an older brother pulled the other four children to school on a little green sleigh. At age six he was transferred to another school in the neighborhood in the basement of a church, consisting of four rented rooms. His father would not have sent him to a public school of lower grades "any more than he would have sent me to jail" (p. 17). The masters at the public schools were reportedly "inferior men" and there was constant talk of "hiding," "cow-hides," and "thrashing."

At about age nine, Hale entered Latin School, where the only fun was enjoyed before the bell rang, so children arrived early, gathered in groups near the school, and talked about the news of the school. Initially, there was no formal or school playground. The room for playing was limited, but there was enough space and time for a game of tag or other contrived games before school began. At eight o'clock in summer and nine o'clock in winter the bell rang in a nearby church cupola and the four or five masters standing on the sidewalk bowed to each other and retired to their rooms. The boys were expected to be in their seats when the bell stopped ringing after five full minutes. Since ringing the bell with the rope was for some reason unsatisfactory, a boy was sent upstairs to strike the bell with the bell tongue for the full five minutes—a tiring but coveted privilege since it allowed degrees of compensation for undesirable behavior or credit for poor recitations. The school system itself was rigid, focusing on extremes of verbal memory.

School life had little to relieve itself of monotony and the only times for play-ing were before school and during the one recess. Some of the boys would rush home after school to join their siblings and friends for trips to the wharves and the excitement of going aboard sea-going vessels, talking with the men, dipping straws into the bung holes of molasses being unloaded and tasting the delicacy, then making their own sailing ships from hemlock bark and sailing them from wharf to wharf. A special treat was going to sea in a soap box. Practically every-thing required for manufacture, creation, and invention was readily obtainable, as well as building tools. There was of course risk and danger in free, spontane-ous play, as when Hale burned his eyebrows by igniting gunpowder with a burning-glass. Their private places, perhaps equivalent to country children's spaces in the woods, were attics, basements, or on the roof which commanded an expansive view of the harbor. There were also the "tame games" of checkers, shuttlecock, cup and ball, battledoor, chess, lotto, etc., but generally only when more exciting games were inconvenient.

All the boys were in touch with nature due to their frequent excursions into the surrounding countryside, and they "could hardly have lived without some sort of gardening at home" (Hale, 1908, p. 63). Some of these gardens were just a square foot and a half each, perhaps inspiring someone to invent present-day "square foot gardening." In the spring, as the snow melted and the sleds were put away, children turned to marbles, kites, hoops, and playing at the Frog Pond. Festivals along Tremont Street and other malls included hucksters of every kind with their tents, tables and stalls, and there were fireworks on Independence Day; these were events to be relished. For many boys there was work to be done at home and children were expected to attend church regularly from an early age. Presumably because of Lucy Larcom's earlier book *A New England Girlhood*, and his own play experiences, Hale focused on the play of boys in his engaging and informative book *A New England Boyhood*.

Playing in the Country: Hunting, Fishing, War, and Recess

Even though people were moving into cities in growing numbers during the late nineteenth century, two out of every three people still lived in the country. Life in the country or on farms differed widely across the developing country but the recreational opportunities—amusements, festivals, sports, gymnasiums—were nowhere equal to those in the rapidly growing cities. Farmers lived miles from their neighbors; earning a livelihood from the land required many hours of back breaking labor by every member of the family strong enough to work, there were no means for rapid communication or travel, and monotony and lack of city pleasures led to drudgery and monotony for many. Dulles (1940) wrote of the simple country pleasures of hunting, fishing, cheap living, pride in labor, and the pleasures of nature, but noted that city pleasures—dancing, gymnasiums, shooting galleries, opera, and theaters—were missing.

The books written by people who lived the experiences they related are most valuable for their accounts of life in a particular era. C. D. Warner's book *Being a Boy* (1877) about childhood in New England is but one of his several accounts of childhood, all valuable historical references. Unlike other writers of his time, Warner devoted more attention to his own gender than to the other. His childhood work and play, set during the mid-1800s, are similar, almost remarkably so, to those (described below) of the present writer growing up during the Depression in the 1930s. For example, Warner describes his literary substitute John driving an oxen team for the first time:

> What a glorious feeling it is, indeed, when a boy is for the first time given the long whip and permitted to drive the oxen ... swinging the long lash, and shouting "Gee, Buck!" "Haw, Golden!" "Whoa, Bright!" ... and all the neighbors for half a mile are aware that something unusual is going on ... I am not sure but I would rather drive the oxen than have a birthday ... I was so little, that it was a wonder that I didn't fall off, and get under the broad wheels ... But I never heard of one who did (Warner, 1877, pp. 2–3)

The differences in our experiences were that John drove oxen and I drove a team of mules, and, while alone driving a wagon, one of my dearest friends at that time fell out and was killed when run over by a wheel. We all reveled in having a horse to ride, cows to chase, and games to play. Before the era of motorized farm equipment young farm boys, just old enough to enter school, took on adult responsibilities, and they especially enjoyed working and playing with animals, frequently making pets of the horses, calves, chickens, goats, and dogs.

> A dog is of great use on a farm ... He is good to bite peddlers and small children and run out and yelp at wagons that pass by, and to howl all night when the moon shines. And yet, if I were a boy again, the first thing I would have should be a dog (Warner, 1877, pp. 37–8)

Play was widely accepted in the New England countryside but only after the chores were done: cleaning out stables, weeding and hoeing the garden, splitting kindling and carrying it to the house, shoveling snow in the winter, sorting out rotten potatoes in the cellar and pulling the sprouts off the good ones, and salting the cattle. Salting the cattle alone or driving them in from the pasture could easily allow time to check for fish in the creek, examine a new bird's nest, or pick some wild berries. Cold weather posed special challenges and taught new lessons, for example learning to turn up large stones on frosty mornings while picking cantaloupes to warm bare feet in the warm soil underneath for a few moments.

Sunday was a day of rest and going to church but hardly a relief for farm children because chores had to be done very early to be on time, and church clothes and shoes had to be put on and worn, making one uncomfortable and conspicuous. Furthermore, Sunday school verses had to be learned and horses rounded up, harnessed, and hitched to the wagon for the trip to church. First were singing and prayers, then the long sermon, then at noon Sunday school followed by lunch while listening to the men talk about cattle, and finally the afternoon service and the trip home for dinner.

Many New England boys, above all else, desired to live by hunting, fishing, and war. Their passion for display—ornament such as that worn by Native Americans and soldiers—was apparently as strong among them as modern boys' devotion to sports heroes. Going out to kill a deer during play without the appropriate trappings would destroy half the pleasure. John and his classmates wove bracelets from the hair of the girls, allowing them to sport trophies equivalent to the scalps carried by Native Americans, the highest respect being accorded to the boy who had the most trophies on his arm. John was determined to become an officer in the military, for officers always stood unharmed in the midst of battle, sword in hand, with the common soldiers falling and dying all around them. John later advanced to the rank of first lieutenant in his village militia.

John named "fair skater," "accurate snow-baller," and accomplished "slider-down-hill" for what he liked best at school during the winter, and among his school subjects he selected history, specifically the history of the Native American wars. School was for endless drill on spelling, arithmetic, and geography, which had to be cleared out of the way before recess. Recess, that traditional bright spot in a school world of discipline and weariness, was alive and well in New England schools:

> But recess! Was ever any enjoyment so keen as that with which a boy rushes out of the school-house door for the ten minutes of recess? He is like to burst with animal spirits; he runs like a deer; he can nearly fly; and he throws himself into play with entire self-forgetfulness ... For ten minutes the world is absolutely his; the weights are taken off, restraints are loosed, and he is master for that brief time ... And there is the noon-ing, a solid hour, in which vast projects can be carried out which have slyly matured during the school-hours; expeditions are undertaken, wars are begun between Indians and settlers ... or games are carried on which involve miles of running, and an expenditure of wind sufficient to spell the spelling-book though at the highest pitch. (Warner, 1877, pp. 67–8)

Such an early love of recess as that embodied in Warner's descriptions reveals an intelligence about play seemingly inherent in children who devote many hours to it each week. He learned early that during recess friendships are formed, "boot" when trading jackknives had to be paid "on the nail," and being honorable sometimes meant that settling disagreements quickly with the fists was better than pretending cheating was fair. He also learned that the delights of reading novels, not approved for children during his time, were perhaps heightened by doing so on the sly, and that spending extra minutes on the way home to help carry a girl's books or to secure a lock of her hair was worth having to explain the delay when arriving home.

By 1890 many farms in areas where living conditions were very hard had fallen into ruin as people increasingly wearied of the long hours of labor and the same routine jobs, and farming became a more demanding vocation. Further, the traditional barn raising, harvestings, rail-splitting, quilting bee, and social visiting were being abandoned, although the young continued to get together while their elders met only at public meetings (Hamlin, 1917). However, the picture in the country was not nearly so dreary as painted by some; farmers still had the independence, the active outdoor life, the occasional social activities, the country dances, the church activities, the county fairs, the holiday celebrations, the occasional traveling circus, and the entertainment and singing schools at the schoolhouse, which were mostly lacking among factory workers and clerks (Dulles, 1940, p. 274). Opportunities for entertainment varied greatly between the more prosperous farm areas and those mired in poverty, just as in the cities. By the turn of the twentieth century the peep shows, penny arcades, and the nickelodeon era were about to be replaced as motion pictures were introduced into towns and cities. As these became more technically sophisticated and widely available, people from the country would flock to them on weekends and to other pleasurable events.

The Western Frontier: Work, Play, Muddy Roads, and Wilderness

Hundreds of thousands of children participated in the westward expansion of America, but their lives and contributions were afforded little attention by historians. Elliott West (1989) searched through journals, letters, novels, and autobiographies to reconstruct and prepare a rich and remarkable account of the failures and successes, troubles and joys of the tough people who settled the frontier. Fortunately, West is grounded in psychology and child development and, consequently, capable of extracting rich meanings from the personal stories of the children. His book addresses the children rather than the real and fictional cowboys, trappers, and traders popularized in both history and novels— those who encountered and eventually tamed the overland trails, rugged towns and mining camps, and isolated farms and ranches. This brief synopsis of frontier children's play tells a special part of the story, exposing their contributions through play and work to family and community and to their own development.

The settlers' living conditions in the frontier West were Spartan at best, with sod and log homes, a world of nature and animals, tragedies, rites of passage, and a continuing struggle to exist in a world subject to the vagaries of nature, illness and injuries, dangerous animals, and sometimes ruthless men. Distances from towns were especially formidable for those unaccustomed to living off the land, for basic supplies could be inaccessible from stores or neighbors for extended periods. Long days were spent during growing seasons planting, harvesting, and caring for livestock in preparation for formidable winters. Every member of the family old and strong enough to work contributed as they were able and had to fit play in between work periods. The work itself provided opportunities for play, as children herded livestock, tended gardens, plowed fields, gathered crops, and fished and hunted game in the outdoors. Household tasks also carried elements of pride and pleasure depending upon the attitudes and helpfulness of the adults, as girls or boys helped with the cooking, sewing, gathering wood, gathering vegetables, tending chickens, cleaning the house, and a myriad other tasks. Evenings, Sundays, and inclement weather allowed opportune times for games, frivolity, and simple celebrations.

When the western frontier settlers moved into a new area, there were no schools, so children were taught at home or in the homes of neighbors, usually by frontier women, scratching out letters and numbers on the dirt floor of a log, sod, or adobe home. When the first schools were established, children would arrive as chores, work, and weather allowed. The teacher would teach two or three at a time and older children would tutor younger ones, for the children, typically aged six to sixteen, were not separated by grade levels. Children drank water from the same gourd dipper, were warmed by a single wood stove, used an outhouse for a rest room, and read an assortment of books, bibles, and McGuffey Readers, focusing on the three r's, history, geography, penmanship, and spelling. The "playground" was the field or forest outside the school building. The teachers earned ten to thirty-five dollars a month. During the 1800s, conditions were quite primitive and there were serious discipline problems and corrective measures in many schools.

> Some teachers were not reluctant to use a rawhide whip. One of them reported that he had whipped thirteen boys the first day of class. Each day thereafter he whipped fewer boys, until finally he was able to put the whip away ... a young teacher named Tom Clay had no problems at all with discipline. The first day of class, he stood up, smiled at the students before him, and placed a six-shooter on his desk. "We're here to learn," he announced. "If anyone misbehaves, there's going to be trouble." (Freedman, 1983, p. 69)

West (1989) assigned the many kinds of play created by frontier children into four categories: the play of exploration from infancy to adolescence, making work into play, playing formal games, and engaging in amusements encouraged by adults. During its first few years the baby's play and exploration of the environment are almost indistinguishable as she practices motor skills and learns to discriminate between objects. Such activity, amply defined by play scholars such as Piaget (1951), is characteristic of all healthy infants, differing with the context, the availability of playthings, and the support of the mother or another adult. The child through such play forms pre-concepts, develops memory, and, as discussed in contemporary scientific literature, apparently stimulates or programs the neural structures. Such exploration and play, however, are not peculiar to infants but continue with growing refinement across developmental periods.

Adults on the overland trails wrote about the innate tendencies of children to watch and wonder at the ever-changing landscapes as they rode the wagons, then eagerly jumping out to explore the scenes and objects they had been watching whenever the wagons stopped—the creeks, pebbles, flowers, small animals, hailstones, animal bones—whatever was novel and interesting. The very young never seemed to tire of exploring and playing. (Some theorists distinguish between the two activities while acknowledging their similarity and relationships.) Gathering objects for playthings and engaging in creative inventiveness, so characteristic of growing children, the older children raced their ponies across the fields, spent long periods at the swimming hole, explored the hills and creeks of the wilderness, the mine shafts and back streets of shanty towns, and found their special play places in the rocks and brush or in snow banks. Despite the ever-present difficult, even dangerous, circumstances, surviving adults writing of their early lives had pleasant recollections of the sensual sensations experienced in mine shafts, woodlands, barnyards, and shanty kitchens. They also loved the muddy streets, despite the encounters with Native Americans, miners, soldiers, and free-roaming animals (Freedman, 1983; West, 1989).

The second category of play, making work into play, was similar to the first, the difference being that children explored their surroundings while performing their chores or assigned work (West, 1989). Just as children creatively, almost magically, transformed their exploratory play into novel forms, theirs was a small task to transform work into play. Like their exploratory play, this contributed to independence and a sense of identity, and helped develop skills that would be needed in the future. Such work/play activities would naturally remind play scholars of the early instinct–practice theory of play proposed by Groos in *The Play of Animals* (1898) and *The Play of Man* (1901), and derived from earlier instinct theories. There is little doubt that mimicking or playing out work roles could indeed contribute to the development of the skills needed for performing future work; however, such play is not performed as training for specific skills but rather leads to mastery of self and environment from a general development aspect (Frost and Klein, 1979). Groos himself seemed to understand the limitations of his theory and extended his perspectives beyond mere mechanical, preparatory for life activities. "I would remark that imitation is almost never merely that; it is creation as well, production as well as reproduction. Close on the heels of imitation comes imagination" (Groos, 1901, p. 290).

Frontier children at work in the fields would liven the work by racing from place to place. Hunting for game to feed the family was little different from hunting for pure pleasure. Hunting for rabbits was remembered by one Oklahoma woman as "about the only good time that we ever had" (West, 1989, p. 105). The availability of game varied by geography: birds on the ponds of the plains, raccoons in the south, deer and bear in the mountains, squirrels in the woodlands, rabbits and coyotes everywhere. One person remembered: "Hunting seemed to me the greatest sport in all creation. Compared with (it) everything else was as dust in the cyclone" (West, 1989, p. 105). A Colorado girl recalled that the chore of picking wild greens and berries was turned into play for she could search out secret places in the hills and valleys and return for future adventures. By age four or five many children were put to riding horses, driving livestock, and delivering messages—all jobs to be enjoyed. Chasing coyotes and cattle on horseback and tending to their special horses and other livestock were common delights, and enjoyed by both girls and boys. Throughout their childhoods, frontier children meshed play and work into one somewhat indistinguishable pattern of playing, working, learning, and developing necessary skills and confidence.

The third category of frontier children's play discussed by West comprises formal games. Beginning at about age five, not seven as proposed by Piaget (1951), children across centuries learned skills such as resolving social issues and controversies and developed physical and cognitive skills through meeting and mastering challenges posed by spontaneous and organized games (see Piaget, 1951; Millar, 1945; Eifermann, 1971). Frontier children played out the games passed on to them by adults and older siblings and others contrived or modified on the spot. Games were played in circles and lines, with sticks and cans, and some involved dancing, chanting, and singing. Boys and girls sometimes played these games together, but the preferred games of their ancestors and their children continued to be selected by the respective genders. "Anti-I-Over," later called "Annie Over" in some locations, was a favorite of both girls and boys.

The universal nature of group games meant that wherever frontier children started at school in the primitive schoolhouses of the early West, they were able to join their new peers in common games and tie firm social links while engaging in the same competitive and cooperative games to which they had earlier been introduced. While children everywhere were playing competitive, aggressive games, eastern children preferred organized sports and "parlor" games and western children played games with more loosely enforced rules such as shinny (perhaps named for the prevalence of bruised shins), anti-I-over, flying Dutchman, and old two cat. The organized sports of eastern children reflected the cooperative individualism of their industrialized culture, while the more spontaneous, flexible games of western children reflected "a society that applauded individual aggressiveness kept within broad rules that were loosely enforced" (West, 1989, pp. 111–12).

The fourth category was play encouraged by adults, a break from previously discussed forms that children either arrived at instinctively, created themselves, or learned from other children. By the late nineteenth century, games in this category were selected to reflect the values of adults. Child rearing manuals were recommended by reformers as good for children and could steer children away from improper or harmful play and amusements. Adults encouraged children to play out roles befitting the respective gender roles characteristic of prevailing cultural norms. Girls, for example, were given sewing materials, cups and saucers, and dolls or scrap materials for making dolls. Boys were to play in the fields, woods, and streets and their toys were guns, lassos, and miniature wagons. This was during the late nineteenth and early twentieth century period to be discussed in the next chapter, when social reformers were pressing for city playgrounds to counter the negative effects of children playing and living in the streets. Perhaps at no time in previous history had the importance of play in preparing children for hard and sometimes cruel living conditions yielded such useful insights for historians. This is best revealed when studying the similarities and differences between the play and work of the late colonial children in the eastern cities and the frontier children of the western country.

The autobiographies written by both Native Americans and European settlers who grew up in eighteenth and nineteenth century America illustrate in great detail the play and games of both European settlers and Native Americans, and simultaneously reveal how their mixing—mutual helping as well as armed conflict—affected the games of children. The original likenesses and differences are indeed remarkable in showing the seemingly natural, inborn tendencies of children to play, and to play in certain ways and for certain reasons.

Most of the Native Americans met by white pioneers on the western trails were friendly at first, often acting as guides. As schools were established by Christian missionaries, some Native American children would attend, allowing Native American and frontier children to pick up vestiges of differing languages and share newly learned games. Most whites remained ignorant of Native American culture, but those who visited their villages would see children playing many games: walking on stilts, spinning acorn tops, throwing and kicking leather balls stuffed with animal hair, riding stick horses, wrestling, and participating in one-legged hopping races, blindman's buff, hunt the button, and Native American versions of football and field hockey. Children of all ages rode ponies and horses and the older boys accompanied war parties on raids. With experience of holding horses, gathering arrows, and collecting wood, they would join in the battles. Girls as early as age five or six helped their mothers with cooking, sewing, weaving blankets, tanning hides, and making bead-work, moccasins, baskets, and pottery. There was no menial work for all was important to the survival of the tribe. Both boys and girls were taught traditional myths, rituals, songs, and dances and learned about the spirits that dwelt in the forests or landscapes around them (Freedman, 1983).

Charles Eastman (1902) wrote of his childhood as a Sioux and never having opportunities for knowing anything about the "Big Knives," as the Sioux called the white settlers, until the terrible Minnesota Massacre of 1862 broke up his home and he was carried into exile. Later he was reunited with his father, who had been imprisoned for his role in the massacre, and lived with him in the citizen settlement in North Dakota where he dwelt among the whites and began his school days. His *Indian Boyhood* is a rich source of information about the play and games of his childhood.

As a Sioux boy among his native people, Eastman joined his elders or his peers in the daily task of hunting for food, and for an occasional medicine dance in the woods. In these dances the boys impersonated their elders, Brave Bull, High Hawk, and others, imitating their dress and their behavior to the greatest detail, no less than modern children who imitate their sports or super heroes. Native American children were also close students of nature, studying the habits of animals and the characteristics of the wilderness, much as modern children study their books in school. They learned early to be independent in the woods, finding their way, securing game, and building fires and cooking wherever they happened to be hunting (Eastman, 1902). A common element among both early Native American children and modern American children is close observation of their respective important adults or role models and learning to emulate them in their play and, ultimately, their lives.

Figure 2.1 Children with an elderly Native American man.
Source: "Nix lui dix" by Roger Cooke. Courtesy of the Washington State Historical Society, Tacoma.

Aside from practicing acts of warfare and hunting, Native American children were masters of their own time. Work was quickly performed and they turned to games and play. Much of the work was hardly distinguishable from play, for the roles assumed were in many respects the same. Existence was perilous, for wild animals and conflicts between tribes posed constant and immediate dangers. Consequently, many of the games mimicked warfare: dividing into groups and choosing sides, sham fights with mud balls, feats with bows and arrows, foot and pony races, wrestling, swimming, and imitation of the customs of their fathers. Games of lacrosse and shinny, still popular in some form today, were common among Sioux children. Arousing bravery and enhancing competition were common elements of play. The "mud and willow" fight, a rather dangerous sport, involved placing mud balls on the end of a springy willow stick and throwing them with great force at the opposing players. This game sometimes involved more than a hundred players. When allowed options and special places, children across cultures are remarkably adept at entertaining themselves through creative, spontaneous play, adapting to whatever materials and spaces are available (Eastman, 1902).

Native American children were also clever at adapting their play and games to climatic conditions. In the winter, having no toboggans, they fastened the long rib bones of buffalo together at the larger end and coasted down hills with remarkable skill. Spinning tops was also an "all-absorbing" winter sport, using heart shaped tops fashioned from bone, wood, or animal horn. They were whipped with thongs of buckskin using a handle made from a stick. Imitating the medicine dance, sometimes considered an act of irreverence, much as "playing church" was among white children, was played in any season. Native American children, like children everywhere, were born imitators. Occasionally the Sioux children played "white man." A variety of pets was always available.

Our knowledge of the pale-face was limited, but we had learned that he brought goods whenever he came and that our people exchanged furs for his merchandise. We also knew that his complexion was pale, that he had short hair on his head and long hair on his face and that he wore coat, trousers, and hat, and did not patronize blankets in the day-time. So we painted two or three of our number with white clay and put on them birchen hats which we sewed up for the occasion; fastened a piece of fur to their chins for a beard and altered their costumes as much as lay within our power. Their merchandise consisted of sand for sugar, wild beans for coffee, dried leaves for tea, pulverized earth for gun-powder, pebbles for bullets and clear water for the dangerous "spirit water." We traded for these goods with skins of squirrels, rabbits and small birds. (Eastman, 1902, pp. 72–3)

The Native American youth was a born hunter. Every motion, every step, expressed an inborn dignity and, at the same time, a depth of native caution. His moccasined foot fell like the velvet paw of a cat—noiselessly;

his glittering black eyes scanned every object that appeared within their view. Not a bird, not even a chipmunk, escaped their piercing glance. There was as much difference between the Indian boys who were brought up on the open prairies and those of the woods, as between city and country boys ... They were, as a rule, good riders, but in all-round physical development much inferior to the red men of the forest. (Eastman, 1902, p. 87)

The Play of Slave Children: "Play Is Fun, Work Is Hard"

Recognizing and comprehending the history of slavery in America are essential to beginning to understand a fundamental yet troubling period in the total American experience. In his book *From Sundown to Sunup: The Making of the Black Community*, Rawick (1972) points out the inaccuracy of the common assumption that slaves, being illiterate, left few written records of their experience. He located and reviewed an extensive body of previously unused material documenting the experiences of those who had themselves been slaves and later had access to schooling. These included scores of autobiographies by slaves, thousands of interviews recorded in the 1920s and 1930s by scholars and federal investigators, and a large number of slave narratives published before and after the Civil War. Rawick's writing helps to illuminate the history of slavery by focusing on the total experience and beliefs of the slaves themselves, especially in that historically neglected sundown to sunup period when they had greater autonomy than when they were at work from sunup to sundown.

Many more slaves than is commonly assumed managed to develop a social life with coherent family structures and many features of other societies. The slave community acted like "a generalized extended kinship system in which all adults looked after all children and there was little division between 'my children for whom I'm responsible' and 'your children to whom you're responsible'" (Rawick, 1972, p. 93). Since both mothers and fathers commonly worked in the fields, older women looked after groups of children and older children often assumed the care of younger siblings. The huts and cabins for slaves were not designed for family life but as sleeping places and shelters from the weather. The slaves spent their days working out-of-doors, cooking was usually done out-of-doors or in cooking sheds, and children played wherever they happened to be—indoors or outdoors. Stephen McCray, who grew up on a plantation in Alabama with 300 slaves, explained how it felt to be a slave:

The coon said to the dog, "Why is it you're so fat and I am so poor, and we is both animals?" The dog said; "I lay around Master's house and let him kick me and he gives me a piece of bread right on." Said the coon to the dog; "Better then that I stay poor, Them's my sentiment, I don't believe in 'buse." (Webber, 1978, p. x)

Thomas L. Webber grew up in East Harlem, graduated from Harvard and Columbia University, and drew heavily on slave folklore and thousands of written or dictated narratives in fashioning yet another rich, scholarly account of one piece of slave culture—education in the slave quarter community of the mid-nineteenth century. In his writing he frequently employs the words of the African-American men and women who were slaves, following the advice of a Tennessee ex-slave: "If you want Negro history you will have to get it from somebody who wore the shoe, and by and by from one to the other you will get a book" (Webber, 1978, p. xiii). Such rich yet meaningful vernacular illustrates the wisdom of people deprived of formal education yet frequently subjected to criticism by those using a different or "cultured" language. Such discrimination is still commonly seen within and across cultures, subcultures, and countries.

The work of Webber (1978), and firsthand accounts of growing up as a slave by Isaac Jefferson, Frederick Douglass, Booker T. Washington, and William Holtzclaw, as contained in Jay David's *Growing up Black* (1968), are vivid, poignant, and saddening accounts of slavery. As slave children grew up, they were put to work in the fields or on such other tasks as might be necessary. In the evening, both boys and girls did the cooking, washing, sewing, and other chores, sometimes staying up through the night helping the women prepare thread for the white folks. Clothing was so scarce that some children would take it off while they slept and put it back on again when it was washed. The clandestine nighttime activities of the quarter adults—hunting, fishing, and attending feasts of stolen food deep in the woods—were treasured social activities sometimes attended by children.

Booker T. Washington wrote: "One of my earliest recollections is that of my mother cooking a chicken late at night, and awakening the children for the purpose of feeding them" (Washington, 1968, p. 96). Given the circumstances, no thinking person could ever accuse his mother of theft. At night the children would sit by the fire with their elders or lie in bed listening to the singing and storytelling. The plantation quarters were typically heated by burning big logs in a fireplace that served as the center of family activity in the winter. Washington and his brother and sister slept among a bundle of rags on a dirt floor. He received no schooling while he was a slave but had to carry his young mistresses' books to the schoolhouse door, feeling that studying in this way was about the same as getting into paradise. His family never sat down at a dinner table, said their prayers, and ate together but foraged for their meals much as animals. They often ate from a skillet or a tin plate on their knees while fanning the flies away.

The harshness of this life was greatly accentuated by the brutality of many masters and overseers. A. J. Mitchell recalled that when his Arkansas master was displeased, "he would make us younguns put our head 'tween his legs and put that strap on us," and former Maryland plantation slave child, James Pennington, said of the overseers: "These men seem to look with an evil eye upon children of slaves, long before they are old enough to be put at the hoe, and consequently under the whip" (Webber, 1978, pp. 20–1). A Maryland plantation slave, Frederick Douglass (David, 1968, p. 85), had a very brutal overseer, a drunkard, profane swearer and savage monster. He armed himself with a cow-skin whip and a heavy cudgel and took great pleasure in whipping and beating slaves. Douglass was often awakened near dawn by the horrible screams of his old aunt:

> whom the overseer would tie up to a joist, and whip upon her naked back til she was literally covered with blood. The louder she screamed, the harder he whipped; and where the blood ran fastest, there he whipped longest. He would whip her to make her scream then whip her to make her hush. (Douglass, 1978, p. 85)

At yet another plantation, Douglass' childhood and that of the other slave boys not old enough to work was spent in leisure time and in small tasks such as keeping animals out of the garden, cleaning the yard, and finding birds as his master shot them. Perhaps because of his attachment to the master, he was seldom whipped and suffered little except from excessive heat and cold, having no clothing except for a coarse tow linen shirt. The children's food was corn-meal mush served in a wooden trough on the ground, where the children gathered like pigs, eating with their hands, oyster-shells, or wood shingles—the strongest getting the best place, the fastest getting the most food, and most going away hungry.

Formal "educational" activities beyond the nursery were virtually nonexistent. Except for Kentucky, the law in slave states forbade anyone to teach slaves to read or write. Violation of this law resulted in very harsh punishment. Consequently, in 1860 only about 5 percent of slaves could read. The earliest "education" of African-American slave children was in the hands of parents after their return from work in the fields, the masters' houses, or other assigned places. During the day and after weaning, the youngest spent their days playing with the other slave children in the nursery. Fenced yards were prepared on some plantations to allow them to play in greater safety while supervised by older children or "nurses." An observer of such a fenced play yard or playground reported that the crawlers were in the pen, toddlers were playing on the steps or in front of the house, and the bigger ones were singing and dancing around a fire they had lit on the ground. The observer recalled that while visiting this and two or three other plantation nurseries she never heard a child cry. Yet another observer saw nursery teachers organizing imaginative games for their children and one teacher ran her nursery like "the kindergarten of today," telling stories, showing children how to make playthings from found objects, and how to set tables, bake mud pies, dress up as flowers, make decorations from natural objects, and catch small animals such as terrapins and keep them as pets. In most nurseries the older children were free to roam the woods and fields and play their own improvised or spontaneous games. In the evening the children joined their families at dinner and doing chores (Webber, 1978, pp. 15–17).

As children of the slave quarters grew older, they were taught traditional games, songs, riddles, and stories by older children and adults. Many of these had been passed from generation to generation in virtually infinite variations, and, as in other societies, these activities were opportunities to learn as well as to be enjoyed. Webber (1978) relates the rich history of slave children's play as extracted from and sometimes quoted verbatim in the rich vernacular gleaned from thousands of written or dictated narratives. Between their light chores, which preceded the dawn to dusk manual labor, children jumped rope, played marbles, tag and blindfold, swung from grapevines, threw horseshoes, walked on stilts, played cards with grains of corn, and made their own toys such as dolls, clay marbles, and bows and arrows. Most of their games are still played in differing formats; today's dodge ball is a variation of slave children's "sheep-meat," "Annie-over" a variation of "once over"; "hide-and-go-seek" a variation of "Ole Hundud." "Us larned to count a-playin Ole Hundud" (Webber, 1978, p. 181). The children also played ring, singing, chanting, storytelling, and riddle games.

On occasional festivities such as Christmas singing and "joyment" were allowed all day, and a fire was built and hog bladders, full of air, were tossed into the fire to "bang" like fireworks. "Hide the switch" and other games were invented to help cope with whippings and evil spirits. At times children were allowed to roam and play in the woods—climb trees, wade in the creeks, fish, hunt, play chase games, and gather berries. Much of the play allowed boys and girls to practice skills they would need later. The girls and sometimes the boys played "grown-ups," making their dolls from scraps and toys such as dishes from broken or castaway items. Just as colonial and Native American children attended and played religious events common to their culture, slave children played "preachin'" and "baptisin'." "We's put 'em down in the water and souse 'em and we'd shout just like the old folks" (Webber, 1978, p. 186).

Accounts of slave life by slaves, observers, the descendants of slaves, and historians reveal more about work, pain, and suffering than about children's play. One reason for this appears to have been the degree of inhumanity and cruelty to which slaves were exposed. Obviously, pain and suffering are illuminated in those who experience it, overshadowing, under such circumstances, the relatively less significant phenomenon of childhood play. Slave children and their elders did play, even under brutal conditions, but as children grew past early childhood and were put to work, play was restricted to briefer periods and work became dominant. Conditions were so brutal on some plantations that some could recall vividly the work and pain, but had little experience or recollection of joyful play. Booker T. Washington, who founded the Tuskegee Institute and earned international recognition as an educator and racial advisor, despite having received no schooling while he was a slave, recounted his recollections of play as a slave child:

> there was no period of my life that was devoted to play. From the time that I can remember anything, almost every day of my life has been occupied in some kind of labor; though I think I would now be a more useful man if I had time for sports. (Washington, 1968, p. 96)

The emancipation of the slaves did not quickly improve their lot to any significant degree. Most had worked on farms or plantations and had no other skills to earn a livelihood, so they turned to sharecropping. William Holtzclaw (1968), a child of such a sharecropper, recalled his experiences on an Alabama plantation during the closing days of reconstruction following the Civil War. Through a verbal agreement with the landlord, William's mother cooked for the landlord's family and his father was one of many farming in exchange for one-fourth of everything he produced. The landlord furnished land, seeds, and mules and his father the labor. The sharecroppers purchased their flour, meal, meat, and tobacco at the landlord's store at his prices, accounted for by cutting notches on a stick.

NOON AT THE PRIMARY SCHOOL FOR FREEDMEN, VICKSBURG, MISSISSIPPI.—[SEE PAGE 308.]

Figure 2.2 Noon at the primary school for freedmen, Vicksburg, Mississippi.
Source: Photographs and Prints Division, Schomburg Center for Research in Black Culture, New York Public Library, Astor, Lenox, and Tilden Foundations.

The few "colored schools" in his area were taught by Southern white men and women, but as the students progressed in their blue-back speller or to about fourth grade, they were made assistant teachers and the white teachers left. When William was four years old, he was put to work on the farm, riding a deaf and blind mule while his brother ran the plow and carried his father's breakfast and dinner to a sawmill where he worked for sixty cents a day. The owner of the sawmill started a school that was open two months a year and invited the colored children to attend. The school building and the benches were constructed of split pine logs, placing the children's clothing and skin at risk from the pine rosin, since the very young children, including William, wore only a shirt. He walked three miles to school every day with his older sister, who carried him when his legs gave out. Their dinner was an ear of roasted corn, wild fruit, nuts and muscadines, and sometimes a possum he and his dogs caught while hunting at night in order to have it for the next day's noon meal. William, like other sharecroppers' children, spent a great deal of time with his dogs hunting possum and coon, especially after he helped "lay by" the crops and time was available. He also spent time with pigs, chickens, mules, and working in the garden, but, like Booker T. Washington, he never referred to any of this as play as children under less trying conditions tended to do. The time for such activities was brief since the cotton-picking season was approaching and school would be stopped so that the children could work in the fields again.

In 1880, when William Holtzclaw was ten years old, his father rented his own farm and struck out on his own, but four years later, deep in debt, with the family decimated by a "slow fever" epidemic and creditors attempting to take their corn, pig, chickens, and vegetables, his father gradually succumbed to his fate and died. But before dying his father set him free in return for William's promise that he would educate himself. He first worked at thirty cents a day and board, and then wrote to Booker T. Washington, Principal of the Tuskegee Normal and Industrial Institute, and gained admission. He later published a newspaper for people in his African-American community and started the Utica Normal and Industrial Institute in Utica, Mississippi, for people of his own race. By 1915 this school had an enrollment of five hundred students.

The distinction between play and work made by different individuals appears to be rooted in the conditions surrounding the activity, perhaps including memories of pain or pleasure and the degree of suffering in one's life. In the words of many contemporary children, "play is fun, work is hard." C. C. White (White and Holland, 1969), an African-American child growing up in the piney woods of East Texas shortly after the Civil War, recalls engaging in many of the activities described by Holtzclaw as work, yet White described them as playful or in pleasant terms, such as singing, playing at recess, picking muscadines, gathering hickory nuts, climbing trees, calling hogs, killing snakes, hunting, cooking pretend meals, smart-alecking at school, cutting wood, playing with chickens, plowing the fields, butchering hogs, milking cows, making butter, and riding mules and horses.

Contemporary studies (Frost, 2005) of natural and other man-made disasters show that play and some forms of work are therapeutic, helping children understand and cope with traumatic circumstances—diminishing the trauma inflicted by brutality or extreme destitution. Children play even under the harshest conditions, and most slave children were not exceptions, though after the first four or five years of their childhood work dominated their lives. Later discussions will visit the play and work of children who suffered extreme adversity or disaster in other eras.

Culture, Circumstance, and Play

The historical characterization of America's early settlers as mere prudes and their children as small adults is no longer viable. The limited data of earlier historians, supplemented later by expansive original data, show that early colonists and settlers of all ages played extensively and energetically in spite of the admonitions of some churches and religious leaders. By the end of the eighteenth century, morality and strict interpretations of the Bible were gradually relaxed and certain pleasures were accepted as appropriate. The play culture of the Native Americans who greeted the early settlers and later befriended and warred with them was rich in scope and expression, and essential for children learning about the work, conflicts, and spiritual roles of their tribes. Their traditional play was unfettered by the massive upheavals already endured by the early settlers and was rooted in a love and appreciation of nature, deep spiritual beliefs, and the requirements of survival. The Native American's culture and religions were deep seated, formed by a long history of relative stability and passed from generation to generation through storytelling, play, work, ceremonies, and close synergy. As European and Native American children gradually joined together in the playgrounds of forest, desert, and school, their play and games became intertwined and each culture came away with new perspectives, some beneficial and some harmful. Perhaps in no other context were the interactions of former Europeans and Native Americans as influential in shaping both cultures as in the deserts and mountains of the western frontier. Here, as earlier in the eastern mountains, a clash of cultures and eventual conflict and domination of territory took place, but not without brushing together a new tapestry of work and play.

The play and work of the children of slaves were remarkable in the face of the terrible assaults—psychological and physical—imposed on their elders. Although forced by conditions of servitude to humble themselves in every conceivable way, adults managed to pass on a culture rich in play—songs, dance, physical contests, storytelling, and opportunities for their children to create their own spontaneous play. Children learned to transform much of their work into play, especially when very young, and all except the very damaged preserved this ability. Just as modern cultures see that children's basic instincts equip them to engage in play in order to survive both natural and man-made disasters, slave children suffered extreme hardships but created or found their own playthings and play environments, and turned to play for strength, comfort, and deliverance from emotional and physical pain and distress.

The remarkable endurance of play and games across centuries, generations, cultures, and countries is quite a story. Both natural and man-made playgrounds change with geography, time, and necessity. Technology, culture, and interest change children's toy choices, but their games, laws, and seasons for playing them endure in modified fashion. Borrowing games among children, across periods of time, and across cultures and geography seems to be natural and relatively unrestricted by adults. Even among cultures that find ways to diminish play, there remains marble time, top time, kite time, ball time, tag time, singing time, festival time, and even time for those games traditionally considered by moralists, puritans, or "polite society" as the darker forms of play—bullying, extreme fighting, prohibited sexual play, gambling, etc. Generations pass them to successive generations and children learn them, play them, and pass them on to others. As we will see in later sections of this book, contemporary adults are finding very effective ways to interfere with traditional play, changing its very culture and, consequently, placing the health, safety, and traditions of childhood at risk.

History does not focus on play alone so much as it places play in rich perspectives of work, religion, culture, family, education, and community. Play's broad, multidimensional meanings emerge from these contexts, and they become play's birthplaces, contexts for expression, and sources of enrichment and growth. Play influences the transference of cultures across generations.

3

The Early Child-Saving Movement
Shame of the Cities

Long ago it was said that "one half of the world does not know how the other half lives." It did not know because it did not care. There came a time when the discomfort and crowding below were so great, and the consequent upheavals so violent ... [that] ... the upper half fell to inquiring what was the matter. (Riis, 1890, reprinted 1957, p. 1)

As the American frontier disappeared, the westward movement declined, and the industrial revolution emerged, an ever-increasing number of rural dwellers moved to cities. This clustering in crowded cities, magnified by the influx of foreign immigrants, led to barbaric conditions of living—poverty, crime, and unsafe conditions for children—and a multifaceted child-saving movement began to emerge. This broad movement embraced several related but separate movements with the common purpose of saving children but with diverse approaches. Collectively, these movements formed the most extensive system previously seen for changing the lives of impoverished, destitute children in America and perhaps the world. One of the common goals of these groups was to improve conditions for children by providing organized opportunities, spaces, and playgrounds for their play, recreation, and learning while protecting them from crime, poverty, abuse, and illiteracy.

This "Progressive Era" emerged during the 1890s and continued through the First World War, resulting in reforms at all levels of government. The reforms during this period were not addressed only to children or play but encompassed a host of government issues and reforms. These reforms included women's suffrage, criminal justice, regulation of commerce, election of U.S. senators, federal income tax, conservation of natural resources, and child welfare, particularly in the fields of child labor, juvenile justice, playgrounds, and health (Marten, 2005). Many of the problems of children and youth addressed by reformers continue today, but, as will be seen in later chapters, the child welfare problems of the Progressive Era related to children's play also continue today, complicated by new circumstances. The Progressive Era of child reforms is best understood when cast in the historical context of the conditions facing children during this period, the changing attitudes to childhood, and changing ideals about constructive approaches to discourse and action. The attitudes and undertakings of Progressive reformers were far more extensive than merely engaging in dialogue and action to improve conditions for children's play and play environments. However, these were critically important issues in formulating policy and practice for improving children's health and development.

During the last half of the nineteenth century, American cities grew in population very rapidly and poverty was rampant. As immigrants flooded into the slums and tenement districts of cities, including New York, preserves were formed by Irish, Italians, Germans, French, Africans, Spanish, Bohemians, Russians, Scandinavians, Jews, Arabs, Chinese, and others. Older, more established groups tended to move away, shift to the outskirts, "go to heaven," or "simply disappear," perhaps joining the heterogeneous element (Riis, 1957, pp. 15–16). Several books and many publications were written at the time by the reformers themselves and by other sympathetic writers (Brace, 1880; Spargo, 1906; Addams, 1909, 1945; Riis, 1913). Perhaps the best modern overview of the plight of city children during this period with links to the playground moveent is Cavallo's scholarly history *Muscles and Morals: Organized Playgrounds and Urban Reform, 1880–1920* (1981). Leading reformers during the late nineteenth and early twentieth centuries awakened the conscience of Americans to the plight of poor and homeless children in the slums of our largest cities, and a child-saving movement was formed.

Victims of a Stolen Childhood

The early social reformers engaged in rescuing children of the working class, ethnic children, and the teeming numbers of orphans from a host of social and economic hazards including crime, homelessness, child labor, child abuse, and abject poverty. A number of factors contributed to these conditions: moral breakdown, unrestricted immigration, unregulated capitalism, and adolescent individuals and gangs engaged in street crime. The movement embraced child welfare programs, including medical programs, volunteer programs, child labor legislation, compulsory education, and the establishment of organizations for boys and girls such as Girl Scouts, Boy Scouts, and Camp Fire Girls (Cavallo, 1981). The recorded history of the plight of girls living on the streets was overshadowed by the more visible plight of boys, though girls may well have suffered the more serious consequences—often left alone without the small security provided by a gang or group, and at the mercy of unscrupulous adults. African-Americans participated in social reforms but they did so in segregated facilities and organizations, lacking equal levels of support. Over time the wider child-saving movement encompassed a number of smaller movements, all with similar goals of saving children from barbaric conditions and some involving common reformers, and all enduring and expanding into the twenty-first century. These, to be discussed later, included the school gardens movement, the nature movement, the children's museum movement, the organized camping movement, and the playground movement. The latter movement, central to the theme of this book, will be discussed in detail in the next chapter.

Charles Loring Brace (1880), a prominent author of his period, worked for twenty years among the "dangerous classes of New York" and documented in great detail the plight of street children, poverty and its consequences, and efforts to ameliorate these conditions. His sources include firsthand knowledge and original accounts by children and leaders in the reform movement that was beginning to emerge around the mid-nineteenth century. Brace speaks with authority and gives straightforward descriptions of the plight of the "young ruffians" living in squalor and homelessness in the slums among New York's one million children at that time, 20,000 to 30,000 of them "vagrant youth." According to the *First Annual Report* of the Children's Aid Society (1854), 1,000 immigrants per day, mostly from Germany and Ireland, were pouring into New York. The consequences were stark:

> Fathers die, and leave their children unprovided for; parents drink, and abuse their little ones ... Thousands are the children of poor foreigners, who have permitted them to grow up without school, education, or religion ... So at length, a great multitude of ignorant, untrained, passionate, irreligious boys and young men are formed, who become the "dangerous class" of our city. (Brace, 1880, p. 28)

The root causes of such conditions were extensive, including ignorance, overcrowding, immigration, lack of work, weak marriages, lack of legislation, and the death of parents. For example, 31 percent of adult criminals were illiterate but only 6 percent of the general adult population; almost 60 percent had lost one or both parents; 65 percent were of foreign birth. When asked about the causes of their downfall, prisoners in the city jail frequently responded that if they had had a trade, they would not be in prison. Homeless boys and girls wandering the streets and involved in juvenile crime commonly identified the loss of one or both parents or abusive step-parents as causes for their crimes, and Brace identified overcrowding of the city as the most formidable source of juvenile crime. Collectively, these abuses and desperate living conditions captured the attention of social, governmental, religious, and charitable groups, and the early child-saving movement emerged.

The reform movement gradually emerged in New York during the mid-nineteenth century. In 1852 the young minister Charles Loring Brace began his career as a missionary among the "dangerous classes of New York" (Fry, 1994, p. 12). Reverend Brace soon called for the establishment of a new organization to carry out his ideas of useful work, practical education, and religious principles to counter the effects of life on the streets. The Children's Aid Society of

New York, formed in 1853, was to be among the most effective organizations in helping children escape from their misery. The first large gift (fifty dollars) allowed them to maintain a small office on Amity Street and they set about developing programs of assistance for New York's street children. Almost immediately, wandering children found their way there:

> Ragged young girls who had nowhere to lay their heads; children driven from drunkards' homes; orphans who slept where they could find a box or a stairway; boys cast out by step-mothers or step-fathers; newsboys, whose incessant answer to our question, "Where do you live?" rung back in our ears, "Don't live nowhere!" ... child beggars and flower-sellers ... all this motley throng of infantile misery and childish guilt passed through our doors, telling their simple stories of suffering, and loneliness, and temptation, until our hearts became sick.

> For the most part, the boys grow up utterly by themselves ... Some live by begging, by petty pilfering, by bold robbery; some earn an honest support by peddling matches, or apples, or newspapers; others gather bones and rags in the street to sell. They sleep on steps, in cellars, in old barns, and in markets, or they hire a bed in filthy and low lodging-houses. They cannot read; they do not go to school or attend a church. Some of them have never seen the Bible.

> The girls, too often, grow up even more pitiable and deserted ... They are the cross-walk sweepers, the little apple-peddlers, and candy-sellers of our city; or, by more questionable means, they earn their scanty bread. They traverse the low, vile streets alone, and live without mother or friends, or any share in what we should call a home. They also know little of God or Christ, except by name. (Brace, 1880, pp. 88–91)

Girls were the most painful figures in all this unfortunate mix of pitiful humanity. The street trades were harder for them because they felt homelessness and friendlessness more deeply, developed earlier than boys, and found themselves at night in lonely tenement rooms or cellars, crowded with filthy people of all ages and sexes in a world of degrading sexual vices. In addition to their fears of sexual exploitation, they often had difficulties fitting into the rough patterns of survival in a subculture dominated by men and boys. Girls also walked the streets as prostitutes and sold themselves at an early age.

> I picked (rags) all day, and didn't make much, and I was cold and hungry. Towards night, a gentleman met me—a very fine, well-dressed gentleman, an American, and he said, "Will you go home with me?" and I said, "No." He said, "I will give you twenty shillings," and I told him I would go. And the next morning I was taken up by the officer. (Brace, 1880, p. 120)

Figure 3.1 Boys playing shuttlecock, or *jianzi*, in Chinatown, San Francisco, about 1900. Shuttlecock is an ancient kicking game dating back thousands of years. The exercise involves all parts of the body and includes jumping and twisting, as well as kicking. This game later evolved into the game of badminton.
Source: Courtesy of the Library of Congress, Prints and Photographs Division, Arnold Genthe Collection: Negatives and Transparencies [reproduction number LC-G403-0165].

Irrational Play: Begging, Picking Pockets, and Outwitting the Police

Despite the vices to which children were exposed, they found ways to eke out some small degree of pleasure, even by means considered unlawful. They looked upon the more mature activities of "flash men" with admiration as they engaged in cockfights, pugilism, picking pockets, swearing, stealing, and gambling, and sometimes joined adults in the pot (drug) houses. Consequently, many learned these same vices, emulated them, and received some satisfaction or pleasure from engaging in them. The small amount of money they earned slipped away in lotteries, gambling, and the low theaters. The child's first lesson was frequently gambling, and stealing was the next (Riis, 1913), both activities that seemed heroic and adventurous to street children. Just when the child's games were of chasing and being chased, the police figured in the child's illegitimate game of stealing and being chased. Froebel, whose philosophy was influencing the development of kindergartens, was not talking about this form of play when he concluded that play built character and through play the child first perceived moral relations. Moral relations were surely built through the illegitimate play of street children, but they were of the wrong kind. Fortunately, as the reader will see, morals, both bad and good, are subject to change.

Free schools were open to everyone in New York, but vast numbers were too destitute and ill clothed to attend without shame, or too busy begging or working in the streets. Consequently, industrial schools were founded by charitable groups, which gathered in the basements of churches or other available places, taught trades, and provided free clothing and meals to those who would behave. Children initially hated school, preferring old boxes and barns to civilized bed-chambers, and developed skill and cunning in thievery, stealing nearby items while all the time pretending to be playing marbles. Life was dangerous on the streets. "The average boy is just like a little steam-engine with steam always up. The play is his safety-valve" (Riis, 1913, p. 233). Many children were run over by carriages and trucks in the street, others were infected by the filth, chased by landlords, or attacked by gangs.

Most teenagers did not attend school but joined gangs in the street-play games of marbles, hide-and-seek, baseball, and countless other improvised games, some relatively harmless and others criminal, even under modern rules of law. While girls played house in the stoops in front of the tenements and took care of younger siblings, boys played among the streetcars, pedestrians, carriages, and pedestrians, attended silent movies for a few cents, engaged in turf wars between gangs, and created their own toys from scrap and junk found in the streets, garbage dumps, and vacant lots (Marten, 2005). A common sight in major cities was that of boys as young as five working as newsboys or fruit vendors for a few cents a day, or of both boys and girls selling in the markets and running errands.

Riis saw a New York child shot down by a policeman for the heinous offense of playing football in the streets. A city ordinance prohibited playing in the streets and even kite flying in certain sections of the city. To the street children, laws were made to be broken and for having fun, for they quickly learned how to treat avoidance as a game. They laughed at the compulsory school attendance and child labor laws. Older children taught two-year-olds how to steal, and the gutters were their playgrounds. Later, with the help of reformers, many street children studied and became disciplined and industrious, and began to show gratitude and affection to their teachers. As the teachers learned that they needed to have some control over the children's out-of-school hours, lodging houses were established, and by the turn of the twentieth century playgrounds were beginning to appear in parks and schools, some even on rooftops. The lodging houses were encouraged and supported by charitable individuals and groups, municipalities, boards of education, churches, and athletics clubs.

Many schools established the "Object System of Teaching," derived from the philosophy and teaching methods of Pestalozzi. This method assumed that the child's mind grasped things rather than names, objects before words, and learned things in wholes rather than parts. The first principle was to exercise the senses through play, which was to employ the sense of touch, weight, and harmony. Eventually, that wonderful symbol of human thought, the written word, was introduced and reading began. Despite the emphasis on play, especially in the kindergartens of New York, some pedagogues held beliefs about play that are strangely familiar to observers of today's schools, holding that teachers:

> organized the life out of it all ... A harassed teacher was vainly trying to form the girls into ranks for exercises ... They held up their hands in desperate endeavor to get her ear, only to have them struck down impatiently ... They did not want to exercise. They wanted to play. I tried to voice their grievance to the "doctor" who presided. "Not at all," he said decisively; "there must be system, system!" (Riis, 1913, pp. 394–95)

Riis then thought to himself: "They have good sense in Chicago, Jane Addams is there" (Riis, 1913, p. 431). The gross misunderstanding exhibited by many pedagogues of the proper role of adults in children's play re-emerged with vigor during the late twentieth century in the illogical processes and broken promises of "No Child Left Behind." Riis later wrote:

> I have no quarrel with the man who would do things by system and in order; but the man who would reduce men and women and children to mere items in his infallible system and classify and subclassify them until they are as dried up as his theories, that man I will fight till I die. (Riis, 1913, p. 431)

We need people like Riis and Addams today to help counter the deleterious effects of "high stakes testing" on children and educators. Despite the problems described above, there were many positive results of schools, although overcrowding, widespread hunger, disease, and crime continued to take their toll during the late nineteenth century. Many boys and girls continued to be corrupted, eventually becoming thieves, vagrants, and vicious people. More radical approaches were needed than those offered by charitable individuals, schools, and churches.

Around the beginning of the twentieth century the views of eminent Progressive educator John Dewey were influencing a generation of educators. He argued that education must meet the needs of the whole child, should be individualized, should engage and meet all her developmental interests and needs, and should be closely connected with the community (Dewey, 1896). Freely chosen, intrinsically motivated pretend play was the primary educational experience for the preschool child, for she must act out ideas before they can be taken into the mental scheme. Such play enables the child to make meaningful that which is of most *interest* to her. Later, Dewey (1916) expanded his views on play, proposing that pretend play was essential for preschoolers, exploration was essential for school-age children, and both were required as models or foundations for free participation in a community of people with shared interests. Reformers turned to the establishment of settlement houses to provide homes for destitute children and to care for their personal, educational, and health needs.

Settlement Houses and Playgrounds for the Poor

In the late nineteenth century, before the wide availability of government-supported social services and welfare options, the problems of the poor led to the establishment of settlement houses. The first, Toynbee Hall, opened in New York City in 1866 and was influenced by earlier ones in London (Woods, 1970). The leaders were aware that poverty had social causes and struggled to secure housing, recreational centers, playgrounds, and basic human needs for immigrants, minorities, and the urban poor in general. The idea spread to the most blighted areas of other cities, and settlement leaders entered the political arena, lobbying for legislation and participating in elections and legislation. Their successful work led to widespread and enduring recognition of urban problems, became essentially the first war on poverty, and laid the groundwork for the New Deal (Davis, 1967).

In the light of Froebel's views on children's creative yet somewhat structured play and Hall's recapitulatory views on children reenacting the evolution of the race, settlement leaders saw the need for kindergartens and public playgrounds. These, they believed, would provide play for delinquents and homeless children who had no safe outlets for their natural "animal" energy. Many other social reformers hastened to join them in meeting these needs. The playgrounds developed by the settlement houses were wildly popular. Children crowded to the playground of the House on Henry Street in Lower East Side New York. Once, when the playground was filled to capacity, a persistent little girl, knowing that mothers with small children were given priority for admission, defended her need to enter, saying, "Yes, teacher, but can't I get in? I ain't got no mother" (Wald, 1915, p. 84). Despite their commitment to playgrounds for such children, settlement workers, recalling their own childhoods in the woods, fields, and among domesticated animals, believed that the best and most creative play took place in the countryside. Consequently, settlements established summer camps and farms as well as kindergartens, and organized playgrounds at schools and other neighborhood sites. For example, Graham Taylor founded Chicago Commons in 1894 and later established the Chicago Commons Farm Camp near New Buffalo, Michigan. Here, among the trees beside the river, around the campfire, and under the stars, balance was to be restored in the lives of those living in the narrow restrictions of the city. The settlement leaders' work with the Playground Association of America added considerable enduring force to the play movement. During the Depression years of the 1930s the settlement houses were to expand their services to include more of the poor and, during the 1950s, the African-American and Hispanic poor.

Many volunteers and prominent leaders were active in the child-saving movement and the development of settlement houses, but Jane Addams and her Hull House were special among this group and serve herein as an exemplar. Addams was active in social work, the settlement movement, child labor reform, and the international peace movement, and she was an important figure in the development of playgrounds and recreation for people of all ages (Butler, 1965). She established the Hull House in Chicago in 1892 with the aims of providing a center for civic and social life, instituting and maintaining educational and philanthropic activities, and investigating and improving conditions in industrial areas of Chicago. She created the first "model playground," tearing down several houses to make way for children's play (Addams, 1909, 1945; Rainwater, 1922; Butler, 1965; Cavallo, 1981). This playground of almost an acre was equipped with sand garden type apparatus, sand pile, building blocks, swings, giant stride, indoor gymnasium, and outdoor games areas to accommodate children, youth, and adults. A student and a policeman supervised the playgrounds.

Figure 3.2 Jane Addams of Hull House, Chicago, Illinois, a leading reformer during the early twentieth century child-saving movement.
Source: Lewis Wickes Hine, 1874–1940, photographer. Courtesy of the Library of Congress, Prints and Photographs Division, National Child Labor Committee Collection, [reproduction number LC-DIG-nclc-04836].

Figure 3.3 The Jane Addams Hull House and playground with a "giant stride" in the foreground.
Source: Robert Hunter, *Tenement Conditions in Chicago: Report by the Investigating Committee of the City Homes Association* (Chicago: City Homes Association, 1901), p. 171. Courtesy of Widener Library, Harvard College Library, Soc 1610, 28.

Addams' international fame added to the nationwide publicity about the playground and other activities of Hull House. In her book *The Spirit of Youth and the City Streets*, she alerted the public to the importance of play in meeting basic human needs and helping counter the effects of poverty and misery prevalent in American cities. She later served as an officer of the Playground Association of America and participated in the playground movement emanating in large part from the activities of that association. Addams was a powerful speaker, experienced world traveler, student of the slums of such cities as London and Rome, and skillful writer. Her persuasive words, oral and written, were instrumental in bringing public attention to the plight of the poor and in securing support for play and recreation. Reflecting on the play and games, religion and patriotism, pageants and festivals of earlier eras, she wrote:

> Only in the modern city have men concluded that it is no longer necessary for the municipality to provide for the insatiable desire for play. In so far as they have acted upon this conclusion, they have entered upon a most difficult and dangerous experiment; and this at the very moment when the city has become distinctly industrial, and daily labor is continually more monotonous and subdivided. We forget how new the modern city is, and how short the span of time in which we have assumed that we can eliminate public provision for recreation ... Never before in civilization

have such numbers of young girls been suddenly released from the protection of the home and permitted to walk unattended upon city streets and to work under alien roofs ... Never before have such numbers of young boys earned money independently of the family life, and felt themselves free to spend it as they choose in the midst of vice deliberately disguised as pleasure. (Addams, 1909, pp. 4–6)

Addams, like many other historical reformers, extended her vision beyond the mere provision of playgrounds for children to encompass broad social, pleasurable, and recreational opportunities for all age groups. She proposed that the many national and local celebrations—marching musicians, public holidays, birthdays of heroes, the planting of trees, changing seasons, dances, public recreation, art, and play and games in their many forms—could all be accomplished through the public parks and the public schools. Not unlike many great historical philosophers who extolled the value of play, Addams cast her plans and actions in a religious context in an effort to help ameliorate the problems of the poverty, homelessness, illiteracy, drudgery, and misery of street children and their families. She viewed preaching and teaching about justice in human affairs as an obligation of religion and morality, such that youth would feel a sense of participation in normal life and social workers would stir the fires of spiritual enthusiasm. Justice could only be worked out by those who would not tolerate inflicting wrong on the feeblest members of society and, in so doing, "make clean and bright our dingy city streets" (Addams, 1909, p. 162).

How country children fared during the child-saving movement is discussed in detail in the next chapter addressed to the play and playground movement. Addams spoke to this, reflecting on her childhood in an Illinois scene of rural beauty. The prairie around her village was dotted with hills of pine trees planted by her father, who no doubt gave thought to beauty. The millstream was contained by high banks that challenged the skills of climbers and were dotted with caves for exploring with candles. She and her stepbrother spent summer after summer carrying on the many games and crusades that only free-roaming children can do, contrasting sharply with the "piteous aspects" of child life in the city, where play, inevitable on the streets, was constantly interrupted, never having continuity, allowing only fragmented dreams, and leading to standing around and horse-play—all so characteristic of city children (Addams, 1945, pp. 16–17). In Addams and other leaders of the child-saving movement, we see the passion and commitment devoted to the American play and playground movement, supporting the many forces (e.g., recreation specialists, education authorities, government) that initiated and implemented, with varying degrees of success, playgrounds and recreational opportunities in many cities throughout America. The common reflections among leaders of the child-saving movement about the freedom, joy, and learning opportunities of living in the country led them to search for and find novel ways to introduce homeless city children to such opportunities. This search led to the sending of thousands of orphans from crowded slums on "orphan trains" to live with farm families in the Midwest.

Orphan Trains, Farms, Coal Mines, and Factories

The Children's Aid Society saw that the best of all asylums for homeless city children might be the homes of farmers with stable families, sympathy for the plight of orphans, and a need for young workers to assist in the many responsibilities of farm life. Between 1854 and 1930 the Children's Aid Society and other organizations loaded on to trains up to 200,000 (some historians say about 100,000) children from orphanages, shelters, and the streets of New York and other cities, and sent them to farms across the Midwest and many other states (Vogt and Vogt, 1979; Fry, 1994; Warren, 1996, 2001; Frost, 2005b). The orphan trains were greeted at train stations by crowds of rural people eager to catch the first sight of these children of misfortune, and they were quickly adopted by childless adults, sympathetic families, and families that needed the children's labor. The Society held meetings in public places such as churches and town halls to discuss the objectives of the Society and something about the history of the children. Those who were able paid the fares of the children or made gifts to the Society. Even the residents of communities and states where children were placed spoke to the positive results. A prominent gentleman in Michigan wrote

Figure 3.4 Orphan train children preparing for a trip to their new families and lives in the country.
Source: Courtesy of the Kansas State Historical Society.

to the Society: "I think it is susceptible of proof that no equal number of children raised here are superior to those you have placed out." A leading judge in Pennsylvania wrote that "they have not known an instance of one of our children being imprisoned for a criminal offense, though we have sent four hundred and sixty-nine [orphans] to the state" (Brace, 1880, p. 241).

As adults, the orphan train children told their stories of pleasant, productive times of work and play on farms. The girls learned household tasks of cooking, sewing, and cleaning. Both girls and boys attended church, milked cows, tended gardens, and had time to play as country children have always played—with dolls, toys, and pets, roaming the woodlands, hunting and fishing, and engaging in the many games common to unfettered children everywhere (Warren, 2001). While acknowledging proudly that he did the work of three grown men, one boy spoke almost reverently about the still, moonlight nights, the pure white snow, and singing coyotes (Fry, 1994). As in the case of many Puritan and pioneer children, the work of children became their play.

The gender differences in play and work were equally apparent. Girls were taught to help with the housework and gardening. They won prizes at county fairs, learned how to tend gardens, make soap, and take care of a home, went to church, and attended school. The boys worked in the fields, tended the horses, cattle, cows, pigs, and chickens, making pets of some animals as they worked, then returning after work to play with their favorites. They also won prizes at county fairs and, like the girls, looked forward to the festivities common to country children. Most of the orphan train children flourished in the country following their disastrous childhoods in the city. In their annual report the Society estimated, based on such criteria as school progress, a success rate of about 87 percent. Many excelled in school, worked their way through college, established families, joined the army, and became successful in farming, business, banking, and politics. In 2007 the Orphan Train Heritage Society, originally located in Springdale, Arkansas, merged with the National Orphan Train complex in Hutchinson, Kansas, where their museum and research center are now located. The society collects and organizes records and disseminates information about the orphan trains and sponsors an annual reunion for riders, now elderly, and other interested people.

Children have always found time, places, and props for play even under extremely harsh conditions (see Frost, 2005b). Yet another example of this spirit and the resiliency of children and their genius in making work into play is found in Bartoletti's *Growing Up in Coal Country* (1996), which illustrates how children as young as five or six worked long hours in coal mines and factories during the early 1900s. They would deliberately jam machines to allow time for play. A group skipped work one day to go swimming, calling it their *strike*. When asked why they were striking, one boy responded, "I don't know, but I'll be damned if we'll give up until we get it" (Bartoletti, 1996, p. 19). After work they played their games much as other children who were not so restricted, making baseballs from string and tape and their own sleds, and playing until dark. Boys fortunate enough to work with the mules did so with pride and satisfaction, treated them as pets, fed them treats, treated their sores, cleaned their stalls, and even shared plugs of tobacco with them. Some used the mules for riding from place to place, both for work and pleasure.

Animals have historically served as friends, healers, and teachers for children (Pattnik, 2004/05). Boris Levinson's (1972) "pet therapy" is now used worldwide in hospitals, schools, and other contexts and has a positive influence on sense of affection, emotional security, and promotion of mental and physical healing. Similarly, horticultural and gardening activities span the play/work/ therapy dimensions. Gardens are naturally therapeutic, places for renewal and connection, places of peace, and places for healing (Bruce, 1999). Moore and Wong's (1997) insightful book *Natural Learning* features a wide range of natural features for schoolyards: water areas, sand lots, animal and plant habitats, also a place for healing. During the early twenty-first century, the famed adventure playgrounds of Europe are integrated into many "city farms" with gardens, plant and animal habitats, and farm animals. Across the United States such features are slowly being integrated into natural playscapes.

There was a vast difference between working on farms in the fresh air with many opportunities for change and individual initiative and working in the dust-laden air of factories and mills under slave-like and monotonous conditions. As many as 2,250,000 boys and girls as young as eight and nine (Spargo, 1906, p. 145) worked up to twelve hours a day, seven days a week. Girls of five or six were found working at night in Southern cotton mills. Spargo watched children hurrying into and away from the mills: "Those receptacles, in too many instances, for living human skeletons, almost disrobed of intellect" (Spargo, 1906, p. 153). One ten-year-old girl told him with pride that she had "worked two years and never missed a day" (Spargo, 1906, p. 151). Malnutrition, sickness, injury, and arrested physical and mental development were common among the factory "slave" children, who were in truth merely vestiges of children—victims of a stolen childhood.

Enduring Elements of the Child-Saving Movement

Many reformers representing churches, park systems, schools, civic organizations, and other organizations and agencies created submovements for saving children that endured and still exist today. These, too, were intended to teach children civic values, honesty, work skills, respect for public property, love of nature, and to provide time and spaces for play, recreation, and learning. These submovements included an organized camping movement, a children's museum movement, a school gardens movement, a nature movement, and a play and playground movement. The origins and early history of these movements are discussed here and they are revisited in the final chapter to show their endurance and benefits for contemporary children. All these movements would become part of the overriding child-saving movement.

Camping out-of-doors has probably always existed. Even the wanderings of the children of Israel would qualify, as would the primitive living of Native Americans, early American settlers from Europe, and the wanderings of homeless people everywhere. Organized camping, on the other hand, was developed for specific purposes, including improving the lives of children suffering from the debilitating conditions of urban living. Organized camping is a sustained, planned group experience, offering creative recreational and educational activities in the natural wilderness, with trained leadership and group living. Such camping appears to have been developed in the United States.

Mixed accounts reveal that an early camp for boys, the Gunnery Camp, was established in Washington, Connecticut, in 1861 and continued until 1879. This camp provided organized opportunities for fishing, trapping, swimming, games, campfires, and storytelling—many activities borrowed from Native Americans. Early settlers learned survival skills from Native Americans which played a prominent role in early camping and survive to the present time, including the virtues of honesty and forthrightness, council fires, dances, and many outdoor skills. There was also sleeping on the ground, living in tents, vigorous hiking, and sports to mimic the life of soldiers (Eells, 1986). Summer camps were part of a back-to-nature trend aimed at providing respite from the moral and physical degradations of urban life. From the perspectives of socially conscious adults, the modern urban world deprived children of their essential childhood, so camps and camp life were intended to compensate for such losses. Changing attitudes toward issues of children's play, health, sanitation, gender roles, and race relations and middle-class Americans' view of the modern roles of children tended to form the structure and lives of the early camps (Van Slyck, 2006).

By the beginning of the twentieth century, the urban, middle-class, idyllic view of children engaging in spontaneous play in the natural beauty of the countryside was fading as the natural wilderness retreated. Children were increasingly deprived of wide open, sunny, wild spaces for active, spontaneous play with natural materials, while overcrowded living conditions and faulty sanitation, crime, and traffic threatened the health of the young. Urban, middle-class Anglo-Saxons were asking: what will prevent urban Anglo-Saxon middle-class children from becoming like immigrant vagrants and ruffians "who would rather haunt the nickelodeon than engage in wholesome play" (Van Slyck, 2006, p. xxii)? What could be done to prevent such objectionable behavior and help ensure that children continued to learn the cultural values of their parents? Summer camps were seen as positive alternatives to children loitering and loafing on city streets, wasting their summer vacations from school, and organized camps were formed throughout the latter 1800s and early 1900s. Camps were also valued for providing a respite from the regimentation of the schools and were seen as alternatives to traditional work on farms that ostensibly promoted character, fitness, and health.

The supporters of organized camps included many of the same leaders who contributed to other elements of the child-saving movement. A brief synopsis of the broad-based child-saving work of Luther Halsey Gulick, as presented in a biography by Dorgan (1934), provides a glimpse of the dedication, skill, and success of one such philanthropist. Gulick engaged in a wide assortment of roles aimed at improving conditions for children and youth, including Lecturer at New York University and Director of Physical Education in the New York City schools. In his writing, Gulick (1909, 1915) promoted a philosophy that play differed from work in that work might be pleasant or unpleasant, done for economic and survival reasons, and focused on ends rather than means. Recreation, in contrast, was rest, recuperation and change from the strenuous parts of life (work), while play is free of the whip of public opinion or the economic lash—self-motivated and free of compulsion of any type. He did not conceive play as simply physical or neuro-muscular activity but as also embracing the things we enjoy during leisure time—art, literature, mother–child play—all the flights of genius and all of social life. Education, he believed, failed if it only equipped one for work (Dorgan, 1934). His commentary on play and education strikes chords strangely familiar today in our era of high stakes testing. Gulick's prominent role in forming the American play and playground movement is discussed in the next chapter, but his influence did not end there. He was also influential in forming organized folk dancing, evening recreation centers, summer playgrounds, vacation schools, and worked with many organizations to improve conditions for play, recreation, hygiene, and education. He is perhaps best known for his and Mrs. Gulick's work with the Luther Gulick camps for girls and for founding the Camp Fire Girls.

Dr. and Mrs. Gulick began enrolling girl campers in 1910 at their camp on Sebago Lake, Maine, a beautiful, natural setting lauded by Longfellow, Whittier, and Hawthorne, populated by many native plants and animals, and blessed with picturesque beauty—a seemingly perfect site for exposing children and youth to the wonders of nature. The camp was named "Wohelo," meaning work, health, and love, and many Wohelo camps sprang up around the country. Daily activities included swimming, sailing, canoeing, crafts, pageants, and caring for the camp—all intermixed with a nondenominational interplay of the spiritual and the physical. Realizing that girls could benefit from the same activities as boys did in the Scouts, the Gulicks and others officially formed the Camp Fire Girls organization in 1912 with Luther as president. Their camps were considered to be the laboratories for the Camp Fire Girls.

Organized summer camps grew rapidly during the early 1900s. The Gunnery Camp was followed during the late 1800s by the first YWCA camp (1874), private camp (1876), and YMCA camp (1885), and in the early 1900s by the first camp for the Boys Club (1900), Boy Scouts (1910), Camp Fire Girls (1912), and Girl Scouts (1912). The American Camping Association was formed in 1910. The early camps were influenced by appreciation of wilderness areas and concerns about their disappearance that were emerging at the turn of the century. Naturalists such as John Muir and Theodore Roosevelt valued nature and helped influence the designation and establishment of protected wilderness land.

The first children's museum was established in 1899 in Brooklyn for the purposes of whetting children's natural curiosity through interactive, hands-on learning and discovery. This was followed by the establishment of children's museums at the Smithsonian and in Detroit, Boston, and Indianapolis. Traditional museums at that time were designed for adults and centered on collecting, preserving, and exhibiting art, natural specimens, and cultural artifacts, essentially for passive listening and observing (Association of Children's Museums, 2005).

Museums designated as "children's museums" were not alone in promoting play and playgrounds. Following the first Annual Congress of the Playground Association of America (PAA) in Chicago in June 1907, the Second Annual Congress was held at the American Museum of Natural History in New York, September 8–12, 1908. One of the main special events at the Congress was an exhibit of playground equipment and activities in the central hall of the museum. The most popular feature was an exhibit of playground models belonging to the PAA, including a miniature municipal playground, a school playground, a private yard playground, a playground and small athletic field for children from less populated cities, a playground for rural schools, and an interior court playground. The walls of the central hall were covered with detailed drawings of model playgrounds and equipment, and maps from many cities showing the location of playgrounds. A series of photographs illustrated the playground system of the New York Parks Department, as well as schoolyard and roof playgrounds operated by the New York Board of Education (Playground Association of America, 1909).

The growth of the playground movement was illustrated by the number of cities participating in the Second Annual PAA Congress—twenty-one from the United States, one from Canada, and one from Puerto Rico. In addition, the movement of manufacturers into the playground equipment field was illustrated by exhibits of playground companies from several cities—Arthur Leland from Templeton, MS; Fred Medart, St. Louis, MO; Narragansett Machine Co., Providence, RI; A. G. Spalding & Bros., New York; W. H. Toothill, Chicago, IL. These and others were prominently advertised in issues of the PAA journal, *The Playground*, throughout its existence.

Advocates of early school gardens in America were not the first to promote educational gardening, for its existence dates as far back as ancient King Cyrus of Persia. American promoters traced the history of school gardens in America back to 1691, when George Fox willed a tract of land near Philadelphia to be used as a playground for children and a garden for them to plant and in which to learn simple skills. During the nineteenth century several European countries promoted active, sometimes mandatory, school gardens (Lawson, 2005). Friedrick Froebel (1902), the German originator of the kindergarten in 1837, was perhaps the most influential person in the establishment of gardens in kindergartens and other school programs in America. His playgrounds encompassed nature itself and were used not only as growing and learning places but also for multiple forms of children's play. Around 1890 the Putnam School garden was established in Boston and continued for about thirty years, marking a burgeoning era of school gardening (Lawson, 2005). The first children's school farm in New York City was formed there in about 1902, and the School Garden Association of America was formed in 1910 to help schools and communities establish gardens and improve conditions for children, especially the very poor. The first public children's gardening program was formed in 1914 at the Brooklyn Botanic Gardens with the intention of teaching horticultural and art and craft projects. All these gardening efforts were directed to fostering multiple skills of cooperation, hard work, and commitment to civic goals (Greene, 1911; Lawson, 2005). During the war years, victory gardens were common expressions of patriotism as well as lifelines for securing food for families, especially those in cities.

H. D. Hemenway, Director of the Hartford School of Horticulture, prepared a manual for teachers and pupils, *How to Make Gardens*, in which he stated that the American school gardens movement started in about 1873, but he does not indicate by whom or where (Hemenway, 1909). School gardening was practiced in some European schools many years before it caught on in America. Some gardens were established to supplement the salary of teachers or provide food for them, and others were botanical gardens where specimens could be studied by pupils. By about 1909 more than 100,000 school gardens existed in Europe, and in several European countries no school qualified for state funds unless a garden was connected with it (Hemenway, 1909).

The creation of school gardens in America was motivated by the desire to assist children, especially those in cities, in their all-round development—learning to use their hands, learning quick observation and decision making, and learning in every branch of study taught in the schoolroom. Mathematics, language, writing, painting, geography, business, and the use of tools are all learned through gardening. In addition, gardening creates in children a love of the beautiful and deters them from petty crimes such as stealing by helping them develop a sense of ownership and responsibility. Gardening was seen as giving play to all of children's motor abilities and was especially valuable for city girls, who were not free to engage in street play and work, as were boys, and who enjoyed too little fresh air and sunlight for sound physical development. Hemenway (1909) claimed that boys doing garden work were 30 percent more rapid in their mental, moral, and physical development than those not having gardens, but does not provide any supporting evidence.

The historical account of garden programs has been traced through a circuitous paper trail of newspaper and magazine articles, mimeographs, pamphlets, committee notes, annual reports, interviews, and books by a contemporary author, Laura Lawson (2005). Her decade-long studies revealed a near continuous presence of garden programs for over a century, wavering between interest during times of social and economic crisis and relative obscurity as public interest declined. Beginning in the 1890s, social reformers created gardens to provide land and technical assistance to unemployed laborers in large cities such as Detroit, New York, and Philadelphia. Education reformers promoted school gardens to correlate with school curricula and teach civics and good work habits. School gardens became a national movement, with offices in the Federal Bureau of Education. This motivated women's groups, civic organizations, and others to promote gardens in vacant lots, window-box gardens, and children's gardens. During World War I millions of Americans planted gardens in backyards and vacant lots to allow more food to be sent overseas (Lawson, 2005). These were so successful that gardening was extensively employed during the Depression years and World War II. Over time, the value of gardening for recreation, play, social reconnection, and the appreciation and conservation of nature came to be recognized.

Such claims for the value of gardening have been reinforced over the past century and continue to support the contemporary gardening movement. Although there were separate movements in school gardening and nature study a century ago, gardening is an aid and ally to nature study and, for all practical purposes, the two can be considered integrated wholes in schoolyard development. Ideally, gardens are formed to complement built playgrounds by providing for a wide range of play, learning, and physical activity needs of children. All in all, the early school gardens were welcome alternatives to the slums and poverty—reducing vice and crime, enhancing learning and development, providing beauty and function to the land, stimulating interest and productive activity for children, and focusing attention back on the farm and the delights of country living. A fundamental motive for the early evolution of school gardens, recreation areas, and playgrounds was to temper the inhibiting pattern of the artificial classroom and book-based learning with active, hands-on learning in the out-of-doors. The nature study movement was closely linked with the school gardens movement in theory if not always in practice.

The nature study movement originated in America's common schools to "open the pupil's mind by direct observation to a knowledge and love of the

common things in the child's environment" and "to put the pupil in a sympathetic attitude toward nature for the purpose of increasing the joy of living"
(Bailey, 1905, p. 4). The movement was a product of elementary schools inspired
by university professors such as C. F. Hodge and G. Stanley Hall as early as the
early 1880s and 1890s. Here again, the influence of great philosopher/educators
over the centuries can be seen. The roots of the nature study movement can be
traced to Socrates and Aristotle and to the great educational reformers—
Comenius, Pestalozzi, Rousseau, and Froebel. G. Stanley Hall, writing in the
foreword to Hodge's book (1902, p. xv), could have been writing in twenty-first
century America when he stated that:

> the work is opportune because it stimulates spontaneous, out-of-door
> interests. It is with abundant reason that we find now on every hand a
> growing fear of the effects of excessive confinement, sedentary attitudes,
> and institutionalizing influences in the school. Such work as is here
> described must tend to salutary progress in the direction of health.

The close ties between the branches of the child-saving movement leave one
to ponder the distinctions between them. This is especially true for the school
gardens movement, the nature movement, and the playground movement.
Even the reformers themselves often tied these movements together under one
umbrella. The Proceedings of the Second Annual Playground Congress of the
American Association for Play carried a paper by Charles Robinson (1908)
entitled "Landscape Gardening for Playgrounds" that helps illustrate these ties.
He asked, "Why should there be gardening in children's playgrounds?" In
answering his own question, he explained that cities grow to such a size that
there are not left any flowers and fields and woods. The idle fields, pleasant
waters for swimming, and snow-clad hills for sledding are too distant for practical usefulness. So what should be done? It is to supply children's want and
need for such places that playgrounds are created. "That is why the grounds are
equipped with ball fields, swimming pools, toboggan slides, and skating ponds.
We are only trying to give to children, city-born as well as country, their rightful
heritage" (Robinson, in Playground Association of America, 1908, p. 65). It was
far easier and less expensive to bring little oases of the country to the city,
making them the children's own, than to take the children occasionally to the
country. Despite this awareness, Robinson maintained that makers of playgrounds brought toys and games of all sorts to the playgrounds and forgot the
flowers and gardens and woods. We tell children to run and jump but never to
look for beauty and natural elements—as though the seals never fall from their
eyes and they never see the delights of nature nor experience its many benefits.
Beauty delights, rests, soothes, and pleases children but generally makes them
no wiser. In playgrounds, the merits of novelty, challenge, and play are added to
the aesthetic benefits of nature and, collectively, they become educational.

In Chicago, where the playgrounds are the best in the world, there is told a story of a little barefoot girl who rang the bell at one of the fine houses and asked, "Please, sir, may I put my feet on your grass?" Playgrounds are too often developed on the theory that she would have asked to swing on the area gate or to slide down the railing of the steps, and never have noticed that there was grass. (Robinson, 1908, p. 67)

Thus we see that a century ago, as the nature study movement was gaining ground, its proponents were in many ways quite modern in their understanding that nature was eroding in American cities, that those places called playgrounds sorely needed a touch of nature, and that, consequently, children were missing fundamental pieces of their childhood. Then as now, the movement was essentially a reaction against the "dry-as-dust" teaching of scientific facts, or science for science's sake. It was an approach aimed at the full use of the senses—of direct experience—to displace the existing "mechanical memory" method common in the schools. By 1905 the nature study movement was widely spread across America and was established in many schools (Bailey, 1905).

Setting the Stage for a Twenty-First Century Child-Saving Movement

The half century following the Civil War and the first quarter of the twentieth century witnessed great change in America's largest cities. People crowded to the cities from the country to find jobs in industry and trade, and a great wave of immigration from other countries, especially in Europe, converged on the overcrowded, polluted streets and gradually forced a movement for play, recreation, and child protection to help counter the devastating effects of crime, poverty, and homelessness. Tens of thousands of ragged, sick, homeless children roamed dangerous city streets, played in open sewers, and struggled to survive. Prostitution, gambling, child labor under primitive conditions, and begging were their common lot, and churches, charitable organizations, and concerned individuals searched for solutions.

Beginning late in the nineteenth century, church, school, and civic organizations began to form movements with similar goals to combat such conditions. They observed and many remembered that children in the country were barely affected by the frenzy of city living, for they had access to virtually unlimited natural playgrounds (fields, forests, streams), farm animals, intact families, were not exposed to constant criminal elements, and were kept busy at farm work. Observing the advantages of rural life over city life, child-saving agencies shipped thousands of orphans from city slums to the country on "orphan trains," where they were placed with farm families eager to help children improve their quality of life and secure an education, and, by various accounts, to have strong and ready hands to help with the farm chores. By all reports, they were successful. The high level of success with the orphan train children was not equaled by the success of the playground movement in general. The diverse developmental advantages of experiencing nature firsthand, so evident in such stories, are being lost to modern American children. Schools, parks, and other providers of play spaces and opportunities for children cannot take the children to the country, but they can transport many of the natural features and habitats of the country to city parks and playgrounds.

Settlement houses were established to house, educate, and care for the homeless, and a number of movements contributing to the overall child-saving movement were initiated. These included the organized camping movement, the children's museum movement, the school gardens movement, the nature study movement, and the playground movement. All of these movements helped to alleviate the plight of orphaned, impoverished, abused, and homeless children, and contributed to the welfare of others. They endured, expanded, are alive and well in the twenty-first century, and are contributing to the remediation of the new and perhaps more serious problems of children, which are discussed in detail in the final two chapters.

The history of the early American child-saving movement is a rich resource for learning about the long history of child abuse and neglect in America, and its links to play and play environments. Children struggled to play throughout American history and often succeeded, sometimes under cruel, barbaric conditions. Since children have little power to create or enforce public policy for themselves, they rely on adults such as those who stepped forward to form the early child-saving movement. Now, in the twenty-first century, they must turn again to adults to rescue them from a perfect storm of events, which are more complex and affecting more children than ever before in America, and which are rapidly resulting in the diminution of their play and play environments and threatening their health, development, and welfare. The early child-saving movement serves as a historical model of caring, aroused adults rising to the aid of distressed children and building a period of innovation that permanently changed the lives of children. The benefits were enormous, teaching children social and work skills, and molding lifestyles of fitness, health, and service to others. These were the reformers whose children conquered the Great Depression and became those patriots, now known as the Greatest Generation, who prevailed in World War II and formed a great industrial and technological revolution. A twenty-first century child-saving movement is sorely needed.

4
The Evolution of the Play and Playground Movement

Playing baseball on the streets of New York is forbidden by a city ordinance. Yet every day during the spring a large proportion of the boys brought before the judge of the Children's court are there for the crime of playing ball ... There were seven games of ball going on at the same time on the sidewalk on one side of a single block ... A streetcar went by with a policeman on the front platform ... The boys slipped away by twos and threes into alleys and cellar-doors. After he had passed the boys reappeared and the game went on ... These boys were not lawbreakers at heart. Their mothers and fathers were sitting on the stoops watching their play, and approving it ... An instinct strong enough to impel boys to play baseball under conditions like these is worthy of attention. (Gulick, 1920, pp. 4–5)

The play and playground movement is closely linked to the primary subject matter of this book. Play and playgrounds were briefly addressed in the previous chapter as one of the fundamental foci of the child-saving movement. Here the play and playground movement is discussed in detail, its history, its influence on the evolution of play environments, and its effects on the play and well-being of children.

In 1994 a friend and prominent play and playgrounds advocate, Fran Wallach, sent me a report found in the archives of New York University entitled "The City Where Crime Is Play," prepared by "People's Institute" and dated 1910–13. The author is unnamed but his/her professional associations are noted as a former agent of the National Child Labor Committee dealing with play and crime issues, investigator for the Russell Sage Foundation, and secretary of the West Side Recreation Committee. In his/her role as investigator for the People's Institute, he/she lived in Manhattan's Middle West Side Hell's Kitchen District for three years. His/her study is a valuable in-depth analysis of the conditions of big city street life that influenced the early play and playground movement a century ago.

Early New York: "City Where Crime Is Play"

New York is described in the report as a "City of the Homeless," and the report names homelessness as "the remedial cause for crime and the need for socialized recreation." The most obvious cause for criminalizing play is laid at the feet of a city government ineffective in meeting the educational, recreational, and civic preparation needs of a city with a population of 40 percent recent immigrants and 78 percent foreign born or of foreign parentage. This report was brought to the attention of the Mayor of New York, Rudolph Giuliani, in 1994, to assist in understanding that the problems of at-risk youth in New York had persisted for decades. The report states that 12,000 children were arrested annually in New York. The 193 cases detailed in the report were drawn from the court records of children arrested and brought to court to face charges. The range of these "crimes" across play and destructive behavior shows that the crimes of children at play in the streets, when prohibited by law, become through normal evolution under street conditions a moral evil and result in criminal types and criminal gangs. The evolution begins with the self-conscious, "illegal" pursuit of spontaneous play in the streets, alleys, and vacant lots and gradually transforms into fighting, stealing, and escaping from the clutches of the police as just another form of play.

Figure 4.1 New York street play, early 1900s.
Source: Photography Collection, Miriam and Ira D. Wallach Division of Art, Prints and Photographs, New York Public Library, Astor, Lenox, and Tilden Foundations.

Figure 4.2 New York children in court in the early 1900s for playing in the streets.
Source: Courtesy of the National Recreation and Park Association.

Table 4.1 Street games of New York children in the early twentieth century

Ball games in the streets	Truancy
Playing shinny	Subway disturbances
Playing with water pistol	Disorderly conduct
Selling papers	Fighting
Snowballing	Attempt at burglary
Throwing stones	Burglary
Trespass	Putting out lights
Pitching pennies	Gambling
Bonfires	Picking pockets
Begging	Shooting craps
Jumping on cars	Intoxication
Kicking the garbage can	Assault
Loitering	Stealing
Destruction of property	

Source: Adapted from The People's Institute (1910) "City Where Crime Is Play," Archives of New York University, 51 page report.

The most common reason for arrests was nearly always the playing of illegal games in the streets. Even singing, marbles, and jackstones were acts leading to arrest—merely play representing perfectly normal childish instincts. Yet children were aware of the law and sent out pickets or lookouts to watch for the police while they were playing, or later committing real crimes. All this led to the formation of gangs and more serious misbehavior such as gang stealing and fighting—even war between gangs that sometimes led to boys being maimed and killed. Fights between two boys and mere gang fights were a "traditional form of play" and not uncommon. Almost a century later, I served as a lookout for teenage boys shooting craps in a city where I was sent to visit relatives and work during the late Depression era. On occasion, my teenage uncles offered me as a combatant in a wrestling match on which they would lay ten to twenty-five cent bets, and which usually concluded when a participant was pinned down and the participants went away friends, but sometimes spilled over into angry blows. This was a means to secure money for an afternoon movie with popcorn!

The problems associated with extreme poverty, especially in large cities with rapidly growing populations, have persisted in America, locking the poor into enclaves of crime and misery. The People's Institute's century-old story of crime and poverty in New York included perhaps the most comprehensive and novel play census ever taken—a "flashlight" study of children playing in Manhattan's Hell's Kitchen area at 4 p.m., Saturday, April 19, 1913. Four hundred civic workers, carefully "drilled" in advance and using tabulation sheets and maps, were assigned to areas of districts and supervised by social workers. They classified the street play of 110,000 children. The number of children and the specific activities of boys and of girls were classified by the activity in which they were engaged. The results were "astonishingly uniform" across districts, resulting in a remarkable compilation of the amazing variety of activities, nearly all a form of play or games, that illustrated the range of creative energy and motivation for play among children enmeshed in a culture of poverty. This sample covered only 28 percent of the total child population of Manhattan, so the entire child population engaged in such play, games, and other activities would be more than three times as large. The ratio of boys to girls observed was about 60 percent boys and 40 percent girls.

Table 4.2 Flashlight survey of street activity in Manhattan's Hell's Kitchen, 1913

Adults idling	30,429
Children idling	27,604
Competitive games (team work and social)	27,482
Competitive play	23,337
Children watching	19,985
Individual play of constructive value	14,156
Adult idlers near children	9,734
Playing games unfamiliar to inspectors	8,538
Children wandering	7,920
Children at work	6,674
Children watching games	5,710
Jumping rope	2,104
Tending babies	1,344
Playing tag	937
Playing handball	618
Roller skating	601
Playing potsey	537
Playing on vehicles	535
Playing marbles	524
Vending	430
Fighting	260
Playing cat	192

continued

Table 4.2 Flashlight survey of street activity in Manhattan's Hell's Kitchen, 1913 *(continued)*

Playing hoople	157
Riding bicycles	86
Playing jackstones	81
Playing with mechanical toys	47
Playing jumping games	39
Examining construction material	33
Friendly tussling (rough and tumble)	26
Playing follow master	7
Playing foot corners	7

Source: Adapted from The People's Institute (1910) "City Where Crime Is Play," Archives of New York University, 51 page report.

Table 4.3 Games played by category

Baseball practice	2,154
Baseball games	1,592
Sand play	317
Playing house	135
Playing ring-around-the-rosy	133
Shooting craps	120
Pitching pennies	94
Playing kick-the-can	54
Dancing	51
Chalk games	51
Building bonfires	41
Playing football	39
Playing Indian and soldier	35
Playing prisoner's base	25
Playing shinny	17
Playing hide-and-seek	15
Playing with tops	11
Playing red rover	10
Tricks with dogs	5
Sewing	5
Playing horse	3
Fishing for hats of pedestrians	2

Source: Adapted from The People's Institute (1910) "City Where Crime Is Play," Archives of New York University, 51 page report.

Thirty-nine constructive games were being played by about 55,000 children during these brief "flashlight" observations taken at a common time (4 p.m.) in a clearly defined environment (Hell's Kitchen). Although the numbers cited are not consistent across categories, the overall data reveal the wide range of play, work, and leisure activities of children, the potential threats from playing in the streets and vacant lots, and the need for intervention by reformers. The data also show the will of children to engage in the biological necessity of play wherever they found themselves and are even more revealing when one considers that the data represent only about a third of the Manhattan area. The streets were literally alive with children playing, working, and struggling to survive. It is significant to note that the most commonly observed activity was "adult idlers in the neighborhood of children," followed closely by "children idling or playing games unfamiliar to the inspectors." Crime was rampant on those mean streets and children were frequently victims. Furthermore, much of children's street activity itself was outside the law and so they devised games to disguise this and escape the clutches of the law. Supervised playgrounds were not available to most of these children.

Conditions such as those described in this report, common in the expansive slums of large cities around the turn of the nineteenth century, were the "straws that broke the camel's back" and spurred social reformers to act on behalf of children. Reform actions, discussed in the previous chapter, resulted in a child-saving movement composed of many elements. None of these were more prominently focused on children's play than the play and playground movement.

The Many Faces of the Play and Playground Movement

The literature commonly refers to a *single* American play and playground movement, beginning near the turn of the twentieth century, but the movement branched into two related movements, each with distinct philosophical sources and influences surviving into the twenty-first century. One was rooted in the physical fitness tradition of the German people, which orignated in Germany and was advocated later in the work of Charles Darwin, Karl Groos, Herbert Spencer, and G. Stanley Hall. This branch of the play movement retained an emphasis on physical fitness and was expanded to include sports and recreation. Over time, it was expressed primarily in public schools, city parks, and recreation areas, and will be discussed in detail in this chapter. The second branch, the child study or child development movement, was influenced by the work of Johan Pestallozi, Friedrich Froebel, John Dewey, and the voluminous research of the child study movement centered in child research stations at major American universities during the early 1900s. This branch of the play movement found expression in early nursery schools and kindergartens, continues to influence early childhood programs in the twenty-first century, and will be discussed in detail in Chapter 5. Some writers active in the movement wrote about the "play movement" and others the "playground movement." Today's perspectives show that the movement focused on both children's play and their playgrounds, and the early authors were talking about the same phenomenon. The terms "play movement," "playground movement," and "play and playground movement" will be used interchangeably in this chapter. At the turn of the twentieth century the term "play" was used with much the same connotation as the term "recreation" (Knapp and Hartsoe, 1979). This broad meaning will be implicit in many of the referenced documents that follow.

A number of writers chronicled the development and evolution of the play movement. The movement was defined as "a mode of collective behavior occasioned by social disorganization or contacts, involving intercommunication of desires, and manifested by an organization of social activities intended to accomplish a common object" (Rainwater, 1922, p. 1). Rainwater explains that a movement is characterized by events involving adjustment to a social condition. As the reader will see, he is referring to the "child-saving movement," characterized by a number of approaches to helping homeless children in major cities around the turn of the twentieth century, and including as one major goal the development of playgrounds in schools and parks. Prominent leaders in the child-saving movement, working extensively with charitable organizations, included Jane Addams (1909, 1945), Jacob Riis (1902), John Spargo (1906), and Charles Brace (1880). The history of the early play movement can be traced through the records of scholars, parks administrators, and others who documented the movement through the last quarter of the nineteenth century and the first quarter of the twentieth century. Notable among these were Joseph Lee (1902, 1929), Everett Mero (1908), Clarence Rainwater (1922), Henry Curtis (1914, 1917), Luther Gulick (1920), and Sapora and Mitchell (1961). The journal of the Playground Association of America, *The Playground*, is one of the most extensive sources of information about the movement—replete with original material and ranging across multiple topics and perspectives. The Archives of the PAA are housed at the University of Minnesota.

During the latter half of the nineteenth century a movement, rooted in Germany, was emerging in several countries that emphasized the health and fitness benefits of vigorous outdoor exercise. This was documented by the German Koch (1908), in an early issue of the *American Physical Education Review*, later translated and discussed by America writers. The purpose of this movement was to counteract the harmful effects of life that threatened mental and physical health, notably the effects of city life and its growing demands. By the turn of the twentieth century common citizens as well as noted philosophers and educators recognized that activities such as gymnastic exercises, outdoor play, swimming, rowing, walking, and bicycling not only developed the muscles but also improved respiration, the nerves, and mental and general health.

The Central Committee for the Advancement of Folk and Child Play is credited with much of the success of the German play movement. Following its organization in 1891, the Committee successfully influenced schoolchildren and later the general population. With the aid of the German Teachers' Association of Physical Education and other organizations, an extensive system of play and outdoor exercises was developed to supplement formal physical training. Gutsmuth, inspired by Rousseau, introduced outdoor play and exercise training in Schnepfenthal, Germany, during the first decade of the nineteenth century. In 1810 F. L. Jahn founded a system of gymnastics, and in 1812 two gymnastics teachers, M. Katharinum and H. Cominus, along with K. Koch, organized the first system of school play. At about the same time, A. Hermann was working to include girls in play and exercises. In 1882 von Gossler, the Prussian Minister of State, added substantial support to the play movement, recognizing not only the health value of outdoor play but also perceiving its great pedagogical importance: "the development of character and the creation of that social feeling which comes only through playing with others on the playground" (Koch, 1908, p. 327). Finally, in 1889 teachers in higher institutions of learning were persuaded to participate in the play movement and the first course for the training of play leaders was established in Gorlitz, Germany.

The first general congress of the Central Committee for the Advancement of Folk and Child Play was held in Berlin in 1891. More than 300 delegates representing 136 civic bodies and several hundred other associations were in attendance. Subsequent congresses were held periodically, the eighth in Strassburg, Austria, in 1907. The Committee's yearbooks contain a repository of information on all aspects of the play movement. The first work of the Committee, training play leaders, was shown in its results. During the years 1890 and 1906, 10,375 male play leaders and 1,089 female play leaders were trained, and a general attitude of enthusiasm prevailed. Additional work of the Committee included the preparation of manuals and rules for various types of play, developing the general physical strength of schoolchildren, and locating large spaces for playgrounds. This latter work was complicated by the gradual disappearance of free open spaces in the cities, a problem that remains today. Despite such problems, the number of playgrounds in German cities with populations over 5,000 increased from 1,166 to 2,092 during the last decade of the nineteenth century, and the available playground space increased from 2,317 acres to 4,587 acres.

The Committee reacted against the "modern trend" toward abandoning the tradition of playing and exercising out-of-doors because of the growth of industry and workers being "imprisoned in factories, workshops, and offices." Consequently, they considered that their ideal and most significant work was to get children and adults to participate in play and outdoor exercises, and they set about influencing new policies and programs for play in the schools.

> Play in the schools shall no longer be accidental, but conducted regularly and under the supervision of the school ... participation by the children may no longer be at the option of the individual pupil, but must be according to a systematic plan ... Just as the formal physical training is compulsory in the schools, so it must be with this play curriculum. Perhaps this is even more essential for girls' schools than for boys', because the physical education of girls and women, particularly in the direction of developing heart, lungs, and nerves, seems to be all the more needful

in view of the unwholesome way of living that has prevailed and that has already had such dire effects upon the general health of girls and women. (Koch, 1908, p. 332)

While the German play movement was gaining strength early in the nineteenth century, organized school and park playgrounds were being introduced into America. The earliest available record reveals that in 1821 a crude outdoor gymnasium was introduced without supervisor or instructor at the Salem, Massachusetts, Latin School (Mero, 1908). Despite this early introduction of outdoor gymnasiums, the introduction of sand gardens in Boston in 1886 is most frequently designated as the beginning of the playground movement (Rainwater, 1922; Mitchell and Mason, 1934). The earliest playgrounds were selections of indoor gymnastic apparatus transported to the out-of-doors, and were called "outdoor gymnasia." Mero attributes this development to New England physical training sources, but at least two events point to German influence. There is, first, the chronological proximity of the initial development of American and German playgrounds or "outdoor gymnasia," and, second, the establishment of an "outdoor gymnasium" at the Round Hill School in Northampton, Massachusetts, in 1825 for play and gymnastics using German-type apparatus and supervised by Dr. Charles Beck, a student of Jahn in Germany (see Koch, 1908; Mero, 1908; Frost, 1989, 1992).

Figure 4.3 The first manufactured outdoor playgrounds in America—"outdoor gymnasia"—were influenced by the German physical fitness movement.
Source: E. B. Mero (Ed.). (1908). *American playgrounds: Their construction, equipment, maintenance, and utility.* Boston: The Dale Association (p. 91).

Hale (1908) witnessed the creation of and played on the first outdoor gymnasium in Boston and discussed the events. The "march of intellect" fad originating in England was adopted in Boston and brought with it German notions about gymnasiums, primarily because two exiles from Germany, Dr. Francis Lieber and Dr. Charles Beck, established a swimming school at the later site of Brimmer Street and an outdoor gymnasium on Tremont Street, then called the "Washington Gardens." The outdoor gymnasium had 200 students the first year, 400 the second, and then dropped to 4 in the third, leading people to question whether a system of fixed apparatus could maintain its popularity unless combined with athletics and rivalry. Hale (1908, p. 30) recalls his feelings of terror when he was taken to the gymnasium in 1826, climbed up the ladder, and was afraid to slide down the pole until a teacher instructed him how to. As the fever for athletics swept over the Latin School, the yard behind the school, approximately 30 feet by 30 feet, was designated a playground and equipped with a vaulting horse, parallel bars, and other gymnastic equipment originally designed for indoor gymnasiums. By this time the term "playground" was used to designate both indoor and outdoor play-places, and "recess" referred to breaks for play.

> *This play-ground (outdoor gymnasium)* was the only play-ground of the school, and was accessible only to the boys in the lowest room. Upstairs we were confined to a very limited passage-way, I might call it, at recess, in which we used to play "tug of war," though we never called it by that name. The recesses were very short, for the simple reason that they did not like to have us in the street. (Hale, 1908, p. 31)

During the period between 1821, when outdoor gymnasiums were introduced into America, and 1886, when sand gardens were introduced, very little progress was made in developing playgrounds for the masses, especially the tens of thousands of children who roamed the streets of major cities and lived in the filth. Following the initial establishment of the Salem outdoor gymnasium in 1821, others were established: Round Hill School of Northampton, Massachusetts, in 1825, and between 1825 and 1830 Harvard, Yale, Williams, Brown, and Amherst Colleges, and the New York High School. These met with limited success, but in 1950 German immigrants, hoping to make their gymnastics system popular, organized gymnastics societies and attempted to incorporate the system into public schools. Later the Swedish system of gymnastics was introduced and both systems influenced subsequent physical education programs in the United States (Mitchell and Mason, 1934). Because of the lackluster interest in outdoor gymnasiums for decades following their initial establishment, compared to the explosive interest after the initial sand garden experiment and the expanding interest of charitable and political groups, virtually all historical documents point to 1886, not 1821, as the beginning of the early American play movement. The sand garden experiments, dating from 1886, marked the beginning of serious efforts by charitable and other organizations to rescue children from the dangers of the slums. As they organized to rescue these children, the resulting "child-saving movement" began to make notable progress in establishing playgrounds and recreation areas and in altering the effects of poverty and homelessness.

The establishment of sand gardens in Boston in 1886 is therefore most frequently designated as the date of origin of the play movement despite the establishment of many outdoor gymnasiums in several American cities more than half a century before that time. H. H. Buxton, reflecting on the relation of sand gardens in 1885 to the rapid development of playgrounds in other cities by 1899, stated in his unpublished Master's thesis: "This was the starting point of the present playground movement in America." In that same year Charles Robinson, a playground architect, also wrote: "the municipal sand piles of 1867 were the first pathetic expression of a need of a playground and of an effort to satisfy it" (Rainwater, 1922, p. 37). Thereafter, most writers adopted this designation despite the many playground initiatives that followed the introduction of the outdoor gymnasiums in 1821.

While visiting Berlin in 1885, Dr. Marie Zakrsewska observed both rich and poor children playing in heaps of sand in public parks under the supervision of the police. Her letter to Kate Gannet Wells, chairman of the executive committee of the Massachusetts Emergency and Hygiene Association, resulted in the placement of a large heap of sand in Parmeter Street Chapel and the West End Nursery in Boston in 1885. Following the enthusiastic reception of the sand by children, piles of sand were placed one year later (1886) in the yards of the Children's Mission Parmenter Street Chapel and Warrenton Street Chapel, and the sand garden experiment began. During these first two years, mothers and other female volunteers supervised the sand gardens. In 1887, when the number of sand gardens was increased to ten, located in one school and several tenement houses, matrons were hired to supervise, and tools for digging and blocks for building were added. By 1899 the number of sand gardens had increased to twenty-one, with twenty of these being located in schoolyards. The Boston city council provided $3,000 annually for their support (Lee, 1915; Rainwater, 1922).

Stoyan Vasil Tsanoff (1897) stated in his book *American Playgrounds* that, at the time he was writing, the playground idea consisted almost exclusively of some articles in periodical reviews and the daily papers, and that his was the first book published in America to deal exclusively with playgrounds. "No books seem to have been written on playgrounds, no organized efforts made to regulate them" (Tsanoff, 1897, p. 1). I have not been able to locate an earlier book devoted exclusively to American playgrounds. Beginning during the first decade of the 1900s, a number of books about playgrounds, to be discussed later, were published by leading figures in the play and playground movement.

A number of these authorities were founders of and participants in the American Association for Play, organized in 1907.

When sand gardens were in their infancy, the chief advantage attributed to playgrounds was their contribution to physical development, particularly that of boys, reflecting the emphasis on outdoor gymnasiums. This narrow focus began to change as sand play and broader provisions were added to playgrounds. Because of the physical development emphasis, playgrounds did not appear to be needed in small towns, villages, and the countryside where ample space and natural play challenges were everywhere available. A similar claim was made for the wealthy classes in cities, who had yards for children's play. Playgrounds, then, were considered necessary only for large cities and mainly in slums and densely populated areas. Tsanoff believed that such arguments represented a very superficial view of play and playgrounds. Playgrounds served very important social, personal, and educational functions for all children, stimulating and guiding life, and developing character in ways not otherwise available. He predicted with accuracy that playgrounds could some day become instruments in educating the "whole man" (Tsanoff, 1897, p. 15).

The sand pile experiments and the rapid growth in sand gardens led from philanthropic to public support for playgrounds. The Boston Parks Department in 1889 appropriated $1,000 for playground work and constructed and ran the Charlesbank Outdoor Gymnasium for boys and men in 1881 and for girls and women in 1891.

> This playground ... was fenced, parked, equipped with swings, ladders, seesaws, a one-fifth mile running track, a sand garden, and provided with wading, rowing, and bathing facilities, all free to the public. Land and equipment were contributed by the park department, operated by private associations ... The children's and women's divisions were entrusted to the Massachusetts Emergency and Hygiene Association. (Rainwater, 1922, pp. 28–9)

This illustrates that thought about the design of Boston playgrounds more than a century ago was quite similar to that of city park playground planners today. Equipment and spaces for both girls and boys of all ages were provided, playground equipment was similar to some that is still available, provisions for organized games were included, and both private and public funding was available. The stage was set in American cities for progress in both the design and scope of playgrounds during the early 1900s, but the Great Depression and World War II would bring such progress to a virtual halt, and, decades later, obsessions about safety, lawsuits, and high stakes testing would interfere in children's play and playgrounds with a hard and heavy hand.

The Boston initiatives to provide playgrounds for boys and girls of all ages, the collaboration of philanthropic and public agencies, and the integration of sand gardens, outdoor gymnasiums, and organized sports areas into one system led at least nine other cities to send representatives prior to 1898 to Boston for consultation about developing their own playgrounds. These cities, Philadelphia, New York, Providence, Brooklyn, Baltimore, Newark, Worcester, Chicago, and Portland, were joined by other cities with the result that the movement developed rapidly and passed from philanthropic to public support, primarily through park and school boards. The stages of the movement were described by Rainwater (1922). The first stage was the sand garden stage, with seasonal use for pre-adolescent age children in densely populated areas of cities, employing both free and directed play, and intended to remove children from the physical and moral dangers of the streets. The second stage, the "model playground" stage, beginning in about 1895, was carried out in several large cities in an effort to attract, guide, invigorate, satisfy, and uplift children and youth and serve as connecting links between home, school, and church (Tsanoff, 1897, p. 18). Rainwater believed that the term "model playground" was first used in connection with playground provisions made by Jane Addams' famous Hull House in Chicago. This model included about three-quarters of an acre, was open to children and youth, and contained sand piles, swings, building blocks, and a giant stride for the children, and handball and baseball courts for boys of adolescent age. The playground was supervised by an experienced student and a policeman (Rainwater, 1922, p. 56).

Tsanoff credited the Culture Extension League as the pioneer in establishing a model playground in the city of Philadelphia. This playground was in response to adults' and children's needs for free play and recreation the year round. Gender specific pavilions were provided for boys and girls, complete with gymnastic apparatus for children and youth, steam heat, showers, and provisions for indoor winter games. The outdoor playground included a play area to be flooded in winter for ice skating and drained in the summer for other games and a race, hoop and bicycle track, and the surrounding area provided grass, trees, walking tracks, benches, fountains with fish, and a special place for leaving babies. Supervision was conducted by playground teachers, whose duties were to be playmates to the children and guide them with civil and gentle manners, while requiring order and decency. Models of supervision differed from city to city and even within cities.

Events leading to the development of the first model playground in New York City were perhaps the most dramatic in the history of the play movement. The efforts began in 1857 with an inquiry by a legislative committee into conditions in the tenement districts or slums of the cities. Nothing of substance resulted from this effort, but in 1887 the New York legislature authorized the city to spend $1,000,000 a year on constructing small parks. In 1894 this power was exercised with the purchase of the Mulberry Bend Park, a two-and-one-half acre site, at a cost of $1,700,000. However, no play provisions were made at this site until a wagon rolled into a cellar and injured several children. Jacob Riis wrote a newspaper article that aroused the citizenry, and the park was "finished," although it contained only plots of grass intersected by concrete walks and with signs warning "Keep off the Grass." Mulberry Bend Park was a failure. A second plot, Seward Park, was acquired, and the land cleared of buildings in 1895, but lack of funds prohibited any further development at that time. In 1899 the Outdoor Recreation League, comprising nineteen societies, opened a model playground in 1899 and, wishing to avoid a repeat of the Mulberry Bend blunder, guaranteed to pay the costs of accidents and damage suits. This playground was designed for people of all ages, cost $2,000,000 and included gymnasiums, baths, spaces for organized games, gymnastic apparatus with instructors, play spaces, and equipment for children. By this time there were thirty-one school playgrounds in New York City, including open-air gymnasiums, kindergarten tents, roof gardens, swimming baths, and evening play centers. At the end of the nineteenth century, the play and playground movement was alive and well in New York City and other large American cities.

Boston, widely known for its much emulated Charlesbank Outdoor Gymnasium of 1889, made a more aggressive attempt in 1900 to develop a model playground with respect to equipment, supervision, and play activities at the Franklin Field site. This project was conducted under the auspices of the Massachusetts Civic League. The annual report of 1901 described the provisions: wooden shelter, bench for mothers, sand boxes, swings, teeter ladders, and carts. Gymnastic equipment for boys included horizontal bars, teeter ladders, fling rings, trapezes, and slanting ladders and poles. Provisions for the girls included sewing and cutting out materials for kindergarten, and space for baseball and other lively games.

By 1900 city leaders in the play and playground movement and scholars were learning that play had educational value, that playgrounds could accommodate both children and youth on the same site, that playgrounds could be used year round, and that public funds should be used to secure playground sites, equip them, and provide supervision and maintenance. Also by this time, the play movement had gained sufficient momentum to move beyond the model playground stage to enter a period of development of small parks patterned after the successful models, but extended to include trees, shrubbery, flowers, lagoons, carriage drives, walks, and large areas of grass. Jacob Riis called them "breathing places," for "one could do little else" (Rainwater, 1922, p. 71). As this emphasis progressed in city parks, the sand gardens and model playgrounds were constructed on private land such as vacant lots, church properties, and schoolyards, all typically barren and unattractive. Such a contrast between the use, function, and appearance of playground sites remains alive in the twenty-first century, yet perhaps to a lesser degree.

Stages of Play Environment Development

The period 1905–12, designated the "recreation center" stage, witnessed the provision of both indoor and outdoor facilities for people of all ages and for all seasons of the year. The manual play of the sand gardens and the physical and manual activities of the model playgrounds were supplemented by provisions for social activities such as dances, clubs, and parties; aesthetic activities such as dramatics, musical programs, and storytelling; and civic activities including health exhibits, public forums, and elections. More expansive equipment was added to meet the needs of crowding and poverty. Parks boards were assigned greater responsibility for developing gymnasiums, libraries, public baths, swimming pools, club rooms, and meeting halls to complement the small parks. There were extensive open days, evenings, summers, and winters. All these provisions, in addition to ball fields, gymnastic equipment, tennis courts, and a multitude of other exercise and games options, as well as recreational provisions, resulted in the need for field house supervisors, play leaders or teachers, janitors, maintenance personnel, and various other personnel.

Between 1912 and 1914 the "civic art and welfare" stage was emerging and involved efforts to regulate and organize play throughout communities and not just in playgrounds and recreational facilities. These efforts were primarily aimed at commercial amusements such as music concerts, theater, dance, dramatics, festivals, and pageantry, which had slowly emerged in previous years. Boston, Cleveland, Denver, Milwaukee, and San Francisco had municipal orchestras and Chicago and Houston had municipal bands. Civic organizations administered and extended much of this work. A "play festival" was held in connection with the first annual meeting of the Playground Association of America in Chicago, on June 7, 1907, and play festivals multiplied in playgrounds and small communities. Christmas and other holiday and seasonal festivals grew in scope, and historical pageants celebrating old customs were revived. The popularity of dancing led to conflicts about young girls dancing in public dance halls, resulting in both social and legal consequences. By 1915 about 158 cities had ordinances regarding play and amusements (Rainwater, 1922, pp. 130–1).

By 1920 the "neighborhood council" stage emerged, as citizens began to develop neighborhood councils aimed at securing greater control over the provision of play and recreational facilities and their operation. Fortunately, there was sufficient cooperation between departments of government and community and voluntary organizations to allow collaboration for mutual advantage. Consequently, the activities of recreation centers were widened to include such activities as town meetings, lectures, motion pictures, cooperative stores, and community days. By this time, there were both theoretical and practical bases for this neighborhood organization stage. Political and social scientists were influencing community beliefs and actions and stimulating change to reflect their theories and studies. People in small towns and in rural areas formed social centers in their school and church buildings. These were cooperative ventures, typically unregulated by any government agencies, but created and operated by voluntary groups within the communities.

The "community service" stage began in 1918 with America's participation in World War I. As military bases and industrial sites mushroomed in number, provisions for play and leisure were inadequate to meet the need. By this time, the Playground and Recreation Association of America (PRAA) had twelve years of experience in training thousands of play leaders on how to administer facilities. The PRAA offered assistance to the Council of National Defense, and the War Camp Community Service was organized. This organization worked largely according to the neighborhood organization pattern, with the community itself taking the initiative in coordinating facility and program planning. The activities, much like those of the neighborhood organization, included a wide range of physical, social, aesthetic, constructive, and civic programs for all ages. By the end of the war, 604 communities had organized recreational resources for the military and about 50 were located near war-related industries (Rainwater, 1922, pp. 179–80).

By the early 1900s formal playground and recreation facilities and programs had expanded to include thousands of city playgrounds at schools and parks in the largest American cities, but in 1914 few country schools had any play equipment in their yards (Curtis, 1914). Curtis proposed that country schools should have sand bins, swings, slides, running tracks, jumping pits, baseball diamonds, volley ball courts, tether ball poles, horizontal bars, croquet sets, and basketball courts. Trees should be planted for shade and gardens for gardening. Curtis was aware of playground hazards, noting that the ground underneath the horizontal bar installed at the end of the swings should be excavated and filled with soft sand. Hard surfaces under such equipment, then as now, would result in broken arms. The equipment was not considered expensive since it could be made by an ingenious member of the community, by older boys using scrap lumber, or sponsored by the mothers' club or school improvement association. If a teacher could raise $20, she could buy a volleyball and net ($6), two baseballs ($2), four bats (50 cents), a croquet set ($1.50), and build a sand bin ($2), leaving $8 to replenish supplies (Curtis, 1914, p. 52).

The country girl was believed to be hindered in her play by clothes and restrictive customs, discouraged in her sports, and handicapped since she "comes up to puberty with only three fourths the lung capacity of the boy of the same age" (Curtis, 1914, p. 65). Curtis could scarcely imagine a boyhood more educative than that of the boy growing up on a farm, spearing fish by torchlight, swimming almost every day, trapping for mink and coon, building log houses in the woods, tending little farms, robbing the nests of bumblebees, caring for farm animals, tilling crops, and playing Native American games. Curtis was not complimentary about the common activities for girls. Many girls did roam the woods, go hunting and swimming, and doll play was more engaging and creative than was realized by those who did not participate. Further, housework was very active, involving far more than washing dishes and sweeping floors, and frequently extending into outdoor activities such as gardening, cutting wood, carrying water, and caring for animals.

> It is all right to play at keeping house, but it is not as exciting or stimulating to the imagination as hunting and fishing. To dress dolls is admirable, but the doll is not very energetic in the matter, and as sport it seems a trifle tame. The girl as a rule cannot go swimming or roam the woods with that freedom that her brother exercises ... Her duties are monotonous and uninteresting. There is not much adventure in washing the dishes or sweeping the floor. (Curtis, 1914, p. 105)

Curtis traveled widely, visiting nearly every state in the union, yet he questioned whether even one percent of the country schools he passed had grounds level enough to accommodate a game of baseball or even a garden. Many were at the edge of wooded hills or adjacent to gullies or swamps. He was heartened to learn that some states were passing laws requiring that all schools have sufficient grounds for a proper playground. Curtis may have underestimated the play value of woods and streams adjacent to schoolyards, having spoken so eloquently of his own play experiences in the woods surrounding his farm home.

The New Psychology and the Institutionalization of Play and Playgrounds

By the time of the war camp movement, a new conception of the purposes and organization of playgrounds was beginning to emerge. The initial sand gardens were piles of sand supervised by people in the neighborhood, who offered no particular scheme or structure to direct the children's play. As sand gardens were expanded or integrated with other provisions during the model playground stage, sponsors continued to operate as though children and youth would develop spontaneously and needed little external influence or interference. This pattern prevailed for an extended period of time as small parks and recreational centers were established. However, the emphasis on playground provision, labeled the "playground movement," was to become a much more vigorous play movement during the early nineteenth century as social scientists, psychologists, educators, and recreation leaders began to examine play and its benefits and to consider both the social and psychological dimensions of providing wholesome play for people of all ages.

The impact of scholars on children's play is traced back to ancient Greece and Rome and continued over centuries, as described in Chapter 1. Darwin's early and mid-nineteenth century work on evolution influenced the thought and theories of scholars active during the American play movement (Johnson, 1907;

Gulick, 1920; Schwartzman, 1978; Spariosu, 1989; Sutton-Smith, 1997; Frost et al., 2005). Although Darwin expressed little interest in play, his findings and views on natural selection and species survival resulted in greater interest in developing a scientific approach to play. Prominent scholars of the late nineteenth century, including Karl Groos, Herbert Spencer, and G. Stanley Hall (later to found the American child study movement), were influenced by Darwin, but they also contributed original theoretical perspectives. The growth of child study that began during the late 1800s was to gain considerable force during the early 1900s, but the "new psychology" was a companion variable in shaping the play movement. Between 1885 and 1910 Americans were redefining their attitudes toward childhood in ways that were quite different from those of the mid-nineteenth century. Following his in-depth historical study of the social reform movement for municipal playgrounds in America, Cavallo (1981) concluded that the theories of Hall, Dewey, Baldwin, and Thorndike emphasized, in distinctive ways, the moral significance of the public, social, and peer group over private, autonomous, moral deliberations. The influence of these men will be discussed in detail in the next chapter. Their theories led to the ultimate conclusion that "an orientation toward public life could be instilled in the young through physical activities, including play" (Cavallo, 1981, p. 151).

The following chronology details major events of the playground movement between 1821 and 1908.

Table 4.4 Chronology of early American playground development

1821	First outdoor gymnasium at the Salem, Massachusetts, Latin School
1825	First outdoor playground and gymnasium with supervision and instruction, Round Hill School, Northampton, Massachusetts
1826	First public outdoor gymnasium in Washington Farden, Boston
1825–72	Period of relatively little activity
1872	First legislative action recognized to purchase land for playgrounds, Brookline, Massachusetts
1876	First park playground, Washington Park, Chicago
1881	First state law authorizing small parks, New York City
1886	First sand gardens established in Boston
1889	First free, equipped, supervised outdoor gymnasium for public use, Charlesbank, Massachusetts (for men and boys)
1890	First New York City playground
1893	First Providence, Rhode Island, playground
1894	First Chicago playground with modern equipment, Hull House
1896	Northwestern University, Chicago, opened extensive scale playground, equipped with apparatus
1898	First Minneapolis playground by Improvement League, in schoolyard
1899	First municipal playground, in New York City, resulting from laws of 1895
1903	Creation of the South Park, Chicago, recreation center idea

continued

Table 4.4 Chronology of early American playground development *(continued)*

1904	Formation of the Department of Public Recreation of the American Civic Union, the first organized national effort on behalf of playgrounds
1905	Opening of the first of the South Park recreation centers, Chicago
1906	Founding of the Playground Association of America; play festival and field day for country children at the organization of the Playground Association of America, New Paltz, New York
1907	First outdoor play festival, at Chicago, on closing day of the first convention of the Playground Association of America
1908	Beginning of extension work by the University of Missouri, Department of Physical Education, to spread playgrounds and physical training to all towns and cities in Missouri; Playgrounds Congress held by the PAA in New York City

Source: Adapted from E. C. Mero (1908). *American playgrounds: Their construction, equipment, maintenance and utility.* Boston: American Gymnasia Co.

By 1910 thousands of organized programs for children had been established around the country, the Playground Association of America had been founded, and between 1880 and 1920 municipal governments spent more than 100 million dollars on constructing and staffing organized playgrounds. The conduct of play and playgrounds was guided (minimally) by child study and the new psychology, but the more dominant factor was "organization" (Cavallo, 1981), labeled "standardization" by Rainwater (1922), intended to structure play on supervised, well-equipped playgrounds owned by city governments. One purpose was centered around institutionalizing play provisions and organizing play experiences, and the second was to utilize modern psychological and biological theories for developing cognitive skills, moral tendencies, and social values (Cavallo, 1981, pp. 2–3).

As groups involved with the model playgrounds, such as neighborhood organizations, schools and parks, and later the War Camp Community Service, assumed more active roles, their opinions, social attitudes, and theories of play became more influential. This gradually resulted in a shift from merely providing facilities and allowing a "laissez faire" approach toward a move to defining standards, rules, or structure and administering them in all aspects of playground design and function. These focused on such elements as conserving behaviors beneficial to the general welfare, developing proper social attitudes, habits, sportsmanship, and control on playgrounds, and adjusting children's play to social exigencies. The increasing structure was in part a function of scholarly influence but led to institutionalizing the development and operation of facilities. The behavior of adults during leisure activities was also of concern, and efforts were directed to the provision of facilities and ensuring the proper behavior of adults, youth, and children. The emergence of structure or standards was to influence not only the operation of facilities and play and playgrounds for children, but also led to organized recreation, festivals, and celebrations for all ages.

The movement to institutionalize grew gradually during the early 1900s, when community and government groups began to provide for all ages and to institute year-round play and functional organization. Commercialization of amusements and equipment entered the picture along with municipal and state legislation, and expert guidance was employed for major programs, playgrounds, and festivals. As hundreds of play leaders were trained, they were sent into public playgrounds and into the streets to mark off play zones, to supplement the limited number of public playgrounds, and to organize and supervise children's play. The trend in the movement was from free play to directed play, from self-selected games to organized games, from a focus on individual satisfaction and rewards to group rewards, including public recognition and team and school trophies. Thus the search for techniques to control, standardize, or institutionalize play became increasingly structured through the application of "science," but a limited understanding of the nature of play and of child development, then as now, restricted progress.

The founding of the Playground Association of America (PAA) was to add considerable strength to the establishment and operation of playgrounds and recreational facilities in cities, but it would have limited influence on understanding and implementing child development research and theory. Implementation of child study was to be the strong suit of the child study movement, which would later exert heavy influence on the creation and spread of nursery schools and kindergartens (see Chapter 5) that would contrast sharply with the "physical fitness" playgrounds of the PAA. By 1906 leaders of the play and playground movement were looking to expand their reach and influence and so formed the Playground Association of America, which was to endure under different organizational umbrellas until the present time.

The Playground Association of America (PAA)

Henry Curtis and Luther Gulick were principal founders of the Playground Association of America (Lee, 1915; Cavallo, 1981). Curtis, a student of the eminent psychologist G. Stanley Hall, earned his Ph.D. in child psychology in 1898 and was appointed director of New York City's playground system. He and Luther Gulick supervised playground programs in the city's poorest wards. Curtis studied recreational administration in Germany and England in 1902 and found the emphasis on "individualistic and militaristic" gymnastics to be objectionable, believing that democratic team games should be the focus in the play movement. Upon his return to America, he was named director of the Washington, D.C., playground system and asked Gulick to join him in forming a national playground organization. In 1905 they met with Curtis Lee and a small group of men and women to consider organizing a course for training those who worked on playgrounds. At one meeting, they discussed organizing a national playground association. On April 12, 1906, in Washington, D.C., the

Playground Association of America was formed. Gulick was elected president, Theodore Roosevelt, a strong supporter of play, physical activity, and nature, was elected honorary president, Jacob Riis honorary vice-president, and Henry Curtis secretary and acting treasurer (PRAA, 1925). Within a year, the association published its first issue of *The Playground*.

The organizers were received by President Roosevelt at the White House and met that same day to develop a play program for the City of Washington. At the second business meeting in Chicago, a Committee on State Laws and the Normal Course in Play was appointed. In June 1906 Seth Stewart, Chairman of the Executive Committee, initiated the publication *The Playground*, a journal that would be instrumental in the growth of the play movement. The main work of the PAA during its first seven years was conducting surveys and providing expert guidance to cities, working primarily through chambers of commerce and other influential groups.

In 1907 Gulick was offered and accepted a staff position with the Russell Sage Foundation, initiated the Foundation's work in recreation, and chaired its Playground Extension Committee. Gulick had already been questioning his plans to enter the ministry while at Oberlin College and decided that organized physical education, like organized religion, would be useful in the contemporary world (Cavallo, 1981, pp. 32–3). He was to become the first president of the Playground Association of America and was the first to arrange the play of children on playgrounds according to age. He broke with tradition by not favoring sharp divisions between various age groups in their games. Based on his extensive observations of children in both American and European playgrounds, he believed that children must learn to govern themselves, since self-government must be acquired as an experience rather than taught as a theory or philosophy. Playgrounds, then, were essential for children in a democracy. In his book *A Philosophy of Play*, Gulick set forth three major conclusions resulting from his years of studying play (Gulick, 1920, pp. xiv–xvi).

1. Play has a greater shaping power over the character and nature of man than any other activity.
2. A people most truly reveals itself in the nature of its pleasures.
3. Each individual recapitulates the history of its kind.

Gulick's first two conclusions gained wide acceptance, but his third received less agreement. A number of prominent leaders in the play movement subscribed to the recapitulation theories emerging from Darwinian ideas of evolution as formulated by Herbert Spencer and G. Stanley Hall. These theories proposed that observing a child would reveal a developmental sequence representing significant stages in the evolution of man, just as the biology of each organism repeated the evolution of the species. Here we see the initial stages of a scientific movement that exerted minimal influence on the early playground and recreation movement but later, with the growing emphasis on research at universities and the emergence of the child study movement, would have a significant impact on play and playgrounds and the educational programs at American nursery schools and kindergartens.

The PAA was instrumental in securing a law requiring every city in Massachusetts to provide playgrounds, and in 1917 the War Camp Community Service was organized. By 1925 the PAA and its successor, the Playground and Recreation Association of America (PRAA), had influenced legislation in thirty-three states that had compulsory physical education components. "The various machine companies [manufacturers] objected to the committee on play equipment and it was impossible to have a meeting of this committee" (Curtis, 1917, p. 16). This will be of interest later in this volume, when the role of playground equipment companies in the present standards movement is examined. At the fourth annual congress of the PAA, Luther Gulick retired as president and Joseph Lee succeeded him. Henry Curtis praised Lee as "the first man to write a book on the subject [a disputed claim] ... If there is any one man who may claim to be the father of the American Playground Movement, it is undoubtedly Joseph Lee" (Curtis, 1917, p. 18), and George Butler, who served on the staff of the National Recreation Association, dedicated one of his books to Joseph Lee with the words: "No man has done more for playgrounds" (Butler, 1936). Butler, having personal acquaintance with leaders in the movement over several decades, wrote in *Pioneers in Public Recreation* (Butler, 1965) a set of personal yet scholarly biographies of more than fifty such leaders. The work is a mini-history of the movement and a valuable reference for students of playground history.

The Normal Course in Play

The Normal Course in Play, spearheaded by the PAA, was to become the inspiration for most of the courses offered by normal schools (early term for teachers colleges) and universities throughout the country. In 1914 the Russell Sage Foundation identified fifty high schools, colleges, or normal schools offering training courses for playworkers. By 1916 this number had expanded to approximately one hundred, with about half being in normal schools, although many of the courses consisted mainly of teaching games. The location of training programs in normal schools was facilitated by the presence of model schools or training schools for children, usually with several hundred children in attendance, making it possible and desirable to have a model playground. Larger universities, such as Harvard and one or more universities in Pennsylvania and Wisconsin, offered play courses in their departments of physical education. Extension departments in other universities offered community institutes on public recreation. In Kansas, forty-two smaller towns, influenced by the University of Kansas, employed a paid director of play, and in Gary, Indiana, girls and boys in high school were assigned to work as apprentices in playgrounds and gymnasiums.

The Normal Course in Play was outlined in a book published by the Playground and Recreation Association of America (PRAA) in 1925. The play instructor was to take the content from such fields as psychology, sociology, child study, anthropology, civics, pedagogy, physical education, dramatics, storytelling, and similar topics, and adapt it in ways most effectively correlated with other courses of the institution. The Normal Course drew fine distinctions between the play of children and the play of adults since many felt that the word "play" should apply only to the activities of children, recreation should apply to leisure, and relaxation should apply to the play of adults. The writers agreed to define play as "what we do when we are free to do what we will," involving "an attitude which may pervade every activity." "Recreation" was applied to "the present-day organized movement to provide community-wide facilities and activities for children and adults" (PRAA, 1925, p. v). The Normal Course, as outlined in the manual, was to be broad in scope, including such topics as program planning, the nature and function of play, play leadership, play facilities, organization and administration, and the history of the community recreation movement.

By the mid-1910s, with 50 daily requests for assistance pouring into the offices of the PAA, the leaders had recognized that the term "playground" was too narrow to capture the broad scope of the movement, and the PAA became the Playground and Recreation Association of America (PRAA). The constitution was revised and the journal was renamed *Recreation*. Consequently, the emphasis on play and playgrounds gradually shifted to an emphasis on recreation, social work, and civic affairs. By 1925 under one-fifth of American schoolchildren had access to playgrounds, but the interests of the PRAA continued to expand to encompass the recreation and leisure activities of citizens of all ages. As America sank into depression in 1930, the PRAA took steps to broaden its conception of recreation even further, completely removing the "restrictive" term "playground" from its title and changing its designation to the "National Recreation Association" (NRA) (Knapp and Hartsoe, 1979, p. 104), and physical fitness, recreation, and sports directed primarily at youth and adults increasingly overshadowed young children's free play. The NRA expanded its services to include the performing arts, training institutes, consultation, research, public information, the ill and disabled, personnel services, and site visits. Amazingly, critics once again thought that the focus of the organization was too narrow, and in 1966 several related organizations—the American Institute of Park Executives, American Recreation Society, National Conference on State Parks— merged to form the National Recreation and Park Association (NRPA) that exists today.

At the time of the organization of the PAA in 1906, forty-one cities were operating playgrounds. In 1924, 711 cities were conducting community recreation leadership and overseeing 5,006 playgrounds, and also employing 15,871 workers (2,783 year-round) to conduct activities at the centers. A recreation specialist, to serve on the staff of the Federal Children's Bureau and the National Conference on Outdoor Education, was called for by President Coolidge in May 1924. Despite this progress, hundreds of communities were still without playgrounds, and studies in twenty cities revealed that 50 to 90 percent of the children observed were on the streets, one half of those idle. The leisure time of young men and women was considered to be an equally serious concern because the attractions of pool rooms, motion pictures, and street corner rendezvous claimed the great majority. In general, the PRAA believed the answer to be the training of leaders, new facilities, and the dedication of volunteers and municipal bodies.

Three ideals of play were considered essential to success in the development and operation of playgrounds, none of which was adequately realized (Curtis, 1917). The first was to provide an hour or two of play for every child every day. This was deemed essential to children's physical, social, and intellectual welfare. The second principle held that children of about the same age, i.e., not more than two or three years difference, and children of the same sex should play together. Finally, the same children should play together every day to allow friendships to develop and to keep down horseplay and loafing. "It is impossible to secure a team spirit unless the same children play together frequently" (Curtis, 1917, p. 31). Neither municipal, park, nor school playgrounds were meeting these ideals.

Playgrounds with four to six thousand children living within a half mile seldom had an attendance of more than four or five hundred children a day, and the most vigorous and athletic children who excelled in the games comprised the largest attendance group. Those who needed to play were most likely to stay away, and during the school year the playgrounds were empty in school hours. This led to playgrounds being overequipped and oversupervised part of the day and underequipped and undersupervised part of the day. None of the playgrounds separated children by Curtis's narrow age prescriptions and the same group of children seldom played together at the playgrounds. Curtis considered the play of girls to be a special problem. Boys would play whether or not playgrounds were provided, but girls would sit around and talk or play simple games like jackstraws, neither activity developing skills in running, jumping, or other physical development. Playgrounds were gradually opened for girls but special provisions and encouragement, such as could be provided by parents, teachers, and play leaders, were slow to change until the late 1900s. Historically, cultural stereotypes and traditions regarding the proper roles of girls at play have proved extremely difficult to modify.

Successes and Limitations of the Play and Playground Movement

The child-saving movement, including organizations such as the Playground Association of America, influenced and shaped the American play and playgrounds movement, but many civic organizations, schools, charitable individuals, and various other groups also made significant contributions, as discussed in the previous chapter. Historians credit reform groups and the PAA for advances during the play movement, because the most valuable material was written by members of these very groups (Hardy, 1982). Consider, for example, the rich volume of material written by officers of the PAA and the leaders in major child-saving organizations as compared to that available from other responsible parties such as neighborhood lobbies, charitable individuals, churches, and various private and public groups. The common, everyday people who worked to forge better communities shared the success of cities in their search for healthy play and recreation for children.

Leaders in the child-saving movement and in the PAA identified the introduction of sand gardens in 1887 as the beginning of the playground movement, but organized playgrounds began in 1821 with the introduction of a German inspired outdoor gymnasium in Boston. The sand garden and the outdoor gymnasiums were eventually combined into more comprehensive playgrounds and expanded to include various types of manufactured play equipment, games areas, sports fields, and broad based recreational areas and opportunities for people of all ages. By the turn of the twentieth century, most major cities had joined the movement, and the growing involvement of government and the organization of the PAA in 1906 were leading to creeping standardization or institutionalization of recreational facilities in American cities. Play leaders were trained, rules for administration and games were formulated, supervisors were hired, and the new psychology of such scholars as Darwin, Groos, Spencer, and Hall began to influence the movement to a growing degree.

The evolution of organized play and playgrounds in America during the late 1800s and the early 1900s progressed through several stages, beginning with merely providing places for children to play. Schools and municipal parks offered respite from play in the streets, under the leadership of trained play leaders. As interests turned to scholarship, especially in psychology, proponents of play argued that play was essential to children's development and should be provided to children every day. This was gradually accomplished in growing numbers of public schools. The focus on play for the youngest children was relatively slow to emerge in America, but play was central to the kindergarten curriculum from its beginning. The play movement had its greatest impact on public recreation, and found expression not only in thousands of playgrounds in cities around the country but also in public gymnasiums, swimming pools, sporting fields, organized music, pageants, historical celebrations, city parks, summer camps, and both public and private schools.

Prior to World War I, one-room schools were spread around the country in rural areas, enrolling children within a few miles and within walking or horseback distance. With the advent of America's entry into the war, national organizations such as Theodore Roosevelt's Country Life Commission argued for changes in schooling, and consolidated schools began to emerge. The success of country schools depended on availability of the means to transport children over longer distances to school, so school buses were brought into service in many areas. The Model T Ford that sputtered and struggled across the rugged roads of the Midwest spelled the end for one-room schools (Grover, 1992). Some scholars later criticized the loss of free-flowing play in nature that had characterized the one-room schools.

At one-room schools in many parts of the country, the playground was the refuge for immigrant children frequently ridiculed for their inability to speak English. On the playgrounds they could speak their native languages and gather in groups for support in understanding their teachers and becoming full-fledged American youth and men and women. Play and social interaction at one-room schools allowed children with disabilities to develop a sense of individuality because their involvement was needed and wanted. Later, in consolidated schools, independence and individuality were not so easily built or retained because graded classes and "chosen up" sides in play tended to favor and result in the greatest rewards for the top achievers. Consolidated schools brought country children to graded schools, and children were ruled by the clock and competition. The more affluent schools installed manufactured playground equipment, and spontaneous play and traditional games were replaced by organized sports and physical education (Grover, 1992).

> Children today need the opportunity to invent their own games, to fail and to succeed with their friends, and to experience the natural world as previous generations did with such unbounded enthusiasm on the playgrounds of America's country schools. (Grover, 1992, p. 204)

The PAA, while achieving a moderate level of success in building and maintaining city parks and recreational areas for people of all ages and for both boys and girls, acknowledged its "failure" to achieve certain basic aims. It did not manage to ensure that children received one to two hours of play time every day (a goal growing in popularity today), that children of similar ages played together, that the same children played together every day to foster sound social development. The "recapitulation theory" on which many leaders relied was later found to be baseless and the views of such intellectual giants as Comenius, Pestallozi, Froebel, and their followers were passed over to be embraced during the early 1900s by the pioneers of the American nursery school and kindergarten movements and the child study movement. In the public parks and public schools, the overriding focus on recreation, organized sports, and physical fitness, extant during the latter periods of the play movement, endures and has contributed to the standardization era of American playgrounds. Conversely, the broad developmental and free play perspectives of many modern preschools, nursery schools, and some kindergartens stand in sharp contrast. The discussion of the child study movement in the next chapter will place this contrast in perspective.

5

Play and the Child Study Movement
Nursery Schools, Kindergartens, and the Developmental Approach to Play

Now, what I want is, Facts. Teach these boys and girls nothing but Facts. Facts alone are wanted in Life. Plant nothing else, and root out everything else. You can only form the minds of reasoning animals upon Facts: nothing else will ever be of any service to them. This is the principle on which I bring up my own children, and this is the principle on which I bring up these children. Stick to Facts, Sir! (Charles Dickens, *Hard Times*)

The late nineteenth and early twentieth centuries witnessed a number of movements to improve conditions for children and provide play and playgrounds. Following the introduction of outdoor gymnasiums and sand gardens in America, two parallel play and playground movements emerged. As seen in previous chapters, the first movement was based initially on the German physical fitness tradition. The physical fitness movement, emphasizing physical development and recreation, grew from the early twentieth century Playground Association of America, but through a series of mergers became the National Recreation and Park Association (NRPA) which exists today. The NRPA continues to champion physical fitness for all age groups, with a stress on safety, following the adoption of national playground safety guidelines and standards during the late twentieth century. Its major audience is urban recreation and park professionals, and its early emphasis on playgrounds for physical development and safety is alive and well in urban park playgrounds and public schools.

Yet another strand or movement, designated herein as the child development movement, had initial roots in the work of Pestallozi, Froebel, and their Renaissance-era predecessors. The founding of Froebel's German kindergarten was a fundamental link to the eventual formation of scientific child study. His ideals or theories of education were introduced into America along with his kindergarten methodology, and they were to become one of the major rallying points for the expression of the differing theoretical positions of child development scholars. Kindergartens would gradually gain strength and diversity from the "new psychology" of such eminent psychologists as Herbert Spencer and

G. Stanley Hall, and would be refined by the work of John Dewey and various other behavioral scientists hard at work in the child study institutes of several universities, utilizing university kindergartens as laboratories for child study and research. All this marked the rapid rise of the American child study movement and, later, the interdisciplinary field of child development.

Through this multifaceted movement, child development was to become a respectable scientific enterprise, and consequently children's play, which would be validated as a central component of child development, would become a subject of scholarly research by a growing class of scholars representing all the behavioral sciences. The child study institutes were not established for the specific purpose of studying children's play, but the resulting research was to be fundamental in positioning play as an essential variable in children's healthy development, and would have a lasting influence on integrating play into children's educational institutions throughout America in nursery schools and kindergartens. In order to illuminate the importance of children's play in child development and education, many of the scientists who contributed to the child study movement are discussed here, and the events surrounding their work are explored. The importance of this discussion will become clear when the contemporary state of children's play is explored in depth in Chapter 8, and we look to history for the causes, consequences, and corrections of questionable contemporary trends in children's play—its dissolution and its evolution into differing forms.

Play and Child Development in Kindergartens

There are traces of kindergarten practice in early educational philosophy dating back to ancient Greece and Rome. Plato and Aristotle recognized the importance of educating children before they entered school at six years of age. The family was to play the principal role in early education. Martin Luther also believed that the family home was the educational institution of primary importance. The emphasis on early education was continued by such prominent philosophers/scholars as Comenius, Rousseau, Pestallozi, Froebel, and Dewey. Drawing from his work at Pestalozzi's school and his keen observations and reflections, Froebel opened the first kindergarten (translated as "children's garden") in Blankenburg, Germany, in 1837.

Froebel's kindergarten was built around the children's inner urges and native impulses, and was to grow out of their natural interests and motivation. The teacher was to place the children in a stimulating learning environment and guide them toward self-direction and self-control. The curriculum called for active involvement of the children with carefully sequenced materials such as the gifts (balls, blocks, cubes, etc.) and occupations (clay, wood carving, painting, weaving, etc.). The gifts were to be handled, counted, examined, manipulated, measured, divided, etc., then used in combination with the occupations for the enjoyable practice of skills such as paper cutting and folding, weaving, stringing, drawing, threading, and painting. The gifts were intended to be discovery oriented and the occupations to foster inventiveness—creating, controlling, modifying, and transforming. Froebel's chief means of instruction was play. However, the limited control exercised over play activities by the teacher and the structured design of the gifts and occupations were to be major points of contention among kindergarten leaders, who would criticize the fixed and formal aspects of his curriculum during the introduction and evolution of the kindergarten in America (Frost and Kissinger, 1976).

The introduction and evolution of the kindergarten in America resulted initially from the work of Mrs. Carl Schurz, a refugee from the German revolution of 1848. Having studied with Froebel himself, Mrs. Schurz opened the first kindergarten in Watertown, Wisconsin, in 1855, initially for her own children. She later met Elizabeth Peabody, who opened her kindergarten in Boston in 1860, intending to demonstrate Froebel's views. Peabody, being of an influential family and a member of the Concord School of Philosophy, won the interest of several prominent leaders in Froebel theories. Among these were William T. Harris, later U.S. Commissioner of Education, and Susan Blow, who would become one of America's most prominent early childhood educators. Harris and Blow opened the first public school kindergarten in St. Louis in 1873. The early kindergartens in America were to survive as philanthropic organizations for a long period before becoming common elements of public education. They appeared at a time when the plight of people in city slums was attracting the attention of philanthropic and religious groups, which early embraced kindergartens as one of the great hopes for ministering to their needs. Kindergartens were:

> located in the worst slums of the cities, and highly cultured and intelligent young women prepared themselves in normal schools supported by philanthropists. These young women entered upon the work with rare enthusiasm and consecration to the cause. No neighborhood was too criminal, no family too degenerate, no child too bad. Into Little Italy, Little Russia, Little Egypt and the Ghettos they went, offering daily care to humanity in its early years. (Hill, 1942, p. 1950)

The lack of funds to meet the overwhelming needs of children of the slums led philanthropic agencies to adopt the kindergarten, use vacant rooms in public schools, and provide financial support. Over time kindergarten became an accepted part of public schools, but these kindergartens did not provide for the physical and health needs of children, and their teachers did not spend their afternoons as social welfare workers for entire families, as did the teachers in philanthropic schools. There were no medical facilities, school lunches, social workers, school nurses, or visiting teachers. Teachers taught both morning and afternoon sessions with different children and had no time for home visits or welfare work. The absence of such fundamental services for young children in poverty was not to be extensively tackled until the advent of the Great Society Programs of the Lyndon B. Johnson presidency. There continue to be wide differences between the ideals of the first kindergartens, based on the Frobelian philosophy of freedom, play, and attention to individual needs and firsthand experiences, and the typical primary school programs of today based on regimentation, memorization, and standardized testing.

By the early years of the twentieth century, the new psychology was influencing schooling from nursery through the childhood years. George Ellsworth Johnson, Superintendent of Playgrounds, Recreation Parks, and Vacation Schools in Pittsburg, Pennsylvania, and a student at Clark University when G. Stanley Hall was President, conducted extensive studies of the theory and meaning of play, the relations between play and work, and the history of play and its value in education. In 1907 he wrote an extensive history of play and games (Johnson, 1907) based on anthropological studies dating back to dim antiquity and including the more recent work of Guts Muths, Pestallozi, Froebel, Groos, Gulick, Lee, Baldwin, and Hall. From these studies and in his writing he not only explained play but also identified more than one thousand of the most important and widely diffused plays and games, and developed a "curriculum of play." In this curriculum he essentially laid out the fundamental play practices of the nursery schools, kindergartens, and, to a lesser degree, primary schools of the early 1900s.

He said that play and work were to be viewed as mutually essential in the educative process and in child development, for all work involves play, and work can and should have playful qualities. There were two ways of using play in education: introducing play into work, and employing play as a means of development. The kindergartens were increasingly introducing play into the school curriculum, for during the first years of life play is the natural teacher of the child (Johnson, 1907). During the early twentieth century, play was considered to have significant educational value, including motor development through motor play, maturation of the nervous system through physical activity, relaxing children through active outdoor play, maintaining attention throughout the day, using instinctive curiosity in nature play, learning to build through constructive play, developing self-confidence, and reducing discipline problems. The play activities of the kindergarten period were intended to reflect the characteristics of development during this period, centering around common objects, free motor activity, experimenting with the senses, explaining, guessing, questioning, imitating, constructing, nurturing plants and animals, cooking, sewing, counting, measuring, rhythms, dancing, and music—all this and more, employing the whole field of the child's interests. Children younger and older than kindergarten age (four to six) were similarly introduced to a play curriculum appropriate to their developmental levels.

John Dewey, the great American "progressive" philosopher/educator, established a laboratory school at the University of Chicago in 1896 to test his educational theories. He disagreed with many of Froebel's educational theories and did not refer to his school as a kindergarten. Over time his agreements and disagreements with Froebel's views were expressed in extensive debates at the International Kindergarten Union. He agreed with Froebel that education should direct the play experiences of the young child toward effective social living, and that ideas were not fixed but changing in different circumstances. He disagreed with Froebel's view that the play processes of the child should imitate the teacher, as with the gifts and occupations, holding that imitation should be arrived at naturally. He would not have a child sweep a make-believe room with a make-believe broom. Instead, he would provide opportunities for children to sweep the classroom floor with real brooms. Similarities are seen between Dewey and Froebel in their valuing of constructive work in the curriculum—drawing, music, nature study, excursions, and gardening. While Dewey was stressing social interaction in kindergarten education, Hall was stressing emotional development, and Thorndike was proposing his behaviorist, stimulus–response, evolutionary concepts of learning in the kindergarten program (Weber, 1969). Froebelian principles, sound in many respects even by modern criteria, were severely tested but remain influential in kindergarten practice.

By the 1920s kindergarten practice had changed to reflect a growing array of research and a new group of scholars. For example, Patty Smith Hill (1923) and her colleagues at the Horace Mann Demonstration School at Columbia University were among the scholars at several of America's largest universities building a curriculum for kindergarten and primary children based on scientific knowledge about the nature and care of young children. Theirs was among the first universities to develop programs to train nursery, kindergarten, and primary teachers for their professions that were the equal of those provided for teachers at high schools and colleges. Beginning in 1905, Teachers College developed experiments with kindergarten children in their Speyer School, led by Luella Palmer, director of public school kindergartens of the city of New York. From the beginning, the teacher was considered a guide, providing opportunities for children to learn from each other though self-government. In 1921 the faculty revised their curriculum, based in part on the writings of Edward Thorndike, with the aim of the school itself becoming a laboratory of democracy, each school subject being "studied from the viewpoint of the desirable improvements in thought, feeling, and conduct" (Hill, 1923, p. xv). Such study was deemed to be successful when habit and character had been established.

The Horace Mann program for the kindergarten was built around work periods, group meetings for conversation, singing and rhythm, preparing for lunch, rest, clean up, story time, games, outdoor play, and excursions. The principal

Figure 5.1 Kindergarten children creating doll-houses at Horace Mann School, 1917. *Source:* Lewis Wickes Hine, 1874–1940, photographer. Courtesy of the Library of Congress, Prints and Photographs Division, National Child Labor Committee Collection [reproduction number, LC-DIG-nclc-05238].

role of the teacher was to supply an environment that would elicit the desired responses of the children. She was to control, without dominating, and raise standards step by step, offering help when needed, supplying necessary materials, and recording the child's individual progress through careful records. In order to meet individual needs and interests, the classroom environment was constantly changing. The "work period" was in reality a work/play period, for materials were provided to enhance physical development, and activities were conducted to help children learn to play with one another, to think through problems, to plan and create using blocks, sand, dolls, clay, construction materials, and to care for plants and clean up.

At the fiftieth anniversary of the Horace Mann School, the emphasis on play was perhaps even more accentuated than before. Spaces and materials for outdoor play had been expanded by the development of a rooftop playground complete with a small garden, adjoining shelter, sandbox, sand toys, slide, swing, horizontal ladder, seesaw, walking boards, packing boxes, bricks, balls, ropes, climb around, wagons, swings, packing boxes, seesaw, walking beams, tricycles, wagons, dolls and doll carriages, blocks, and an assortment of toys (Garrison et al., 1937). Materials and spaces for physical science and exploration had expanded to include an aquarium and fish, cages of different sizes for resident and visiting animals, gardening seeds, tools, and containers, and special science materials such as magnets, magnifying glasses, hour-glasses, and thermometers. There were also construction areas with small and large building blocks for constructing buildings, rooms, and models, and assortments of art materials, woodworking tools, and special work areas and tables. Opportunities, spaces, and props for play dominated both the indoor and outdoor classrooms. The indoor area included a block area, house play corner, project play blocks, piano, gym, doll corner, workbench, tables, and jungle gym. Reading, writing, spelling, and arithmetic were integrated into the overall play/work curriculum, based on children's experiences, real-life problems, excursions, stories, and interests.

From the inception of American kindergartens, "outdoor play" rather than "recess" was the term commonly used to denote a special portion of the day. The best kindergarten teachers never considered outdoor play as recess, break, downtime, breathing spell, interlude, or halt from the normal patterns of indoor activity during which children were free and active within reasonable boundaries and their "work" could hardly be distinguished from their play. Such freedom within limits was intentional, planned, and consistent with the emerging science of the child study movement. The preeminent, contemporary early childhood programs throughout much of the world continue the play emphasis in the kindergarten curriculum, but political events of the late twentieth and early twenty-first centuries are placing such freedom and creativity at risk, countering decades of scientific research in child development.

The Child Study Movement and the New Psychology

Over time, the work of educators who favored a developmental or "whole child" approach focusing on all aspects of child development—social, intellectual, emotional, and physical—and that of psychologists who engaged in "scientific" studies of children became intertwined. The new psychology emerged, a child study movement was born, and eventually child study research centers would be established around the country.

During the late 1800s and early 1900s G. Stanley Hall was the leader in promoting scientific study of the child; he was the most influential figure in the child study movement. The movement gradually gained considerable support among many groups and agencies, including the leaders of the Playground Association of America and the leaders of the child-saving movement, but it was greeted with indifference and scorn by most scientists (Smuts, 1985, p. 110). Hugo Munsterberg, a Harvard psychologist, said that he would love his children but never study them (Hall, 1923, p. 392). Hall was one of the most prominent psychologists of his time, founding the American Psychological Association and four psychological journals, yet he was never able to establish an enduring child research organization (Hall, 1923, p. 583). He encouraged many scientists to study children, but others viewed his work as unscientific (Siegel and White, 1982). Hall followed in a line of psychologists influenced by evolution theory. William James (1890) set forth theory rooted in "laws" of evolutionary natural science that viewed human neurophysiological structure as having evolved from lower animals, and E. A. Kirkpatrick (1903) tied child development to working out the instincts of the evolved mental structure of the race.

The early child study pioneered by Hall and other prominent scholars failed to gain momentum, and by the end of World War I the scientific study of children was in "a sorry state" (Smuts, 1985, p. 110). A survey revealed that only three psychologists and two psychiatrists had a primary interest in children (Jones, 1956, p. 239). Hall stressed that sound mental development depended upon sound physical development, and his theory was biological and evolutionary. In embracing the recapitulation theory of his predecessors, presuming an evolutionary hierarchy for the development of the mind, and failing to understand the powerful role of culture and sociology in development, Hall was a victim of his times. His promotion of free play for young children arose from his belief that ontogeny, or individual development, recapitulates phylogeny, the development of the race. Each biological and behavioral stage should be lived completely in order to achieve normal growth and prepare for the next stage. Believing that understanding the abnormal or defective mind could instruct in understanding the normal mind led Hall to promote the study of abnormal patterns of growth and development—a belief that would be challenged by the work of scholars at the Iowa Child Welfare Research Station. Most of the scientific study of children between 1900 and World War I focused on abnormal or subnormal children, but the Iowa Station, established by the Iowa legislature in 1917, studied only normal children (Cravens, 1993). Bird Baldwin, the appointed director, was committed to studying normal children, and during 1918 initiated a program to survey the health and well-being of Iowa children during wartime, resulting in the recording of dental and physical measurements for 140,000 Iowa children.

Arnold Gesell opened the Yale Psycho-Clinic in 1911 and later initiated studies of normal child development. The growing gap between child welfare and child research programs, increasing interest in the social sciences, and philanthropic interest in science led to the development of the new policies of the Laura Spelman Rockefeller Memorial Fund (LSRM) during 1923-4. The principal goal of this fund, when founded in 1923, was to "further the welfare of women and children," but this was changed to "the application of the social sciences for the purpose of reform" (Smuts, 1985, pp. 110–11). Lawrence Frank was appointed chief executor of programs for child development research and parent education.

In 1924 the first child development institute was established at Teachers College, Columbia University, by the LSRM, and the Iowa Child Welfare Research Station was awarded a grant to expand its programs. During the following three years, major LSRM institutes were founded at universities in Minnesota, Berkeley, and Toronto, and Gesell's clinic, renamed the Yale Clinic of Child Development, was awarded a five-year grant (Smuts, 1985, p. 111). In addition to these major child research institutes founded by the LSRM, Merrill-Palmer was established in 1922 and Fels was established in 1929 (Sears, 1975). This extensive network of child research institutes was devoting previously unparalleled attention to research in child development and would have a lasting influence on programs for young children.

Following World War I, philanthropic and child welfare organizations became increasingly exuberant about the potentials of science for improving the lives of all children. The impact of science and technology in transforming industry during the war lent validity to the view that research in the social sciences could improve the lives of all people. Drawing energy and insight from the emerging child research institutes, the stage was set for the scientific study of children to take off. Several emerging national professional organizations were to have lasting influence on child study, education, and child development research and practice. From the beginning, the leaders of those organizations discussed here were active in the child study movement, and their ongoing activities included research and the practical applications of children's play. The history of the movement and of children's play, especially with respect to advocacy, is deeply intertwined with the history of the professional organizations discussed below.

Applying the New Psychology to Education

Beginning around 1890 and continuing through about three decades of the twentieth century, the new psychology, based on the work of such figures as G. Stanley Hall, William James, Edward Lee Thorndike, Luther Gulick, Francis Parker, Herbert Spencer, Arnold Gesell, and John Dewey, influenced the work of child-saving agencies, governmental agencies, nursery schools and kindergartens, and, to a lesser extent, public schools. Their affiliation with universities and their writing and teaching were leading to the discovery of inconsistencies in earlier views of child development. As the new psychology gained adherents, the "conservative" group of educators who followed Froebel were opposed by a younger group of scholars, and vigorous debates ensued, which were not to result in a degree of mutual understanding until about 1910, when both groups united under the direction of all the recognized leaders (Hall, 1923; 1953–4).

In 1895 G. Stanley Hall, President of Clark University, center of the child study movement, invited kindergarten leaders to participate in a summer session to study kindergarten education. Thirty-five prominent leaders attended the opening session but thirty-three of the thirty-five in attendance left when Hall criticized the work of Froebel and his American disciple, Susan Blow. Anna Bryan and Patty Smith Hill remained to plan an "ideal scheme" of kindergarten education with Hall and William Burnham. Following several years of controversy about the proper procedures for kindergartens, the International Kindergarten Union (IKU), at their tenth annual meeting in 1903, appointed a Committee of Three, Susan Blow, Alice Putnam (President of the IKU), and Lucy Wheelock, who were to select fifteen members to form a Committee of Nineteen. The members of the Committee, representing both conservative and progressive views, were to study their differences and prepare a unified report or, failing that, a brief opinion. After a decade of study, discussion, and vigorous debate at meetings of the IKU, the two reports were published in one volume prepared by several of America's most prominent kindergarten leaders (IKU, 1913). Lucy Wheelock wrote the preface, Annie Laws the introduction, Susan Blow a report on the conservative position, Patty Smith Hill a report on the liberal position, and Elizabeth Harrison a brief report on the Froebel kindergarten.

With respect to play, the report of the conservative (Froebel) faction stated:

We hold that the highest form in which the native activity of childhood expresses itself is play. We accept the Froebelian definition of play "as self-active representation of the inner life from inner necessity and impulse" … We are earnest in our conviction that kindergarten exercises must preserve the form of play … Through his studies of childhood, Froebel became aware that some plays point toward the practical arts, some toward the fine arts, some toward science and literature, and some toward the ethical life of man as embodied in social institutions. (IKU, 1913, pp. 108–9)

The conservative position held that the kindergarten should not impose restrictions on symbolic or pretend play wherein children make believe they are another person or an inanimate object such as a stick is a horse. They considered that all make-believe play is valuable for understanding meanings and activities and for developing individuality and intelligence. "All children should have plenty of time and opportunity for free play and in free play should be interfered with as little as possible" (IKU, 1913, p. 113).

Speak to a child of heroism, social interdependence, or patriotism, and you might as well speak to a deaf person. But tell him the story of David, let him play such games as the farmer, miller, baker, carpenter, and wheelwright … and you not only stir the emotional equivalents of these ideals, but prepare the way for their definition to intellect. (IKU, 1913, p. 116)

Americans were not alone in their establishment of programs for young children and studies of child behavior, including play. Nursery schools and kindergartens were growing in popularity. Emile Jacques Dalcroz, a teacher in Geneva, Switzerland, devised procedures that influenced the early English nursery schools. His system was intended to develop bodily expression through music with the aim of coordinating the muscles, senses, nerves, and emotions into an integrated response. Rachel and Margaret McMillan started a nursery school movement in England by opening the Deptford School Clinic in 1909 as a private philanthropic organization, primarily to provide health and physical care to children of the poor. These motives were similar to those of the leaders of the American child-saving movement when they opened schools for children of the city slums. Early on, the English nursery schools adopted modern psychology and developed environments that allowed full expression of feelings and ideas and avoided repression of appetites and instincts. The nursery school was intended to allow freedom of movement and expression but without oppression and harsh discipline. Children's free drawings and their play were used as guides to understanding the young child. The tenet that "all behavior is caused," and the belief that nursery school teachers could learn the underlying motives of children's behavior through direct study of that behavior, led to child study activity well into the twentieth century (Weber, 1969).

The Ruggles Street Nursery School was organized by the Women's Education Association of Boston in 1920. Abigail Adams Eliot, a student at Radcliffe, studied the McMillan Nursery School in England and opened the Ruggles Street School to working class children. Patty Smith Hill, a major leader in the kindergarten movement, was also active in promoting nursery schools. By the 1920s nursery schools were accepting children as young as 18 months. Kindergartens were becoming part of public schools, and the age range of children accepted was further narrowed from ages 3–6 to ages 4 and 5. Nursery schools were much slower to gain a foothold in schools. By 1934 kindergartens were available to one child in four, but there were only about 500 nursery schools in the entire country. However, the emergency nursery schools sponsored by the Federal Emergency Relief Association began to change this picture rapidly (Iowa Child Welfare Research Station, 1934).

By the end of the first quarter of the twentieth century, nursery schools were established at the child research centers of Yale, the University of Iowa, Teachers College, Johns Hopkins, Minnesota, and Merrill-Palmer, and by 1928 laboratories for the study of young children had been established at the Iowa Child Research Center. During this gestation period, nursery school practice, like that of kindergartens, was influenced by a number of emerging psychological rationales, including behaviorism and psychoanalysis. The works of Darwin, Hall, Dewey, Gesell, and Freud were known, and vigorous efforts were made to condense their philosophies into practice. But it was about the mid-twentieth century before such scholars as Lawrence Frank, Daniel Prescott of the University of Maryland, and Arthur Jersild of Teachers College were successful in establishing child study and nursery and kindergarten principles addressed to the "whole child."

Figure 5.2 Outdoor play at Cornell Nursery School, 1924.
Source: Courtesy of the Division of Rare and Manuscript Collections, Cornell University Library.

Play and the "Whole Child"

Play was a central component of the child research center nursery schools just as it was in the kindergartens, for students of child behavior were developing programs focusing on the "whole child." The Iowa Child Welfare Research Station opened the first of the child research nursery schools in 1921 as a logical extension downward of public education. Expanding knowledge of child development led to a break with the old criterion of age of entrance and ability to master the three R's and a focus instead on more "wholistic" principles of guidance in physical growth, health, behavior patterns, methods of learning, personality development, and social and civic growth. Both nursery schools and kindergartens were to work closely with families and supplement family and community life. Play materials and expert supervision of play, not commonly found in homes, were provided. Fundamental patterns of eating, sleeping, and play were carried out under the tutelage of trained professionals. The children were separated into four sections by maturity and age—twos, threes, fours, and fives—and their classroom spaces were specially designed according to levels of maturity.

The indoor play space for four-year-olds had six large windows to allow for sunlight and ventilation, colorful curtains and furniture, shelves for flowers, a cloakroom with low hooks, a low blackboard and bulletin boards, a bench for observers, and cupboards and shelves for storage, including play materials.

The play areas of the room included a horizontal bar with rings that could be alternated with swings, flying rings, a trapeze, and a knotted rope simply by snapping them into place. Ladders and a slide could also be attached to the horizontal bar, making the area very flexible and easily adapted for swinging, climbing, sliding, and the development of motor skills.

The outdoor playground was located on a hill overlooking the Iowa River. A wooden play platform accommodated several types of play equipment—inclines and a perpendicular ladder for climbing on to the platform, packing boxes, a portable ladder, a horizontal iron bar to accommodate a slide, removable swings, trapeze, and rings. The platform was surrounded by a gravel walking path, and a square sand box was placed at the exit of the slide to serve as a landing for children sliding down. A tree house was built around two large trees and had substantial railings and a ladder for entry. A storage facility was provided for the large variety of movable equipment. The children's health and safety were carefully monitored, with regular inspections by a nurse and ongoing attention by the teacher for potential health and safety problems, followed by incidental and planned discussions with the children. For example, when a child was seen throwing sand or gravel at another child's face or, when using carpenter tools, a child began waving a saw around in a dangerous manner, the teacher stopped the activity, brought the children together, and asked, "Is that a good thing to do?" or "How should you do that?" The children themselves were guided into making a few simple rules for use of the sand or the saw. The Iowa Child Research Station's *Manual of Nursery School Practice* (1934) was remarkably modern in its approach to nursery school practice and illustrated surprisingly modern thinking about the role and influence of play in development and the role of adults in providing for its expression.

The Great Depression placed enormous stress on families throughout America from its beginning in 1929 until industry geared up for World War II and employed thousands of unemployed and underemployed workers. During this period, emergency nursery schools were authorized by the Federal Emergency Relief Administration (FERA), sponsored by the United States Office of Education (USOE), to employ needy teachers and support personnel and to provide educational and health services to people suffering from social and economic difficulties. To help public schools prepare for and operate nursery schools, the FERA announced offers of assistance from the National Association for Nursery Education, the Association for Childhood Education, and the National Council of Parent Education. Representatives from these organizations worked with the USOE to prepare bulletins of "best professional advice" for schools and families on setting up and operating nursery schools (USOE, 1933a, 1933b, 1936).

These early nursery schools, true to their philosophical roots, could aptly be called "play schools," for both the indoor and outdoor spaces were designed and used to allow a broad range of free, spontaneous play for children aged from two to six. The indoor play room was inexpensive yet effective, offering a place of function and beauty, gaiety and color: simple and neutral areas for house play, music, storytelling, dramatic play, art, and cots and tables for resting and working with table materials. The outdoor space, roof, or playground was also arranged and equipped for various forms of play: sandbox, seesaw, jungle gym, balance board, slide, ladders, blocks, saw horses, planks, storage sheds, pedal and wheel toys, stacking materials, equipment for swinging and climbing, and a central open space for active running games and boisterous play. Even during this early period, safety was carefully evaluated and provisions were made to protect children from injury. The slide exited into a pit of fine gravel to absorb the shock of falling on to a solid surface, equipment was sized to the ages and developmental levels of the children, and when blocks were brought out for play, the swings were detached from their frames to prevent children from being hit by them. Play equipment for indoors and outdoors included both manufactured and self-built items and was frequently constructed by handymen and carpenters using scrap material. The USOE bulletins included drawings for building both indoor and outdoor equipment at reasonable cost. Stacks of cut logs, for example, could be arranged for climbing, and empty kegs could be used for rolling activities. As in later Head Start programs, a nurse was available, medical care, food, and sanitation were provided, and attention was given to ensuring that children had access to fresh air and sunshine indoors and out.

Federal authorization for emergency nursery schools dovetailed with nursery school experiments at universities, research at child study institutes, the influence of fledgling professional organizations, and the overall impact of the new psychology. Collectively, these forces built the philosophy and practice in nursery school programs for our youngest children that have survived in large measure to the present time. Operation Head Start, arguably the most successful of Lyndon Baines Johnson's Great Society Programs, proved highly successful for young children and families and reflected the influences of these early groups (see Cravens, 1993).

Three disciplines or professions grew rapidly during the latter 1800s and early 1900s—medicine, social work, and education. The Department of Education was established in 1867, becoming the U.S. Office of Education in 1929. Normal schools for training teachers became widespread, and major universities established schools of education (Sears, 1975). Between 1870 and 1910 the proportion of children enrolled in elementary school rose from 57 to 73 percent.

The Demonstration Play School, conducted in the summer of 1913 at the University of California, illustrated the influences of the new psychology, emerging child study, and the play movement on indoor and outdoor curricula for elementary age children. The school was built around the idea of uniting the spontaneous play of children with societal demands for education. This was to be accomplished by combining the functions of the play center with those of the school, hence the name "play school." The organization and activities of this school were different in emphasis from those of other private and public schools, but had demonstrated success in numerous schools, playgrounds, and boys' and girls' organizations. Play schools emphasized a wider interpretation of the nature of the child as a spontaneous, active being, motivated by internal needs, not merely a reflexive mechanism responding to external stimuli. Play, nature's method of education, was learning through living and experience, representing practically the only method for infants, and, as the child's development proceeded, was gradually supplemented with work as outlined by academics. In such activity and with appropriate leadership, the younger children would educate themselves through broad, rich, wholesome, spontaneous play. Work, an "externally compelled activity," played an increasingly important role for youth (Hetherington, 1914, p. 687).

The Play School philosophy embraced the need for children to acquire the tools of cultural adjustment, including the three R's, but warned against such an emphasis for children as young as four or five. The school rejected the traditional, harsh practices of many schools of the era:

> The time has come when men are beginning to realize that the stifling of the child's developing enthusiasms in life through a back-warping, chest-cramping, nerve-breaking, mind-deadening desk and schoolroom program of "studies" is as cruel as the Spanish Inquisition. (Hetherington, 1914, p. 697—how timely these words during the high stakes testing movement—ever creeping down to younger and younger children!)

The Play School was proposed as the next step in the evolution of the American elementary school. Its goals (abbreviated) were: 1) to organize opportunities for a complete play life; 2) to provide leadership in order that the capacity for work may be established; and 3) to connect play with materials and activities needed for success in society. The portion of the curriculum devoted to the child's play life included not only spontaneous indoor and outdoor play but also environmental and nature activities, subsumed under excursions and nature experimentations. For the little children, short trips included free play and opportunities for sensory experiences, collecting, learning the names of natural objects, simple observational games, and some direct instruction. For older children, excursions included hikes, weekend camping, scouting, arts, trips to the woods, fields, streams and lakes, farms, historic places, industrial locations, and public service centers. Nature experimentation included: 1) playing and experimenting with physical energy—water, air, heat, mechanical devices, sound, light, and electricity; 2) playing and experimenting with animals—playing with pets, feeding and caring for animals, and raising and taming wild animals; 3) playing and experimenting with plants—planting, tending, and conducting gardening experiments. (Almost a century later such principles reemerged in headlines, websites, and scientific research.)

Fortunately, vestiges of this philosophy remain in many American preschools and in the child development departments of universities, but it never fully succeeded in securing a firm foothold in America's public schools. One probable reason for this difference may be found in the professional training of early childhood center faculty and administrators as opposed to public school faculty and administrators. The former are typically trained in college and university departments of child development that remain true to their roots in that field; the latter, trained in departments of curriculum and instruction or in departments of education, may receive little or no formal training in play and child development since their training focuses on teaching academic subjects. Consequently, public schools typically allow brief or no recess periods for play, and, except for play in public school-sponsored preschools for Head Start programs and kindergartens, physical development is limited to physical education classes. Currently, steps are underway to increase the academic focus and high stakes testing in public school preschools and kindergartens, driving yet another nail into the coffin of children's spontaneous play.

Child Development Becomes a Scientific Discipline

Technological advances implemented in World War I by such organizations as those forming the child-saving movement, as discussed in Chapter 3, were instrumental in invigorating interest in child study. Following the war, a combination of foundation money and massive federal funding replaced the philanthropic funding of the 1920s and 1930s, and a new generation of scientists revived the earlier enthusiasm.

The early pioneers of the child development movement—Hall, Thorndike, Watson, and Terman—were all psychologists. Hall was the first president of the American Psychological Association, and Thorndike, Watson, and Terman in turn later held that office. The cross-disciplinary field of child development was to grow from the work of scientists in various specialized disciplines of behavioral science. Robert Havighurst, for example, created a cross-disciplinary doctoral Committee on Human Development at the University of Chicago in 1941, but the students continued to specialize in specific fields (Sears, 1975). The child study institutes were instrumental in forming and expanding the field of child development, and the work of Piaget, emerging during the 1920s, was to have a profound effect on both child development as a field of study and the specialized disciplines from which it was formed, e.g., psychology, sociology, education, anthropology, and medicine. His book *Play, Dreams, and Imitation in Children* became a classic in its field and opened up new insights into the nature of children's play.

G. Stanley Hall moved from his professorship at Johns Hopkins to the presidency of Clark University in 1889. Here he developed the child study movement, incorporating child development into educational practice, and held summer workshops in child study for teachers and school administrators. Play was among the many child-related topics he and his students studied. Arnold Gesell, famous for his development of normative descriptions of child development, and Louis Terman, known for his work on intelligence testing and gifted children, were among his students. The history of play can be traced through all of the disciplines comprising the interdisciplinary field of child development. Two of these disciplines will be discussed here, one drawing from the monumental work of the anthropologist Margaret Mead, and the second addressing the work of pioneering psychoanalytic play therapists Melanie Klein, Anna Freud, and Virginia Axline, who followed the psychoanalytic methods of Sigmund Freud and Carl Jung. The contributions of scholars in other social/behavioral disciplines will be explored later.

Scientists in several specialized fields contributed to the emerging discipline of child development and added to the body of knowledge about play and child development during the early 1900s (Murchison, 1931). Margaret Mead conducted cross-cultural research in the South Pacific—New Guinea, and many other places. Her doctoral dissertation resulted in a book, *Coming of Age in Samoa* (Mead, 1928), which remains a bestseller today. She worked with the American Museum of National History from 1926 until her death, maintaining that studying people in faraway places helped Americans better understand themselves. This perspective could be applied to the work of scientists in the many disciplines contributing to the interdisciplinary field of child development that gradually emerged from the work of early pioneers.

Mead's findings about the cultural transformation of the Manus of New Guinea during a twenty-five year period exemplify the profound contributions that scientists of various disciplines can make to a collective understanding of child development, and, more specifically, illustrate the influence of children's play on the formation of culture. When she first visited the Manus in 1928, Mead found a primitive culture, quite literally living in the Stone Age and existing within a culture of taboos and sanctions. When she returned in 1953, the Manus had made a giant step from a primitive to a civilized culture. During World War II nearly a million Americans passed through New Guinea, leaving ideas for a new way of life. Several conditions made this transformation possible: experience with Anglo-Saxon law, religious ideas of brotherhood, an exceptionally gifted leader, and the Australian plan for self-government (Mead, 1956).

Mead's classic ethnographic studies of the natives of New Guinea offer compelling insights into the rich, natural methods of child rearing and of children's play that have become nostalgic artifacts in a world of stress, plastic toys, and excessive indulgence for some and debilitating poverty for others. The child rearing patterns and play of Manu children are rich exemplars of a natural life that stands in stark contrast to many of the stories of desperation already told in this book.

During Mead's 1928 visit to the Manus, the adults were:

a driven, angry, rivalrous, acquisitive lot of people who valued property and trade above any form of human happiness except the maintenance of life itself, the children were the gayest, most lively and curious, generous and friendly, that I have ever known. (Mead, 1956, p. 110)

In the Manu child's world, property was communal, not stored, and available for all to use—canoes, paddles, spears, bows and arrows, beads, occasional tobacco, betel nuts. Unlike their elders, children quarreled very little, followed their leaders, avoided feuds, and were friendly and generous. While their parents made the village ring with abuse, the children continued their play in the moonlight. The child's whole world was a play world. A Manu child described his play life as thinking about little else than his little canoe. He could think of nothing else in the morning than getting his spear and arrows and paddling out to spear fish, and in other times he and his friends would talk of making something they could use. His mind was "set on play only."

Manu children's play world was carefully supervised yet remarkably free, devoid of nagging by adults and arranged to allow small mistakes from which they could learn better judgment and circumspection. They were never allowed to tackle tasks that were outrageously difficult or to make mistakes that could result in serious injury, permanently frighten them, or inhibit their exploration. Techniques for teaching young Manu children included applauding every ambitious attempt, gently pushing aside too ambitious projects, ignoring small errors, and punishing large ones such as breakage and carelessness. The major segments or "departments" of knowledge expected to be mastered by all the small children were "understanding the house," "understanding the fire," "understanding the canoe," and "understanding the sea" (Mead, 1956, p. 127). In the physical world, children learned by doing (reminiscent of Dewey), endless activity, and experimentation. The repetitive Melanesian language was taught by playful repetition, as were singing, dancing, drumming, fishing, handwork, and the art of war, often modeled by older children. Children's play was provided with all the necessary equipment, safe and pleasant playgrounds, and joyful companions of all ages and both sexes. As the reader will see, modern day play leaders or playworkers on adventure playgrounds adopt such natural roles in their interactions with children on the playgrounds.

There is indeed much to be learned and emulated from such significant studies, but Mead was puzzled as to why children with such rich play lives and strong adult oversight were so unimaginative. For example, when given paper for drawing they would draw endlessly about their play world but not show a spark of fantasy. In a culture where adults were preoccupied with unseen spirits, the supernatural, and ghosts, none of these were reflected in their drawings.

The children participated fully in the adults' mechanical world and could understand and handle handicrafts and machines, for they had imitated these mechanical processes throughout childhood. However, they did not imitate the feasts, spectacular dances, marriages, or funerals. There was no loving imitation of the adult world, its work or ceremonies (Mead, 1956), merely endless repetition of the units of activity. For example, they did not imitate or play at war but did imitate the mechanics of spear throwing. Mead's work demonstrated that play was a central component in the education, cultural understanding, and eventual behavior of Manu children, and exercised considerable influence on their values, attitudes, and developmental skills.

Mead was also puzzled as to how children who grew up in such an idyllic fashion could be transformed into and become the driven, hostile adults their parents were. She was to conclude that in any primitive, untouched, homogeneous society the result would be the same—little Manus become big Manus and little Indians become big Indians. In other words, in any homogeneous culture "any method will do." So long as every adult in contact with the child is saturated with the traditions of the culture, the child will also become saturated. However, such homogeneity would not apply to changing cultures but would change according to exposure across generations. Mead's work demonstrated the power of play in transmitting culture, and she raised many pressing questions about the educative process, child rearing, and broad issues of political and social structures. For example, how did immigrants to America with such striking differences eventually become Americans? Somehow, something happened to adults that was transmitted to their children. And why is the assimilation of African-Americans and Hispanics so fraught with difficulties, and the attempt to forcefully "democratize" Iraq, Afghanistan, and other countries so slow and fraught with risks? Mead's powerful work begs an answer to both questions, and the answer to the second may well reside in the questionable notion that something must be *done to* people in order for cultures or political systems to assimilate. People must *want* to change rather than merely submit to being changed. The interdisciplinary work of scientists during the child study movement, gaining strength through the child research institutes, posed such questions, as child development became a powerful scientific discipline.

Mead's observations and conclusions about cultural assimilation were also relevant in some respects to the problems and issues encountered in integrating multiple social and behavioral sciences into one overriding discipline of child development. There were notable cases where serious philosophical differences emerged, but overall the eminent leaders and scholars were able to work as a unit to create and maintain the child study movement and, eventually, to form a cohesive umbrella field of child development that would change international perspectives on child health, welfare, education, and our understanding of children's play. However, before the end of the twentieth century changing patterns of adult culture changed children's play and education in remarkable ways, resulting in the crises forming the thesis of this book.

In yet another discipline comprising the field of child development and the study of children's play, the eminent pioneer in psychoanalysis, Sigmund Freud, opened new vistas through his work on motivational and emotional variables that grew from his psychoanalytical theories. This element gained strength and focus following Hall's invitation in 1909 to Freud and Carl Jung to attend Clark University's twentieth anniversary celebrations and deliver a lecture series. Following World War I, psychoanalytical studies of children that would lead to the creation and refinement of play therapy for children internationally were being carried out in London by Melanie Klein, and in Vienna by Anna Freud. Their studies in play therapy resulted in an expansive body of theory and practice intended to provide therapeutic benefits for child victims of abuse, war, natural disasters, illness, emotional and physical injury, and trauma in general.

Freud is widely credited with founding psychotherapy, but the approach was developed by a number of scientists. Freud himself credited Josef Bruer for bringing psychoanalysis into existence (Freud, 1938). The International Psychoanalytic Association was formed in 1910, with Jung as president, and the first American group was formed the following year under the name the New York Psychoanalytic Society. Freud was not credited with developing the field of play therapy but his *Little Hans and the Rat Man* (Freud, 1909/1955) was the first published casework describing a psychological approach to working with a child. He believed that play had cathartic effects, allowing children to purge themselves of the negative effects of traumatic events (Frost et al., 2004).

Hermine Hug-Hellmuth (1921) was one of the first therapists to propose that children's play was useful in child analysis, and he proposed that play materials be employed for children's self-expression. However, Melanie Klein (1932) and Anna Freud (1946) were the brilliant early pioneers who constructed approaches to play therapy based on the psychoanalytic tradition. In building play therapy for children, Klein substituted play and play materials for Freud's free verbal association commonly employed with adults. She proposed that children lived through and worked out their anxieties and phobias by making connections between play experiences and original or fantasized ones (transference). Klein's therapy setting was a child-sized table with simple toys—bricks, houses, carts, trains, carriages, wooden people, paper, scissors, and pencils. As the child played freely with these toys, the therapist observed the manner of play, gained insight into complexities, offered prompt interpretation, and uncovered the roots of the child's problems, thus reducing the child's resistance and anxieties. Despite her overreliance on the significance of early sexual anxieties, Klein advanced play therapy practice well beyond its original state.

Anna Freud, Sigmund's daughter and a contemporary of Melanie Klein, agreed with Klein that her play therapy method was needed for children too young to verbally express their emotions during psychotherapy. She disagreed with Klein's tendency to see underlying symbolic meaning in virtually all play, proposing that a particular play activity may have a simple, harmless explanation. For example, the child who plays out shutting a purse tightly may not be symbolically closing her mother's womb to prevent her from having any more siblings, but may simply be playing out previous experiences with such play materials. Freud also focused on developing positive emotional relationships with the child, for she believed that really effective play therapy took place only through positive attachments between therapist and child. Her methods included observing children's play using toys, art materials, and storytelling, during which she gradually shifted from play to verbal interaction, while helping the child understand her feelings.

Virginia Axline, a student of Carl Rogers, worked with him in developing one of many approaches, nondirective therapy, that perhaps became the most widely used method of those developed since Freud's and Klein's pioneering work. Collectively, they were successful in shifting the therapeutic focus from the therapist to the child. Axline (1947a, 1947b) believed that play is therapeutic because it can promote a secure relationship between child and adult, allowing the child to state himself in his own terms, just as he is, and in his own way. The child's playing out is equivalent to the adult's talking out and is necessary because children may not have sufficient maturity to express conscious or unconscious inner conflicts verbally, but can do so through free play. In other words, the young child's play is a means of expression; skillful adults can learn from observing play, and can express children's feelings back to them in ways that aid understanding. The child is the most important person in the process. The therapist is accepting and understanding, and there is no prying, criticism, nagging, or directing. The child is psychologically free to express herself and to direct her own growth. Axline (1947b) established eight basic play principles that guide child-centered play therapy today. In condensed form, they are shown in Table 5.1.

Clark Moustakas (1953) and Garry Landreth (1991), influenced by Rogers and Axline, were instrumental in interpreting and expanding nondirective or child-centered play therapy. Landreth, a professor at North Texas State University,

Table 5.1 Axline's eight basic play principles

- The therapist accepts the child just as he is.
- The therapist forms a warm, friendly relationship.
- The therapist creates a permissive relationship in which the child is free to express her feelings.
- The therapist reflects back the child's feelings to help her understand her feelings.
- The therapist respects the child's ability to solve her own problems.
- The therapist does not attempt to direct the child. The child leads; the therapist follows.
- The therapist does not attempt to hurry therapy.
- The therapist sets only the limitations necessary to help the child accept responsibility in the relationship.

heads the largest graduate program in play therapy in the U. S., and was instrumental in forming the Association for Play Therapy, as discussed later.

The Emergence of Professional Organizations Advocating Play

The reader will review in the final chapter the work of organizations, agencies, and groups in reintroducing free, spontaneous outdoor play and developmentally relevant school curricula to children's lives. Throughout their existence, a number of professional organizations helped formulate and stuck firmly to a "wholistic" approach to child development, schooling, and child rearing, and challenged the forces that attempted to reduce play, arts, and humanities to an afterthought. The foci of this book would be incomplete without a brief history of a few of the major actors in these roles. The International Kindergarten Union (IKU), founded in 1892, was the parent organization of the Association for Childhood Education International (ACEI). Following its founding, the IKU existed to serve the kindergarten movement for many years (IKU, 1913; Hill, 1942; Wortham, 2002).

At the time of the establishment of the IKU, the kindergarten movement was already underway. Kindergartens were sponsored or operated by public schools, philanthropic or parochial organizations, and training schools were preparing teachers. However, philanthropic support was dwindling and public schools still resisted the concept of kindergarten. In 1924 a new magazine, *Childhood Education*, which still exists today, was launched as the official journal of the IKU, and a national headquarters was established in Washington, D.C.

In 1929 the IKU appointed a committee on reorganization to include various levels of education, and a year later, in 1930, the IKU adopted a new constitution and the name Association for Childhood Education (ACE), and joined with the National Council of Primary Education. ACE added "International" to its name in 1946 to indicate its concern for children throughout the world. Following World War II, it sent lay and curriculum materials, toys, and books to liberated and occupied countries. For more than a century the ACEI explained and promoted the developmental values and conduct of children's play in kindergartens and later in nursery schools and elementary schools. Its publications regularly carry research and practical articles on play and play environments, and its annual conferences feature special workshops and addresses about play. Its books about play include Frost and Sunderlin (1985), Frost et al. (2004), Burris and Boyd (2005), and Ferguson and Dettore (2007).

The National Association for the Education of Young Children (NAEYC) is the premier organization for early childhood professionals, having grown out of a loosely formed committee of nursery school advocates in 1926 into a powerful international organization of more than 100,000 members at the turn of the twenty-first century. The National Association emerged from the National

Committee on Nursery Schools (NCNS) in 1929, resulting in the formation of the National Association for Nursery Education (NANE). Prior to this time, many nursery school proponents, including Patty Smith Hill, worked within the Association for Childhood Education. The early leaders of the NANE were professionals supporting a "whole child" orientation to child development, and their organization helped break the stress on habit training and promoted all aspects of education and child development. From its inception to the present time, the NAEYC has made children's free play one of its keynotes, giving it special attention in its publications and conferences.

The name was changed to the National Association for the Education of Young Children (NAEYC) in 1966, and by this time the headquarters of the Association had moved from New York to Washington, D.C. Since then, the NAEYC has been a powerful voice in public policy at all levels, including the federal level. No other organization has been a stronger advocate for creative children's play. Through its massive conferences, extensive publications, mini-conferences, and direct involvement of staff and members, the NAEYC has achieved unequaled success in influencing and securing the rights of children to play—in preschools, kindergartens, and early childhood programs worldwide (Hewes, 1976; NAEYC Website, 2007).

The founding of the Society for Research in Child Development (SRCD) in 1933 was yet another signal event in the child study movement. Its history is closely tied to that of the child research institutes, dating back to the founding of the National Research Council (NRC) in 1916. In 1922 Bird Baldwin, director of the Iowa Child Research Station, was appointed chairman of the NRC to advise government agencies, and Lawrence Frank was named executor of the Laura Spelman Rockefeller Memorial Fund (LSRM) programs for child developmental research. Both these men were exceptionally strong advocates for children's research, Frank considering child development research "the most effective method for dealing with our social difficulties" (Smuts, 1985, p. 111). The NRC, affiliated with the National Academy of Sciences, established the Committee on Child Development (CCD) in 1924, with Baldwin as chairman, to respond to national defense needs and to coordinate academic, industrial, and governmental research (Dupree, 1957).

Following extensive and heated controversy between the chairman and members, the CCD was disbanded in 1933 and the Society for Research in Child Development was established. In June 1933 almost 100 researchers, including many anthropologists and sociologists, met to form the SRCD at the fourth CCD conference in Chicago. Consistent with the original purposes of the CCD in 1925, those of the SRCD continued "to stimulate and support research and to encourage cooperation among researchers in many fields." These purposes are extremely relevant to the study of play and play environments since play is among the most complex phenomena studied by researchers. The implications for its successful expression are often misunderstood, and its influence on health and learning widely underestimated. Over the years since its founding, SRCD scientists, representing the disciplines of psychology, sociology, anthropology, education, and medicine, have added substantially to the body of research on children's play and have kept the child development emphasis alive in many social and educational contexts in America and abroad.

The International Play Association (IPA) is the leading international organization committed to the major purpose of promoting the child's right to play. The IPA was founded in 1961 as the International Playground Association at a conference called for that purpose in Denmark. The first world president was C. Th. Sorensen of Denmark. Stina Wretlind-Larsson, Max Siegumfeldt, Jens Sigsgaard, and Lady Allen of Hurtwood laid the plans for the conference and were leaders in the ensuing organization (Wretlind-Larsson, 1979).

A second international conference was held in Zurich, Switzerland, in 1964 and membership included both play leaders and "professionals." During the following three years, the membership grew by fifty, with a few from non-European countries (Abernethy and Otter, 1979). Mrs. Thomas Hess of Greenwich, Connecticut, was the first American member, and Pacific Oaks College and Children's School in Pasadena, California, was the first American organization member. The Pacific Oaks outdoor program is one of the better models of play leadership and of developmentally appropriate materials and practice in America.

By the early 1970s IPA membership had grown to the point that national correspondents/representatives were selected in countries with a large membership. Paul Hogan, a deeply committed proponent of volunteer- or community-built playgrounds, was the first American representative. He was followed by Donna Seline, and in 1985 Joe Frost was elected to that position. A few months later the membership approved bylaws for formal organization as the American Association for the Child's Right to Play and a board of directors was established through election: Joe Frost became president and U.S. representative; Sue Wortham, treasurer; Marcia Guddemi, newsletter editor; Jay Beckwith, Harris Forusz, Roger Hart, Robin Moore, and Barbara Sampson, board members.

During the late 1970s the name of the international organization was changed to the International Association for the Child's Right to Play to reflect interest in a much broader field of concern than merely playgrounds (Bengtsson, 1979). The name is now the International Play Association, Promoting the Child's Right to Play (IPA/USA). By 1987 the IPA included members from fifty countries, and twenty-five Americans attended the World Congress in Stockholm. Robin Moore was the first American to be elected president of the international organization.

During the early 1970s the original vision leading to the organization of the Anthropological Association for the Study of Play (TAASP), later to become the Association for the Study of Play (TASP), pulled together scholars from different disciplines to promote research into and a better understanding of the nature and function of play. Such prominent scholars as Brian Sutton-Smith and John Roberts had already been exploring possibilities for forming an organization. This influenced Alyce Cheska, Howard Nixon, and Edward Norbeck to organize mini-conferences in Minneapolis (1972), Burlington, Vermont (1973), and New Orleans (1973). The success of these meetings resulted in a May 1974 meeting of more than thirty scholars in London, Ontario, chaired by Cheska, to discuss the formation of a professional organization on play. These scholars built a framework for the emerging organization, elected a steering committee of twelve (Salter, 1976), and elected officers that same year. Allan Tindall was elected President-Elect at these inaugural meetings in London, Ontario, and drafted the TAASP Constitution (Stevens, 1977). He became President in 1975, represented the organization skillfully and faithfully, presided over the Annual Meeting in Atlanta, and died shortly thereafter (Stevens, 1977).

The First Annual Meeting of the Anthropological Association for the Study of Play (TAASP) was held in Detroit. At this meeting, anthropologists, educators, psychologists, and sociologists came together to discuss play topics of mutual interest, and a multidisciplinary organization was set to flourish. The published proceedings of this meeting (Lancy and Tindall, 1976) established an enviable level of scholarship and range of published play topics. The first proceedings included 27 scholarly papers covering a great variety of topics—theoretical approaches to studying play; ethnographic studies of children's games; linguistic and ethnographic analysis of play forms; expressive aspects of play; observational studies of play in primates and young children; socio-psychological aspects of play and humor (Stevens, 1977). In 1988 the *Conference Proceedings* were replaced by the annual book *Play and Culture*. Members and publication topics represent anthropology, education, history, sociology, recreation and leisure studies, folklore, dance communication, the arts, kinesiology, philosophy, cultural studies, and musicology. In 2007 the Strong National Museum of Play became the permanent headquarters of TASP.

The Association for Play Therapy (APT) was envisioned by Charles Schaefer and formed in New York in 1982 by Schaefer and Kevin O'Connor. Garry Landreth joined them on the initial board; the aim was "to provide a forum for professionals interested in developing a distinct group of interventions that use play as an integral component of the therapeutic process for children in need" (APT website, 2007). In 1984 the first annual conference was held by O'Connor in New York City, followed in 1987 by an annual conference held by Landreth in Texas. This was the first APT conference held outside of New York. The conferences that followed were rotated between eastern, central, and western regions of the U.S. The *International Journal of Play Therapy* was established in 1992 to promote and disseminate research in play therapy. In this same year the first chartered branches, Texas and Oregon, were established, and, in 1993, Registered Play Therapist and Supervisor programs were initiated.

The professional organizations discussed here represent only a few of those committed to play research and child development. The more expansive list includes the American Psychological Association, the American Academy of Pediatrics, the American Anthropological Association, the American Sociological Association, the American Alliance of Health, Physical Education, Recreation, and Dance, the National Recreation and Park Association, and the Child Welfare League of America.

Decades of Promise and Gathering Storms

The subject of child study—the new psychology and the discipline of child development focusing on the "whole child"—emerged rapidly during the early twentieth century, and play came increasingly to be regarded as a central process in social, cognitive, physical, and emotional development. Froebel made major contributions leading to the twentieth century development of American kindergartens, play schools, and nursery schools. Behavioral scientists such as Hall, Spencer, Gesell, Thorndike, James, and Dewey made significant contributions that were realized in America's early twentieth century child study research institutes and research on play.

This work led to the establishment of university programs for nursery school, kindergarten, and primary school teachers and administrators. Programs for nursery school and kindergarten were typically found in departments of child development. The training in these departments emphasized the whole child and the full range of children's developmental attributes, including play. Programs for primary through elementary school were typically housed in education departments focusing on academic subjects with minimal attention to child development and play.

Child study and research on play gradually mushroomed in scope and became respectable disciplines of inquiry. Schools and caretaking institutions followed precedents in promoting play and play environments, and many child development centers continued to subscribe to the whole child philosophy. During the late twentieth century, the hounding of public schools in accord with the whims and illogical principles of politicians attempting to shape education into industrial-type models, the standardization of curricula, changing patterns of child rearing, the abuse of technology, and other factors, led to the diminution of traditional play and a growth in the negative consequences of play deprivation. As will be seen in the final two chapters, this growing storm of factors radically altered children's play and children's access to traditional play environments—undermining decades of hard-learned lessons about the care and education of children. The dawning of the twenty-first century would see a growing backlash against such patterns. A nationwide movement to preserve traditional play and play environments would emerge, and the play and child development research of the twentieth century would again gain respect.

6
Play during Hard Times
The Great Depression

Well, we still played ball. We'd go to the show for ten cents. The girls played house. We sewed. We made quilt blocks or dolls. Some kids had roller skates, I didn't have any ... oh a lot of times grandma would make biscuits and give us the last nickel she had to go buy candy. I can remember that, during the Depression. You'd get one pair of shoes and as soon as it got summer, you went barefoot, except when you went somewhere. We were happy and we didn't know what we were missing. (Oral history by Betty Robling, a Depression era child, in Thompson and MacAustin, 2001, unnumbered.)

The child-saving movement beginning around the turn of the twentieth century was a broad-based, integrated movement encompassing many leaders and actions intended to improve conditions in the slums of America's great cities—conditions appropriately called "the shame of the cities." The agony of the cities eventually brought together a small army of charitable workers who formed the unprecedented child-saving movement described in Chapter 3. This movement spilled over into organized efforts to create opportunities for children's play and spaces for their urban play environments nationwide, as discussed in Chapter 4. Then, in Chapter 5, the burgeoning professional and scientific communities took up the challenge and broadened the movement to improve conditions even further, changing the very nature of education from strict authoritarian rule and rigid subject matter to educating through a developmental approach focusing on the whole child. But just as the future was looking brighter, a new crisis, the Great Depression, brought slum-like conditions down upon the entire nation. We pick up the story there.

The Great Depression hit in 1929 with the crash of the stock market, resulting in the economic ruination of most American families. No previous calamity, war, or conditions of poverty impacted on so many and produced such pain and misery among America's old and young, rich and poor, rural and urban. By 1930 America was economically busted and millions of Americans lost their farms, homes, furniture, livestock, life savings, businesses, jobs, and whatever rosy outlook they held for the future. The decade before the Depression was

138

much like the latter decades of the twentieth century and the early years of the twenty-first century—people buying cars, banking on the stock market, maxing out their credit, and chasing pleasure. Factories were increasing in number, people were working, and school dropouts were declining. Although 21.5 million of the 27.5 million families in America earned less than $3,000 a year, they were buying clothes, cars, houses, furniture, radios, and many other goods on credit (Wormser, 1994). The more they bought, the more the factories produced, and the higher the stock market rose, but disaster waited on the sidelines. Now, in October 2008, America and countries around the world are once again seeing their economic futures slipping away in a beehive of greed, graft, deceit, and mismanagement. We have lessons to learn, for, once again, children will be the victims of such gross errors, lending even greater urgency to the resolution of the current diminution of play and play environments and the consequences for children's health, fitness, and well-being—for their futures.

Bursting the Economic Bubble and the Dreams of Americans

On October 24, 1929, the bubble burst and stocks fell through the floor, leading to total panic among those with stocks, mortgages, loans, and money in banks. Some committed suicide due to their desperation and others because of their illegal dealings. Companies went broke, banks folded, and workers lost their jobs. By 1933 more than 15,000,000 Americans were unemployed, including more than 80 percent of workers in some cities. The sale price of farmers' produce followed the free fall, making it more expensive to grow crops than to sell them. People were evicted from their homes and sought shelter in tents, shanties, railroad cars, under bridges, and with relatives. Lack of money to pay teachers resulted in many schools closing and others reducing the number of days and months of operation. Bread lines sprang up in cities; farmers banded together to help one another as they saw their friends' farms, livestock, furniture, and machinery auctioned to the highest bidder; World War I veterans were denied promised bonuses, and farmers and workers were denied economic assistance. President Hoover maintained a hands-off policy, believing that "depressions were natural and normal under capitalism, and that things would soon get better" (Wormser, 1994, p. 9). However, he provided capital to some big businesses, which infuriated many people. As a result, "Hooverville" became the contemptuous moniker of the makeshift living quarters thrown together by the homeless.

Millions of poverty stricken families were devastated by the ravages of the Depression. Children, youth, and minorities were most vulnerable. Having limited education, maturity, and job experience, youth could not compete favorably in the limited job market, and their unemployment rates soared, reaching 40 to 70 percent in many cities and states. In 1935 nearly 80 percent of the sixteen-year-olds out of school could not locate jobs (Cohen, 2002, p. 6).

Children too young to work for pay and totally dependent on their parents had no place to turn for relief and were frequently hungry, subject to disease, and unable to afford medical care. Consequently, malnutrition and disease were rampant in the most depressed areas such as city slums and impoverished coal mining regions. Even the very young, not able to work for pay, were put to work by their parents in whatever manner they could contribute—picking cotton, caring for babies, helping with household chores, feeding livestock, gardening, picking up rags and reusable castoffs—whatever they could do. In response to the question, "When did your parents put you to work?" some Depression era survivors, now elderly adults, answer, "As soon as we could walk." The Depression spelled "ravaged childhood" for countless children across America. There is very little mention of children's play and playgrounds in some of the best-known books about life during the Depression. Rather they speak of the devastating consequences and the prevailing hope among even the most seriously affected that they could find a way and the future would be better—tragic yet inspiring in its insistence on dignity and honor.

Figure 6.1 Girl picking strawberries on the Kendle H. Sigmon farm, Springdale, Arkansas.
Source: Howard Clark, photographer. **Courtesy Shiloh Museum of Ozark History, Caroline Price Clark Collection (S-2002-72-1132).**

In his classic *The Grapes of Wrath* (1939), John Steinbeck weaves a story around the horror of the transformation of millions of lives into poverty conditions, yet he describes a real-life American drama perhaps unsurpassed in its eloquently presented mix of reality and majesty. Studs Terkel's *Hard Times: An Oral History of the Great Depression* (1970) captures all the real-life excitement and bitterness of Depression era life, leaving the reader with a sense of nostalgia and admiration for the toughness, resourcefulness, and prevailing hope that served Depression era children into old age. The dozens of Depression era survivors from all walks of life that Terkel masterfully interviewed as adults spoke little about play and pleasure but rather of hardship and hope. In his *Uprooted Children: The Early Life of Migrant Farm Workers*, Robert Coles (1970), the prominent Harvard psychiatrist, describes how migrant farm workers, a quarter century after the Depression ended, still lived and worked under Depression-like conditions of poverty, hardship, and stress. These lowest paid American workers continue today to suffer the consequences and rootless-ness of poverty—conditions described by Coles as "a human condition, a fate really ... that is remarkable and terrible and damaging ... almost without description" (Coles, 1970, p. 123). Coles talked to children about their paintings and games, revealing their nostalgia and hopes for better times, and he spoke extensively—and eloquently—about hope and help.

In his book *An Hour before Daylight: Memories of a Rural Boyhood*, President Jimmy Carter recreated his Depression-era boyhood on a Georgia peanut farm. He wrote in great detail about his family, his African-American and white boyhood friends, and about work and play—the closely knit, twin adventures of virtually all children of that era. "Although I had a lot of work to do around our house and yard, at the barn and in the fields, my playmates and I found time to do other things" (Carter, 2001, p. 90). They picked fruit and nuts in the woods, milked the cows, tended the fields, churned butter, fed the livestock, and engaged in the seemingly unending work of the farm. They devised many of their own playthings. Among the toys of choice were hoops from wooden kegs propelled by a hand-held stiff wire, rubber band slingshots, darts made from nails embedded in one end of corn cobs with feathers embedded in the other end for guidance, spears, and rubber guns with spring clothespins. Some of the boys had riding ponies, and everyone Carter knew could swim, although this favorite activity was sometimes interrupted by the presence of water moccasins (poisonous snakes). Making and flying kites, tree climbing, riding goats, hunting possums and raccoons, playing in tree houses, capturing lightning bugs in jars, playing baseball, looking for Native American artifacts, hunting and fishing, learning to use firearms, and going to the movies were all common activities. All these forms of play were remarkably similar to those of other children living among the farms and hills during the 1920s, 1930s, and 1940s.

These and many other writers focused on and drew attention to the magnitude and debilitating consequences of the poverty and hopelessness during the Depression, but most paid scant attention to the striving of children to play. Children's play seemed to many adults a trivial matter under such debilitating circumstances. Commonly seen throughout history as frivolous, unimportant, and associated with pleasure, children's play seems even more inconsequential when grueling conditions of extraordinary poverty, abuse, neglect, and blind disregard by governments hold sway.

Even the children of the Depression fixed their attention on work and basic survival needs over play, not implying that they did not play, for indeed they did—as children have always played during times of distress. Childhood ended early and with it opportunities for leisure and play were often overpowered by survival motives. What did the Depression mean?

> It meant a life of picking cotton or working in a factory ten hours a day instead of going to school or playing. For others, it meant pretending nothing was wrong so the neighbors wouldn't know their father was broke or on the verge of suicide. It meant not being able to call a doctor when you were sick, not having the heat of a fire when you were cold, not having food when you were hungry. One child remembered: We didn't have anything to eat for a whole week but potatoes ... My brother went around to the grocery store and got them to give him meat for his dog— only he didn't have any dog. We ate that dog meat with the potatoes. (Wormser, 1994, p. 11)

Children themselves thought mostly of work and survival. Their stories were told in thousands of letters to Franklin and Eleanor Roosevelt asking for financial and material aid. Eleanor received more than 300,000 items of mail in response to her radio invitations to hear from ordinary Americans. Most of the letters were from the working class seeking aid, and hundreds were from children and youth, mostly girls. These were letters about need and pleas for help, but they were also letters about dignity, embarrassment, and hope.

Mena, Arkansas, June 3, 1939

Dear Mrs. Roosevelt:

I certainly am ashamed to sink so low as to have to write this. Please don't say anything about this to anyone, please. Mrs. Roosevelt, I have written to you for help if you will help me. My father has a job in the little plainer [sawmill] here and the largest check he has ever drawn was fifteen dollars (one week). There is four in our family ... We use three or four dollars for groceries and Dad spends the rest at the pool hall. I have been trying to get work for about three months and I can't find a thing. Maybe it is because I look so shabby ... Mrs Roosevelt, why I have written is, I plead that if you will, would you send me ten dollars for a few cloths, please would you. If you would I will tell God how good you were ... Please never say a word about this to anyone, please. If my parents find out about this they would kill me ... I am still trying for a job and if you help me and I ever get work I will try to pay it back.

Respectfully yours, (Cohen, 2002, pp. 57–8).

The Depression era child writing to Mrs. Roosevelt was from Mena, Arkansas, nestled in the beautiful Ouachita Mountains, a thinly populated area of wooded hills, swift creeks and rivers, and small farms in the river bottoms. She, like hundreds of others writing to Mrs. Roosevelt, spoke of despair and need and hope. These children played, but virtually no play was mentioned in their letters. Pride had something to do with this. One is less likely to focus on play when survival is at stake or one is begging for help. The reader who wishes to capture the feel and the spirit of the daily lives of children during the Depression should see the book-length collections of photos by Thompson and MacAustin (2001) and Alsberg (1934).

Pleasant and Not-So-Pleasant Memories

Here I add reporter to my historian role and supplement the written accounts of others about their childhood experiences during the Depression with my own vivid memories of growing up during the 1930s and 1940s on a small farm in the Fourche River Valley in the Ouachita Mountains of Arkansas near Mena (as in the letter to Mrs. Roosevelt above). My Depression era experiences were extended to other geographical areas and other types of life when my family traveled one summer by rattle-trap bus in the migrant farm worker stream to live in a tent and work in the vineyards and orchards of "Californey" along with Arkies, Okies, and Hispanics. For two further summers, I lived, worked, and played with relatives and their neighbors in a large Texas city and in rural Texas cotton country. In gathering material for this chapter, my wife, Betty, and I interviewed people in their late seventies, eighties, and early nineties about work, play, and "getting by" in the years leading to and during the Depression. Betty grew up during the Depression with her tenant farmer family on small cotton and cattle farms in Arkansas and "Grapes of Wrath" country near Sallisaw, Oklahoma. They "kept the road hot" in trips with parents, uncles, grandparents, and cousins over the long unpaved stretches to Arizona and "Californey" in primitive broken-down cars to work in the fruit harvests. The people interviewed grew up in various geographical areas of the country in large cities, small towns, and rural areas.

Figure 6.2 Depression era children playing with scrap materials.
Source: Courtesy of the Franklin D. Roosevelt Presidential Library.

Just as we have seen in previous chapters, no matter what the circumstances—war, deprivation, natural disaster, work, discrimination, or abuse—children struggled to play during the Depression and were adept at creating and copying games to match whatever playgrounds they found, constructed, or were made available to them—city, country, streets, fields, barns, barnyards, vacant lots, creeks, hills, manufactured devices; whatever the playground, biology took over. They "made do" and they played. Much play was virtually indistinguishable from work, for children were ingenious in finding time and toys for their play and tended to find or create bits of pleasure, imagination, and magic, even in the midst of hard work. When plowing an open field near a stream, we would stop to search for arrow-heads or go to the stream and clean out a special spring for cold drinking water, check fishing poles "set out" on the bank for fish, or play with captured insects and animals. We set traps for fur-bearing animals and would "run the traps" to kill and remove the possums and raccoons, skin them, stretch them on homemade stretching boards, and sell them at the store for a few cents. All this activity seemed to flit between play and work, joy and burden, necessity and recreation.

Shooting or trapping wild animals for food was a kind of necessary game, and butchering hogs with adults at "hog-killing" time was more festival than work because neighbors would come to help, engage in humorous storytelling, chase the flies out of the kitchen with "dish rags," eat a noon meal called "dinner," consisting of fresh "tenderloin" (pork chops), and everyone would take meat home in return for their help. The children carried water, started fires under "wash pots" to boil water for scraping off hog hair and making lye soap, and the youth would learn how to shoot the hogs in the brain with one rifle shot, slit the throat to bleed the animal, hang it from a tree limb, and pour on boiling water to loosen the hair. Then they would scrape it all off and cut up the hog for salting, sugar curing, and smoking in the ever-present smoke house. These were times when older children could demonstrate their experience and wisdom to younger children, for they had been carefully instructed in the art of butchering hogs. None of this seemed cruel, brutal, or unusual to children who had experienced such activities all their lives. There appeared to be little or no carry-over of such lack of sentiment about animals to humans, for most children gave loving care to several pets—calves, chickens, dogs, cats, and horses that doubled for farm work. Modern children, youth, and many adults, never having experienced such events or faced hunger in their absence, would likely never understand how such "orgies" could be a form of "festival" and a place for play and storytelling.

Many people on small farms in the Southern hills, mountains, river bottoms, and along the bayous, hardly noticed the changes when the Depression hit. They were "dirt poor" before the Depression and remained that way. Many farms had been passed down through families and no debt was owed. The rural people who owned no land and those who lost their land to the banks bore the heaviest burden and lived a "hand-to-mouth" existence or turned to the migrant stream for relief. Families were large and children, in many cases both boys and girls, worked in the fields alongside adults, contributing to their livelihood. My father's income from the farm and part-time jobs amounted to about $400 a year. We would buy salt, sugar, flour, and kerosene (for the lamp) from the country store on credit and pay when the "crop came in." The rest of our food came from the garden, canned and placed in the cellar, the milk cow and hogs, and hunting and fishing. Some elderly mountain women, telling stories of their pre-Depression era childhoods, said they never played much except when they were able to make the three mile walk along muddy roads to school and enjoy recess, or paddle a boat across a river to catch a pickup (mail truck) or rattle-trap bus to school. Many schools closed during the Depression due to lack of money to pay teachers, but such rural children were accustomed to missing school to work or simply because of the difficulty in getting there. Some of the roads were so muddy that when children walked in the ruts where wagons had traveled, their lunch bucket (if they had one) dragged on the ground. Teachers were accustomed to frequent absences and sometimes kept children in a grade an extra year before "promoting" them to the next grade.

Nearly all healthy children worked, and even illness did not always keep them from their daily tasks—feeding chickens, gathering eggs, slopping pigs, milking the cow, and chopping and carrying wood. Girls were more frequently involved in tasks related to household chores such as preparing food, washing clothes in "wash pots" and "wash tubs," sweeping with "homemade" brooms, and caring for babies and toddlers. Many girls and boys worked in the fields all day and did household chores in the evening. Food came from gardens and livestock and, minus modern conveniences of electricity, cars, tractors, and other expensive items, very little money was earned and almost all was spent on necessities—plows, horses or mules, a milk cow, pigs, chickens, and assorted other farm animals. Dresses and shirts were made from feed sacks. The boys and men wore "store bought" bib overalls and "brogans" (ankle high work shoes) during the winter and boys went barefoot in the summer. Girls and women made most of their dresses and underwear. Some women wore home-made "bonnets" to protect against the sun, and some girls wore long, brown socks during the winter to hide their "long handles" (long, warm underwear) that could be seen through the holes in their socks.

Many of the adults knew almost nothing about the stock market except that it had crashed and taken rich people's money with it, did not use banks, and had limited means to read or hear national or world news. The Depression, to many, was just another familiar period in a long struggle for survival. Surprisingly to moderns, these same people spoke lovingly of strong family ties, the ability to "make do" with what they had, support of neighbors, pride in work, special church and family activities, close ties with special friends, and feelings of pride and competence in "doing what had to be done." When radios began to make their appearance in isolated country houses, neighbors would gather at night to hear news of the Depression and later of World War II. President Franklin Roosevelt became very popular when he initiated the New Deal and even more so when America entered World War II, generating many jobs in factories and the military.

Country dwellers would converge en masse at county seats on Saturdays to see double-feature "cowboy movies" and newsreels and stroll up and down crowded sidewalks transformed into social affairs for whole families. At first they arrived by wagon, left their teams of mules or horses at the "wagon yard," sometimes slept on hay overnight in or under the wagons and, as roads were improved, drove their jalopy cars and trucks to town. Early movies at theatres in county seats attracted people in ways never before seen. They were immensely popular for all ages and a quarter (25 cents) would purchase admission, a coke, and popcorn. Another quarter would buy a plate lunch or 15 cents a hamburger at the Rock Café or McGaugh's Café. Traveling carnivals would make their way to such towns and the Saturday county seat festivals would extend into the night. The theatre in Scott County, Arkansas, where the author viewed his first movies during the Depression, was renovated and reopened to large crowds in 2007.

During the Depression of the 1930s and the World War II years of the 1940s, the school play and work of country and small town children continued much as they had during the Colonial period. Country schools had mid-morning and mid-afternoon recess, an hour at noon for bacon and biscuits, and play for some, but for the poorest there was only play. For example, the percentage of underweight children in mining areas of the country ranged from 20 percent in some schools to 90 percent in others (Thompson and MacAustin, 2001, p. xii). Waiting for the primitive bus to make its morning and evening runs over muddy roads extended play to five periods. During this time, some kids roamed the hillside behind the school to find hickory nuts to crack with rocks and eat. There were improvised games of war, chase, building dens and forts, shinny, building dams in the stream, dog pile, hot pants, catapult, baseball with home-made balls, and improvised and traditional games, many passed on for centuries. Rules were subject to argument, negotiation, and threats of physical persuasion.

Teachers usually stayed indoors except to watch or stop a fight. When we played war on the side of the mountain behind the school, one kid would be stationed at the back of the school to run up the mountain and alert players when the teacher rang the bell. There was no playground equipment until the Works Progress Administration (WPA) installed four devices during the mid-1930s—a tall slide, two swings, and a merry-go-round. The playgrounds were a barren field in front of the school, a stream running behind, and a tree-covered mountain emerging beyond the stream. The reader should remember that in this book "playground" is not simply the name of a space equipped with manufactured playground equipment but refers primarily to all those outdoor places where children gather to play. Country children had access to more than one "playground"—the hillside and creek, the open field, and the WPA equipment.

Girls tended to play house, jacks, jump-rope and other relatively safe, social games in the clearing in front of the school, but occasionally entered into the games played by boys, except those involving physical contact or obvious hazards such as wrestling, vaulting from a distant launching point over a person bent over holding his ankles, shinny, war, and tackle football. Teachers prohibited them from going up the east half of the mountain where the boys played, but they sometimes engaged in girls-only games on the west side of the mountain. I do not recall ever seeing anyone violate this rule. There was very little animosity between girls and boys, and both groups seemed to enjoy the games that everyone played—Annie over, red rover, deer and dog, kick the can, and, occasionally, baseball played with a homemade ball and a piece of lumber. Girls did not play tops, in part because "gambling" for marbles was sometimes involved, and many parents' strong religious feelings did not allow this in any form. Boys only rarely jumped rope or played jacks with the girls because the girls were far more skillful, and engaging in "girls' games," already considered "sissy" by most boys, would expose them to losing to a girl and being teased.

Wrestling matches were common and sometimes evolved into fist fights. Children would gather round to watch, but unfair fighting—older boys picking on younger, the use of weapons of any kind, or two picking on one—was not tolerated by the older onlookers. When teachers in their classrooms saw a crowd gathering through their classroom windows, they would usually stop the fights. The principal would sometimes paddle those who "started" the fight. The most extreme bullying involved children walking home from school who would be "waylaid" by older boys, who threatened, stole valuables (knife, lunch bucket, marbles), and occasionally insulted and threatened the younger boys, or made rude, suggestive remarks to girls. All the boys who could find a way to secure a pocketknife or jackknife carried one at work and school and used it for opening sacks, whittling sticks, making toys, sharpening pencils, fixing harnesses, or playing mumble peg. Using or threatening to use a knife in a fight would exact consequences from other children, perhaps a "licking" by an older boy, a whipping by the principal, and yet another whipping by the boy's father. Most boys aged eight to ten had access to a .22 rifle and/or shotgun, were instructed in its use, and developed some degree of skill in killing animals and fish for food. Parents and neighbors did not tolerate dangerous use of guns. All adults in the community were expected to correct and guide misbehaving children.

Many "boys' games" were games of skill and strength, sometimes hazardous and occasionally violent. War games included children from first through eighth grade, chosen by leaders who appointed themselves. Generals and captains created the rules and made final decisions to resolve arguments. The younger children quickly learned to opt out of certain games. One of the most realistic games took place when dead limbs fell from pine trees, covering the ground. The two chosen armies would gather on opposite sides of a small clearing among the trees, face the opposition, and hit limbs against tree trunks. The ends of the limbs would break off and fly toward the "enemy," filling the air with flying sticks, much like the flight of arrows in movies depicting the storming of a castle. Despite the protection of the trees, an occasional child would be hit with a stick and everyone would stop the game, gather round, wipe off the trickle of blood with a dirty handkerchief or shirt sleeve, make sure their wounded playmate was OK, and then resume playing.

In the game of dog pile, a group of boys would walk around the playground looking for a candidate; someone would yell "dog pile" and all the boys would jump on him. The victim would join the dog pile team to look for the next victim. If you were a "snitch," or did not play or fight "fair," you would be subject to repeated dog piles until you changed your behavior. Some kids seemed to enjoy this attention. I recall that one boy offered his lunch bucket, previously used for lard, to the dog pile leader if the team would dog-pile him. This was the largest boy in the sixth grade. He had been retained twice, mainly because he missed so many days of school. He was assigned to the back seat of his row in the schoolroom so he would not block the view of shorter kids. He was only dog-piled at his request.

Following rains, boys and girls would build dams in the stream behind the school and let the torrent loose to wash out another group's dam downstream. This was some of the most intense play in my memory, perhaps what today's writers have in mind when they speak of deep play, flow, fully functioning, and transcendental play. Apparently, the more creative the play was, the greater the interest and the more fascinating and useful the results. When the bell rang, everyone would troop into the school, some barefoot, with pants or dresses dripping wet, proud of their dam achievements, and rarely admonished for tracking mud on the floors. Creeks and mud holes were common play places and served to wash barnyard slush off feet from early morning chores done before going to school.

"Hot pants" was one of the few games banned by teachers as soon as they learned of its existence. In hot pants, all the boys chose up sides and the players on each side stood in separate lines. A piece of paper was inserted into a back pocket of each player and set on fire. The player would run as far as he could before stamping out the fire and his progress was marked as the starting point for the next player. The greater the distance covered by the entire team determined the winners. A teacher stopped this game after its initial production. The "tattle-tale" was dog-piled a few times.

The country doctor treated occasional cuts and bruises. The only recess injury during my elementary school years that required hospital care occurred during a catapult game on the mountain. Older boys would climb a pine sapling, pull the top to the ground, and coax a younger boy to hold on while they released it, instructing him to let go when he was about head high. One boy did not understand the instructions and was shot into the air, resulting in concussion. The principal whipped the older boys and the victim recovered. The whipping and the little kids' refusal to play again permanently stopped the catapult games.

Games tended to emerge and stay popular for extended periods or seasons. Shinny was among these. All the players would go to the woods and find sturdy limbs to use as shinny sticks. A large tin can would be located, teams chosen, and a "hockey type" face-off would begin with flying sticks and serious efforts to defeat the other side. Skinned shins were common but there were no serious injuries. Games prohibited today in many schools—dodge ball, chase, rough and tumble, tackle football, and other games involving body contact and possible injury to the psyche—were common. Both boys and girls considered such games sufficiently tame for girls to participate. The "better teachers" would occasionally hold special play times, take their classes to the open field, join in "choosing up" sides, and play baseball with the children. The ball was made from many yards of string from feed and flour sacks wound tightly around one of the small, hard rubber balls used for playing jacks, and the bat was a tree limb with the bark removed. No one, not even the catcher, had a ball glove.

On the small farms, war game contestants employed long slender sticks with sharpened ends and mounted green persimmons that could be thrown for long distances into ditches where combatants took shelter. After such games, opponents would gather round and look for other exciting options—perhaps a fight with corncobs or a real rodeo in the barnyard, riding half grown steers. The rodeos frequently attracted adults, who would urge on the riders and laugh when they fell in the barnyard muck.

After crops were laid by in Arkansas, I was twice sent to visit relatives in a Texas city where we played in the vacant lots and in the streets, worked in an uncle's junk yard, and learned how to banter with the police to keep them away from the older boys' crap games in the alleys. Two of my several uncles were teenagers who tutored the younger boys in such matters. They rigged wrestling matches for us with older boys, hoping to win ten to fifteen cents per match until the price for a movie and popcorn for our group was earned. These were playful times, tempered with hard work and tough play, but clearly instructive and, in the main, joyous, exciting, and filled with comradeship.

Recesses at school were the main times for children to play but, despite the grinding hard work of most mountain children before and during the Depression, they also played at home. The word "recess," as applied to play and playgrounds, is traditionally reserved for the open play spaces at school equipped with manufactured or built play equipment. In reality, and as used here, recess refers to breaks or respites from work, as in schoolrooms, factories, and other settings where activity is prescribed, monitored, structured, and frequently unpleasant.

Sunday morning was reserved for Sunday school classes and long sermons, and evenings for yet more long sermons, frequently given by a traveling preacher selected (or, more accurately, allowed) to preach, if he acknowledged that Jesus Christ was our Savior and the Bible was true and infallible. This left all Sunday afternoon for swimming in the river, riding horses bareback into the hills (few children had saddles), making dens in the hay in hay barns, making rubber guns (guns made from pieces of boards, a clothes pin and pieces of tire inner tubes), stick horses, and other toys, playing with neighbors and relatives, and sometimes joining people from several communities in "singing and dinner on the ground" events at a camp ground, church, or river bank. Walking home along the dirt road at night after church was a compelling experience, for the heavens were bright with stars, the animals in the wetlands and nearby hills were singing their songs, and the lightning bugs (fireflies) were lighting up the roadsides with millions of their tiny lights. These were times to capture some in fruit jars to place by the bed at night and marvel at their flash and glow. Our play was traditional, even eternal in some respects, but re-created as though it had never existed before we invented it. Rules had to be made and changed to suit our fancy or accommodate the play props we discovered or created—an old cultivator could easily become a car or airplane, an old oak tree with huge limbs the site for a Tarzan-like tree house, safe from our enemies and subject to our play choices.

Country children learned early to live by certain unwritten rules. People working in the fields could take one watermelon or cantaloupe from a neighbor's field with impunity, but only if they did not damage the vines or other melons. Such charity applied to most readily available sources of food, especially if the owner knew the disposition of the boys and they "borrowed" only what they would immediately eat. Under such conditions, this was not considered stealing but merely "looking out for one another in hard times." Actually, the Depression did not change much for small farm families who owned land "free and clear," probably passed down from parents and grandparents. There was no electricity or running water; many even had no outdoor toilets before the WPA built them throughout a community. But they had a milk cow, shared milk when a neighbor's cow "went dry," butchered hogs in the fall for winter meat, canned garden vegetables, and bought only basic supplies such as sugar, flour, salt, and kerosene (for lamps) at the community store. Those who went hungry in farm country were often those with fathers who abused alcohol (labeled "drunks") and wasted what little money they made at the sawmill or in the fields on moonshine, failing to invest in a few cows, plant a garden, or plan ahead for the long, cold winters.

My father farmed 20 acres with a team of mules, spending a full week just "turning" (plowing) the ground in preparation for planting corn, cotton, or peanuts. When I was seven or eight years old, he bought a second team of horses and a small turning plow for me. One of my most memorable days of childhood was when I first followed him around the field, turning a foot or two of ground each time I circled the field. Today this would be called "child abuse." Then, such was the same pattern that my father had learned from his father and expected of any member of the family. Everyone "old enough to walk" helped support the family, but hard labor was not without its rewards. I could ride a real horse like the movie cowboys, join my friends in rides into the hills and into the sawmill town of Forester, Arkansas, and play and swim "jay-bird" (naked) with the boys from the "black" community nestled in the woods near clear, swift-flowing, Big Cedar Creek. Forester was "the town that moved away," apparently resulting from sawmill owners' objections to their workers' efforts to unionize. The site of Forester is now a pine forest where former residents still hold an annual reunion. We rounded up cattle, explored the hills, fished in the river and creeks, carried our .22 rifles on hunting trips "like Indians," held horse races, searched woods for muscadines and huckleberries, shot game and fished for food, and learned to give our horses special care. These were opportunities to develop pride in work and gain the respect of family and neighbors. In summers we would stop by a cool, clean running creek or river to "cool off" and swim after work was done. These alternate rhythms of work and play were in many ways indistinguishable.

The families that lived under the most primitive conditions—old shacks nestled up into the hills among the rocks on land that resisted giving up vegetable crops—survived by hunting and fishing, doing odd jobs, and raising a few cows or pigs in the woods. When I went to one of these houses to play with their children, we were sent to a bank of clay (dirt) by their mother for lunch because there was nothing in the house to eat. Here I watched in amazement as the children ate dirt and instructed me on the technique—"don't chew it, but squish it around in your mouth with spit until it goes down." I was invited several months later to join this same family for supper (evening meal). They were having "possum and dumplins," but by the time we arrived, the possum, which we had never tasted, had been eaten, so we ate dumplings. We ate at an old handmade table, sitting on handmade chairs in a kitchen with a handmade cabinet and a wood stove with oven. As he completed eating, the father raised his plate, licked it clean, and instructed us to do the same to save having to "draw water" from the well to wash the dishes. In those days you did not disobey your elders. We complied, and he stacked the plates in the cabinet, ready for the next meal. At yet another home "way back up the holler," we five boys were "rocked out" (with thrown rocks) of the yard by our friend's mother when she learned we had eaten the pot of beans she had cooked for her husband's supper when he came home from the sawmill. Having experienced such brief frenzies of anger before, we simply jumped the fence and took our play to the barn. The mother later went to a tree and brought apples to the barn for each of us.

The play, playgrounds, and recess periods of children living in small towns differed little from those of children living in the surrounding country and, as in the case of families on small farms or patches of land, adults with unencumbered businesses in small towns managed to support their families without resorting to food lines and falling into homelessness as seen in large cities across America. Small business places lined the main streets of small towns, and they were crowded with people from the countryside on Saturdays. Here they spent what little spare change they had for amusement and necessities, and this money fed the families of merchants. Most small farmers and country residents bought food staples from small country stores "on credit," and most paid in full when the "crops came in."

Stories from Children of the Depression

Interviews with men and women who grew up during the Depression provide rich personal experiences about their childhoods. John Shaw, a retired IBM executive, grew up in Depression era, small town Durant, Oklahoma, and saw his father bumped from his railroad job and forced to live apart from his family in a distant area of the state in order to secure a job. His mother kept her job with the telephone company. After two years, his father returned to Durant and established a fruit stand with his brother and worked a second job as night jailer for extra money. John sold newspapers, helped at the fruit stand, and attended a public elementary school enrolling Durant children. Many of the children had bicycles and, like children everywhere in America, created their own games and played traditional games at school. His elementary school playground was equipped with a slide, merry-go-round, monkey bars, and a giant stride. Children played at morning, noon, and afternoon recess periods, teachers stayed inside during recess, and small town children enjoyed the same freedom to play as children in smaller country schools.

As in hundreds of other small towns, farmers, sharecroppers, and others from the surrounding countryside arrived in Durant on Saturday mornings, some coming late Friday and sleeping in or under their wagons. They converged at the "Mule Yard," set up a "market," and sold farm produce from their wagons. Choctaw Indians living in the area joined the crowds walking up and down main street, going to the movies, eating hamburgers at the cafes, and shopping for necessary odds and ends in the local stores. Movies were very popular. Durant, a town of about 10,000 people, had three movie theatres and two drive-in theatres. John later graduated from college, played in a military band, and became a program manager for IBM.

Eddye Cruze was born in 1930 and adopted by a Christian family from a Dallas orphanage when she was six weeks old, despite the fact that she had rickets and was covered with sores. She was taken to live in their home in Miles, Texas, a town of about 800 near San Angelo. Her father owned gas stations and held a government job, so they weathered the Depression in much better economic condition than most people in their vicinity. He did lose much of the money owed to him by farmers to whom he delivered gas, and also lost the money he had invested in a bank that "went busted." The family lived on a railroad line and "hobos" would drop off the trains to beg for food from her family and others, frequently doing work in exchange. Her mother never sent anyone away hungry and gave food to her less fortunate neighbors. This led to greater than typical traffic to their house.

Eddye's school was consolidated earlier than many rural schools, so children in grades one through eleven attended her school, located about a mile from her home in town. She was taken to school and picked up because her family owned a car and four trucks. The school held two recesses and a lunch period. The games were red rover, hide-and-seek, Annie over, kick the can, jump rope, softball, baseball, and football—with real factory-made balls and a few ball gloves. Nearly all the boys and some of the girls carried jackknives and used them for mumble peg and various other games and work. Eddye's mother used hers to cut corns off her feet and for other essential tasks. The school play-ground was equipped with very tall manufactured play equipment—slide, merry-go-round, giant stride, swings, and trapeze. Eddye was one of the tomboys, frequently choosing organized ball games over the games more frequently played by girls. There were no obese children in their school but, as in other small town schools, there were bullies. She did not recall any serious injuries to children while playing on the school playground.

At home children would create games based on movie characters seen at the local theatre—cowboys and Indians, and cops and robbers. Their evening entertainment was listening to the radio and playing Chinese checkers, Monopoly, jacks, cap pistols, and paper dolls and dolls purchased out of a Sears catalog. Like children everywhere, they created games such as saving tin foil, rolling it into balls, inserting it in a tobacco can, burying it, and searching for the "hidden treasure." Many communities had baseball teams that would play on weekends. Eddye's father designed play equipment for a backyard play-ground and had a local metal artisan construct a swing and swinging bar. Neighborhood children came there to play.

Dust storms were so common that every child brought a towel or handker-chief to school so they could wet it and hold it over their faces to protect against the sand. Despite the drought and dust conditions, many farmers managed to continue tending gardens and crops. Eddye raised chickens, a neighbor pro-vided milk, and her parents were able to buy food essentials. They had electric-ity throughout the Depression.

Durward Shreve was born in 1920 and grew up in Marion, a small coal-mining town in southern Illinois near Carbondale. His dad suffered from a slow, painful illness (thought to be cancer), was confined at home, and died when Durward was nine years old. This was the year the Depression hit, leaving him and his remaining family, already very poor, in a state of near starvation. They struggled to survive, receiving occasional unsolicited help from neighbors and relatives, and helping others butcher hogs for portions of the meat. Although most of the families in Marion received welfare assistance during the Depression, his mother would not accept "charity." Neighbors sometimes donated their excess government-issued powdered milk to the family, resulting in Durward's family consuming "mountains of gravy." Later, his adult children persuaded him to write all the "doings" of his life. I was privileged to read his story, entitled "Doins of Dad."

With the exception of having very understanding and supporting teachers in first and sixth grades, Durward's elementary school experience was a long nightmare of borderline failure and humiliation. He believes that being among the poorest of the poor helped account for his "setting the record" for whip-pings by teachers, receiving three in one day, and hardly a day passing without his receiving one. His fifth grade teacher humiliated him in front of the class, and he "just passed." Thanks to a caring sixth grade teacher, his grades were among the best in that grade and he continued to excel in school.

Children walked to Durward's five-room Marion Elementary School, and a "before school" playtime for early arriving students was supplemented by mid-morning, noon, and mid-afternoon recesses. He "didn't know what toys were" except for the ones they traded for or made themselves—scooters from old skate wheels, cars from various junk, hoops from wagon wheels and barrels for rolling with sticks, clothespin rubber guns, beat-up Pet Milk cans for balls, sticks for bats, burlap or "tow-sack" tents, marbles, tops, and his special sling shot, used both for play and killing chickens. Boys and girls played the traditional games seemingly played everywhere, such as chase, hop scotch, pitching washers, leap frog, climbing trees, building tree houses, whittling, and mumble peg. Many of the games were "dangerous" and kids were scratched, cut, and bruised but none suffered a serious injury.

When World War II arrived, Durward was drafted into the air force and served as a combat intelligence officer in various European countries. He served three years, two and one-half in combat, and left the service as a full Colonel (Eagle Colonel) with nine battle ribbons and three presidential citations. He attended college and became a successful businessman. Despite a childhood of extreme poverty and years of bitter war, Durward said: "We managed—more important, there was love among the family." He believes that the people living during the Depression and World War II were indeed "the Greatest Generation," and that today's children, in contrast, are "selfish, want too much, and get too much."

Russ Kyler was born in 1924 and spent his Depression era childhood in Huntingdon, Pennsylvania, where his father worked for the water department. Their neighbors were "hard hit" during the 1930s, but his father was able to keep his job and his family "went about life about the same during the Depression as any other time." A key to their success was owning "free and clear" a house in town and a farm, operated by a sharecropper family, just a short ride away by Model T or Model A "Ford flivver." Their house in town was located three blocks from the train depot, and hobos, seemingly knowing in advance which houses were good targets for a hand-out, passed up other houses to get food from his mother. "Mom always fed them. Dad said, 'Never send anyone away hungry.'" The Kyler family lived in town during the winter, but Mom and the three kids went to the farm as soon as school was out. In the country they planted a garden, helped care for livestock, took fruit and vegetables to sell door-to-door in town, and canned vegetables for the winter. All the children worked and turned over the money they earned to their parents. Russ, his brother, and their friends played and hunted in the woodlands, climbed trees, threw rocks at birds, picked wild berries, swam, dived from a rope swing into the creek, and drank the creek water, which was considered clean. Boys in the country typically had a single-shot rifle before they left elementary school, were carefully instructed in its safety and use, and were expected to bring home game commensurate with the number of shells used. Russ received his first .32 caliber, single-shot rifle when he was five years old and was told, "Don't point at anything you don't want to kill." At age six he was allowed to hunt rabbits and squirrels and bring them home for food.

Playgrounds, natural and built, were plentiful, ranging from the woodlands and barnyards in the country to the park playground, school playground, and two movie theaters in town. Hoot Gibson, Hopalong Cassidy, and Tim McCoy cowboys livened the screen and set the stage for later imaginative cowboy— Indian play with cap pistols and "rubber guns." Ten cents bought the popcorn and the stage was set for serials, newsreels, and double-features—typical fare in Depression era small town theaters. Here children saw big city "soup kitchens" on the newsreels but had no firsthand conception of their meaning. The park playground, two blocks from home, was the setting for traditional games and organized games of baseball, football, tennis, and swimming, and included equipment for exercise play—giant stride, trapeze rings, and swings. Many of the play materials were created by the kids—rubber guns, hoops and sticks, and wagons made from castoff wheels. In the winter there was sledding on the hills with his Christmas gift sled, and, beginning at age twelve, Russ rode his own bicycle with other fortunate friends.

Russ attended both a one-room country school and later a consolidated school in town. There were no school buses so children walked to the one-room school, which had eight rows of desks, one row for each grade, one through eight. A teacher was always on the playground during the morning and after-noon recesses and during the lunch period that also allowed time for play. They "made up" many of their games and played such traditional games as tag, chase, mumble peg (with pocket knives), kick the can, and hide-and-seek. Girls and boys played together much of the time but the girls also played jacks and hop-scotch, on occasion with boys. There was no playground equipment on the school grounds. Later, in the consolidated town school with separate rooms for each grade, the recess and lunch period traditions remained, and a large bell planted on the roof of the school alerted everyone to the times for indoor and outdoor events. Russ did not recall any child being seriously injured while play-ing in town or country, and he did not recall seeing any obese children in his schools.

Russ volunteered for the air force early during World War II, flew P-47 fighter planes out of England, and was credited with destroying 10 enemy air-craft, plus one probable German jet. Now in his eighties, he travels from city to city speaking about his war experiences to gatherings of pilots and others inter-ested in aircraft. He is treated as the hero he is everywhere he goes. My wife, Betty, and I traveled to Phoenix in 2007 for one of his addresses and came away full of pride for his achievements and the camaraderie he shared with his military peers and other aircraft enthusiasts.

Paul Drescher was born in 1928 on a sharecroppers farm near Giddings, Texas. His father bought a 250-acre farm for $3,400 with a bank loan of $1,700. When the house burned they were "taken in" by another farm family and lived upstairs over the space for the farm animals. He and his five brothers and sisters worked on the farm and attended a one-room school with about 20 students in grades 1 to 7. Paul was the only pupil in third grade so the teacher had him teach the second graders. They played traditional games during the two recesses and noon hour at school, much as described by other country children at that time.

Drought and economic decline resulted in the farm being repossessed by the bank in 1934. A second bank took the livestock and farm equipment worth taking but "didn't bother" with the "worn out" furniture. "When you are poor and the bank takes everything, times don't get any better." The children's clothing was "hand-me-down rags" patched together, and bare feet were the summer style. They moved from sharecroppers shack to sharecroppers shack and eked out a bare subsistence. Other sharecroppers, including friends among the African Americans, shared food with them. As early as age ten, children walked the dirt roads to seek out work in the fields and would hoe cotton for ten-hour days for six cents an hour. They bought essentials "on credit" at the country store. When a second house burned and mules died, payment was delayed and they turned to a second store for credit. At home, work dominated everyone's time and Paul's memories of play were overshadowed by memories of hard work.

Like so many with lives overturned by the Depression, Roosevelt's New Deal programs and America's entry into World War II brought relief to Paul's family. With the New Deal, relief workers visited homes to determine who qualified for assistance. People hid what food they had to help ensure approval. Paul's older brother worked in a Civilian Conservation Corp (CCC) camp and sent $25 a month home and his father walked eight miles into town to build out-houses for a Works Progress Administration (WPA) program. Paul volunteered for the army when he was seventeen and sent money home.

Double Trouble: The Great Depression and the Dust Bowl

A "can't-put-it-down history" (Walter Cronkite), *The Worst Hard Time*, of what has been called "our nation's greatest disaster"—dust storms that devastated and terrorized America's great plains during the 1930s—was written by Pulitzer Prize winning author, Timothy Egan.

At its peak, the Dust Bowl covered one hundred million acres. Dusters swept over the northern prairies as well, but the epicenter was the southern plains ... More than a quarter-million people fled the Dust Bowl in the 1930's ... John Steinbeck told part of the story, about getting out, moving somewhere green. Not much was heard about the people who stayed behind, for lack of money or lack of sense, the people who hunkered down out of loyalty or stubbornness, who believed in tomorrow because it was all they had in the bank. (Egan, 2006, pp. 9–10)

It hadn't rained more than a few drops in the Panhandle for five straight years. One day the wind started to blow, and every day it blew harder and harder, as if nature were playing a cruel joke on the Okies. The wind blew the dry sod into the air, and every morning the sun rose only to disappear behind a sky of red dirt and dust. The wind knocked open doors, shattered windows, and leveled barns. (Stanley, 1992, p. 4)

During the double whammy of the Great Depression and the Dust Bowl, futures were not nearly so secure in rural areas and small towns of the Midwest, populated by thousands of farmers with mortgaged lands and bank loans used to buy equipment. Foreclosures were epidemic, and farms, farm equipment, livestock, and even furniture and cars were auctioned to the highest bidder, and families were forced to hit the road. Many joined the migrant streams to the West, some men left their families and roamed the country looking for work or as "hobos," begging for a handout, and whole families went to live with relatives. Entire extended families searched for work, joining the never-ending stream of jalopies on the road to California. If they failed, they turned back "home" again to face the same dismal future, then turned yet again toward California in never-ending rivers of miserable lives of futile searching and lost promise.

Poor dirt farmers, made paupers by the blowing dirt and the Depression, headed to California to pick cotton and work in the orchards, but arrived to find few jobs available to the masses who had joined them on the trek. Most of these migrants were poor, with limited education, wore baggy, ragged clothes, and were desperate in their search for work. The Californians called them "Okies" and "Arkies"—derogatory terms—and often refused them either jobs or charity. Route 66, the main highway from the Plains to California, teemed with old jalopies making the perpetual run to the "promised land" and, failing there, going back again to the reality or illusion of "home." Despite all this, for most Depression and Dust Bowl families, hope never died and they survived to become the adults whom Tom Brokaw (1998) called "The Greatest Generation."

In the summer of 1939 I was six years old and lived with my grandparents and most of their children (five boys and five girls) in a three-room, clap-board, sharecropper's house on the remnants of a cotton farm near Muleshoe, in the Texas Panhandle. Grandpa bought and sold junk from old cars, hauling it from place to place in a rickety old truck. We boys would ride with him and work as

Figure 6.3 Dust storm in Rolla, Kansas. "Dear Mr. Roosevelt, Darkness came when it hit us. Picture taken from water tower one hundred feet high. Yours Truly, Chas. P. Williams."
Source: Courtesy of the Franklin D. Roosevelt Presidential Library.

junk sorters so he could get the best prices for the various metals or usable car parts. We were avid sorters because we could keep an occasional usable or fix-able toy from the piles of junk and begin lavishing attention on it as we made the long trip home. These were the only manufactured toys in the family. Two of the older boys were teenagers, who still lived at home but walked the Muleshoe area almost daily in search of odd jobs. They would pick cotton in exchange for chickens, leave them in the farmer's coop until Saturday, then take the younger boys on the three mile walk to town to see a movie. En route we would occasionally stop to pick up three or four chickens owed to my uncles (on occasion, possibly "borrowed"), cook one in a gully to eat on the spot, then sell two others in town for money to buy movie tickets. The next day (Sunday), our play was all about choosing up sides and playing the roles of cowboy heroes in the movies. Our most prized toys from the junk yards were beat up toy guns and one real revolver with most parts missing. This "real gun" was a possession prized by all; a little play time with it could be traded for a few marbles or a beat up top.

In summer, we boys slept in the yard on metal cots without mattresses, but we would sleep on quilts spread on the kitchen floor during cold or rainy weather. One late afternoon, the adults began to yell for the children to get in the house, and looking toward the west we could see a huge dark reddish and black rolling cloud beginning to blot out the sun, emitting a kind of train engine roar. This was a dreaded dust storm—a massive wave of sand stripped from the once fertile fields, bearing down on us and threatening every living thing and every house and barn in its path. Chickens were making their last run to the chicken house, for, by morning, many would succumb to the smothering sand. We all stuffed rags in the cracks around windows and doors, and our grandparents bundled everyone under quilts, gave us a wet towel or "dish rag" to hold over our noses and mouths, and told us to stay there. The house shook and dirt blew in through the cracks, but eventually we fell into a fitful sleep. Next morning, noses were filled with grit, teeth crunched together, and the usual breakfast of oatmeal, kept in bags or boxes, was filled with sand. Only the milk, sealed in jars and kept in a bucket in the well, survived the penetrating missiles. Floors were covered, sand was heaped on the west side of the house up to the windows, the chicken coops were destroyed, and the few surviving hens and roosters were wandering or staggering around pecking at the litter. Within a few hours things had returned to normal, and work and play resumed. For a time our playgrounds were the smooth, undulating rivers of sand blotting out any remaining vegetation, but throughout that summer we were fearful of walking far from the protection of home, and we listened for the ominous roar and looked to the west in fear that another dust monster would bear down on us.

During that same summer, the stresses of need, despair, and misplaced hope led my mother to take me to find work in West Texas, walking the dusty back roads, asking for food and work at farmhouses, keeping a lookout for windmills to refill our "fruit jar" (water jar), and sleeping in haystacks. We met others "walking the roads" from time to time, and sat talking and resting in the shade of trees. These were among the times I recall that children were too exhausted to play. (We could sleep in the shade of a tree, at the end of a cotton row, or, as I later learned, standing up in a crowded bus hanging on to the luggage rack during a four-day trip from Arkansas to California.) We finally found a short-term job working in the fields, with rent-free living for a few weeks in a two-room abandoned shack equipped with a wood cooking stove, rickety cabinet, table, two chairs, and an iron "bedstead." I carried a lard bucket down the hill in the afternoons to the barn where men were milking cows and separating cream from the milk. They generously filled my bucket with whey (cream-free milk) and fed the rest to the hogs. We walked to a country store to buy kerosene for the lamp, flour, sugar, salt, and other basic food supplies. I spent days helping in the fields and hanging out at a nearby house, playing with a girl about my age. We soon "caught a bus" back to Arkansas, having learned that life on a small farm in the green Ouachita mountains was far better than anything offered in the arid plains of West Texas.

Between 1930 and 1940 the number of farmers in the Dust Bowl states declined by about 400,000 and the unemployment rate in Arkansas, Oklahoma, and Texas soared to 30 percent. Almost half of the farms in Oklahoma were sold in bankruptcy court. If a farmer could not pay and refused to move, a tractor arrived to tear down his house and "force him out." This contributed heavily

Mrs Oklahomans reach Calif. via the cotton fields of Ariz.

Figure 6.4 Oklahoma Depression, dust bowl migrants, San Fernando, California, 1935.
Source: Photographer, Dorothea Lange. Courtesy of the Library of Congress, Prints and Photographs Division, FSA/OWI Collection [reproduction number LC-USZ62-56051].

to the largest migration in U.S. history, with more than a million migrating from four Dust Bowl states to California between 1935 and 1940—some hitch-hiking, some "ridin' the rails," others in old jalopies (Stanley, 1992).

As a child, my wife Betty made several trips with her parents and grandpar-ents over the dirt roads from Guthrie, Oklahoma, and Van Buren, Arkansas, to Arizona and California in search of work. They slept on the side of the road, cooked fried potatoes, gravy, bacon, and eggs over campfires during the best of times and gathered fruit from orchards when available. Betty had a small rubber doll and a rag doll her mother made for her and doll furniture made from scraps of wood by her grandfather. She carried on conversations with the dolls in the back seat of the old car and played cards with her mother during the long days of travel. When they were stranded for car repairs or met other families on the road, she joined other children in games of chase, marbles, hopscotch, chasing "lightening bugs," and drawing pictures in a Big Chief writing tablet. In the evening they sat listening to the tall tales and true-life stories related over and over by the men around the campfires. Betty's father related many of these same exciting, real-life stories to me during the 1960s, seemingly embellishing and extending them as his memory allowed and impact demanded. They were sometimes stories of despair and failure, but more often stories of hope, impending success, and the "good old times." When work was available, usually picking cotton or fruit, the children would work alongside their parents. Betty's memories are filled with pleasant times. She always felt loved by a closely knit family and remembered vividly the joyful play and hard but rewarding work. Early during World War II the family returned to work small farms in Arkansas and Oklahoma and began to rebuild their lives. Here they had livestock to feed and a horse to ride. The common qualities of our childhoods must have formed much of the cement that has held our marriage together and happy for 56 years.

History books and documents never seem to quite convey the full meaning of growing up in the mountains, rolling farmlands, or unspoiled deserts, fail to express adequately the full meaning of close knit families, and rarely capture the essence of free, spontaneous play in the wonders of nature. Some of the eloquently written children's books about growing up in the Depression era seem to do this best. One can hardly read such works as Cynthia Rylant's moving *When I Was Young in the Mountains* without feeling the nostalgia and pride inherent in living, working, and playing in such captivating places.

> When I was young in the mountains, I never wanted to go to the ocean, and I never wanted to go to the desert, I never wanted to go anywhere else in the world, for I was in the mountains. And that was always enough. (Rylant, 1982)

The wonderful children's book *Roxaboxen* is a celebration of children's active imaginations and their ability to create magical play places, even out of the most unpromising materials. *Roxaboxen* is a true story about the author's grandmother, who grew up near a hill in Yuma, Arizona, when Yuma was a small town.

> It looked like any rocky hill—nothing but sand and rocks, some old wooden boxes, cactus and greasewood and thorn ocotillo—but it was a very special place ... A town of Roxaboxen started to grow ... Once there was a great war, boys against girls ... The girls had Fort Irene, and they were all girl scouts. The boys made a fort at the other end of Roxaboxen, and they were all bandits. (McLerran, 1991)

And a classic children's book by Wilson Rawls, *Where the Red Fern Grows,* is a story related countless times over among those who recall their early lives in the mountains.

> Our home was in a beautiful valley far back in the rugged Ozarks ... In the spring the aromatic scent of wild flowers, redbuds, papaws, and dog-woods, drifting on the wind currents, spread over the valley and around our home ... I roamed the hills and river bottoms. I knew every game trail

in the thick canebrakes, and every animal track that was pressed in the
mud along the riverbanks ... My (hunting) dog-wanting became so bad I
began to lose sleep and my food didn't taste good any more ... Papa set me
on his lap and we had a good talk. He told me how hard times were, and
that it looked like a man couldn't get a fair price for anything
he raised ... He said he'd do anything if he could get some good
hounds for me, but there didn't seem to be any way he could right then.
(Rawls, 1961)

These simple stories express the sentiments, nostalgia, and longing of sur-
vival-bent people during the Depression, making the long tortuous trips to the
"promised land," but always hearing the call of a simple, natural life where children worked and played and never longed to live anyplace else. This is the
essence of a way of life that has disappeared and is unavailable to most contemporary children, for their exposure to the wilderness has been displaced by life
in the jungles of cities, the torturous drills of test driven classrooms, and the
cyber playgrounds of their private rooms and home entertainment centers. It is
their form of life that must have prepared country people to cope with the hard
knocks they would endure during the Depression.

Play and Play Environments of City Children during the Depression

The play of city children was similar in many ways to that of country children,
but the playgrounds and objects for play differed according to the availability of
natural, junked, bought, or self-made materials. Children in families "with
means," whether in city or country, continued to play much as they were accustomed to playing. These were the families that managed to retain property, jobs,
or money, and those fortunate enough to continue attending school. Dwellers in
city slums continued to live and play under the most wretched conditions, and
those forced to join the bread lines or the migrant stream lived a "hand to mouth"
existence. Many were abandoned by their families or orphaned by their parents'
deaths, and turned to living in the dangerous streets. Others were constantly
exposed to new challenges, new playmates, new schools (or no schools), and created their own play objects and opportunities as they joined the migrant stream.

There were major differences between the lives of people living in low to
middle income areas of large cities and the lives of people living in the slums.
The child-saving movement focused on these most depressed groups—the
homeless, orphans, dispossessed immigrants, child laborers, ignored minorities, and others who found themselves in seemingly inescapable conditions.
The Depression simply exacerbated conditions for the poorest among poor city
dwellers, resulting in bread lines, increased unemployment, wandering the
country, and homelessness, driving many to the brink of despair. Charitable
agencies of the child-saving movement continued to serve many such people.

Earlier chapters outlined the conditions of immigrants and others exposed to the most wretched conditions prior to the Depression. Many living in other areas of cities continued to have sufficient to meet limited but basic survival needs. The following stories from people growing up in the more affluent areas of cities contrast sharply with the earlier descriptions of big city slum life.

Stuart Brown recalls the play and pleasures of his Depression era childhood in suburban Chicago in a letter. Stuart, a medical doctor and psychiatrist, spent much of his adult life studying play and the effects of play deprivation on humans and animals.

It used to be that self-organized play was all kids did. Most adults over the age of 45 will likely have memories of exploring on their own, through puddles and fields or on city streets, told only to be home before dinner or before dark.

The games of my own youth were typical of those that spontaneously cropped up back then in vacant lots and parks across the country. They were anarchic, and didn't always end well, but they had their own style and etiquette, were full of interruptions, reversals, flexibility, rule changes. Despite the seeming anarchy, these games existed within an overall, agreed-upon sense of structure and fairness. They were undertaken with an accepted, minimal risk of damage, and had some safeguards. Although there was considerable mayhem and noise during the course of these games, I remember that they were exciting, and there wasn't naked aggression. It was OK to cry if you got hurt but not OK to cheat or whine. Not OK to make fun of one of your own team members, but OK to ridicule someone on the other team. If team members changed in the middle of the game, OK to try and humiliate the former teammate then.

Looking back now, these play-inspired portraits feel more real and persistent as continuing aspects of my current self-image than most other remembrances. My studies of the play deprived and the research of others confirm that these and other rough and tumble play experiences have significant life-shaping consequences.

My last trip to suburban Chicago and the old neighborhood revealed no empty lots, no pick-up games, a lot of adult supervised youth sports, busy kids and parents, many more and much nicer cars, less street noise, clearer air, mixed ethnic groups in sidewalk restaurants, and multiple families living in the big Victorian houses. Not the same world. I believe that kids, even on the soccer and little league fields today, create their own, private play domains. Nature's design for play is just too strong to be pushed aside completely. They will find their own, new ways of asserting their own community, socialization patterns and individuality. One journalist recently wrote about driving his kids and their friends from one activity to another when he noticed a strange silence among the group in back. Upon further inquiry, he discovered that they were all texting each other on their cellphones so that they could speak frankly and secretly in the presence of the adult.

Paul Hogan's (1995) delightful book *Philadelphia Boyhood: Growing up in the 1930s* reveals the joys of childhood in a large city among extended families, street peddlers, organ grinders, the iceman, and the butter and egg man. During the latter half of the twentieth century, Paul was a prominent leader in the growth of playgrounds and the establishment of the International Play Association/USA. He planned and created community-built playgrounds in many states and was a spark plug at conferences of people working for children's play and playgrounds. His Philadelphia family did not live in the poverty-stricken city slums described in previous chapters and managed to retain means for providing necessities. In his book about the Depression era, he spoke of the special tree house, comic book heroes, self-made toys, early movies, and the vacant lots for digging, sledding, sliding and popular games. A large lot across the street from his family's and Wilt Chamberlin's alma mater was covered with hills and valleys, kept clean of trash and free of dumping, and was used as a playground for children and for cookouts by families. In the winter they would sled down the hills on their Flexible Flyers, and in the summer they would sled down on cardboard boxes. Football, baseball, and even basketball were played on the level dirt areas. Kids dug tunnels and forts in the hills and made their own fire pits for cooking chicken and potatoes or hotdogs, rolls, and corn in the husk. Paul claimed that "Colonel Sanders would have starved had he started his business anywhere in range of our 'finger lickin' good chicken.'"

One fateful day, city engineers, architects, and politicians visited this delightful, natural playground and doomsday was not far off. The lot was to be developed into an official playground. Horse powered equipment moved in and leveled the hills and valleys, a fence and iron gate were installed, and the entire site was covered by a foot of sharp cinders that lacerated knees and feet. Both children and adults stayed away in droves from such a barren, forbidding place. A "half-baked" gym was opened but it soon closed. Throughout the history of America, oft well-intentioned changes, cloaked as "progress," have conspired to destroy nature and children's best playgrounds. Decades later, Paul's early playground site contained a large, clean, well-managed swimming pool.

Dorothy Stuemke grew up in Chicago, near the present site of Midway Airport, during the Depression. Her earliest recollections were of living with her family in the basement of her grandparents' house. Her father worked nights as a part-time railroad dispatcher and both he and Dorothy's mother found part-time jobs to supplement the family's income. He slept most of the time when at home, did not spend time with the kids, and never spanked her. On one occasion he took his children to a park to play in the pool, remembered by Dorothy as a very special experience. People of low-income status lived in the apartments in the several neighborhoods where she lived and had only limited social interaction with their neighbors. Dorothy's out-of-school play places were the sidewalk in front of her house and the very small backyard behind her apartment building, but her favorite special place to play was the stairway leading to her family's apartment. Here she played dolls and bounced balls up and down the stairs, playing mostly with her brother. They did not know their neighbors because they moved almost every year. They shared bathrooms and washtubs with other families in the buildings. The sidewalks were painted green to resemble grass and clothes-lines were used for the intended purpose of hanging clothes but also for making play tents. The children received a toy or two for Christmas, but most of their toys were found or homemade. In the winter they would make snowmen, using a shovel and a wagon.

Dorothy's family rarely left the neighborhood, and she had little understanding of what the Depression meant. Even though her family lived only a few miles from the soup lines and concentrations of homeless people in inner city Chicago, she did not know about "poor people" and "soup lines." She walked two or three miles to school with her "large" brother who picked on her, but defended her from other large kids. His behavior and getting into trouble caused them to be moved from school to school. Her teachers included both "good" and "bad," but there was always a teacher supervising play at recess. Their play periods or recesses were similar to those seen in schools everywhere, a morning and afternoon recess, punctuated by a long lunch period with time for play. Dorothy and her friends used the jungle gym, merry-go-round, and slide, and played jacks, marbles, pick-up-sticks, and Red Rover, but rarely with boys. Boys played ball games with balls and bats brought from home. The boys were too rough, "always pushing and tugging in hordes, like a herd of cattle." They even went into the building first, followed by the girls and little kids.

Dorothy does not remember seeing any "fat kids" in her school and was unaware of any children suffering serious injuries. She had almost no experience with plants, gardens or nature areas, and did not play in vacant lots, tree houses, or forts. Her dad did not want her to ride or have a bicycle, and her mom was very protective and warned her about strangers and kidnapping. She had a "lot of jobs and responsibilities," but she loved to sing and play with imaginary friends, go to church, and never felt lonely. When the war started, her father was deferred and her brother went into the service at age 16. Dorothy was later a successful elementary teacher for four decades.

The poorest and most distressed people of New York, Philadelphia, Chicago, and other large cities were the very poor or homeless before the Depression, now joined by thousands more who had suddenly lost everything and had little economic, social, or educational means to recover. The slums remained slums and children's play continued in the streets, vacant lots, abandoned buildings, junk yards, and all such places that creative children discovered and claimed for their playgrounds. As wretched as Depression conditions were for people everywhere, they were even worse for recent immigrants, minorities, and those with serious disabilities. "Civil rights" were still a dream and decades away. During the Depression, African-Americans continued to suffer the consequences of discrimination, lack of education, extremely high unemployment, lack of basic essentials for housing and health, and all the misery that followed.

Having a disability, especially mental, meant severe discrimination in riding public transportation, attending school, or securing jobs. Many families hid their disabled children away in attics, basements, back bedrooms, or other out-of-the-way places. I knew about a young girl in my community who was kept locked in a cellar when visitors came to her house and when the family was away from home during the day. When she died, the immediate family buried her in a family cemetery in the woods near their house without any announcement of her funeral.

"Store bought" toys were rarely seen in abundance, and children with several toys were those whose fathers had steady jobs. A holiday was just another day of work unless it fell on Sunday. Christmas was celebrated by decorating a small tree with rings of paper colored with crayons and pasted together with flour glue to form "ropes" that were hung in circles around the tree. In cities, almost any object resembling a tree would be erected, and families tried to have one present for each child—a few marbles, a piece of candy, a coin or two, an apple or orange—placed in a sock and hung on the mantle (if available) or placed in a small box or sack under the "tree." Many parents or older siblings would carve dolls from sticks or make them out of socks stuffed with rags or cotton. Adults knew that children loved and needed toys but food and shelter had to be given priority. Many contemporary children, in stark contrast, are overwhelmed with toys and expensive electronic gadgets that isolate them from playmates and keep them indoors. Children then re-focus from creative, active outdoor play to sedentary, physically passive, indoor play, often suffering the consequences of diminished social and physical activity, and risking their fitness and health.

The letters to Mrs. Roosevelt in Robert Cohen's *Dear Mrs. Roosevelt* came from all parts of the country; they were filled with requests for basic essentials such as clothes, medical needs, and small amounts of money for paying debts. The young writers, mostly girls, asked for help for their entire families, showing great devotion and concern for their welfare. The children were proud despite their living conditions and frequently asked that their letters remain confidential to avoid shame for the family or punishment for themselves. Among the hundreds of letters asking Mrs. Roosevelt for help was one from Philadelphia.

Dear Mrs. Roosevelt:

I am asking you for your charity, asking you to send me and my two sisters suits for Easter. It is not only that we have nothing to eat but also nothing to get dressed into. Easter is coming nearer and nearer but I do not think it will be an Easter for me. It will be another dull and unpleasant Easter like last year. It is supposed to be a time of rejoicing but I know I shall not be rejoicing for I have nothing to rejoice about ... You notice the big sizes. That is to last us for a few years. If you do send them just let this be a secret between me and you, please do not tell anyone. During this time God bless you a thousand times.

Yours truly,

p.s. Mrs. Roosevelt please send mother one of your old dresses that you do not wear now if it is size 40 please!

Occasionally a child would ask for a toy:

Dear Mrs. Roosevelt,

I am 6 years old this is my first year in school I am a little colored girl my name is B.J.R. I wish you wold please send me a Sherley temple Doll because my doll got broke I will take good care of the doll if you sen me one please Answer. My daddy helped me to writ you yours with lots of kisses XXXXXXX.

Among the many volumes about life during the Depression, a moldy old copy of *The Lost Generation* by Maxine Davis (1936) is very special to me. Davis was a newspaper and magazine writer in Washington during the Depression and recorded the experience of the social, economic, and political problems of that period. She set out on a three-month long, 10,038 mile trip across America in a secondhand car, talking to boys and girls of "every kind and condition" and to others who were in contact with them. Her purpose was to learn about the characteristics, ambitions, hopes, attitudes, and needs of boys and girls facing "the most difficult situation which has ever confronted youth in the history of this nation" (p. ix). She found them everywhere and talked to them in their homes and schools and in their work and play. Children during that period had little fear of adults and heard few warnings about the "dangers" of talking to strangers, so Davis gained children's time and attention without stint.

Boys and girls who have grown up playing marbles and jackstones on city pavements have the same fine detachment and lack of responsibility of their country and their community that a snooty English governess has toward a slum child perilously stuffing his stomach with pickles and peppermints. It's not their baby. The reverse is true in the rural areas. Out in the corn and hog country, out where the alfalfa scents the air, where the wheat is a yellow sea, young men and women have a sense of possession and of obligation which is in vivid contrast to the cities' children. (Davis, 1936, p. 48)

Davis quoted a study by Anne Davis (a relative?) of children's activities in Chicago during the Depression. She pointed out that this could have been any large city—Cleveland, Newark, Minneapolis, or Boston. The results of Anne Davis's study are found in Table 6.1.

The 1930 White House Conference on Child Health and Protection, called by President Hoover, led to numerous recommendations directly affecting recreation. The government and private citizens were realizing that outdoor play, recreation, and amusements such as movies and radio were beneficial to both mental and physical health—not only for children but for entire families. Play and recreation were seen as antidotes to juvenile delinquency and were vehicles for transmitting the values of the older generation to children and youth. Among the nineteen provisions of the 1930 Children's Charter were:

1. wholesome physical and mental recreation for every child from birth through adolescence, with teachers and leaders adequately trained;
2. for every child, provision by communities for safe and wholesome places for play and recreation, and social and cultural opportunities;
3. extension to rural families of social, recreational and cultural facilities; and
4. extension and development of the voluntary youth organizations for the benefit of all children "to return to them those interests of which modern life tends to cheat children" (Grotberg, 1975, p. 304, White House Conference, 1930).

These recommendations would later influence the construction of many recreational areas and playgrounds. Participants at the 1930 White House Conference had agreed that no field was more in need of scientific investigation than early childhood recreation and play. Consequently, emergency funds made available during the Depression contributed to scientific studies on play and recreation. Within the first two years of its operation, the Civilian Conservation Corps (CCC) workers had completed 20,000 construction

Table 6.1 Chicago children's Depression era activities

- 383 spent some time in public libraries, and 2,841 never went inside one.
- 1,118 sometimes visited a park, but 2,110 never found them attractive.
- 536 frequented Chicago's beaches, and 2,687 did not.
- 277 spent some time in supervised clubrooms, but 2,930 never spent time there.
- Only 60 boys and girls were lured to Chicago's famous settlement houses, and 3,163 had never been there.
- 45 said they had spent some time at the YWCA or the YMCA, and 3,171 said they had not been there.
- 136 said they had read one library book, only one had read five or more, and 2,961 had never read any.

What then do they do? They told the investigators, "Just fool around."

projects, including 131 stadiums, 532 community centers, and innumerable wading pools and playgrounds. Play streets, vacant lots, and dump heaps were cleaned up, spaces for play were prepared, and hygiene was improved. In addition, provisions were made for doubling the number of recreational personnel.

Although President Hoover was the object of much criticism for his leadership during the Depression, he had surprisingly modern views about preserving the environment, providing for children's play and play environments, and introducing children in cities to the natural advantages of the country. Contemporary Americans at every level are only now, with the threat of global warming and children's disconnection from nature, awakening to some of his warnings.

> *The child of the country is handicapped by lack of some cultural influences* extended by the city. We must find ways and means of extending these influences to the children of rural districts. On the other hand, some of the natural advantages of the country child must somehow be given back to the city child—more space in which to play, contact with nature and natural processes. Of these the thoughtless city cheats its children. Architectural wizardry and artistic skill are transforming our cities into wonderlands of beauty, but we must also preserve in them for our children the yet more beautiful art of living. (Hoover, 1930)

The Awakening

During 1933–4, the worst school year in history, the Federal government came to the rescue of these orphans of the Depression. By then the gravity of the situation was so serious that only a quarter of children were attending schools, with school terms even half what they should have been; hundreds of schools did not open at all, 200,000 certified teachers were unemployed, and other professions were suffering similar shortcomings (Davis, 1936). Franklin D. Roosevelt was inaugurated as president in March 1933, and in his inauguration speech spoke his famous words, "The only thing we have to fear is fear itself." Americans looked to him for change, even salvation from their misery, but although Roosevelt's New Deal was criticized by many as being too slow in effecting widespread change, on November 9, 1933, his Executive Order creating the Federal Civil Works Administration (CWA) effectively declared war on the Depression. By that time about fifteen million were unemployed. Within a month, more than four million men and women had enlisted and work began in remote mountain areas, city slums, and Depression impacted areas throughout America.

By January, 4,040,000 workers were employed. Schools, playgrounds, hospitals, roads, water mains, sewer lines, and many work projects were underway. Playground sites were leveled and manufactured playground equipment was being installed. Unemployed men and women from many professions and vocations found work, and hardly a community failed to reap the benefits. On March 31, 1934, the CWA was terminated, but the CCC and later the Works Progress Administration (WPA) operated in every area of the country.

The CCC was a work relief program established on March 19, 1933, by Roosevelt to combat poverty and unemployment, and it became one of the most popular New Deal programs. For $1 per day plus housing and meals, workers erected buildings, improved city, state, and national parks, constructed logging and fire roads in forests, and planted millions of trees. A percentage of their pay was sent home to families. Workers lived in CCC camps, including 143 segregated camps enrolling 200,000 workers. There were also separate camps for Native Americans. As unemployment declined, the CCC ended in 1940, just before America entered World War II in 1941 and shifted attention from domestic to war issues. Reports from individuals and records indicate considerable success for the CCC.

The WPA, largest of the New Deal agencies, was created in April 1935 and was operational in almost every locality in the country. This program was never as popular as the CCC, apparently because of poor management, political patronage and manipulation at both national and local levels, and a record of workers being paid without working. WPA came to mean "We Piddle Around." By November 1938, 3.3 million were employed by the WPA at a rate of $19 to $94 per month. Despite its record of bureaucracy, the WPA established an enduring heritage that continues today—building highways, roads, streets, public buildings, hospitals, schools, educational programs for both adults and children, parks, forests, recreation areas, and playgrounds. The program also provided commodities to the poor and school lunches for many schools, and improved or created recreation areas. In January 2009, as we faced a devastating worldwide economic meltdown, we saw the influence of President FDR in the sweeping reforms proposed by President Obama, the nation's first president of African-American descent—a Harvard educated president with an obvious grasp of history.

The living conditions of the Depression era remained in a state of slow, gradual improvement until the beginning of American involvement in World War II in 1941, when men left for the military and women worked in factories to support the war effort. Many historians identify the war as the principal factor that rescued America from the grip of poverty. The New Deal was successful in helping to reduce unemployment and improve standards of living, but the war accelerated job growth and set the nation on a path of rapid economic recovery. During the war, American children continued to play much as they had played during the Depression, but they had new toy weapons to create, new war games to play, and new heroes to emulate—soldiers, sailors, and air force pilots. The shortage of steel to build playgrounds apparently had little effect, for children were still free to explore the woods, fields, and vacant lots where their unbridled creativity took over. By the end of the war in 1945, American culture was changing in unprecedented ways, eventually leading to a scientific and technological revolution, new views of the family, and a new culture of childhood. The stage was being set for radical changes in children's play, new views of what constitutes playgrounds, and all the consequences that followed.

As stated in the opening section of this chapter, we have lessons to learn from such crises as the Great Depression, not only how they influence the play of children but also how leaders and dedicated citizens working together can bring resolution and reconstruction to human needs and broken promises. Roosevelt's New Deal worked, slowly at first, but gained energy over time. Hardly a community failed to benefit as solutions similar to successful war programs were employed, but radically different in yielding construction rather than destruction. Every form of technical skill was brought to bear in the war against the Depression—by scientists, farmers, engineers, architects, teachers, lawyers, doctors, nurses, politicians, mechanics, and carpenters—all contributing to common goals. All this, coupled with the rapid rise in employment with the onset of World War II, set America on the road to unprecedented prosperity and new approaches to child rearing. The lesson learned, applicable to the current play, fitness, and health crisis, is that massive problems require massive, coordinated solutions.

7

Natural, Built, and Adventure Play Environments
Back to Nature

My aim was clear and correct—to give children in towns the same chance for creative play as those in the country. (C. Th. Sorensen, 1968, p. 9)

Adventure playgrounds are where the craft and the practice of play-work are applied in their purest forms. But with clever planning and well-considered modes of intervention and sound, reflective, analytical practice, we can support the playing of children even within the tight confines of a school playground. (Penny Wilson, U.K. playworker, 2009, p. 277)

The best European playgrounds probably represent the "future today" in conceptualizing play environments. The concept of playground, limited in scope, will eventually be replaced by a more vital and comprehensive concept of outdoor environments for people of all ages, combining elements of nature, a wide array of play activities, and involving all family members in specially designed environments within their own immediate neighborhoods. (Joe L. Frost and Barry L. Klein, 1979, p. 204)

Children's grounds for play over the centuries previous to the initiation of built or manufactured playgrounds during the 1900s were the wilderness and farms of rural dwellers and the streets, vacant spaces and nearby forests, waterways, and fields of city dwellers. Natural playgrounds in a schoolyard emerged in Froebel's German kindergarten schoolyard during the mid-1800s, including gardens and a wide variety of plants and features, about the time the German outdoor gymnasia playgrounds were introduced in America. The early history of America's built playgrounds—outdoor gymnasia, sand gardens, and earlier variations of playgrounds featuring manufactured equipment (Manufactured Appliance Era)—was discussed in previous chapters. Here we revisit early built playgrounds and pick up the story of playgrounds following the establishment of the American play and playground movement of the early 1900s.

Playgrounds built for children, such as those designed by architects or produced by manufacturers, and those created with children, are commonly seen in backyards, child care centers, schools, and city parks. These feature playgrounds

173

that differ substantially with respect to philosophy, built or manufactured materials and equipment, space, natural materials, and play leadership or supervision. All are intended to be used for children's play, and those in public places may be used by a common core of children, especially those living in the vicinity. Built playground equipment can complement natural materials, nature areas, and gardens in the confined spaces of child care centers, schools, and backyards, especially for motor skills such as climbing, sliding, brachiating (overhead activity), and providing props for make-believe play. These playgrounds should be supplemented with spaces for organized games, sand play, water play, construction play, and storage facilities for tools and loose parts. Natural features and materials are complementary and essential and should be available to all children. Trails, hills, water works, butterfly gardens, animal habitats, greenhouses, wetlands, gardens for growing flowers, vegetables, and herbs, etc.—all contribute to child development through work, play, aesthetic appeal, sense of wonder, and learning. Play environments should be selected or prepared with children to stimulate all the senses, promote the full range of normal play phenomena, and lend magic to the psyche and the soul. Good play environments are a matter of balance and attention to natural forms of play, not an issue for either/or arguments by adults. We can learn much about magical playgrounds by observing children and engaging them in their creation and recreation, for playgrounds are never finished (see Talbot and Frost, 1989, on magical playgrounds).

Children's found, built, formal, or designed play environments have taken many forms over the past century, evolving across time and differing by geography, the ideas of their creators, and the varied interpretations of scholarly work by professionals representing many disciplines. Here we divide natural and built play environments into periods, beginning with the "Natural or Wilderness Era" extant over centuries. This was followed by the "Manufactured Appliance Era" that evolved around the beginning of the twentieth century and continued through the "Adventure Playground Era," popular in Europe since World War II; the "Novelty Era" of the 1950s and 1960s; and the "Modern Era" of standardized playgrounds, beginning in the 1970s and 1980s (Frost, 1992). Yet another era, herein designated the "Postmodern Era," featuring a reemergence of play in nature and natural play environments or playscapes, is taking shape as this is written.

Natural Play Environments: Wilderness, Vacant Lots, Habitats, and Gardens

As America entered the industrial age and the rural families of America and immigrants from other countries flooded the large cities, Americans turned to the examples of European reformers to bring nature back to children. Froebel's German kindergarten was a model of self-active processes such as experiment, construction, discovery, and invention. His love of nature and his belief that children should have opportunities to develop freely led him to engage them in gardening and take them on frequent excursions into the countryside. His children were to grow as naturally as flowers in a garden, and the very name kindergarten or children's garden was intended to suggest children's growth in the open air with rain and sunshine. This was to happen under the guidance of an intelligent and caring gardener who interferes only when the plants need pruning or transplanting (Hill, 1942). Froebel's kindergarten was significantly different from schools emphasizing memory recitation, receptivity and quies-cence of mind and body rather than learning through self-activity, including play and nature study. His nature and garden playgrounds or grounds for play pre-dated the rise of the American play and playground movement by several decades. They provided a model that should not be overlooked by contempo-rary "back to nature" advocates who strive to re-create in city schools, parks, and neighborhoods some elements of nature and the wilderness.

Froebel's great living whole—God, nature, and humanity—was interpreted and expressed fully in the early American Froebel-based kindergartens such as the example given by the authors of the International Kindergarten Union's (IKU) Committee of Nineteen report. Generally, the proponents interpreted Froebel to mean that the child should be so treated that she will feel that what is provided for her corresponds with her own inmost nature and needs. The first thing the child was expected to learn was what she must do to become an acceptable member of the kindergarten community of fifty or more four- and five-year-olds. This meant learning the proper ways to treat comrades and the play materials. It meant being active, industrious, polite, kind, and contributing to the care of the kindergarten (ideas reminiscent of those of Maria Montessori). There were moralistic fairy stories that exemplified such virtues, and games wherein children rendered service to classmates, plants, and animals.

The educational process moved from concrete experiences (e.g., caring for plants) to representations in stories and play. For example, the teacher watched the children at the sand play table building their villages and caves, digging their wells, and tracing their roads, and opened up opportunities based on their spontaneous play. This included such matters as providing shells to substitute for holes in the sand, providing alternate colors, sizes, and types of beads for stringing, and, as skills developed, rolling balls to a particular child for eye and arm exercise. The gifts and occupations were fundamental for such activities as introducing children to vertical lines, sinking and rising objects in water, and the classification of geometric objects (IKU, 1913, pp. 146–7). The Froebel-based kindergarten was not totally free but guided by trained teachers who allowed a large degree of freedom as a base for observing (child study) and introducing increasingly complex alternatives.

The American Froebel kindergarten utilized the entire day for inculcating its values. Even the daily luncheon gave occasion for developing cleanliness, courtesy, and neatness, and the simple opening prayer and hymn for cultivating the devout spirit. The child created a spiritual environment in his play world that faithfully caricatured the greater world. The plays of the children were in part reproductions of experiences but were also opportunities for children to have experiences. As the year progressed, the classroom gradually became the embodiment of a happy, functioning community as each new experience was assimilated and interpreted through pictures and treasures collected on excursions or made by the children.

Excursions were a central component in the Froebel kindergarten, as children traced backward the sources of their food through visits to farms and bakeries, and themselves planted corn and wheat, made bread, and brought vegetables and fruit to the classroom to sort, classify, cut, draw, and paint. Exploring nature to learn about the homes of animals and the benefits of wild plants, and tending gardens to learn about the mystery and beauty of life, were fundamental experiences. The vast experiences of the children were periodically represented in simple drama with dances and choruses. Holidays and festivals were opportune times for special celebrations, national songs, stories of heroes, and summary experiences (IKU, 1913). Collectively, the school could be seen as a play school. To the casual observer, the daily activities would appear to be mere play, yet the careful or trained observer would see the deliberately guided development of pre-concepts underlying later academic subjects as well as the more obvious social and moral advantages of play and nature.

Following in the footsteps of Froebel and other lovers of nature, the early American nature movement of a century ago was addressed to getting children back to nature so they could reap its many benefits. This would help provide children in cities with the advantages available to those in rural areas. Reformers knew that the whole playground conception was fundamentally flawed without the flowers of the woods, the grass and blossoms of the fields, the waters of the brooks, the sand of the seashores, and the presence of their animal habitants. Instead, the ideal playground was seen by most, even by many designers and educators, as a barren desert of rocks and sand, equipped with paraphernalia for children's exercise. Yet even then, the ideal playground, in the minds of thinkers and observers of children, would be more nature and less city, more God and fewer policemen—a place where water runs and can be touched, where miniature beaches lap into the sand and small dams can be built, where castles are built from sticks and stones, where children can observe in awe and wonder the miniature bugs and bees and butterflies, where miniature forests provide cover for dens and forts—yet places where fairies can be found, dirt pies can be made, muscles can be tested, and the thrills of sliding and spinning and climbing can be experienced.

The school gardens movement originated in association with the nature movement of a century ago. The early school gardens were intended to foster cooperation, hard work, and civic goals, and to contribute to sound physical

Figure 7.1 Returning to natural play.
Source: Courtesy of Shutterstock Images LLC.

development, school learning, use of tools, sense of ownership, overall development, and a love of the beautiful. Necessity prompted the extensive cultivation of "Liberty Gardens" during World War I, "Depression Relief Gardens" during the Great Depression, and "Victory Gardens" during World War II. Community garden programs gained interest during the 1970s, and gardening is growing rapidly in the early twenty-first century during the economic recession. Gardening contributes to children's play, work, learning, and development in both indoor and outdoor contexts. Although nature has always played a central role in children's play and play environments, contemporary children are rapidly losing touch with the essential qualities of nature that teach, sustain, and heal, and are turning to artificial substitutes in their enforced absence from free, active, outdoor play.

Throughout the twentieth century, built playgrounds were employed as a substitute for the natural play environments of previous centuries. As nature disappeared from schools and other common play venues, built playgrounds were created to provide exercise and challenge, and to accommodate children's natural forms of play. They became increasingly popular, due in part to the limited availability of other spaces, but they squeezed out all signs of nature in far too many places. The story follows.

Manufactured Apparatus Playgrounds: Steel and Stone

The Manufactured Apparatus Era began with the erection of the first outdoor gymnasium at the Salem, Massachusetts, Latin School in 1821, and grew slowly for several decades until sand gardens were introduced into Boston play yards in 1886. Inventors and manufacturers entered the field and began producing playground equipment in volume around the turn of the twentieth century. The impetus for built playgrounds increased as major cities developed supervised, equipped playgrounds for public use in city parks and schools, and the Playground Association of America (PAA), founded in 1906, became vibrant and influential during the following decade. In 1910 the PAA published recommendations for supervised playgrounds (Playground Association of America, 1910), and playground manufacturers promised to settle playground problems "with a scheme of material appliances." Manufacturers featured iron, steel, and wood in their catalogs, advertised in the PAA journal, *The Playground,* and were credited with "rendering distinguished service as a propaganda agency in the American playground movement" (PAA, 1910, p. 272).

The PAA recommended apparatus for boys under ten years of age and girls of all ages, yet many early built playgrounds had separate playgrounds for boys and girls. The apparatus prescribed included: 1 sliding board; 2 giant strides; a sand court; 4 rope swings, 10 feet high; 2 teeter boards or teeter ladders; 4 sets of ring toss or quoits; and balls, bats, nets, bean bags, and similar materials. Most contemporary manufacturers do not manufacture, sell, or recommend portable materials or "loose parts" such as the latter materials. The area recommended was 100 × 200 feet with an average capacity of 150 to 200 children.

During this early period, play leadership was considered essential, not only for supervision but for maintenance, organization and administration.

Figure 7.2 Steel pipe playground, 1900.
Source: From the collections of the Texas/Dallas History and Archives Division, Dallas Public Library.

Such accessories as drinking fountains, toilets, seating areas, shaded areas, shelter and storage rooms, landscaping, lighting, water sprinklers, and space for maintenance equipment were recommended and actually included in many of the early city park playgrounds. Attention was given to various design elements of play equipment, such as the advantages of wood versus metal, a controversy that continues today. Contemporary safety guidelines and standards reveal major hazards in this early equipment: excessive heights, heavy moving objects with battering ram effects (e.g., animal swings, trapeze rings), shearing devices in rotating apparatus, head entrapments, and hard surfacing (e.g., concrete, asphalt, packed cinder, and hard-packed earth) under equipment (Frost, 1986b). Since no two playgrounds, built or natural, are identical, it is not possible to assign absolute values to any one type. Much of the early manufactured equipment was extremely hazardous and has been modified or deleted from playgrounds. Manufacturers have modified most early equipment designs and still distribute many types. For example, merry-go-rounds, originally open in the center, with shearing elements at the axles, now have a solid seat base and speed controllers. With careful attention to knowledgeable selection, modern equipment can serve many useful play needs. However, this equipment does not substitute for natural materials.

The first quarter of the twentieth century was one of optimism about children's play and the expansion of playgrounds, especially in large cities, and scholars were raising awareness about the value of play for child development (Lehman and Witty, 1926; Lee, 1927; Lloyd, 1931). However, there was only limited change in the design of playground apparatus before the Novelty Era of the mid-1900s. Manufacturers continued the pattern of producing traditional swings, slides, merry-go-rounds, jungle gyms, seesaws, and giant strides, with only minor design changes—ostensibly to attract customers. Modified equipment advertised in *The Playground* included a merry-go-round type device, the Medart Ocean Wave, that rocked and rotated simultaneously; a ball-bearing Flying Swing that rotated as two children swung at each end; and a Merry-Whirl swing combination of merry-go-round and swing.

Separation of playgrounds for boys and girls continued, and separate parks and playgrounds were maintained for African-American citizens. These patterns were gradually modified through the Great Depression of the 1930s. During World War II, the coeducational activities of unemployed youth and adults expanded, with sports fields sharing space with playgrounds and children's play. Play and recreation specialists were recommending smaller equipment for younger children and separate play zones to accommodate different types of equipment. After the war, when metal was again available for playground equipment, the same type of equipment manufactured before the war re-emerged and, by the 1950s, the Novelty Era was emerging.

Figure 7.3 County fair in Georgia. White children were admitted free one day, African-American children the next.
Source: Jack Delano, photographer. Courtesy of the Library of Congress, Prints and Photographs Division, FSA/OWI Collection [reproduction number, LC-USF33-021216-M2].

The Novelty Era: Dennis the Menace

The Novelty Era was the most innovative period in built playground design since the early playground movement. By the mid-1900s the "playground movement" had become essentially a recreation movement, influenced in part by the redesignation of the Playground Association of America as the National Recreation Association, and later as the National Recreation and Park Association (NRPA). At each stage the organization shifted emphasis to broader goals and broader activities. Children's play became an adjunct to recreation for all ages, and children's playgrounds to multiple facilities and environments for recreation, with an emphasis on a wide range of sports. (The NRPA has once again begun to place greater emphasis on children's play.) Despite these changes, 1950s and 1960s designers, handymen, architects, artists, and manufacturers began to notice children's needs and the potential economic benefits of playgrounds and playground equipment, and new designs captured the fancy of play advocates. Physical fitness, aesthetic qualities, and manufacturability motives were clearly emphasized over child development concerns despite the

Figure 7.4 The novelty era featured historic structures, art objects, and animal and space age devices.
Source: Author.

avalanche of new, imaginative designs (Musselman 1950, 1956; Shaw and Davenport, 1956).

The advocates of novelty or fantasy playgrounds substituted more appealing structures for the standard municipal playgrounds featuring paved surfaces, fences, and the classic steel appliances—slides, swings, sand, and jungle gyms— and to compensate for the amusement park concept of "amusement for amusement's sake" (Nichols, 1955). The Museum of Modern Art, *Parents Magazine*, and Creative Playthings sponsored a national competition for play sculptures intended to capture children's imagination (National Recreation Association, 1954). The criteria for judging the entries were play value, aesthetic quality, safety, and manufacturability. A New York City painter captured first place and a prize of $1,000 with square, block houses, five feet tall, with windows, ladders, climbing ropes, peek holes, and an attractive color scheme.

The structures entered in this competition and many featured in novelty playgrounds were fixed, concrete formations, abstract, resistant to change, movement, or action by children. These presumed worthy motives were frequently more appealing to adults than to children (Frost and Wortham, 1988; Frost, 1992). I visited parks in two major cities featuring the playground sculptures of a recognized national architect and an internationally recognized artist. The architecturally designed playground was an arena of rock and concrete pyramid-shaped domes supplemented with massive, relatively fixed vertical timbers.

The artist-designed one included a climbing tower with a spiral slide, several additional slides, swings, fixed cubes, and geometric, artistic structures set in a city park. When we arrived at this latter site, we saw no children playing on the equipment or sculptures but heard children in the surrounding woodlands, and found them sliding down a hillside on cardboard boxes!

The advocates of novelty playgrounds acknowledged the existence of nursery school playgrounds, and praised their spontaneity and interesting materials, typically created from a child development perspective. They claimed that the modern "foxholes" and "air raid shelters" of the "sculptural" playground would not have been possible in the early 1900s when the nursery play yard emerged, but agreed that all the common types of playgrounds contributed to the intellectual, social, and leisure needs of children (Nichols, 1955). From the beginning, playground designers represented many disciplines or professions and worked from the perspectives of their disciplines or crafts rather than observation of children at play or research about children's play.

During the Novelty Era, many cities joined the trend toward more imaginative playgrounds, many related to historic events in history such as the Wild West, and various scientific achievements such as the launching of Sputnik. Stagecoaches and rockets were depicted with the expectation of enhancing children's learning, interest, and imagination. The novelty trend spread around the country; Philadelphia's recreation department developed sixty playgrounds, parks and squares, tailoring each playground to the presumed needs of the community (Crawford, 1956; National Recreation Association, 1959). These included streets closed off for playgrounds (play streets), toy lending, theme equipment for imaginative or make-believe play, and sculptures intended to be used as play equipment. The City of San Mateo, California, transformed a drab playground into a bright happy one by installing a multicolored sand box, colorful concrete culverts, a red and blue drinking fountain, and an equipment hut decorated with a painted-on carousel with nursery rhyme characters, all "filled with youngsters" (Shaw and Davenport, 1956). This was all done to stimulate children to associate with their "dream world thoughts."

That was just the beginning, as many other cities followed this pattern of appealing to the imaginative instincts of children at play. The Los Angeles Parks Department designed, built, tested, and implemented novel slides, western theme villages, multiple function exercise equipment, and shark and octopus rockers (Frederickson, 1959). Hank Ketchum, the creator of "Dennis the Menace" cartoons, designed a "Dennis the Menace" playground for the City of Monterey, California (National Recreation Association, 1957). The East Orange, New Jersey, Recreation Commission installed two fourteen-foot cabin cruisers on a playground, added a lighthouse, built a jetty and dock from telephone poles, and used sand to create a "nautical playground" (National Recreation Association, 1958). By the mid-1960s rocket play structures inspired by Sputnik were springing up around the country (National Recreation Association, 1960), and play manufacturers were predicting a rosy future for the playground industry (National Recreation Association, 1962).

These predictions turned out to be surprisingly accurate. Two decades later (Frost, 1989, 1992), action oriented equipment was a chief priority; steel was the primary material for exercise-play equipment; plastic was replacing steel in play sculptures (animal figures, etc.) and was being used as molding over steel frames to add color, comfort, and protection from the sun; traditional swing seats were increasingly replaced with sculptured animal figures; equipment was lower in height and designed to accommodate various age groups; tanbark and other resilient materials were added under and around equipment in a growing number of playgrounds. The popularity of these changes was predicted accurately, but manufacturers failed to predict the popularity of wood equipment, the hazards of heavy, animal sculpture swings, the injuries inflicted by novel rotating mechanisms, and the widespread reluctance of manufacturers and consumers to provide resilient safety material under equipment or the reluctance of consumers to maintain it. By the mid-1960s complex climbing structures combining various play options or events were beginning to become available, but these were relatively simple compared to the adventure playgrounds that emerged in Europe during World War II and the huge, multifunction, linked super-structures and accompanying play devices that would emerge during the Modern Era.

Adventure Playgrounds: Tools, Pets, Junk, Loose Parts, and Gardens

Long before World War II, city children were playing in vacant lots and construction sites, garbage dumps, and junk heaps. They sorted the building materials from the junk, borrowed tools and loose parts wherever they could find them, created their own special forts and houses, and laid siege to rival gangs with shields of garbage can lids and swords of slats from orange crates. Abandoned cars became castles and palaces, caves and tunnels were dug, and food would be roasted over bonfires. In the evening, parents would have to drag their children home (Frost and Klein, 1979). Some enterprising individuals noticed the freedom that children enjoyed, the intensity of children in their creative play in nature, and began to question the efficacy of substituting manufactured appliance playgrounds for such creative enterprise. One such individual, Professor C. Th. Sorensen, a Danish landscape architect, would capture the attention of play advocates around the world with his conception of "junk playgrounds."

During the war, many European cities were under constant attack and entire city blocks were reduced to rubble, the common stuff of city children's creative playgrounds. Children played their games of war among this devastation, using selected bits of rubble for their guns, vehicles, fox holes, ships, airplanes— whatever was needed to defeat the enemy and to release the pent up trauma of constant stress. Construction areas were also common sites for such play, and were regarded by children and some adults as superior to traditional iron and steel equipment fixed in the ground. Sorensen, who had designed many playgrounds, noticed that children enjoyed playing on bombed out sites and construction sites more than on finished playgrounds. They played more creatively and for longer periods of time than with the equipment made for them. This observation led to the establishment of the first "junk" or "waste" playground near a public housing project in Emdrup, Denmark, in 1943, during the German occupation. The name "adventure playground" came later (Bengtsson, 1972; Frost and Klein, 1979; Frost, 1992).

Lady Allen of Hurtwood introduced the junk playground concept in the U.K., coined the name "adventure playground," and created several adventure playgrounds for "handicapped" children. These playgrounds had provisions for all children, whatever the disability, to have specially designed carts or wheelchairs to move about the playground. The play structures or natural play areas were also specially designed for them. One such provision is seen in Figure 7.5d. The water area, like other provisions, was appropriate for wheeled vehicle travel. Years would pass before adventure playgrounds spread widely to other European countries, Asia, and the United States. Their history in America has been perilous at best, having never gained solid acceptance, but their promise is so great that no account of the history of play and playgrounds would be complete without calling them back, over and over again, to both doubting and dedicated readers. At the time of writing in 2009, signals once again indicate growing interest in their re-emergence.

Adventure playgrounds were not the invention of one individual, and indeed their growth and acceptance in several countries can be traced to the efforts of many individuals and groups of people concerned about the welfare of children. Mainly, children themselves were the discoverers or creators, for they had found and created playgrounds from junk for centuries. As seen throughout this book, the forms of play and the stuff of play that made adventure playgrounds such special places for children were created by children long before an individual "discovered them." Well before adventure playgrounds were established, adults who were sensitive to children's play needs had been observers of children's play and supported their drives for creative play with malleable materials, but Sorensen went well beyond the usual efforts in his aim to "give children in towns the same chance for creative play as those in the country" (Sorensen, 1968). In 1931 Sorensen wrote the following:

> Perhaps we should try to set up waste material playgrounds in suitable large areas where children would be able to play with old cars, boxes and timber. It is possible there would have to be some supervision to prevent children fighting too wildly and to lessen the chances of

injury but it is likely that such supervision will not be necessary. (Sorensen, 1968)

If adults had bothered to ask children or simply watch them play, they would have helped create and value adventure playgrounds long before the Emdrup experience.

The Emdrup playground took form under the leadership of architect Dan Fink and a nursery school teacher and ex-seaman, John Bertelsen, the first play leader. Soon people were flocking to see this first adventure playground, and such playgrounds were beginning to be established in other areas of Denmark. Lady Allen of Hurtwood visited Emdrup just after the war in 1945 and set up several junk or adventure playgrounds in bombed out sections of London. Trails led to all the special play areas and components, allowing children with various abilities or disabilities to access and play in and with all the elements on the playground (personal observations). Later, the concept spread to other European countries and to the United States.

As the adventure playground concept spread, they began to be recognized as places where children could mold and shape their own play environments, using junk, scrap material, and tools. Play leaders were employed, scrap materials and tools were solicited from industry and individuals, and children had alternatives to fixed, un-malleable play environments. The London Adventure Playground Association (Jago, 1971) offered this description:

> An adventure playground can best be described as a place where children are free to do many things that they cannot easily do elsewhere in our crowded urban society. In an adventure playground, which can be any size from one third of an acre to two and a half acres, they can build houses, dens and climbing structures with waste materials, have bonfires, cook in the open, dig holes, garden, or just play with sand, water and clay. The atmosphere is permissive and free, and this is especially attractive to children whose lives are otherwise much limited and restricted by lack of space and opportunity. (Jago, 1971)

One of the early play leaders, Jack Lambert, worked as a play leader in several Danish adventure playgrounds and understood, as few adults do, the differences in the views of the architects who design playgrounds and the children whom they intend to play on them. His delightful story of the development of a modern housing estate reveals how architects noticed that children were always playing with the building materials, so they decided to build them a playground. After failed attempts at planning the playground, they decided to ask the children how it should be designed. But after more attempts the architects were still unhappy, for the children had many more ideas than the architects themselves. Eventually they decided to give children the tools and scrap materials and let them build the new playground themselves. In this manner, they could see what the children really wanted, then build it properly. So the architects sat down, watched, and waited—and waited. After a quarter century, the playground was still not finished and the architects were still waiting in case one day it might be finished and they would know what the children really wanted (Lambert and Pearson, 1974, p. 9). Most Americans have never seen an adventure playground or observed children at play on one. Consequently, they have little basis on which to judge their value. Children are often better judges of good places to play than are adults. Trained playworkers engage children in making decisions about what is to be built and what is to be played. Lambert carried his philosophy and experiences to the U.K. and then to the United States, where he expressed to me his consternation that Americans had made virtually no progress in embracing and spreading the adventure play movement that had met with moderate success in several European countries.

What did Lambert believe was the perceived problem with adventure playgrounds that hindered their acceptance? Basically, his answer reflects on the limitations of adult sensibility about the way *they* should provide for children's play. Committees, councils, designers, and manufacturers scratch their heads in puzzlement about what facilities and equipment would be best for children. Swings? Climbers? Merry-go-rounds? They plan, design, purchase, and build for children elaborate made-to-order playgrounds, cut the entrance ribbon, and wait for children to be amused. Children rush to their new toys and all the adults are delighted, until they see children returning to the streets to play or dragging loose materials to the designed site so they can create for themselves. Why not, Lambert asked, provide a space—a vacant lot, part of an existing playground, corners of garden plots, pieces of parks, in woodlands? He asked good questions. Why not let children learn to use tools, create from natural materials and scrap, learn to cook over open fires, tend animals and gardens, build dens and forts, find and enjoy secret places, play in the water and sand—just imagine, create, build, enjoy? These are among the magical activities that appeal to children, build skills, and enhance development.

From the beginning, adventure playgrounds depended in no small degree on the presence of trained play leaders. Given the nature of the play leadership or "supervision" that children were accustomed to, the presence of an adult "leader" was initially seen as intrusion into how they should play. So at first the informed or "trained" play leader might sit alone drinking tea, allowing the children to initiate contact and then, as they learn that the leader has some knowledge of building, entice him to join in their constructions. The leader does not need to tell children to build, for they simply need the opportunity, the tools, and the materials. Building was Lambert's entry into the children's world, for in every playground where he served this was the central point of communication. The first play leader at Emdrup, John Bertelson, learned this lesson early—children are sovereign and the initiative must come from them.

Figure 7.5a Children's willow den in the Old Quarry Adventure Playground, Knottingley, U.K.
Source: Courtesy of the Old Quarry Management Committee.
Figure 7.5b Children playing and tending fires at Hanegi Adventure Play Park, Tokyo, Japan.
Source: Courtesy of Tim Gill, photographer.
Figure 7.5c Working with play leaders or playworkers, children in Copenhagen create villages and streets with gardens, animal hutches, play materials, and tools.
Source: Author.
Figure 7.5d Children playing in water at a specially designed Lady Allen of Hurtwood adventure playground for children of all abilities in London.
Source: Camilla Jessel Panufnik, Fellow of the Royal Photographic Society, photographer.

The roles of play leaders, now called "playworkers" in Europe, have been quite different from those of contemporary schoolteachers and park personnel since the inception of formal training programs for leaders at adventure playgrounds:

- supporting play in unrestrictive settings;
- refereeing when conditions warrant;
- being friends but maintaining order;
- ensuring that the playground is well equipped with tools and materials;
- attracting volunteers to assist on the playground;
- allowing children to pursue their own play agendas;
- introducing flexibility and adaptability;
- teaching skills when asked;
- talking to children whenever needed;
- making suggestions without demanding.

(Adapted from Allen, 1968; Nicholson, 1971; Bengtsson, 1972; Benjamin, 1974; Frost and Klein, 1979; Lambert, 1992)

In 1979, after visiting adventure playgrounds in several European countries, I concluded that the concept should be adopted in the United States and set about working toward that end by incorporating many adventure play ideas into school and child care center playgrounds, serving on the board of the Houston Adventure Playground Association, and corresponding with Bill Vance, founder of the American Adventure Playground Association. Because of the effects of national safety guidelines first published in 1981, potential lawsuits, and a widespread belief among parents and school administrators that such playgrounds were messy and hazardous, the adventure play idea was largely abandoned in the United States. Now, early in the twenty-first century, there is a groundswell of opinion aimed at bringing adventure concepts and nature back to playgrounds. This is a welcome change of direction, for the best adventure playgrounds of Europe are much more developmentally appropriate than playgrounds stocked only with a standard superstructure and swings.

Adventure playgrounds have continued to be popular in many areas of Europe. By the turn of the twenty-first century, they had diminished to near oblivion in the United States except for vestiges that proponents managed to fit into more conventional designs. In general, they never flourished because of objections to their junky, untidy appearance, the emergence of national playground safety standards, unsubstantiated claims that they were hazardous, and a failure to understand their value for children's play. In April 1976 the American Adventure Playground Association (AAPA) was formed by park and recreation professionals, educators, and commissioners in southern California, with Bill Vance as president. By May 1977 the AAPA identified sixteen adventure playgrounds in the United States, but an undetermined number were not identified in Pennsylvania, New York, California, Texas, and Georgia. Many of these emphasized children building with scrounged and natural materials but lacked trained play leaders. The AAPA disappeared within a decade, but other groups continued to sponsor sites (Frost, 1992).

One such group developed a demonstration adventure playground in 1979 at Mountain Park in Houston, Texas. The playground was located on eight acres and featured a garden and nature center, storage areas, animal habitats, a sand and water center, an arts and craft area, a picnic area, an office area, and a courts and games area. The play leaders/program leaders received three months of training, and facilitators received a one-week orientation. The staff concluded that: "There probably has never been a playground as professionally staffed as the Mountain Park Adventure Playground" (Sarahan and Hager, 1980, p. 100). The staff included educators with master's degrees, professional actors, artists, special educators, bilingual educators, and environmental educators. However, the organizers were not satisfied with mere credentials. Ongoing training was required of all staff members to help meet the goals of the program. Within four months of opening, about 15,000 people had used Mountain Park but, despite its success with parents and children, the Mountain Park experience endured for only a few years (Frost, 1992).

The spirit survived and the Mountain Park group reorganized as the Houston Adventure Playground Association (HAPA), which established two new adventure playgrounds in 1986, one at Mark Twain Elementary School and the other at Freed Park in Houston. These functioned until lack of funding, safety concerns, and general malaise led to their dissolution in about 2002. The children at these sites were "latch key children," with reduced opportunities to develop positive social and problem solving skills, and with special needs for adult guidance. Surveys and standardized tests revealed that parents and teachers supported the program, children's aggressive behavior was reduced, problem solving opportunities increased, and children made significant gains in social responsibility and social problem solving (Mauldin and Giles, 1989).

The most revealing opinions about the worth of the HAPA playgrounds were those of children and their parents.

> What I liked best about it was that everybody got to do what they wanted to do. There was something for everybody ... we did not have to stand in line. (B. M.)

> My favorite part was the carpentry because I built an airplane a little longer than my arm and it weighed three pounds. My next favorite thing was playing with that big ball. I had the best time of [my] life, funnier than Astroworld. (K. F.)

The following comments were from a parent and a teacher:

> Somebody should have thought of this years ago. Wonderful experience for urban children, fabulous experience for children of all ages. (S. B.)

Thousands of children in our city lack the opportunity to discover what is possible for them to do, to know what reality permits and what it prohibits. Kids everywhere need to experiment, to build and tear down, to find out what works and what doesn't, to plan and discover, to predict and be surprised, to copy and try something new, to succeed and fail; and then try again. Jumping and running, hammering and sawing, climbing over and under, singing and performing, working in groups and going it alone, helping and receiving help, tasting disappointment and knowing joy, these are the tasks of childhood. (J. E. C.)

Until recently, children in the country enjoyed the advantages of adventure playgrounds in their everyday play lives. Traffic was rarely a danger. There were trees to climb, dense bushes to create hiding places and forts, woods for exploring, fires to be made for cooking, animals to be chased, and tree houses to be built. Raw materials for tools and building dens and forts were everywhere. Rivers, creeks, and ponds were available for swimming and fishing, and adults working in the fields and hunting in the woods were frequently available for advice and models. But all this changed as country kids joined their city peers in the mass exodus to indoor cyber worlds. The "Modern Era" of standardized playgrounds, designed and manufactured to meet national safety standards, and generally devoid of the natural advantages of adventure playgrounds, trumped virtually all other choices, including adventure playgrounds.

The Modern Era: Standardized Playgrounds

During the 1970s and 1980s most public park and public school playgrounds in America continued to perpetuate decades-old designs—hazardous and ill suited for the broad developmental play needs of children. The public school designs had multiple hazards and were suited primarily for exercise or motor play. Public park playgrounds followed essentially the same pattern as those of the public schools—collections of swings, seesaws, jungle gyms, and merry-go-rounds—with little thought for materials and spaces to accommodate symbolic or imaginative play, play with natural materials, or constructive play. Overall, they were light years away from the developmentally focused playgrounds of America's best child development centers. These differences can be attributed to the pioneering leadership of professionals grounded in principles of play and child development traceable, in part, back to the early tenets and ideas of Froebel and Dewey inspired schools.

The first national surveys of playgrounds, sponsored by the American Association for Leisure and Recreation and conducted during the late 1980s, confirmed the above conclusions. Public school playgrounds were described by the investigators as a "national disgrace" (Bruya and Langendorfer, 1988). Park playgrounds were hazardous and ill suited for children's developmental needs (Thompson and Bowers, 1989). Although deficient overall in provision for the broad play needs of children, preschool playgrounds were generally safer and more developmentally appropriate than those of public schools and parks (Wortham and Frost, 1990). However, among all the preschool playgrounds surveyed, the "worst of the lot are accidents waiting to happen, sterile in play value, and essentially unfit for children's play" (Frost et al., 1990, p. 91).

By the beginning of the 1970s the generally unsafe, developmentally sterile school, park, and preschool spaces serving as children's playgrounds were leading designers to reconsider their novel, imaginative play structures, and manufacturers to rethink their manufactured steel appliance equipment. In rapid succession, modular wood equipment featuring multiple decks and play options was designed and made available by manufacturers, including Columbia Cascade, Big Toys, Landscape Structures, Mexico Forge, GameTime, and Iron Mountain Forge, and rapidly spread to other manufacturers. From this period to the present time, many of the equipment innovations resulted from one manufacturer observing the innovations of a competitor and creating a device of similar appearance, function, and appeal. The Annual Conference of the National Recreation and Park Association (NRPA) features play equipment exhibits by many companies and is perhaps the largest and most popular venue for viewing new designs and for sharing ideas among manufacturers, city park personnel, playground consultants and designers, and many others interested in children's built playgrounds. The NRPA is in a unique leadership position for the present century because of its long-term emphasis on play, recreation, and built and natural environments.

During the 1980s modular designs, composite units, and super-structures became ever more popular and began to mushroom in size, expense, play function, and popularity. Jay Beckwith was an inventor of post-deck-attached play structures featuring modular equipment and linkages of play events that allow continuous movement by active children. "Designs in this format were emerging as the new standard for playground equipment, replacing traditional swings, slides and climbers that have remained unchanged for the last half-century" (Beckwith, 1985, p. 209). Beckwith pointed out the need for creative play experiences and listed the qualities that good playgrounds should exhibit: complexity, linkage, social function, flexibility, challenge, developmental challenges, durability, and safety. By this time, growing interest in children's play and play environments, and the realization that children were losing something very vital in their play lives, was leading to a surge in productivity among students of play.

The growing interest of scholars and students of play in the United States and other countries led to an International Conference on Play and Play Environments at the University of Texas in 1983. This was reputed to be the largest group of play scholars ever convened. Keynote addresses, group presentations, and tours of play environments were featured. Prominent playground designers among the attendees prepared plans in advance and the participants spent two days creating a playground from junk that endured for several years before succumbing to the threat of safety standards and lawsuits. The conference was sponsored by fourteen state, national, and international professional organizations, and attracted the maximum 500 participants representing the United States, Republic of China, Denmark, the Philippines, England, Greece, Canada, Korea, Mexico, Germany, Australia, and Japan. The speakers and authors of the proceedings included Joe Frost, Director, Sue Wortham, Co-Director, Greta Fein, Brian Sutton-Smith, Celia Genishi, John Galvan, Margaret Garza, Sandy Briley, Stuart Reifel, Betty Beeson, Ann Williams, Tony Simon, Peter Smith, Shu-Fang Lo Chia, Catherine Cooper, Deborah Edward, Teresita Aguilar, Sheila Campbell, Eric Strickland, Heather Naylor, Lawrence Bruya, Connie Steele, Marjorie Nauman, Suzanne Winter, Michael Bell, Pauline Walker, Michael Henniger, Gwen Myers, Jacqueline Myers, Gary Moore, Marian Monroe, Jens Pedersen, Jay Beckwith, Paul Hogan, Ellen Church, James Talbot, Nancy Dill, Sharon Teets, Charles Wolfgang, Steven Silvern, Peter Williamson, Terry Countermine, David Fernie, Carol Woodard, Elizabeth Hrncir, Robert Collier, Cynthia Wade, V. T. Gershner, L. Moore, Francine Nichols, Tim Nicosia, Michael Willoughby, Barbara Hatcher, Judy Nicosia, Betty Wagner, Thomas Yawkey, and Margaret Yawkey. These speakers and authors published papers in the Conference Proceedings (Frost and Sunderlin, 1985). During this conference, plans were laid to formalize the bylaws and board of directors of the U.S. affiliate of the International Association for the Child's Right to Play and hold the first election of officers. The organization is now the American Association for the Child's Right to Play (IPA/USA).

The addresses at this conference served as a summary of the state of play and play environments in 1983. Play was historically viewed as wasteful and harmful, or frivolous and unimportant—but allowed for the pleasure it gave children. Only a few scholars over the centuries had given play its due credit, and some historical theories—cathartic, repetitive compulsion, and surplus energy—were ways of excluding children from the richer dimensions of play, thus saying that play is unimportant. By the time of this conference, scholars were recognizing play as the central social, intellectual, and cultural activity of infancy and the preschool years. Froebel, Huizinga, Caillois, and others had explored the philosophical, social, and cultural dimensions of play, but it was left to such scholars as the incomparable Piaget to focus on play's significance for intellectual development and set the stage for twentieth century scholarly interest. Brian Sutton-Smith continued to offer unparalleled depth and breadth to our understanding of children's play. Yet, despite growing interest by scholars, Americans generally disregarded play, allowing sports, "basics," and misunderstanding of play to leave most public schools and other venues a wasteland for play and play environments—eventually preparing the way for a new era of play environments centered on child development, the natural play tendencies of children, and getting children back to nature.

The Postmodern Era of Play Environments: Back to Nature

Growing interest in preserving the planet and getting children back to nature, spurred by Al Gore's book *An Inconvenient Truth* (2006) and his Academy Award winning documentary by the same title, and Richard Louv's bestselling book *Last Child In the Woods* (2005, 2008), stimulated new nature programs nationwide. The Children and Nature Network is reconnecting children with outdoor play and nature. In just a few months during 2007, state and regional campaigns started in at least twenty-two cities and several states. Slogans and groups such as "Leave No Child Inside" and "Life's Better Outside" are bringing like-minded people together from many disciplines to develop nature initiatives, provide news and research, and institute outdoor play and nature programs for children. In April 2007 the states of Washington and New Mexico signed "No Child Left Inside" (NCLI) Initiatives into law and California legislation was in progress. These initiatives were designed to promote the development of natural play and learning environments and to ensure children got time for outdoor play in nature. The No Child Left Inside Act, sponsored by a broad coalition representing environmental, educational, and public health organizations, was approved by the U.S. House of Representatives on September 18, 2008. The National Wildlife Federation sponsors training for integrating wildscapes and gardens into outdoor classrooms and playgrounds and operates a nationwide certification program for schoolyard habitats. Information about such programs and those to follow is readily accessible on the Internet by entering the name of the organization and following the cues.

A number of authors speak to the value of integrating habitats, gardens, wild places, and nature areas into schools, neighborhoods, and cityscapes (Frost and Klein, 1979; McKibben, 1989; Nabhan and Trimble, 1994; Rivkin, 1995; Moore and Wong, 1997; Stine, 1997; Hart, 1997; Frost et al., 2004; Kellert, 2005; Louv, 2005; Spencer and Blades, 2006; Tai et al., 2006; Goodenough, 2007, 2008; Frost et al., 2008;). Such works rekindle our attachment to nature and alert us to its value and rapid destruction. These authors help us understand what detachment from nature is doing to children and compel us to unplug our kids and let them again roam the wild places. In *The Ecologist*, Gill (2005) observed: "children are disappearing from the outdoors at a rate that would make the top of any conservationist's list of endangered species if they were any other member of the animal kingdom." A decade ago, speaking about effects of the destruction of nature and the importance of children's participation in sustainable development, Hart (1997, p. 3) wrote: "people's relationship to nature is the greatest issue facing the world at the turn of the century." Let us pray and work to ensure that the damage we have already done to nature will not be its final kick in the

Figure 7.6 Mt Greenwood Playground, Chicago, a boundless intergenerational playground for all children, including those with disabilities.
Source: Photo courtesy of Tom Norquist, Gametime.

pants, as McKibben's *The End of Nature* (1989) warns; let us pursue a course to remedy the environmental ills and human errors that have brought us to this place in history.

City kids in confined schools and neighborhoods, especially those in slums and barrios, cannot be taken to the wilderness regularly, but thoughtful, innovative adults can bring exciting chunks of nature to city schools, neighborhoods, and parks. Some playground planners are doing just that by helping child care centers, parks, and schools rebuild their stark, fixed parks and playgrounds and integrating nature into limited spaces. Over a ten-year period,

Table 7.1 Mt Greenwood Playground, Chicago, Illinois

This special playground was a Boundless Playgrounds project in cooperation with local and national donors. Provisions are made for all children and designed to meet national regulations for access and playability. Features include:
- expansive swings in both the preschool and school age areas that include adaptive seats in both areas to meet the needs of all children
- ramp accessible 2–5 play area in lower left-hand side of photo
- water sprayground in lower right-hand side of photo
- custom musical instruments provided by a local artist
- mosaic decorated columns, "modern totem poles"
- elevated hill covered in soft surface poured in place with custom mounds
- hillside slide
- universal climber
- ramp accessible 5–12 play area with integrated "hybrid" Xscape fitness based equipment
- beautiful large shade trees and green areas
- many tables and benches throughout for family picnics and gatherings
- large accessible parking area nearby to help all users into park area

Moore and Wong (1997) transformed an asphalt schoolyard playground into a naturalized environment or "environmental yard." Their research and work with children are a profound expression of the value of play and natural habitats and a powerful example of qualitative research. Numerous other professionals (Rivkin, 1995; Stine, 1997; Burriss and Boyd, 2005; Greenman, 2005; Spencer and Blades, 2006; Keeler, 2008) are lending their research and experience in transforming sterile, fixed playgrounds into integrated play yards featuring materials and natural environments that accommodate a wide range of developmental needs.

The University of Texas Play and Playgrounds Research Project (Frost et al., 2004, 2008, 2009 in press) operated continuously at Redeemer Lutheran School in Austin, Texas, since 1973. This research site features three play environments with both manufactured and contrived equipment to accommodate various forms and levels of play, games, vegetable and herb gardens, butterfly gardens, gazebos, greenhouses, and animal habitats. The butterfly garden was certified as a "Schoolyard Habitat" by the National Wildlife Federation. The overall environment is a science laboratory, a place for relaxation and reflection, a challenging playground for a wide range of children's play, and a site for scholarly research by university students and professors. The most popular natural area is a half-acre wetlands created from a retention pond extensively refashioned to become a wilderness wonderland. One of the children affectionately dubbed it "the land down under," a name that has been adopted by the entire school. In the Redeemer playscapes and wildscapes, spontaneous play and hands-on work blend into one integrated, outdoor compendium of physical, social, and intellectual activity with all the accompanying fun and learning. Recess and physical education are available every day, and the cafeteria features a salad bar and organic food, some from the school gardens. The overweight/obesity rate is very low at this school, in a state where the overall rate is 19 percent (Frost et al., 2004; Frost, 2008b; Frost et al., 2009, in press).

There are both likenesses and differences in the developmental values of typical built play environments, schoolyard habitats or gardens, and natural playscapes. Studying and working in natural environments are complementary to the physical activities of playing in play yards. Children need both nature study and free, spontaneous play on physically challenging play spaces and equipment. Schoolyard gardening and nature study provide healthy physical activity and build knowledge. Playground apparatus builds skills in hanging from overhead apparatus, swinging, running, sliding, chasing, throwing, catching, climbing, and playing traditional games, not readily available in most school gardens and nature areas. Both natural and built play areas are needed for the fitness and healthy development of children.

Creating play environments that mirror children's natural play tendencies and enhance their broad developmental needs involves selecting from the many material options—natural and built—to form integrated play yards. The initial step is studying the developmental forms of play that evolve as children experience and mature. Next, the materials for play—natural and built—are selected to complement these play forms: toys, rattles, bells, mobiles, etc., for the sensorimotor play of infants; grasping toys, blocks, push-pull toys, textured materials, etc., for the object play of toddlers. Preschool and school-age children differ widely in their play needs. Taking into account such differences, they need composite structures, slides, swings, climbers, overhead apparatus, balancing units (natural and built) for exercise/gross-motor play; play houses, wheeled vehicles, vehicle tracks, sand, water, loose parts, etc., for make-believe or symbolic play; tools, scrap lumber, blocks, sand, water, etc., for construction play; balls, nets, goals, grassy fields, paved areas, etc., for organized games; storage on all playgrounds to accommodate the wide range of loose parts or portable materials needed for all forms of play. All this, integrated with animal habitats, gardens, greenhouses, natural hills, and ever-changing natural vegetation, will result in rich, vibrant play environments for play, work, and learning.

City farms, sometimes integrated with adventure playgrounds, are growing in popularity in many regions of the world. The European Federation of City Farms promotes environmental and agricultural projects where children and adults work, play, and learn about the natural environment and its interrelationship with plants and animals (Ginsberg, 2000). The city farms movement started in the 1970s and resulted from the desire of people all over Europe to counter the alienation of people from nature. Presently, there are eight city farm federations in Europe, and they are spreading around the world. The gardening movement is expanding in America, with community gardens spreading and home and school gardens becoming more popular, partly because of rapidly rising food prices but also due to concern about the potential health consequences of processed food and additives, and the need for children to develop the social, emotional, intellectual, and physical skills resulting from gardening. Fortunately, gardens do not require extensive spaces and can be integrated into schoolyards, playgrounds, backyards, vacant lots, and city parks.

During the late twentieth century the nature of children's play evolved from free, spontaneous, self-chosen outdoor activity in natural and found environments to directed recess play on manufactured play equipment and adult led games and indoor technology play. Beginning early in the twenty-first century, pressures built for a return to free, outdoor play and play and learning in nature. This circular pattern, unlike any ever before seen, evolved during the short time span of a few decades.

The arrival of the twenty-first century brought with it an awakening to the effects of twentieth century change on the security of the natural planet and the well-being of children. Scientists everywhere acknowledge that the natural ecology is disintegrating at an ever more rapid rate, due to the excesses of its human residents. Many of these same forces are impacting children's play and playscapes, resulting in deprivation of traditional forms of play and natural grounds for play. The benefits of play and the consequences of play deprivation are elaborated in the next chapter, and the growing movement for remedial programs in the final chapter.

8

The Value of Play and the Consequences of Play Deprivation

Play for young children is not recreation activity ... It is not leisure-time activity nor escape activity ... Play is thinking time for young children. It is language time, problem solving time. It is memory time, learning time, investigating time. It is organization of ideas time, when the young child uses his mind and body and his social skills and all his powers in response to the stimuli he has met. (James L. Hymes, Jr., from an unpublished paper)

Life without play is a grinding, mechanical existence organized around doing the things necessary for survival. Play is the stick that stirs the drink. It is the basis of all art, games, books, sports, movies, fashion, fun, and wonder—in short, the basis of what we think of as civilization. Play is the vital essence of life. It is what makes life lively. (Stuart Brown with Vaughan, 2009, pp. 11–12)

For centuries, children's play was free, self-chosen, and characterized by creation, imagination, and intense emotional involvement. The outdoors was its stage—the ultimate playground. Playgrounds for rural children were the wild places of the countryside and, for children in towns and cities, the lots, streets, and surrounding countryside. During the last quarter decade of the twentieth century, outdoor play, playgrounds, and recess began to fall out of favor in the schools and neighborhoods of America and were replaced by sedentary, indoor cyber play and organized sports. Fast on the heels of declining outdoor play came declining fitness, obesity, and unprecedented consequences for children's health and fitness. Since then, the tempo of change has increased and new obstacles have emerged to bring about the diminution of traditional outdoor play. By the turn of the twenty-first century, the consequences of play deprivation for children's health and fitness had reached a crisis stage. Advocates for children were awakening to the need for something to be done to counter the prevailing view that play is frivolous, inconsequential, and purely for fun. The accelerating threats led to research and dialogue intended to inform the nation about the developmental values of play and the consequences of play deprivation.

The rapid diminution of traditional play and play environments, coupled with poor nutrition, obesity, and associated disease, are potentially more damaging for American children than any other crisis in our history—medical or natural. How did we arrive so quickly at such a state of mediocrity in children's play? Why are play and play environments valuable for children's development? What are the consequences of not playing, and what can be done about it?

The Rush to Distinction and Mediocrity

When World War II ended, Americans began to rebuild their lives, but work, travel, and cultural experiences had forever changed and broadened their world perspectives, and most would never be the same again. Technological advances resulting from waging war also resulted in new manufacturing techniques, new views of entertainment, and greater comfort in everyday living. Before long, the Cold War emerged, the Space Race followed, and an emerging technology revolution brought an unprecedented standard of living. The rapid changes revolutionized home conveniences, transportation, communications, industry, education, and politics, and the fallout found its way to children's play and playgrounds.

During the final three decades of the twentieth century, centuries-old outdoor play and traditional games began to change, a process that accelerated in the twenty-first century. Manufactured toys replaced toys created from scrap and found materials; computer play, video games, cellphones, and an unprecedented array of sedentary, indoor high-tech games and cyber playgrounds supplanted spontaneous outdoor play and games in natural and built playgrounds. By the turn of the twenty-first century, impediments to traditional play had accelerated in scope and consequences. Constant media bombardment warned paranoid parents about the dangers of children playing in the streets, vacant lots, and other neighborhood venues, so children were instructed to stay indoors. Children were happy campers, preferring to play with their cyber toys near the indoor electrical outlets and the refrigerator well stocked with junk food. The diminution of outdoor active play at home was rivaled in scope and consequences by the reduction of play and physical activity at school, as time-honored recess fell out of favor and physical education became optional. The reasons for this are discussed in detail in this chapter.

Throughout America's history, children in both city and country schools enjoyed the reality of minor bruises and "skinned-knees recesses," typically mid-morning and mid-afternoon, usually extended by a long period for lunch. In 1989 a survey by the National Association of Elementary School Principals found that 96 percent of school systems still had at least one recess period, but another survey a decade later found that only 70 percent of kindergarten classrooms, which historically emphasized play as a foundation of education, had a recess period. In 2006 the International Play Association/USA reported that

40 percent of American public schools had either deleted or were considering reducing recess. Forty thousand schools no longer have recess (Marano, 2008). In yet another study of more than 11,000 children, lead researcher Romina Barros (2009) of Albert Einstein College of Medicine and colleagues found that 30 percent had little or no recess.

The dissolution of traditional, free outdoor play occurred remarkably rapidly in the United States, but it was also falling out of favor in other countries too. Interview information gathered from the mothers of 2,400 children in 16 countries in North America, South America, Europe, Asia, and Africa showed that lack of free play and experiential learning opportunities (learning by doing) were eroding childhood in all these nations (Singer et al., 2009). Children's major free-time activity across these countries was watching television despite their histories of industrialization and educational opportunities. The study indicated that an increasing similarity of information and entertainment sources may have resulted in increased homogenization of children's activities and the attitudes of parents.

Not since the administration of President Theodore Roosevelt, honorary President of the Playground Association of America and the force behind the establishment of 5 national parks, 150 national forests, 4 national game preserves, 51 federal bird reservations, and many other natural treasures, have play, recreation, conservation, and outdoor living been given anything more than cursory attention by national policy makers. Sports and organized physical education dominate the thoughts and actions of national policy makers when considering the fitness levels of American children and youth, and such matters as free play, recess, and outdoor play environments are rarely mentioned. After learning the results of a report that the fitness of European children was superior to that of American children, President Dwight D. Eisenhower established the President's Council on Youth Fitness in 1956. In 1963 President John F. Kennedy changed the name to the President's Council on Physical Fitness and expanded its mandate to all Americans. In 1966 President Lyndon B. Johnson changed the name to the President's Council on Physical Fitness and Sports and expanded the Council's mission to include sports. President George W. Bush "stayed the course," establishing a "reinvigorated Council" with football legend Lynn Swann as chairman. Through its partnership with federal, state, and local agencies and with private agencies and nonprofit organizations, the goals of the program were addressed—vigorous daily activity, training for fitness and health, and sports and sportsmanship.

The focus on organized activity such as sports, scheduled fitness routines such as walking, jogging, "working out," healthy eating, and physical education, though commendable and critical for health, was too little too late to match the expanding storm of elements diminishing traditions that kept American children and youth active in play and work. Now America faces a fitness, obesity,

Figure 8.1 Toddler play in a natural playscape: building pre-concepts, motor skills, and enhancing development.
Source: Courtesy of Rusty Keeler.

and health crisis described by medical specialists as an epidemic that, if unchecked, could become a pandemic. Consider a far-out scenario such as that depicted in the animated Walt Disney film WALL-E, which was released in June 2008. The world is devastated by human excesses that have destroyed nature, leaving the earth wrapped in trash and populated by one lonely cockroach and a robot garbage compacter called WALL-E (Waste Allocation Lo Lifter Earth-Class). All the remaining earthlings had centuries earlier vacated earth on a massive spaceship, where they lived for 700 years before their probe ship visited earth and brought WALL-E back to the mother ship, carrying one newly discovered growing plant with him. Here the descendants of earthlings had continued their sedentary life styles, doing "nothing," supported by unbelievably complex robots that cared for their every physical need, leaving them to spend all their time eating, drinking, sleeping, and lounging on levitating cushy couches. Babies, youth, and adults appeared as clones, all clinically obese, unable to walk and totally dependent on their created robotic creatures. The way of life on this massive spaceship was remarkably similar to certain of the patterns seen on today's cruise ships. People of all ages are wired to their electronic devices, engaging in 24-hour indulgent gastronomical gorges, many so obese they must cruise the ship's buffets and casinos on electronic carts and be lifted on and off tender boats when visiting port destinations. WALL-E's discovery of one lonely living plant from earth inspired the overjoyed spaceship residents to return to earth and begin the process of renewing the earth's natural resources. The simple pleasures and complex values of free, challenging play in nature had passed them by.

Developmental and Therapeutic Values of Play

On few educational or child development issues is the body of evidence more substantial—free, spontaneous play and outdoor playscapes, both natural and built, are essential for the fitness, health, and development of children and for their adaptation to their culture, society, and world. To the extent that children are deprived of this inherent need, their development is damaged. Beginning with the practices and views of the great reformers of the pre-twentieth century era, and continuing through decades of scholarly research, philosophical and scientific conclusions were consistently pro-play and playgrounds. Decades of research conclude that play promotes cognitive development, social development, language development, physical fitness and health, learning, and coping with trauma (Frost, 1997). The centuries-old traditional games of children played in both natural and organized playgrounds carry extensive developmental benefits. Researchers who immerse themselves in the play lives of children seek out play events unseen by the common eye and words unheard by the common ear that amplify the deeper meanings and values of children's age-old games (Callois, 1961; Opie and Opie, 1969; Sutton-Smith, 1972; Howard, 1977; Sluckin, 1981; Opie, 1993; Darian-Smith and Factor, 2005).

The body and mind building power of traditional games or folk games may be overlooked when designers and keepers of play environments create playgrounds for children. As children approach school age, their play evolves from symbolic or imaginative play and simple games into increasingly elaborate, organized, and invented games, both traditional and contemporary. Games contribute to understanding the customs and institutions of various cultures (Callois, 1961). They become intertwined with daily life, and are imbued with competition and risk taking and mimicry or acting out roles. Children's active, spontaneous, exuberant, contrived games represent and yield skills of calculation, strategy, negotiation, contrivance, physical skills, and creation of rules and subordination to those rules. The implications for adaptation to society and preservation of culture are profound. Development through play is a cumulative process, with learning from earlier forms lending power, intellect, and motivation for engaging in later forms. All this begs diversity of playgrounds to accommodate the natural forms of play engaged in by children of differing developmental and age levels.

Play that is beneficial to children is play that is active, creative, and social, engaging the body in fine and gross motor development, and the mind in negotiation, problem solving, imagination, and flexibility. All this requires play environments that are flexible and adaptable to the various forms of play and types of play materials that children naturally choose. Play encourages autonomous thinking and environment building, provides opportunities to

Figure 8.2 Developing social skills and fitness: negotiating, planning, swinging, climbing, jumping, running, brachiating, inventing games, and playing chase and organized games. *Source:* Courtesy of Redeemer Lutheran School, Austin, Texas.

practice new skills and functions, promotes flexibility in problem solving, develops creative and aesthetic appreciation—all in a context of minimum risks and penalties for mistakes (Cole-Hamilton et al., 2002, p. 15). These findings are supported by more recent research reviews by prominent organizations. A clinical report by the American Academy of Pediatrics (enter AAP Play in an Internet search engine) supports the above conclusions and adds benefits in creativity, healthy brain development, development of multiple competencies, developing social and leadership skills, and engaging in joyful imagination (Ginsburg, 2006). This report attributes the decline in outdoor play and recess to high stakes testing, hurried lifestyles, and changes in family structures. This will be further explained in what follows.

A Stanford University study (2007) and a research review by the American Heart Association (Marcus et al., 2006) add extensive health benefits: prevention of obesity, high cholesterol, high blood pressure, and heart disease—all factors implicated in shortened life spans. The Stanford scientists concluded that inactivity among children may result in this generation being the first in American history to have a shorter life span than their parents, and that physical education and recess at school and outdoor play at home are essential to healthy child development.

Play is essential for cognitive, social, physical, and emotional development, and added contributions to general health and well-being, creativity, working in groups, dealing with challenges, exploration, engaging in childhood passion and imagination, and brain development. Play provides opportunities for parents to engage fully with their children, but hurried lifestyles, changes in family structures, and an increased emphasis on academic subjects have reduced recess and places for self-directed play. Regular physical activity is essential for children's health. This can be in the form of structured play or unstructured, free play, both essential to preventing obesity, but also for cognitive, social, physical, and emotional development. However, free recess play at school carries developmental, academic, and health benefits not secured by structured, adult-directed activity (Cole-Hamilton et al., 2002).

Research involving 11,684 kindergarten through eighth grade students in 1,055 schools, sponsored by the highly acclaimed Robert Wood Johnson Foundation (2007), makes a compelling case for school recess. What happens at recess is just as important as what happens in the classroom when dealing with such issues as depression, violence, and obesity. Since only 36 percent of America's children meet doctors' recommendations for physical activity during the school year, recess offers our greatest opportunity to meet these needs. Children from poverty and minority homes are the most shortchanged. Children need teachers who get involved in facilitating play and introduce traditional games that are all but lost to modern children. Trained adults can assist with conflict avoidance and resolution, and teach healthy nutrition. Growing numbers of children do not know how to play in the out-of-doors and, consequently, fail to develop social and cognitive skills needed to relate positively with peers. Adults responsible for children in school should indeed be trained play leaders, but such training should not unduly interfere with children's age-old rights and needs to engage in and learn through free, creative, spontaneous play. Unfortunately, loss of outdoor play and recess has resulted in a generation of children who have a greater need for supervision by adults when playing because they have had too little opportunity to learn through experiencing play on their own.

In addition to the developmental values of play, its therapeutic benefits, indoors and outdoors, are extensive, operating wherever play occurs and contributing to a wide range of healing processes. The effects are most evident and documented in children's hospitals, centers for disturbed children, and places devastated by natural disasters and war, but play carries healing power wherever it is practiced—classrooms, playgrounds, woodlands, streets—indoors or outdoors (Frost, 2005b). In institutional contexts, play therapists work to help children express themselves through play in ways they cannot do verbally. An extensive body of research demonstrates the effectiveness of play therapy in helping traumatized and disturbed children (Landreth, 2002; Frost et al., 2008).

Play, Brain, and Play Deprivation

Neuroscientists and the medical professions around the world are connecting the dots between children's play, physical activity, and brain development, leading to insights unanticipated just a few decades ago. Free, spontaneous play is associated with improved memory, problem solving, creativity, imagination, and formation of synapses. Severe play deprivation is associated with depression, social vulnerabilities, emotional dysfunction, problem solving, and formation of abnormal synapses (Frost and Brown, 2008; Brown with Vaughan, 2009).

Decades of research on the value of play and playgrounds is supported by the research of neuroscientists concluding that play is essential for brain development. Research during the 1960s supported the view of brain plasticity (ability of the brain to change with experience) and the importance of early activity such as play (Frost, 1975). In 1974 the President's Committee on Mental Retardation sponsored the National Conference on Early Intervention with High Risk Infants and Young Children at the University of North Carolina in Chapel Hill. At this conference, early plasticity theories were documented with physical evidence from relatively primitive (by today's standards) brain imaging. There can be too much stimulation or too little stimulation—either leading to negative consequences in behavior (Lipton, 1974). Photographs of brain tissue from infants who died a few weeks after premature birth revealed remarkably abnormal (retarded) brain development for those who survived for a few weeks, apparently due to being isolated and deprived of stimulation.

During the 1990s the phenomenon of play, historically viewed by many as frivolous and unimportant behavior serving no apparent purpose, gained respect as biologists, neuroscientists, psychologists, and other scholars learned that play is as important as other basic drives. Advanced tools of brain imaging allowed unprecedented insights into the role of experience, including play, in human development (Chugani, 1994; Sylwester, 1995). Begley's (1996) review concluded that unused neurons do not survive, synapses are not formed, and the child fails to reach his potential. Research at Baylor College of Medicine concluded that "children who don't play much or are rarely touched develop brains 20 percent to 30 percent smaller than normal for their age" (Nash, 1997, p. 51). Brain development is truly a "use or lose it" process. Early experiences determine which neurons are to be used and which are to die, and consequently whether the child will be brilliant or dull, confident or fearful, articulate or tongue-tied (Begley, 1996). Because of rapid advances in imaging tools and compelling results, the 1990s were aptly called "the decade of the brain."

Deprivation of play, absence of warm, early emotional ties with parents, abuse, and debilitating conditions of poverty can jeopardize early brain development and result in immature social and emotional behavior, impulsivity, violence, and reduced capacity for later learning. The classic case of 3,000 Romanian orphans adopted by American parents between 1960 and 1996 after living in almost total neglect illustrated this connection years ago (ABC News, 1996). Scientists at the Denver Children's Hospital learned from PET scans that these children's brains were remarkably different from those of normal children. Some were so severely damaged that one mother described hers as the "child from hell." Some never learned to talk, read, feel pain, or love. Play therapy resulted in measurable progress but they never developed like normal children.

The evidence that play is a central process in brain development is gaining new respect with each passing year. One neuroscientist suggests that there is a dedicated circuitry in the brain equivalent to its love and fear circuits (Johnson, 2004, p. 125). In primates, the amount of brain growth between birth and maturity is a reflection of the amount of play engaged in by each species (Bekoff and Begley, 2001; Smith, 2005). The scientists who study play and the brain are no longer viewed as strange and immature. They have revealed that early brain development is programmed by nature, and the effects of sensory and motor experience begin early—some believe before birth. Unique cultural experiences, such as playing games, reading, and using computers continue the programming and reprogramming (Hirsh-Pasek and Golinkoff, 2003). Information received in a positive emotional environment is a powerful factor in brain development. Vigorous social involvement, as in rough-and-tumble play, and creativity with sand, water, and other natural materials are perhaps the strongest positive emotional involvement for young children once basic bodily needs are met (Johnson, 2004).

The effects of physical activity, including play, continue to be discovered and are seen in enhanced physical performance, brain function, self-esteem, energy levels, and relief from boredom (Scheuer and Mitchell, 2003). For the first time, scientists at Massachusetts Institute of Technology (MIT) have seen neurons in the brain of a living animal change in response to experience (MIT News Office, 2006), opening up pathways for future studies about how the brain responds to stimuli, both positive and negative. Physical activity, exercise, or active play benefits specific brain functions, positively affecting the hippocampus, a brain structure essential for memory and learning (Society for Neuroscience, 2000). As the brain continues to generate new brain cells throughout life in both animals and humans, challenging environments offering social interactions and physical activities are essential to their growth. Voluntary activity, such as spontaneous play, is enough to trigger a boost in brain cell proliferation. These advantages of physical activity are complemented by its power to reduce or prevent the negative effects of chronic stress and to boost the brain's defenses against infection. Keeping active and playful from birth through old age has profound benefits that are only now beginning to be discovered.

Norman Doidge (2007), M.D., psychiatrist, psychoanalyst, and researcher at Columbia University and the University of Toronto, has written a fascinating synopsis of the new science of neuroplasticity (changeable, malleable, modifiable brain) and the emerging promises of neurorehabilitation for the debilitating effects of brain damage, injury, memory loss, learning disabilities, and emotional disorders. Doidge alerts the reader to the phenomenon of "the plastic paradox," the power of the flexible brain to accommodate not only to flexible behaviors but also to rigid behaviors. Scientists moved from the view of a fixed, "hardwired" brain and the belief that most brain damage is fixed and permanent, to understanding that the brain has remarkable powers to transform itself. The transformations seen in young brains can continue to operate throughout the lifespan. Cultural influences, positive thinking, exercise, activity—all influence the structure and workings of brains from birth to old age. For example, immigration or immersion in a new culture for children or adults is a challenge to the plastic brain for it involves cultural change—learning new things, taking things away, adding new neurons, and losing unused ones—resulting in social integration or social rigidity. Such can influence children's getting along on the playground or adults' creating war because of cultural differences.

The rapid changes in children's play, sports, and outdoor activity patterns were becoming increasingly evident during the late 1900s but were ignored or given only cursory attention by policy makers. Sedentary life styles, coupled with increasing consumption of junk food and reductions in recess, outdoor active play, and work were contributing to a nation of flabby, short-winded kids with elevated blood pressure and cholesterol and declining heart–lung endurance and strength (Winston, 1984). Beginning during the 1980s, findings of increasing obesity were complemented by fitness level studies by the President's Council on Physical Fitness and Sports, the American Academy of Pediatrics, the U.S. Department of Health and Human Services, and studies by the American Alliance for Health, Physical Education, Recreation and Dance (Ross and Gilbert, 1985; Dennison et al., 1988; Frost, 1992).

- Forty percent of 6 through 12-year-old boys could not do more than 1 pull-up.
- Seventy percent of 6 through 17-year-old girls could not do more than 1 pull-up.
- Fifty percent of American children were not getting sufficient exercise to develop healthy heart and lungs.
- About fifty percent of 5 to 16-year-olds could not run a mile in less than 10 minutes.
- Forty percent of 5 to 8-year-old children had at least one of three risk factors for heart disease—high cholesterol, elevated blood pressure, or physical inactivity. (Ross and Gilbert, 1985)

The benefits of play were recognized by eminent philosophers centuries before twentieth century scholars and national organizations turned their attention to the consequences of not playing. Stuart Brown's studies of the genesis of the violence of Charles Whitman, the 1966 University of Texas sniper and mass murderer, and his later studies of animal play for *National Geographic* drew new attention to the consequences of play deprivation, which include aberrant, even violent behavior (Brown, 1994, 1997, 1998, 2008). Whether a child becomes a violent adult appeared to be related to the existence of healthy attachment to adults and of positive early play behavior, including the opportunity to play extensively in supportive, playful contexts (Brown, 1994, 1997, 1998; Perry, 1996). These studies of the genesis of Whitman's violence, and Brown's follow-up studies of convicted Texas murderers and drunks who had killed themselves and others, revealed striking commonalities in their childhoods. As a child, Whitman secluded himself on the playground, and his father did not allow him to play at home. The childhoods of 90 percent of the murderers were characterized by either the absence of play or abnormal play such as bullying, sadism, cruelty to animals, and extreme teasing. None of them engaged in rough and tumble play as children—a normal, healthy form of play important for developing good relationships. Seventy-five percent of the drunk drivers had play abnormalities. Brown conducted interviews over several years with several thousand humans (Brown with Vaughan, 2009). This research, coupled with his extensive studies of animal play, led to his forming the National Institute for Play, a forum for searching out and communicating research on biological processes and play.

> Neuroscientists, developmental biologists, psychologists, social scientists, and researchers from every point of the scientific compass now know that play is a profound biological process. It has evolved over eons in many animal species to promote survival. It shapes the brain and makes animals smarter and more adaptable. In higher animals, it fosters empathy and makes possible complex social groups. For us, play lies at the core of creativity and innovation. (Brown with Vaughan, 2009, pp. 4–5)

Extremes in play lead to the conclusion that there is play that is good for children and play that is bad for them—both with consequences. The task of rearing nonviolent children is complicated by constant media violence—television, video games—and, in many city neighborhoods, actual criminal activities that influence children. Many children's games arise from and gain force through such exposure, and the values learned conflict with those of traditional intact, loving families. The absence of adults with positive values and the view that a little "quality time" can effectively substitute for extensive periods with supportive adults who shape values and provide opportunities and appropriate places to play are significant in creating violent youth. Children are permanently shaped through their participation or nonparticipation (Frost and Jacobs, 1995).

During the 1980s the deleterious effects of inactivity were emerging not only in low levels of physical fitness but also in deficient perceptual modalities for transmitting information to the brain for organization and response. Fewer than half of first grade children and fewer than one-fourth of sixth grade children could pat or walk to the beat of a musical selection, mimic movements presented in sequence, or execute movements to verbal instructions (Weikart, 1987).

> In addition to extensive TV viewing and abuse of junk food, several other factors were contributing to this state of affairs. The absence of adults during the daytime due to divorce, both parents working outside the home, and associated fear of violence reduced the availability of support, encouragement, and availability of outdoor physical activity and nourishing food. Education reforms typically emphasized "academics" and "extended school hours" over play, play equipment, and physical education. (Frost, 1992, p. 44)

What a remarkable and disturbing change from the time, just a few decades earlier, when children benefited from the reality of blistered hands and skinned-knee recesses. Their out-of-school hours were filled with outdoor play and work, and flabby, weak kids were rarely seen.

Obesity, Illness, and Dying Young

By the year 2000 the second most preventable cause of death in America was overweight and obesity, accounting for about 15 percent of all deaths, and second only to smoking which accounted for about 18 percent (Mokdad et al., 2004). During the first decade of the twenty-first century, such data were spurring government agencies and professionals in many disciplines to pay closer attention to the burgeoning obesity and fitness crisis. A report by the National Health and Nutrition Examination Survey (Ogden et al., 2006; National Center for Health Statistics, 2008) showed that in 2003–4 an estimated 17 percent of children and adolescents aged 2–19 years were overweight. About 14 percent of 2–5 year olds, 19 percent of 6–11 year-olds, and 17 percent of 12–19 year-olds were overweight or obese. These rates were four times the rates for 6–11 year-olds in the 1970s and triple the rates for other age groups. If the rate of increase in obesity and overweight continues at the current pace, 75 percent of adults and 24 percent of U.S. children and adolescents will be overweight or obese by 2015 (Wang and Beydoun, 2007).

Despite major efforts to resolve the crisis facing children and the nation, the picture remains grim. A comprehensive, scholarly report by the Trust for America's Health and the Robert Wood Johnson Foundation (Levy et al., 2009) reveals that obesity, perhaps the key indicator of the severity, scope, and consequences of America's play, fitness, and health crisis, continues to grow unchecked. The epidemic is real and is threatening to become a pandemic. During 2007 the obesity rate increased in 37 states and rose for a second consecutive year in 19 states, with no state showing a decrease. In 28 states one-quarter of the adults are obese. An estimated two-thirds of adults are overweight or obese, and an estimated 23 million children are either overweight or obese.

Rural children are as likely to be obese as urban children. Rural African-American children had the highest level of overweight (44 percent) and obesity (26 percent) compared to other racial and ethnic groups. As family income increased, the percentage of overweight children decreased significantly in both rural and urban settings. Children in poverty lack resources to support physical activity and healthy eating. Baby Boomers had a higher prevalence of obesity and became obese at younger ages than their predecessors, the "silent generation." Evidence is growing that documents the association between obesity and poor mental health.

The rapid growth in obesity is evident internationally, with 22 million children under age 5 being overweight across the world, especially in countries where westernization of behavioral and dietary lifestyles is evident (Deckelbaum and Williams, 2001). About 70–80 percent of obese children will be obese adults (Robinson, 2000). One in four children in England is obese, and schools were scheduled to begin testing children for excess weight in 2008, to be followed by letters to parents alerting them to potential long-term health damage and emphasizing the need for children to get at least an hour a day of active play time (Green, 2007). A two-year U.K. study by prominent scholars Richard Layard and Judy Dunn (2009) concluded that a changing culture of childhood, spurred in the U.K. by "excessive individualism," led to an ethos of parents putting themselves first and placing low priority on children. The researchers maintained that British children are the unhappiest among children of any industrialized nation, rivaled only by American children, reflecting a breakdown of the nuclear family in both nations.

Professional organizations are searching the underutilized research spelling out the inactivity trends of American youth and the potential health effects. The National Recreation and Park Association, the YMCA, and the National Association for Sport and Physical Education, organizations whose forebears helped organize the Playground Association of America a century ago, came together to commission the Stanford University School of Medicine to review the research on physical activity among children and prepare a landmark report (Stanford University, 2007). This report demonstrates the value of play, physical education, sports, and other forms of physical activity in the prevention of obesity, and its positive effects on the general health of children and longer life expectancy. The Centers for Disease Control predict that the current generation of children may be the first ever to have a shorter lifespan than their parents. The predicted effects of obesity on shortened life expectancy were supported by University of Washington and Harvard University scholars, who found that in about 1,000 counties or 12 percent of the women in the United States, women's life expectancy was shorter than it was in the early 1980s, and men's life expectancy had declined by about 4 percent (David Brown, *Washington Post*, April 22, 2008). Could this be the leading edge of the effects of obesity on longevity?

The extensive research reviewed in the Stanford report and data from the Centers for Disease Control confirm that childhood obesity is associated with health risks for children and later as they grow into adults. The consequences include depression, low self-esteem, discrimination, abnormal cholesterol, cardiovascular disease, Type 2 diabetes, sleep apnea, arthritis, asthma, anxiety, depression, and cancer. Being overweight as a child can accelerate the development of heart disease processes that typically take decades to develop. This same generalization about disease acceleration in childhood applies to other obesity-related disorders—digestive, metabolic, respiratory, skeletal, and psychosocial—that are now appearing in children either for the first time or with greater severity and prevalence (Daniels, 2006). The medical professions acknowledge that the childhood crisis revolving around inactivity, poor diet, and obesity is an epidemic of major proportions.

Just as Americans were awakening to the reality of widespread child obesity, the Centers for Disease Control (CDC) and European researchers announced that a new condition, childhood rickets, had re-entered the scene after having been virtually eliminated decades ago. Rickets was widespread at the turn of the twentieth century among the poor living in polluted industrialized cities, but was checked when vitamin D was discovered and the anti-rachitic properties of cod-liver oil were put to widespread application by the 1930s. On October 11 and 12, 2001, scientists, health practitioners, and policy makers from the CDC, the American Academy of Pediatrics, academic and professional institutions, and government agencies met in Atlanta to discuss vitamin D supplementation and related issues of rickets, research needs, and the role of sunlight in preventing vitamin D deficiency (Scanlon, 2001). Government tests indicated that a surprising number of Americans no longer get enough vitamin D, especially African-American adults whose dark-pigmented skin does not produce as much as is needed from sunlight. Nine out of every million babies aged six months to one year, mostly African-American, were hospitalized for rickets during the 1990s, and doctors began recommending vitamin D supplements for breast-fed babies until they were switched to fortified formula or milk. The links between low levels of vitamin D and cancer, osteoporosis, diabetes, multiple sclerosis, and high blood pressure are widely documented. Fear of developing cancer from excessive sunlight is weighed against the possibility of developing rickets from not getting enough sunlight and/or not receiving enough vitamin D supplements (Scanlon, 2001; Rajakumar and Thomas, 2005; National Institutes of Health, 2008).

This news about the reemergence of rickets comes at a time when some physicians and other health professionals are warning about the risks of cancer from exposing children to sunlight, and parents everywhere are slathering their children with sunscreen whenever they spend a few minutes in the sun. But other physicians and researchers who presented papers at a National Institutes of Health conference in November 2003 warned that sunscreen blocks ultraviolet rays and prevents the body from getting vitamin D directly from the sun, and advocated responsible and regular exposure (www.nih.gov). The average Caucasian in Boston needs 5–15 minutes of exposure to sunlight two to three times a week during the summer before applying sunscreen, but the average African-American may need up to ten times that much to produce the same amount of vitamin D (Scanlon, 2001). Those who advocate sensible, limited exposure to sunlight recommend that time of exposure be regulated and extremes leading to sunburn be avoided. Now parents and educators are faced with the dilemma of placing children at risk for rickets from too little sunlight or at risk for cancer from too much. Such dilemmas are the stuff for creating further adult paranoia about the health and safety of children.

The president of the American Academy of Orthopedic Surgeons warned that a 10 percent bone mass deficit during childhood can increase the later risk of osteoporosis and fractures by up to 50 percent. American children suffer fractured arms more frequently today than four decades ago—girls 56 percent more and boys 32 percent more (Neergaard, 2008). This increase does not appear to be caused by children engaging in riskier play. The history of children's play demonstrates that play has become increasingly tame during the past three to four decades. Those who advocate the elimination of "risky" play should consider the causes of playground injuries, which have increased from about 117,000 in 1976 to about 225,000 in 2007 (Consumer Product Safety Commission, CPSC.gov). This increase is not due to children taking greater risks, exposure to new forms of play such as skateboarding, or manufacturers replacing antiquated playground equipment with safer versions. The evidence grows that recess play is tamer than it was during the 1970s and children are becoming less fit, obese, and weaker.

Obese, poorly coordinated, weak kids are unsafe in any outdoor play environment. The growing pattern of overprotecting children from "risky" play such as dodge ball, chase, rough and tumble, and contact games has been extended into a national trend to "dumb down" children's play—standardizing play equipment, restricting play, and constructing artificial shade structures—all debatable from both economic and health perspectives. Indeed, children accustomed to air conditioned schools, cars, and homes tend to abandon open, sunny play spaces on playgrounds during very hot weather, seeking shade wherever it can be found, even under the play equipment. Planning playgrounds that include trees and other natural features that provide partial shade as well as challenging play venues in the sunlight appears to be a more sensible pattern. Public health campaigns and vitamin D supplementation virtually eliminated childhood rickets during the early twentieth century, so the National Institute for Health is currently debating whether to modify recommendations for vitamin D.

Probable correlates between obesity and disease are extended even further by the knowledge that accumulation of fat in the liver cells, or nonalcoholic fatty liver disease (NAFLD), is a common, relatively unnoticed disease among children. A study of 742 children, aged 2–19, who died in San Diego County between 1993 and 2002 found that fatty liver was present in 13 percent of those children (Schwimmer et al., 2008). Over time this disease can result in the need for liver transplants, even among children. The prevalence of NAFLD increases with age, is more prevalent among boys and Hispanics, and overweight and obese children accounted for 81 percent of all cases. Leading pediatricians predict that about one-fourth of children with fatty liver disease will develop hepatitis before age 20. Mayo Clinic researchers identify obesity as the major cause of chronic liver disease, which is related to affluence, diet, and lifestyle. There is no present cure and the rate is growing among children in several countries. Pediatricians and research scientists are serving up extra helpings of research showing that hauling around excess pounds is taking a heavy toll on children's health. Fatty liver disease is only one of the syndrome of diseases— others are diabetes, elevated cholesterol, hepatitis, hypertension, heart disease— linked to play deprivation, bad diet, inactivity, and obesity.

The state of childhood fitness and health in America has declined to a level that calls for radical state and national attention. A 2007 report from the Trust for America's Health ranked Texas sixth among states with the highest levels of obesity among children aged 10–17, with 19.1 percent considered obese, exceeded by the District of Columbia, ranked number one, with an obesity rate of 22.8 percent. Alarmed by such statistics, the state of Texas ordered a comprehensive physical assessment of its students.

During the program's first year, 2.6 million of almost 3.4 million Texas students in grades 3–12 were tested, using a FITNESSGRAM Test created by the Cooper Institute of Dallas. This test assesses measured body composition, aerobic capacity, strength, endurance, and flexibility. The results, published online July 1, 2008, by the Texas Education Agency (2008), revealed that fitness levels decline with each passing grade level, corresponding with a decreasing emphasis on physical activity in upper grades. The preliminary results show that 32 percent of third-grade girls and 28 percent of third-grade boys reached the "Healthy Fitness Zone." In seventh grade, only 21 percent of the girls and 9 percent of the boys met the health standards. The children in schools in poverty areas scored lowest on the tests and those in high income area schools scored highest. The Texas legislature passed weak mandates for physical education and recess during the 2007 session but, fortunately, the Texas Education Agency test results were a wake-up call for the entire state, and legislators began to draft additional legislation to counter the threats to children and youth, the economic stability of the state, and the health of its citizens. Consistent with popular views, provisions for recess and free play are subordinated to structured physical education, and this is in turn subordinated to high stakes testing on limited "academic" skills.

In some respects, in America the current obesity epidemic, which is spreading around the industrialized world, represents yet another crisis for children that has already had deleterious effects that far exceed those of the industrial age on the health and welfare of children. Growing indicators show that the obesity crisis will affect far more children, result in more disease, and reduce the life spans of far more children than suffered the morbid conditions of the factory child worker or the hard labor of farm children a century ago. Ironically, the industrial age children's condition was the result of malnutrition from overwork and starvation; today's children are the victims of the malfeasance of excessive structuring, standardizing, and regulating of their lives, and their enforced estrangement from nature and outdoor play and playgrounds. In both periods, play deprivation entered prominently into the picture. The causes are complex and intertwined.

The Causes of Play Deprivation: A Perfect Storm

Some fundamental factors emerge from the extensive data about the causes of play deprivation and its consequences on fitness, obesity, and health. Poverty and education levels are deeply implicated. Lack of knowledge of and access to information about the effects of nutrition and activity on the human body and the resources to act on that knowledge appears to be deeply implicated in the high rates of obesity and low levels of fitness among children living in poverty. Modern lifestyles contribute to the imbalance between the calorie or energy availability, appeal, and intake of energy-packed, high calorie foods and the expenditure of excess, empty calories in physical activity. Children who eat more calories than they expend are at risk for becoming obese. A multitude of factors enter into this picture: processed food; fast food venues; working families; school lunches; pampered children; sedentary living; replacing physical activity with technology; lack of knowledge among adults about play, nutrition, and exercise and their effects on children's health.

Just how American children were removed from free, outdoor play and are suffering the consequences is a story told throughout this book and is resulting in an eventual backlash to be described in the final chapter. Initially promising but ultimately destructive influences—cyber play, paranoid, hovering parents, national playground safety standards, the threat of lawsuits, and high stakes testing—have collectively generated a perfect storm, reducing centuries of traditional, free, creative, outdoor play to a mere shadow of its former state, resulting in serious consequences for the development, health, and fitness of children. The technology revolution of the mid-twentieth century is deeply implicated in this diminution.

Out-of-Control Cyber Play

The effects of imagination on children's real lives were widely known long before the advent of television and other electronic media. As early as 1909

Jane Addams (1909, p. 93), a great reformer of the early twentieth century child-saving movement, related the story of three boys, aged nine, eleven, and thirteen, who played out the adventures of outdoor life influenced by the theater, spending weeks planning to lasso, murder, and rob a neighborhood milkman. They saved to buy a revolver, adopted a watchword, "Dead Men Tell No Tales," covered their faces, and "ambushed" the milkman. Fortunately, his horse shied, the shot missed, and his life was saved.

> The theatre is the only place where they (youth) can satisfy that craving for a conception of life higher than that which the actual world offers them ... The theatre becomes for them a "veritable house of dreams" infinitely more real than the noisy streets and the crowded factories ... The drama provides a transition between the romantic conceptions which they vainly struggle to keep intact and life's cruelties and trivialities which they refuse to admit. (Addams, 1909, pp. 75–7)

The theatre remains, and the media, greatly expanded in complexity and drawing power by miracles of technology, continue to exert unparalleled influence on the imaginative play of children, some of it beneficial, much of it damaging.

Following the introduction of television in the late 1940s after World War II, as production shifted from tools of war to tools of leisure, major changes were seen. The increasing affluence of families contributed to the wider availability of television for influencing children's imaginative play and led to "showering" them with ready-made toys, eventually expanding into computer play and the Internet communication and games revolution. Early television programming for children was intended to create inexpensive entertainment, attract young viewers, and provide a public service, but such lofty purposes were to be replaced by commercialization aimed at children. Children's programs became so popular that they began to substitute for active outdoor play during out-of-school hours. From the beginning, physicians questioned the possible physical effects of extensive television viewing on young children's bodies and minds, and issues, both pro and con, were voiced by social scientists about the possible educational consequences.

As early as 1985 the National Coalition on Television Violence (1985) compiled 850 studies, including subjects from twenty nations, showing the harm of children's viewing television violence. The results included increased anger, verbal aggression, fighting, dishonesty, desensitization toward violence, and willingness to rape. A hearing on Neurobiological Research and the Impact of Media, called by Senator Sam Brownback in 2003, featured prominent researchers who presented studies reinforcing extensive earlier research on the negative effects of violent and sexual content on children's behavior and development (Brownback, 2003). University of Michigan researchers reporting at the hearing found that exposure to violence during childhood predicts aggressive behavior of both sexes during early adulthood. Other studies reported at the hearing found that pretend or virtual violence affects brain development in much the same ways that real violence does. Such effects on children begin early and accumulate over time. More than two hours of daily TV/video use by preschool children is associated with obesity and adiposity (Mendoza et al., 2007). The American Academy of Pediatrics issued national guidelines for parents, recommending that television viewing by children two years of age and older be limited to one to two hours a day and that only television of "high quality" be allowed.

Arguably, the most extensive body of interdisciplinary research on children and television ever reviewed is reported in *Children and television: Fifty years of research* (Pecora et al., 2007), covering more than 2,000 research reports. This book summarizes the growth and "wisdom" of the first fifty years of television and may portend the next revolution in electronic media and their influences on children. Pecora visits each decade from the 1940s to the present time, illustrating how television during the first decade of the twenty-first century competes with the Internet, video games, instant messaging devices, and other electronic media for children's attention. Selective use, monitored by wise adults, can contribute to learning the forms and formats of electronic media, making judgments about program content, building pre-academic skills, and improving academic achievement. Spreading six hours of daily time multitasking across a range of technology raises serious issues about the possible consequences of giving up so much free time traditionally used for active, spontaneous outdoor play.

Electronic play is a study in contrasts. Computers offer virtual glimpses of the world and open great libraries and scholarly research for instant access. In tech play, children sit for long hours, trading outdoor play with peers for junk food and sedentary entertainment. Organized sports fill the gaps for many, but these are typically created, organized, and dominated by adults. Now a "balanced" diet is a cookie in each hand, and the venue for a special meal is a fast food venue or an eat-all-you-can-hold restaurant. Play is dominated at home by solitary, virtual socialization with unseen faces, video games, WIFI, Wiis, text messaging, and chat rooms. This home entertainment is supplemented by cruising malls with the ever-present "umbilical" cellphone or iPod attached to the ear and playing video games in the noisy, garish, entertainment complexes—with or without parents in tow. The sedentary pastimes of children at home and school, especially the engagement with electronic media, contribute substantially to inactivity. Ten to sixteen-year-olds are engaged in vigorous activity for about thirteen minutes a day and spend more than ten of their waking hours relatively motionless.

All this reflects willingness, even support, from parents or caretakers who themselves may be addicted to the virtually unlimited attractions of high-tech play, sometimes disguised as work. Parents typically purchase the devices, determine where they will be placed in the home (public or private areas) or car, and may allow unlimited access by children. Many utilize tech toys and tech play as baby-sitting devices for the very young and allow children to substitute cyber play for meaningful conversation, outdoor play, and collective family activities. Combine all this with other intrusions on children's traditional play, such as high stakes testing, and the storm grows.

As technology rapidly advances, countries worldwide look to its tools to enhance their industrial, educational, political, and economic processes and products (Swaminathan and Yelland, 2003), and adults look to high-tech devices to entertain and instruct their children. In many respects, the technology promising to revolutionize the education of children is far behind the research about its long-term consequences. For example, research on the influence of computers, the Internet, and virtual reality on children's brain development is still in its infancy, yet promising to re-create the way children learn (Frost et al., 2008). Early neurobiological research is showing that, with time and use, electronic media change brain development and modify the ways children think (Healy, 1998, 1990; Hirsh-Pasek and Golinkoff, 2003).

Homes are sprouting every imaginable electronic device for adults and children, and more are rushed to the market every year. The array now includes media rooms, computer networking systems, cable TV, satellite systems, security systems, remote control appliances, humidity control systems, home theatres, cellphones, video games, and countless other cyber gadgets intended to provide in-home access to nonstop entertainment and communication with peers. Parents' concerns about outdoor predators and environmental hazards result in children being restricted to the indoors and engaging in social networking with faceless others. Many children become the pawns of their cyber toys and never learn the age-old joys and skills of creating for themselves. Little about sex and violence is left to the imagination, for high-tech offerings originally designed for adults are easily modified and sold for children, or children simply apply their considerable technology skills to access such fare for themselves on the Internet, as they often have computers in their bedrooms at home or carry them in pockets and backpacks wherever they go.

Ready access to computers at home and school leads to what Oppenheimer (2003) calls a "culture of the flickering mind," meaning a generation poised between becoming confident, creative problem solvers and becoming victims of computerization and commercialization careening out of control. During the 1990s the emergence of the Internet was seen as the long-awaited savior for American education, promising to revolutionize the nation's failing schools and prepare students for a high-tech future. Like many other educational fads, such as the No Child Left Behind Act and high stakes testing, reality quickly set in and the results were "crushingly discouraging" (Oppenheimer, 2003, p. xiv).

Modern mixtures of politics and commercialization tend to bode poorly for children's success in school and, in the present context, contribute to a changing culture of children's play. Clever entrepreneurs are quick to capitalize on the naivety of lawmakers, school administrators, and parents about the promises of technology, selling them a "bill of goods" about transforming children's rearing and education. Classrooms have become test factories, titillating entertainment has replaced spontaneous play, and computers have become babysitters at home and messiahs at school.

The fallout has produced two opposing camps—those who see promise and those who see danger and the destruction of humanistic and scholarly traditions. The differences revolve around whether children will sharpen their powers of observation and imagination, engage in active exploration and creative thinking, learn to solve complex problems, develop empathy for others, and sample broadly and reflect about important matters such as the nature of knowledge and the meaning of values. Computers can be invaluable research tools—and tools only—for such educational ends. The great philosophers and educators of past centuries would add to the educative process a familiarity with such educational materials and sensations as mud and water, hammers and nails, sticks and stones, taste and touch, plants and insects, wheels and gears, paper and pencils, and hugs from caring adults. The real world of reasoned balance should take priority over the virtual world in classrooms and playgrounds.

The upsides and the downsides of technology as a tool for play are extensively studied and debated. Dorothy and Jerome Singer (2005), long-respected

Figure 8.3 Genesis of cyber play.
Source: Courtesy of Shutterstock Images LLC.

observers of children's play, creativity, and imagination, examined in detail the long debated effects of electronic media on children's cognitive and moral development, confirming that the toxic effects of media violence are as real as many have believed. However, they argue that, with appropriate guidance from parents and teachers, electronic media can contribute positively to creativity, imagination, empathy, and even promote school readiness. Pretend play, supported by traditional play materials such as blocks, dolls, and soft toys, or through combining toy play with incentives of television, computers, stories, and songs, can lead to increased imagination and the love of play. All this, of course, should be supported by the adult caregiver's touches, smiles, words, and simple suggestions. When teachers or parents become active participants in children's television or computer play, they can prompt the child to construct and elaborate, and thus encourage play and learning. Such simple, unstructured "scaffolding" of the child's play with electronic media contributes to the use of television, computers, video games, and other electronic media in constructive ways. These caveats, applicable to adult monitored play and learning, should not overshadow the volume of research findings confirming the devastating, toxic consequences of giving children free rein in making all their own choices and having unlimited access to electronic media.

The first national survey of its kind found that 97 percent of all American teens aged 12 to 17 play games on computers, cellphones, or consoles, with at least half playing on any given day. Much of the play is social; most teens play with others in the same room some of the time, but 27 percent play with people over the Internet (Lenhart et al., 2008). Such play robs teens of opportunities to learn social skills through face-to-face play in more constructive settings and opens up opportunities for engaging in sexually explicit and violent content, and the growing risk of exposure to teen bullies and adult predators. About a third of teens play games designated as appropriate only for older players. The content learned, the oft sedentary and solitary activity, and the loss of active, outdoor play in challenging play environments are all implicated in the current problems of children and youth. Ironically, the same day this study was released, September 17, 2008, a science fiction writer, Bruce Sterling, delivered a keynote address at the Austin, Texas, International Game Developers Conference, giving the international audience a peek into the possible future of computers—a dish rag from General Electric that would ostensibly connect to future cloud networks with the power of more than eight million of the best current laptops. He speculated that computers of the future would be ubiquitous enough to be incredibly boring, like toothbrushes, bricks, and forks, and would be scattered among everyday household and workplace devices, such as door knobs.

In her acclaimed book *Endangered minds: Why our children don't think*, Jane Healy (1990), psychologist, educator, scholar and mother, raised provocative issues about why children had problems with concentration, information analysis, reasoning, problem solving, and other forms of complex thinking. Drawing from both research and experience, she pointed to electronic media, fast-paced lives, unstable families, environmental hazards, and educational practices as being implicated in how children think and how their brains are built. The "couch potato" brains of kids addicted to cyber play are affected by the chemicals they eat in their fast foods—leading to upsets of brain chemistry and resulting in attention and learning problems. Learning problems and attention deficits are consequently treated with more chemicals, leading to risks of even more bizarre behavior.

Bodies and brains are connected, so frail bodies are associated with frail brains. Occasional organized sports and daily hours of cyber play are feeble substitutes for daily outdoor play on challenging playgrounds—as in recess— and daily physical education that builds bodies and sharpens brains for the academic tasks of the classroom. Overprogrammed and underexercised children are increasingly developing the attention deficits and other behaviors associated with ADHD, depression, and anxiety. Even adult writers enjoying the benefits of computers for rapid, comprehensive information searches find that zipping along in a swiftly moving stream of particles is chipping away at their concentration and contemplation (Carr, 2008). Hopping along from source to source of written information, a form of skimming activity, and rarely returning to visited sources, may be making people "stupid." The longer they use the Internet and the more sources they locate, the more difficult it is to concentrate. Such observations suggest possible long-term problems, as schoolchildren lean on computers for both knowledge gathering and entertainment and avoid immersion in books and outdoor play. Deprivation of spontaneous outdoor play is a fundamental contributor to the breakdowns in school behavior reported by the nation's teachers. Out of control cyber play is joined by other forces such as ever-expanding safety standards that work together to diminish beneficial forms and venues of play.

The Perpetual Evolution of Safety Standards

In the early 1900s playground materials for young children were sand play areas with awnings for shade, sand buckets and shovels, bean bags, and low benches. and the manufactured playground equipment for older children of that era included giant strides, horizontal ladders, swings, tether poles, and teeter boards. More elaborate playgrounds included baseballs, basketballs, slides, merry-go-rounds, and jumping ropes. A major hazard was excessive height— swings and trapeze bars 15–20 feet high, slides 10–15 feet high. Hard surfacing was common—concrete, asphalt, packed cinders, and hard-packed dirt. Open base merry-go-rounds and crowded conditions added to the hazards. Details for reducing hazards were spelled out in the literature of that period well before any organized effort to develop safety standards. By 1917 playground specialists recognized the "miserable state of playgrounds," and Curtis (1917, pp. 121, 123) called the playgrounds of many cities "a disgrace to the systems to which they belong ... The school trustees apparently finish the building and forget all about the playground ... I suppose that this surfacing must have been chosen by the janitor."

Such criticism and awareness of hazards and injuries among leaders in the field led to the first formal effort to develop standards for playground apparatus. This was done by the Committee on Standards in Playground Apparatus, commissioned by the National Recreation Association (NRA). Seventeen recreation executives from ten states prepared a guide for communities in selecting playground apparatus (NRA, 1931). The essential elements to consider were location, arrangement, erection, regular inspection, supervision, designated apparatus zones, care of ground under apparatus, and instruction on use of equipment. Specific preschool apparatus for the exclusive use of younger children and elementary school age children was prescribed, as were provisions for separate playgrounds for boys and girls.

Early playground leaders recognized a century ago that falling on to hard surfacing was a primary factor in playground injuries and requested that the National Recreation Association (1931) appoint a committee to study the issue. The NRA responded by appointing a committee of eleven recreation leaders from the United States to conduct a study of playground surfacing problems. Data were collected from more than twenty cities with extensive playground experience, and a two-part report was published in the August 1932 and September 1932 issues of *Recreation* (formerly *The Playground*). The materials recommended for areas under and around equipment (fall zones) were tanbark, sawdust, shavings, and sand—all to be spaded and raked frequently. World War II redirected the energies of playground proponents, and serious development and application of safety regulations or standards would await a new round of committee actions by national groups.

In 1969 the chairman of the Committee on Accident Prevention of the American Academy of Pediatrics met with a group in New York to prepare voluntary standards for playground equipment (correspondence dated September 14, 1972, between the Accident Prevention Laboratory of the University of Iowa and the American Academy of Pediatrics). Their purpose was to "establish a nationally recognized safety standard for children's home playground equipment" (Committee on Accident Prevention of the American Academy of Pediatrics, 1969). The draft was sent to committee members for comment but the standards were not adopted and the effort was abandoned in 1971. The absence of comprehensive research data hampered the work of early playground safety professionals, but a milestone was reached in 1972 with the introduction of the National Electronic Injury Surveillance System (NEISS).

The NEISS comprised a sampling of hospital emergency rooms throughout the United States and its territories, providing national estimates of the number and severity of injuries associated with, but not necessarily caused by, consumer products, including playground equipment. During the same year (1972) that the NEISS was implemented, two separate actions intended to result in mandatory standards for playground equipment were initiated.

First, the United States Food and Drug Administration's (FDA) Bureau of Product Safety issued a report, *Public Playground Equipment* (BPS, 1972), revealing a dismal picture of playground hazards and injuries. The FDA requested that the Consumer Product Safety Commission (CPSC) support a study of public playground equipment by the University of Iowa. The Iowa investigators (McConnell, 1973) studied injury data prepared by the NEISS, the National Safety Council, and the CPSC. They utilized accident data on ages and sizes of children and data on children's behavior at play such as misuse and horseplay. The results of this report led to additional studies by the University of Michigan on anthropometric data and strength of children that contributed to accidents and injuries, as well as studies of playground surfaces by the Franklin Testing Institute. The reaction of school districts to the documentation of fatalities and injuries on playgrounds was mixed. One large Southern city removed all the swings from its elementary schools because too many children were being injured from falls on to asphalt surfaces.

During the period when the Iowa Study was in progress, the Playground Equipment Manufacturers' Association was working with the National Recreation and Park Association to develop proposed safety standards intended to be used by the CPSC as a voluntary standard. The resulting draft was circulated by the CPSC (1973) for comment. In 1974 Elayne Butwinick, a member of the task force and a public school teacher, petitioned the CPSC to develop consumer product safety standards for playground slides, swinging apparatus, and climbing equipment (Butwinick, 1974). Her petition was supported by reports on 4,094 accidents and several fatalities from one recreation department and two public school systems. She noted that the playground fatality of a six-year-old in Los Angeles in 1951 was the eleventh playground death in that school system over a twenty year period. The school system installed rubber surfacing under and around playground equipment and, as of 1965, ten years later, "had had no further fatalities."

A second petition by Theodora Sweeney (1974), chairperson of an Ohio public school, was used by the CPSC to support Butwinick's petition. In 1974 the CPSC, operating under the Federal Hazardous Substance Act, issued a call in the Federal Register for proposals to develop a standard for both home and public playgrounds. The National Recreation and Park Association, the only bidder, was awarded a contract, and a committee of citizens and industry representatives formulated a report, *Proposed Safety Standards for Playground*

Equipment (NRPA, 1976). Manufacturers feared that adoption would result in high retooling expenses, and designers were concerned that creativity would be stifled. The CPSC identified technical problems and contracted with the National Bureau of Standards (NBS) to revise the document. Two reports emerged from their work, and the CPSC decided to issue the NBS reports as handbooks rather than mandatory standards. Two handbooks for public playground safety were eventually published in 1981 (CPSC, 1981a, 1981b).

In 1990 the Americans with Disabilities Act (ADA) was passed into law, mandating that all public services and accommodations, including playgrounds, be inclusive, that is, accessible to all children, regardless of disability. The access board developed accessibility guidelines (ADAAG) for play areas on making playgrounds accessible. At the request of the CPSC, the American Society for Testing and Materials, a major national producer of consensus safety standards for materials, products, systems, and services, developed a play equipment standard in 1993 primarily directed to manufacturers and intended to be consistent with the CPSC guidelines that were primarily directed to consumers. In 1989 the CPSC contracted with the Comsis Corporation to evaluate the technical rationale for the 1981 handbooks and make recommendations for changes. This resulted in perhaps the most extensive review of playground safety ever conducted.

During this same period (the early 1990s) the issue of preparing and implementing play equipment safety standards was further complicated by the development of standards/guidelines by other organizations, including the American Public Health Association, the American Academy of Pediatrics, many state department agencies responsible for regulating child care centers, several cities, and state departments of education. The present author reviewed all these actions in detail and concluded: "If all of these (and other) groups initiate and enforce playground safety regulations, play equipment designers, manufacturers, installers, and groups responsible for maintenance and supervision will find themselves in legal, technical, bureaucratic log-jams of major proportions" (Frost, 1992, pp. 204–5). (One common, consistent safety standard for manufactured equipment is needed but, except for "unseen" hazards such as toxic materials detectable only by laboratory tests, safety in natural environments should be left to parents, playworkers, and teachers who oversee playgrounds.) The predicted logjam materialized and contributed to the diminution of children's play and playgrounds. One striking consequence is the growth of playground injury lawsuits.

A Litigious Society

As attorneys grew aware of the potential consequences of national safety guidelines and standards, they quickly became the "standard of care" for resolving injury lawsuits, and lawyers entered the fray in growing numbers. Manufacturers standardized and "dumbed down" (for child development) their playground equipment in efforts to meet ever expanding, inconsistent safety standards, and schools began to abandon recess and shut down playgrounds.

Although not generally known or acknowledged, playground injury lawsuits date back for many decades. The playground developers of the early twentieth century were not easily swayed by the threat of lawsuits as they are today, but as early as 1915 the parents of a boy injured in a fall from a swing sued the Tacoma, Washington, school board. The child's parents prevailed in the suit and the school board was required to pay damages for the injury. As a result, playground equipment was removed from many schools in the state of Washington (Curtis, 1917). Removal of play equipment from playgrounds following lawsuits has been a common practice and is at an all time high during the first decade of the twenty-first century. During the 1930s interest in playground injury lawsuits reached such a level that an address on reducing injuries and liability was made to California recreation workers and published in *Recreation* (Jacobson, 1940). The recommendations were surprisingly modern, dealing with selection of equipment, observing for defects, developing inspection systems, keeping records, supervision, and signage. The author (Jacobson, 1940) was very perceptive in noting that signs such as "Not Responsible for Accidents" are absurd. One cannot escape one's legal responsibility by a sign saying, in effect, that one chooses not to be obligated. Such logic would protect bank robbers who attach a sign to their bodies alerting tellers that they are not responsible for their actions!

The growth of lawsuits and the closing of many playgrounds around the beginning of the twenty-first century are closely linked to the ever-growing scope and complexity of playground safety standards. The CPSC playground safety guidelines grew from 13 pages in 1981 to 43 pages in 1997, and 51 pages in 2008. The ASTM safety standards grew from 26 pages at their inception in 1993 to 56 pages in 2005. These documents have become essentially the "national standard of care," meaning that they are influential in most playground injury lawsuits. With each passing revision, additional inconsistencies are built in, consumers are increasingly frustrated, lawyers gain additional fuel for litigation, and school and park administrators struggle with decisions about keeping playgrounds in place. National standards which usually influence legal decisions are inconsistent with state regulations, but in March 2009 Texas legislators drafted a bill that would require compliance with ASTM and/or CPSC for purchases of playground equipment using state funds. Yet problems would remain, for wide-ranging interpretations of national standards in lawsuits have led to litigation as remotely connected to playground equipment as falling over a stump in a grove of redwood trees adjacent to a university laboratory school playground.

The author addressed some of the current problems resulting from playground safety standards and made recommendations for improvement: revising standards to focus on hazards demonstrated by research and scientific data to result in serious, disabling injuries and fatalities, and leaving the protection of children from low level hazards to parents and trained professionals; limiting standards to manufactured products and leaving safety in natural, wild environments to parents and responsible caretakers; improving safety training for play leaders; making state and national standards mutually consistent; broadening participation in standards committees to include a range of professionals; requiring safety inspector certification to include practical experience on playgrounds; simplifying and condensing standards yet utilizing the extensive body of research on child development and play. Decisions about the safety of nature and natural play materials on playgrounds should be left to the adults responsible for children, except when such life-threatening issues as toxic contamination, identifiable by scientific tests, are in question (Frost, 2004, 2005a, 2006b).

Lawsuits are a two-headed beast, resulting in the fortunate removal of several types of antiquated, severely hazardous, life-threatening playground equipment from American playgrounds, yet having a much more extensive record of involving schools, child care centers, municipal parks, and individuals in years-long litigation about injuries that, just a few decades ago, would have been blamed on the carelessness of children and the natural consequences of growing up. School administrators fear both lawsuits and test failure. This is evidenced in news reports of school systems around the country that no longer allow time-honored playground games that include physical contact, such as dodge ball, chase games, tag, and rough and tumble play. The ultimate insult to children's play came when a school installed a warning sign on their playground: "NO RUNNING, PUSHING OR SHOVING." Some schools no longer build playgrounds, and a growing number have deleted or reduced recess to avoid injury and allow more time for testing. Fear of lawsuits is an ever-present concern.

"The notion of a riskless society is a peculiarly American one" (Andrews, 1998, p. D-1). Thousands of adventure playgrounds throughout Europe, especially in Scandinavian countries, England, and Germany, are more challenging, more fun, and more developmentally beneficial than most American playgrounds, but in the eyes of most Americans they are messy and hazardous. The European playground safety standard (European Committee for Standardization, 1998), prepared by representatives of eighteen countries, wisely excludes adventure playgrounds from the standards because they are fenced and secured, operated by trained playworkers or play leaders, use self-build equipment, and have better safety records than traditional playgrounds. Key factors contributing to their safety record appear to be the quality of play-leader training and the existence of extensive opportunities for children to engage in challenging play, leading to improved cognitive and physical performance and, consequently, improved ability to recognize and cope with potentially hazardous conditions.

Figure 8.4 "Dumbing down" the playground.
Source: Author.

The European and American systems have radically different views of risk and responsibility. Europeans place greater responsibility on children and allow risk taking because it is essential for development. They believe that improper or excessive supervision can hinder opportunities for development. The European position is amply supported by research. For example, risk is inherent in all mammal (including human) behavior (Brown, 1997). Play itself enhances risk and the more active and adventuresome the child, the more risk she may assume or be prepared to safely assume.

Tim Gill (2005) would return play and playgrounds to their early primal state of "den-building, bug-hunting, and pond-dipping." Gill, a former director of the Children's Play Council at the U.K. Children's Bureau, reports that the U.K. is "light years behind" cities in Germany, Denmark, and much of northern Europe in providing natural playgrounds for children. Yet, accident claims in the U.K. remained static in recent years and then fell in 2004 by 9.5 percent. U.K. courts are "no more likely today to hand down daft judgments than they were 10, 20, or 100 years ago" (Gill, 2005, 2008). However, the culture of fear is increasing, and paranoid parenting is making rapid inroads into childhood culture in the U.K.

Frank Furedi (2005), described as the most influential sociologist in Britain and author of *Therapy Culture, Culture of Fear, and Paranoid Parenting*, maintains that child safety in the U.K. is impacting adults and children in ways never seen before. The list of safety regulations appears to be growing every day as a new security state is being erected around children. It is no longer fashionable or desirable to be adult or "grown up." Many prefer to look young, act young, and never come to grips with the positive values of becoming mature people. This contributes to a world of witchhunts and adult insecurities about pedophiles on every corner and potential injury, bullying, or worse, on every playground and in every game involving human contact. Sports could be the next form of play destroyed by the child protection industry. The prevailing message in today's society is:

> do not trust adults. ... To genuinely believe that adults cannot help but abuse humanity represents a profoundly negative understanding of what humanity is really all about ... Other people's children are becoming a no-go area for adults ... The biggest danger to children is when adults absolve themselves of the responsibility of looking after them. (Furedi, 2005, pp. 5–6)

The changing safety and litigation scene in the U.K. is similar in many ways to that in the United States. A major difference is that many play specialists, scholars, and parents in the U.K. embraced the adventure playground movement and saw a generation of children who played there regularly benefit from the freedom, activity diversity, and play leadership of trained playworkers. A second difference is the organized playwork training programs in the U.K. that have no equivalent in the United States. These U.K. people, not unlike Americans familiar with adventure playgrounds and playwork programs, now find themselves in the position of attempting to rescue children from those who smother children and impose ever more restrictive standards on their education and play.

Christina Sommers, resident scholar at the American Enterprise Institute in Washington, D. C., author of *Who Stole Feminism?*, *The War against Boys*, and, more recently, *One Nation under Therapy*, writes eloquently about the current "therapism" generation of American "gloom-sayers" (Sommers, 2005). She rejects the assumption that America's youth are a mess, most needing therapy and at risk of being declared officially nuts. Rather, she maintains that most Americans, young and old, are happy and surprisingly sane despite the conditions to which they are exposed. Because of the common assumption that today's children are an emotional mess—weak, wimpy, and unable to protect themselves—many parents, educators, and other professionals take unprecedented measures to protect them from the stress and "dangers" of centuries-old playground games. Hurting feelings and risking bumps and bruises are *out*; hovering, protecting, setting ridiculous rules or standards, and suing for offenses are *in*. However, unless radical changes are made in the emotions and thinking of American adults, most American children may have permanently lost their rights to play unsupervised in the parks of our cities and the wild places of the countryside.

The effects of lawsuits on play and playgrounds are intertwined with other compelling factors contributing to the diminution of outdoor play—high stakes testing, excessive, contradictory safety standards, and the changing, regimented lifestyles of American families. These factors, collectively and independently, contribute to the reduction of creative, absorbing play in natural contexts and to negative consequences for physical and emotional health. The solutions reside in political action (for which this author has limited experience or expertise), scholarly research, which is in abundant supply, common sense, and the will of people to make changes to excessive regulation and failing governing systems. Parents themselves carry heavy responsibilities in ensuring that their children have opportunities to engage in spontaneous, active, outdoor play that contributes to their health and development.

Under-parenting and Over-parenting: Baby Boomers to Generation XXL

Contemporary parenting practices and the play of children were influenced by major generational changes, especially those beginning with the Baby Boomer generation, and the present generation will in turn contribute to form the next generation, perhaps to be known as the XXL generation. Characterizations of different generations are generalized and should not be viewed as accurate for everyone, but they provide a general sense of the culture existing during successive periods.

The Baby Boomers were born during the post-World War II period between 1946 and early 1964. During that period, 76 million babies were born in America. As veterans returned from the war, they went to work, and many women left their wartime jobs to keep households and raise children. Theirs was known as the "silent generation." Having lived through the Depression and the war, most had known hard times with all its economic restraints but now, with growing affluence, they sought to expand their boomer children's freedoms, idolizing them and attempting to provide comforts they themselves never knew. However, the label "silent generation" seems a misfit to me and to those I interviewed who grew up during that period. Rather, we would characterize them as resorting more to action than to words, getting things done, doing the "right" thing, accomplishing their intent, and teaching their offspring by example and unambiguous words to plan ahead and hold off the tragedies of poverty they had experienced. Thanks in part to President Franklin Roosevelt's New Deal Depression recovery programs, and his leadership during World War II, the "silent generation" spoke as a group through dedication, commitment, and resolve—and they prevailed.

As Boomers grew into youths, their growing affluence and unprecedented freedom resulted in social movements for civil rights, feminist rights, gay rights, and disabled rights. Yet, despite these seeming concerns for fellow citizens, many were commonly considered to be whiners, slackers, and even the "doom generation." The Cold War contributed to their haste to enjoy the good life before the feared calamity of nuclear war. In 2008 they were aged 44–62, many moving into retirement but worried about social security, a decline in home values, terrorism, war, energy, and the economic futures of their children and grandchildren. The Boomers scrimped and saved for the "good life"—bigger houses, fitness, entertainment, health—and for their Baby Boomer babies— cyber toys, good education, college, cars, and other advantages their grandparents—the silent generation—never knew or only dreamed about. Play, playgrounds, and entertainment became ready-made, structured, standardized, and generally consisting of things to be bought and places to be hauled to in parents' cars in a never-ending schedule of organized sports, hobbies, and lessons. Occasional vacations substituted for traditional time with parents as both parents entered the work force to buy their own toys, prepare for retirement, and enjoy the status of work and affluence.

Today's babies of Baby Boomers are known as the Echo Boomers, Generation Y, and/or Millennials, born between 1982 and 1995. Many are hovered over by "helicopter parents" and shuttled by their working moms and sometimes dads to a never-ending array of scheduled sports and lessons. Some are victims of over-parenting by overanxious "überparents" who coddle and protect them at home, school, playground and on into adulthood, enabling them to become emotionally and physically "weak" and remain in the nest indefinitely. In reality, the labels "weak" and "overanxious" best fit the parents themselves, who bear responsibility for the fragile condition of their children, whose lives are structured by others—parents, teachers, and coaches—all directing what they can do and how to do it. Many are different from their indulgent, self-centered, ladder-climbing parents but are remarkably media proficient with an amazing array of electronic devices—all used for endless hours of entertainment, communication with peers and strangers, and occasional school work. Many Echo Boomers are group thinkers, leaning on their peers for information, feedback, and support, and capable of teamwork but remarkably naïve about reflective thought and planning for oneself. Rather, many seek praise and instant gratification, and rely on parent figures for the hard decisions. Since theirs is an indoor world, many are semi-helpless out-of-doors and, deprived of play, recess, and playgrounds at school, may gain little appreciation or understanding of nature and everyday outdoor tasks, and do not know how to play common, traditional games or use simple yard tools.

Today's children are into "what's hot," pop idols, shopping, video games, text messaging, the Internet, chat rooms, computers, and websites. Some are the most protected children in history—trophy children—restricted to home after school and when parents are working, protected by seat belts, air bags, and helmets, and they take more shots, medications, slap on more suntan lotion, and receive more warnings about potential illnesses and injuries than any generation in history. The unseen threats are seemingly everywhere: constant noise from entertainment devices places them at risk for early hearing problems; lack of sunlight and vitamin D are leading to an increase in childhood rickets, while too much sunlight results in cancer; and lack of physical activity and excessive junk food contribute to a growing childhood obesity epidemic. All this reduces free, spontaneous, active, challenging outdoor play to a threatened relic of past generations.

Thanks to the fragile economy, high stakes testing, and a nonstop media blitz about child predators, many of today's parents fear their children will not pass the tests, be retained, fail to get into college, get hurt in the street or on the playground, or become victims of violence. Which is the greater threat, becoming one of the few dozen children kidnapped by a stranger each year, or becoming one of the millions of overweight or obese adults facing premature health problems and shortened life spans? Worldwide media bombardment following virtually every child kidnapping and serious child abuse case adds almost daily to growing parental concern or paranoia about the safety of their children. Today's working parents have limited time and little excess energy to spend with their children and may also tend to be sedentary, so indoor technology play is seen as a safe substitute for outdoor play.

Contemporary children increasingly prefer unlimited access to indoor electronic toys, computers, and refrigerators stocked with junk food. Parents require their children to stay indoors for safety reasons, and many struggle to enroll them in organized, supervised sports as an alternative to outdoor free play in natural and built environments they consider dangerous. Consequently, growing numbers of children are more technologically literate than their parents but know little about initiating spontaneous play or playing with peers. Quick to seize on a perceived need and an opportunity for sales, electronic game designers create indoor games that get kids moving while they play. Such artificial substitutes for the forms and venues of spontaneous play and traditional games, enjoyed by children for centuries, beg the attention of play proponents and scholars everywhere. All this was to be further complicated and children's play placed at even greater risk by the passage of the No Child Left Behind Act.

No Child Left Behind: A Flawed Political Mandate

The coup de grâce for free play arrived with the passage of the No Child Left Behind Act that substituted high stakes testing for play, physical education, and the arts in schools across America, and contributed to an epidemic of child obesity and related health issues. No organized program is inflicting more damage on children's free, creative, spontaneous playground play, physical education, the arts, and recess than high stakes testing. Enter "High Stakes Testing" or "No Child Left Behind" in a search engine such as Yahoo or Google and see millions of hits and voluminous evidence against this illogical, ill informed, politically inspired practice that has given the "boon" to boondoggle.

High stakes testing is contrary to a century of research on education and child development. It is based on mechanized, industrial-type models for producing spinach, dog food, and industrial products. If it were about excellence, it would be about educating highly creative individuals, capable of reflective, visionary thought and action. It would be about ambition, pride, collaboration, thinking, and imagination. Einstein's wisdom seems appropriate here: "He who joyfully marches in rank and file has already earned my contempt. He has been given a large brain by mistake, since for him the spinal cord would suffice."

High stakes testing in its present form is rejected by many major professional education and assessment organizations. Evidence of its faults is voluminous. For example, the position statement of the Association for Childhood Education International concludes: "To continue such testing in the face of so much evidence of its detrimental effects in regards to motivation to learn, learning itself, and the narrowing of curriculum is irresponsible and inappropriate" (Solley, 2007, p. 37). Professional organizations and research scholars conclude that high stakes testing is illogical, damages morale, and fails to result in better education for students (National Association for the Education of Young Children, 1988; Association for Childhood Education International, 2001; Amrein and Berliner, 2002; Popham, 2002; Berliner, 2005;). Two of the most prominent researchers into the effects of high stakes testing, working at the Arizona State University Education Policies Study Center, conducted and summarized exhaustive research to conclude that negative consequences multiply as time on testing grows (Nichols and Berliner, 2007, 2008). High stakes testing is taking the joy out of learning and failing to close achievement gaps. Curriculum is narrowed, teacher and student relationships are undermined, motivation is reduced, teachers are demoralized, and students are bored. School thus becomes uninteresting, punitive, and damaging.

Latino scholars write that high stakes testing is damaging for poor, minority, non-English-speaking students, and argue for assessment that is fair, impartial, and uses multiple criteria rather than culturally biased procedures and content. They find no truth in claims of widespread success, especially among the poor and minorities (Valenzuela, 2005). Some schools are rated "unacceptable" because their students start from the deepest hole, while children in other schools are deposited at the schoolhouse door in their parents' limousines. Pressure is on to extend testing to younger and younger children, including preschool and Head Start ("Head Start Resists Efforts," 2003; Frost, 2006), despite the questionable utility of such testing for young children.

Samuel Meisels, President of the Erikson Institute and one of the nation's leading authorities on assessing children, and Sally Atkins-Burnett (Meisels and Atkins-Burnett, 2004) critiqued the federally created instrument used to test four- and five-year-old Head Start children in 2002. Never before in the history of America have so many young children been subjected to a standardized achievement test. The test showed a stunning lack of appreciation for the broad, comprehensive goals and activities of the highly successful Head Start program, operational since 1965. "This test is not good early education practice. It is not good psychometric practice. It is not good public policy. And it is certainly not good for young children" (Meisels and Atkins-Burnett, 2004).

Politicians are deeply implicated in the testing movement, creating the No Child Left Behind Act and extending failed testing policies into preschools and Head Start. Young children throw up on test papers and older ones secretly dope out on parents' prescription drugs to get through the tests. In 2008 a Texas school district held a workshop to help families learn how to handle the stress of students taking the Texas Assessment of Knowledge and Skills. Some teachers and administrators are pressured to manipulate data or cheat to save their school's or their own reputation and qualify for bonuses, while recess, physical education, and the arts are set aside to make way for teaching the test driven curricula. A poverty area public school in Texas that closed in 2008 for failing to meet test requirements reopened that same year under a new name. The principal, who had a Ph.D. and had led the school to progress each year during her tenure but failed to meet minimum standards, was quickly hired to administer a school in a nearby district.

Young teachers are leaving the profession in record numbers, lamenting the deluge of questionable teaching requirements—preparing for tests, dealing with discipline problems, managing medicated, stressed out kids, communicating with children who speak little English, meeting with disgruntled parents who fail to understand that if they do not raise responsible children, teachers cannot reach them or teach them. Older teachers long for the day they can retire, yet fear that their retirement checks may fail to sustain them in a faltering economy. All the while, politicians and administrators struggle to raise academic standards ever higher, grasping at failed policies and seeking miracle cures through catchy techniques such as paying bonuses or rewards to teachers who manage to outdo their peers in raising test scores. This, they assume, can be accomplished by "cutting frills"—recess, playgrounds, P.E., music, literacy, history, etc.—in exchange for spending days drilling on the expected test items, and motivating students with pep rallies, pizza parties, and posters. When all this fails, some schools resort to data manipulation and cheating.

Stress on the youngest students is perhaps most objectionable—no room parties, no nap time, reduced or eliminated outdoor play—in sum, an unhappy place for both children and teachers. During this national flurry of political maneuvering, few seem to understand that a single standard should not apply to all children in all schools. Three public schools in one Texas School District were recently rated "unacceptable" because a few special education students did not reach the minimum passing score on a standardized test. Children are not cookies to be cut by the same mold, chickens to be graded, or commercial products to be built on an assembly line. For decades, research has shown and teachers have known that the schools in poverty areas receiving the least professional and material support enroll the children least prepared to achieve upon entry and the most likely to fail. At the opposite extreme, most children in schools located in high income neighborhoods have little difficulty passing high stakes tests, yet suffer the consequences of being denied a broad curriculum addressed to the development of the whole child and to preparing them for entering major universities.

Following the publication of *A Nation at Risk* in 1989, a number of states developed their own versions of high stakes testing, and a few started testing during the 1970s. Obviously, there was little consistency among the states regarding expectations, nature of testing, criteria for "success," or results. The No Child Left Behind Act of 2002 failed to change this pattern and is fundamentally flawed. A review of results from twenty-six states by the prestigious Fordham Institute (Cronin et al., 2007), aptly entitled "The Proficiency Illusion," found that the states do a bad job of setting and maintaining standards of student proficiency. Two-thirds of American schoolchildren attend schools with mediocre (or worse) expectations about what children should learn. "Proficiency" varies wildly from state to state, with "passing scores" ranging from the 6th percentile to the 77th. Further, "passing" scores vary within states across subject areas, with mathematics being consistently more difficult than reading tests, and tests in higher grades more difficult than tests in lower grades. The goal of No Child Left Behind—to achieve 100 percent proficiency—was as far away in 2007 as it was in the first year of its implementation. In an interview with the *New York Times* on October 3, 2007, Diane Ravitz, a professor of education at New York University and Assistant Secretary of Education for Research from 1991 to 1993, described the No Child Left Behind Act as "fundamentally flawed," declaring that a main goal of making every child proficient in reading and mathematics by 2014 is "simply unattainable." There have been no gains in eighth grade reading in a decade. The obsession with standardized testing has reduced the time available for other important school subjects and goals, and has subjected schools, students, teachers, and administrators to ever more onerous penalties. On October 9, 2007, Daniel Koretz, a professor at Harvard's

Graduate School of Education, weighing in during a *New York Times* interview, stated that the tests were based on the idea of getting a good test in place and beating people up to raise scores so they would learn more, but questioned whether the tests were anything more than a shell game. Leaving the states to develop their own definitions of proficiency results in measurements without meaning.

The illogical emphasis on high stakes testing and a creeping national curriculum—the so-called basics—emerging from standardized, narrow criteria, deny children opportunities to reflect and learn about the complexities of a chaotic and rapidly changing world. Learning to cope in the midst of change is not accomplished by drilling on a limited set of test items. Rather, creativity, imagination, and reflective thought are essential to understanding the present and preparing for continuous, accelerating change. Learning beyond ordinary boundaries is cultivated early through play, and is inspired by play, as opposed to rote teaching (Frost et al., 2008). Consider the initiatives explored in the fascinating book *Imagining the Impossible: Magical, Scientific, and Religious Thinking in Children* (Rosenberg et al., 2000) and the challenging views about change and learning in *Presence: An Exploration of Profound Change in People, Organizations, and Society* (Senge et al., 2004). We radically underestimate children's powers to learn through magical episodes of imaginative play and to expand visions of change and society through spontaneous social interaction with peers. Little of this is tapped in the structured context of standard tests. There is little controversy regarding the need for a rational form of national achievement standards and assessment that is reliable, cumulative, and comparable. That is not the issue. The argument is over a failed, politically inspired system that shows no consistent promise for improving the education of American children and youth. It is about a system that systematically denies the poor equal educational opportunity. Even closer to the context of this book, the argument is about subjecting the young to a system that denies children's rights to free play, creative thought, and artistic enterprise, and erodes their health, fitness, and well-being.

In 2009 the Texas legislature, recognizing that the high stakes testing movement was only an "illusion of progress," began work on bills to eliminate such testing for grade advancement, focusing on progress in student performance and flexibility in course offerings rather than one-time test scores. The Texas testing system was originally used by President Bush as a model to develop the later, seriously flawed and failing, No Child Left Behind Act. In Texas's high school graduating class of 2007, almost half were not college-ready, almost none were prepared for workplace jobs, and one-third dropped out before graduation, essentially ensuring a lifetime of low-paying jobs and assistance from social services. Legislators are now opening the gate for a return of the arts, humanities, physical education, and recess, and preparing students for either college or the workforce. Such action, multiplied many times nationwide, is bringing common sense back to schooling and leading to an unprecedented drive to revitalize the culture of childhood.

Needed: A Twenty-First Century Child-Saving Movement

The values of free, creative, spontaneous play and challenging built and natural outdoor play environments are supported by decades of research. This research is rivaled in scope by findings that, during the latter decades of the twentieth century, the potential benefits of play and play environments were diminished by play deprivation. The shift from outdoor play to indoor electronic play, the decline of recess and playground play, threats of lawsuits, parental fear of child injury, and excessive regulations and testing are all ample reasons for deliberation and a compelling stimulus for inquiry and action. The effects of such factors on the health, development, and well-being of children are confirmed as a crisis of accelerating disease by the medical professions and a host of other scientific disciplines.

Other elements of a "perfect storm" of forces contribute to this state of affairs—lack of opportunity and access to places for physical activity, lack of knowledge and motivation among both adults and children, the appeal of leisure activity over active lifestyles, "fast food nation" diets, and, for many, the grinding consequences of poverty. Generational changes in the lifestyles of modern Americans, spurred by the technological revolution and the media and information explosion, also contribute to the crisis. All this could be improved by creating activity-friendly neighborhoods, safe, challenging places to explore and play, using mass media to educate the public, providing health and physical education classes in all schools, reinstating daily recess for elementary schools, and reducing significantly the time children spend with recreational technology—the cyber playgrounds.

Growing numbers of play and medical professionals believe that children need at least one hour of vigorous physical activity each day, with half taking place in physical education and recess at school, but ninety minutes of activity may well be a more realistic recommendation. William Dietz (2001), a leading Centers for Disease Control expert on nutrition and physical activity, said in a *British Medical Journal* editorial that spontaneous play may be the only requirement for increasing physical activity of young children. Play is indeed a fundamental requirement for increasing physical activity, but there is no single "magic bullet" for the multifaceted attack on the many health and development issues facing children.

The intertwined factors that deprive children of the play they need are multiple and complex, each begging the efforts of numerous disciplines and a level of coordination and care not yet seen in the history of childhood issues in America. Three brief decades of mounting physical inactivity have created a crisis that will take years to resolve, and that will only happen if national, state, and local organizations and agencies come together to combine their resources and form a coordinated plan of action. Present efforts, though promising and expanding, lack the coordination and commitment needed to reverse current patterns. Not unlike the crisis of children in the slums of American cities a century ago and the resulting child-saving movement, America now needs and may be setting the stage for a twenty-first century child-saving movement.

9
Toward a Contemporary Child-Saving Movement

Long ago it was said that "one half of the world does not know how the other half lives." It did not know because it did not care. There came a time when the discomfort and crowding became so great, and the consequent upheavals so violent ... [that] ... the upper half fell to inquiring what was the matter. (Riis, 1957, p. 1)

I repeat the quote by Riis above that opened Chapter 3, for I have seen no other statement that so appropriately introduces the need for a contemporary child-saving movement. The history of childhood in America holds no more compelling story than the late nineteenth and early twentieth century child-saving movement. A century later there are growing signs that a new child-saving movement is taking root, echoing the same forgotten refrain—half the nation seemingly not knowing, nor caring, until the discomfort became so great and the consequences so savage that adults, once again, fell to inquiring what was the matter! What the current generation of adults failed to notice was their children's health, development, and fitness slowly being squandered by changing lifestyles, abuse of technology, and a changing culture of affluence, parenting, schooling, and society, resulting in a changing culture of childhood (see Frost, 1986a, 2003, 2005, for the evolution of these changes). What adults seemingly failed to know or care about were the consequences of children being deprived of centuries-old traditions of free play and unrestricted access to play in the playgrounds of the wilderness, the neighborhood, and the schoolyard—all factors implicated in a complex web of modern day diminution of play—for their children's health, fitness, and well-being.

A century ago, when the upper half—individuals, organizations, and charitable, governmental, and professional groups—finally noticed the perilous lives of the forgotten orphans and street children of city slums, they established movements and organizations, many still alive and well a century later, that changed the lives of hundreds of thousands of children. These visionary reformers of the early twentieth century established and built a complex ecosystem of private, charitable, and governmental groups comprising a child-saving movement of unprecedented proportions. They were the forerunners of the Greatest

Generation—those patriots who conquered the Great Depression, fought and won World War II, and gave birth to an expansive economic, cultural, and industrial revolution. Following the successes of the early child-saving movement and the social and political movements that occurred during the second half of the twentieth century, a technology revolution was born, affluence flourished, the culture of childhood changed in unprecedented and unexpected ways, child advocates began to awaken, and a twenty-first century child-saving movement began to slowly take form. A century ago, the issues were lack of housing, food, shelter, schooling, and playgrounds, resulting in crime, illiteracy, disease, and hopelessness. Compared to now, the triple blow of immigration, industrialization, and urbanization had harsh effects on the very poor in cities. Now, the issues are even more comprehensive, profound, and potentially damaging, affecting not just the destitute children of poverty, but the children of every socioeconomic and ethnic group.

Lessons from the Past

Would a new child-saving movement be sufficiently strong, coordinated, and comprehensive to overcome the ravages of a chaotic, postmodern culture of child rearing and schooling gone wrong? Elements of heartening change are falling into place—signaling reconsideration by child rearing institutions, showing weak but promising signs of saving play, natural and built play environments, and recess, and *possibly* reversing patterns of deteriorating health and fitness among American children. The problems that led to the organization of the early twentieth century child-saving movement were relatively simple compared to those now faced by people seeking to bring common sense and resolution back to the culture of childhood and save play, recess, and nature.

For centuries, the inherent need for play and the antidotes for obesity and the other consequences of play deprivation were supplied by playing in nature, engaging in productive work, and securing food directly from the land. With the advent of the information age, the technology revolution, and the accompanying affluence during the latter decades of the twentieth century, the culture of childhood changed from relatively simple, yet successful, patterns of existence to extraordinarily complex ones. The signals for a changing culture of childhood picked up force with the "hippie generation" and the age of technology during the 1960s, and were everywhere apparent by the 1970s and 1980s. What adults seemingly overlooked about the deteriorating culture of childhood was that public institutions failed to compensate for fragmented family lives and families themselves failed to take charge of their children's fitness and dietary patterns. As a result, children shifted their time from spontaneous play and meaningful work to sedentary TV watching and computer play. Having a cookie in one hand and a sugary drink in the other is not a balanced diet, and substituting TV and computer entertainment for active, outdoor play does not build fit bodies. The consequences of play deprivation and disrupted families go well beyond such matters as fitness, affecting children's social and cognitive learning and consequent behavior in schools. As one teacher aptly said, "If parents don't parent them, we can't teach them."

As recently as the 1950s and 1960s, educators and child development professionals were speaking in glowing terms of achieving "the golden age of childhood." The scenario of the American family a quarter century later, in 1985, was an expanding pattern of divorce, one-parent homes, or two working parents, various child care arrangements, increasing amounts of sedentary activity, television viewing, including heavy episodes of sex and violence, use of illicit drugs and tobacco, and children birthing children (Frost, 1986a). In 1979 the U.S. Bureau of the Census reported that children involved in divorce during 1979 numbered about 1,181,000, more than triple the number in 1957. In March 1980, 14.6 percent of 8,530,000 families were maintained by female householders, doubling since 1960, and soaring to 25 percent in 1985 (Stengel, 1985). According to the Neilsen Report on Television for 1980, children watched television 30 to 31 hours weekly, more than any other activity except sleep. By graduation day, the average high school student had seen 18,000 murders in 22,000 hours of television viewing (*U.S. News and World Report*, 1985).

A quarter century ago studies showed that watching TV makes kids fat (Dietz and Gortmaker, 1985). The pattern of family breakdown was already well established and we are now playing catch-up. Sedentary lifestyles and junk food, coupled with increased emphasis on academic subjects (due to failing children) and reduced emphasis on play, physical education and physical work, was leading to a nation of short-winded kids with elevated cholesterol and blood-pressure levels, and declining strength and heart–lung endurance (Winston, 1984). To further complicate matters, the rate of American teenage pregnancy in 1985 was the highest among developed nations—at 96 per 1,000 for 15 to 19-year-olds and more than 5 per 1,000 for 14-year-olds (*Education Week*, 1985).

The growing pattern of child rearing a quarter century ago was one of parents losing touch with their children, leaving parenting to machines and surrogates, and shifting the school's traditional modes of instruction and authority—direct and personal—to legal and contractual, and their curricula from comprehensive and individualized to narrow and standardized. Schools and teachers were being sued by parents for common playground injuries and parents were intervening or even suing to have children's failing grades changed to passing grades, even though their children had excessive absences during the school year and did not complete their work. This "modernistic" ethic eventually permeated both family and school. Many hovering parents overprotect their children, despite moralistic and ethical breakdowns in their own behavior, and remain mute in the face of such illogical, failing "innovations" as "No Child Left Behind" and high stakes testing (Frost, 2003). Such modern thought and action led young teachers to abandon the profession in unprecedented numbers and left older teachers eager for the day they could retire. The time for radical reform was upon us, and the American public at large still "didn't get it," but, with the opening of the twenty-first century, a tide of dissent, concern, and action was rising.

The Postmodern Era in Children's Play and Play Environments

During the last two or three decades of the twentieth century, a slowly rising tide of dissent arose against the diminution of play and the standardization of playgrounds. Policy makers questioned the worth of high stakes testing. National and local media spoke to the futility of such practices, and, thanks to the unfortunate, unintended consequences so painfully visible, such as the growing rate of obesity and other health-related problems among children, the public grew more concerned and better informed. Some states are suing the Federal government for failing to fund the No Child Left Behind Act, some are proposing legislation to require recess and physical education in schools, and both state and national politicians are reexamining the No Child Left Behind Act. In June 2007 the Texas legislature passed a bill, signed by the governor, that established minimum periods of time for physical education and/or recess in schools, as well as a second bill that mandated replacement of the current high stakes tests with end-of-course exams. Several other states were taking up similar issues, and organizations are being formed at an unprecedented rate to inform about the nature and value of play and to reintroduce children to outdoor play and play environments. By 2009 all fifty states and the District of Columbia had passed laws relating to physical education and/or physical activity in schools, but only thirteen states included measures for enforcement (Levy, et al., 2009).

Many of the submovements of the early twentieth century child-saving movement have endured and are expanding their influence. Will these be sufficient to overcome the disappearance of children from their traditional play environments of past centuries? Will the rapid diminution of children's outdoor play continue to result in unhealthy, weakened children? Will the many groups and organizations attacking these problems work together to form a twenty-first century child-saving movement to match that of a century ago in protecting and saving children and preserving their right to play? The time is overdue but momentum is building.

Building on the Early Child-Saving Movement

Here I briefly revisit the emergence of the early child-saving movement of the late nineteenth and early twentieth centuries, which was a compendium of several movements or submovements, several having common sponsors and workers. I will trace their enduring elements and progress toward resolving current issues. I then describe recent innovations intended to resolve the current play, fitness, and health crisis among American children. Although many etiologies are implicated, saving children's recess, free outdoor play, play environments, and nature are key factors in attacking and resolving the modern crisis and restoring children's rights to play and access to play environments. Several early twentieth century movements contributed to the overarching child-saving movement of that era—the play and playgrounds movement, the school gardens movement, the children's zoo movement, the nature study movement, the organized camping movement, and the children's museums movement. These movements endured throughout the twentieth century, remain alive and well, and are contributing to an emerging twenty-first century child-saving movement, and, hopefully, a reconstituted culture of childhood.

The Play and Playground Movement

The American play and playground movement, growing from German influences, began slowly in the mid-1800s and reached groundswelling proportions by the turn of the twentieth century (Chapter 4) as reformers turned their energies to saving children. By 1906 hundreds of playgrounds had been constructed in city parks throughout major American cities, and the Playground Association of America (PAA) was being formed under the leadership of prominent individuals who would inspire other submovements intended to save children from the perils of America's city streets and slums. The playground movement fizzled during World Wars I and II, but was reinvigorated in the 1950s and 1960s during the novelty era, reaching new levels of interest and activity during the modular era of the 1970s and 1980s and the standardized era of the 1990s. The turn of the twenty-first century saw growing criticism about the "dumbing down" of American playgrounds, leading designers and manufacturers to reach deeper into their creative resources to make playgrounds more exciting, risky, challenging, and attractive to both adults and children.

Modern playground equipment is safer, more developmentally appropriate, offers more challenges, and, when wisely selected and supplemented, meets a wider range of children's play needs than did the old "prison yard" playgrounds featuring "manufactured appliances." Americans have choices, not only in terms of the types of equipment selected, but also in the overall design of playgrounds. They have cookie-cutter playgrounds because they tend to choose from limited, standard perspectives of what makes a good playground, or they are simply uninformed about children's needs and the wide array of choices that can be bought, built, or created by children. There are many options. Further, modern playgrounds should be supplemented with nature areas, gardens, animal habitats, and other elements intended to foster exploration, creativity, and imagination and to help ensure physical fitness, social competency, and learning. We need to reinstate recess, get kids back to their outdoor play, and relinquish the strangleholds of excessive technology, hovering and unconnected parents, and illogical, irresponsible academic testing that keeps children from free, active play.

In reality, playgrounds at the turn of the twenty-first century were already giant steps ahead of early twentieth century playgrounds. Many adults, recalling their pleasant experiences playing on traditional swings, merry-go-rounds, seesaws, giant strides, and tall, steep slides, but seeing the effects of play deprivation on children in recent years, criticized the demise of such equipment. In reality, all of these devices, in safer form, are still available and supplemented with a host of new, challenging apparatus. The problems are frequently in the minds of adults who "design" or select equipment for a playground and are motivated simply to fill vacant spaces with the largest, most expensive equipment available rather than create a playscape attuned to the developmental play needs of the children. Let there be no mistake, playgrounds, including both manufactured equipment and natural materials, are sorely needed to meet children's play and learning needs (Frost, et al., 2004). Unfortunately, there is precious little chance that children in mega-cities will have regular access to the wilderness playscapes of earlier generations. Traditionally, children's play was balanced with meaningful work, so most were physically active in the outdoors and ate natural foods, void of chemical additives and processing, directly from the land. Few were obese, and symptoms of early heart disease, diabetes, and related diseases were rare. The paucity of research did not deter early reformers from observing the health benefits of open air and exercise. When reformers finally saw the effects of immigrant families and American farm families flooding into cities, they began to act, taking some of the advantages of the countryside to children in crowded urban areas.

The School Gardens Movement

The school gardens submovement of the child-saving movement, initiated as a children's school farm, was formed in New York City in about 1902, and the children's gardening program was created at the Brooklyn Botanic Gardens in 1914. The National Gardening Association (NGA), formed in 1973, aimed to influence the establishment of a garden in every school. The NGA helps children and adults to establish links between plants, gardening, food, and health, and learners to become connected to the environment. A national NGA survey found that in 2007 more than $35 billion was spent on gardening, an increase of more than $1 billion over 2006. In December 2007 the National Farm Bill that passed the Senate included $10 million to establish pilot programs for community school gardens, helping ensure that school gardens would grow and prosper. The garden movement is alive and growing—in schools and communities throughout the nation.

Figure 9.1 Children tend herb/vegetable gardens to provide herbs to Meals on Wheels and food for the school cafeteria.
Source: Courtesy Redeemer Lutheran School, Austin, Texas.

The realization that children are losing touch with the wonders and learning opportunities of nature is also inspiring organizations to consider the developmental disadvantages of losing touch with natural habitats. These include the Children and Nature Network, the National Gardening Association, the American Horticultural Society, the Partnership for Plant-Based Learning, the No Child Left Inside Movement, the Sierra Club, and the U.S. Forest Service. The National Wildlife Federation emphasizes the developmental and learning values of plants and gardens, and extends its interest and influence to natural habitats for plants and animals and preserving the earth's ecosystem. Many educational programs and professional organizations promote the contributions of nature to science, mathematics, social sciences, and literacy, and to related areas such as physical fitness and mental health.

As the movements discussed here continue to spread across America, they are increasingly evolving from stand-alone attractions into complex ecosystems for play, development, learning, and aesthetic qualities. Many botanical gardens, prepared for people of all ages, have special gardens and other natural features for children. By 2007 at least ten botanical gardens were accredited by the American Association of Museums (AAM). For example, the Chicago Botanic Garden is a member of the American Public Gardens Association and is also accredited by the AAM, recognizing its collection of 2.4 million plants, 23 display gardens, 3 native habitats, a 100 acre natural oak woodland, and animals of many species. This 385 acre garden is visited by more than three-quarters of a million people each year.

The Children's Zoo Movement

Yet another submovement with ancient roots is presently flourishing and awakening to the need for children to be reintroduced to outdoor play and learning. The London Zoo, founded in 1938, was the first children's zoo in Europe, and the Philadelphia Zoo was the first to open a special children's zoo in America. Zoos have grown beyond mere places to see exotic animals to become powerful settings for connecting children and adults to nature—protecting endangered species and wildlife habitats, conservation, recycling, energy conservation, and providing educational programs. The Association of Zoos and Aquariums, formed in 1924, was dedicated to animal care, wildlife conservation, education and science. In 2005 it had more than 200 accredited members drawing more than 145 million visitors during that year. Many have sections for children's zoos, also called petting zoos and children's farms, since they feature both hands-on contact with animals, mostly domesticated, and gardening and plant propagation. Many have also developed playgrounds with both commercial equipment and natural play features such as water and natural habitats.

One shining example is the San Antonio Zoo's Tiny Tots Nature Spot, established in 2007, which occupies a special corner of the grounds and includes both indoor and outdoor play venues—a sandy sea shore for wading, natural and built play equipment, nature walks, a mammoth cave with giant aquariums, special waterways for exotic birds such as flamingos, a miniature lake with floating docks, indoor spaces for water play, and transparent walls for

Figure 9.2 San Antonio Zoo, Tiny Tots Nature Spot, Children's Beach—sand and water play.
Source: Photograph courtesy of Brandi Cross.

observing prairie dogs in a natural outdoor habitat. The zoo is connected to Brackenridge Park, a vast wonderland for children, replete with woodlands, playgrounds, picnic areas, and playing fields, with the clear headwaters of the San Antonio River flowing through it. The San Antonio Botanical Gardens, the Japanese Gardens, and the Witte Museum are also nearby, making this a magical, contiguous ecosystem for children's play and learning.

The Nature Study Movement

This movement, closely allied with the garden movement, was inspired by university professor C. F. Hodge and the eminent psychologist G. Stanley Hall in the late 1800s to combat the growing fear of excessive confinement, sedentary attitudes, and the institutionalizing influences of schools—motives not unlike those of present advocates of getting children back in nature. The early playground movement was tied to the nature study movement by early reformers, both philosophically and in practical terms. They understood it was far easier and more productive to bring little oases of nature to the city for children to use in their play, learning, and appreciation than to take them on occasional trips to the country—how modern this sounds! This, they believed, was the reason that playgrounds, ball fields, pools, and parks should be created in cities. Cities were growing to such a size that fragrant flowers, clear creeks, and mysterious woods were becoming scarce. Even a century ago, reformers recognized that multiple places for children's play should be provided that are complementary in value. The accuracy of these assumptions is presently striking home as child advocates come to understand that no one solution to the play and playground crisis will meet the need to reintroduce children to outdoor play and playgrounds. Ideally, playgrounds, like play, take many forms—built, natural, or, more appropriately, a mix of elements to challenge, inspire, and foster creativity, imagination, learning, development, fitness, and health.

Such diversity need not crowd out playgrounds for testing and strengthening motor skills, playing chase games, rough and tumble, climbing, sliding, brachiating, and pulling wagons. Nature needs little space to enliven a playground, for it clings to life around the boundaries and fences and entrances, needing little room to become a flowering creation or a shaded wonderland. Collectively, a well equipped, thoughtfully created, miniature ecosystem of toys and nature resonates with children, can be condensed into small backyards, neighborhoods, and school play spaces, and can include many of the play features once found only in vast wild places, city streets, junk yards, fields and barnyards, or the wonderfully creative adventure playgrounds popular in Europe.

The Organized Camping Movement

Yet another submovement entered the scene over a century ago and grew during the early child-saving movement to complement and enhance other venues for play. The organized camping movement, initially for boys, was developed for essentially the same reasons as the other movements—to improve the lives of children suffering from debilitating living conditions in cities, develop civic responsibility, sharpen physical and social skills, bond with nature, and enhance the intellect. An early camp was established in 1861, as a back-to-nature trend patterned after the vigorous survival skills of Native American children. Additional camps were formed rapidly during the early 1900s, not only in response to the challenges of city streets but to provide respite from the regimentation of schools. The work of naturalists such as John Muir and Theodore Roosevelt helped direct attention to the need for preserving the wilderness and concern for its disappearance. The early camping movement and its leaders influenced the creation of the Boy Scouts, Girl Scouts, and Camp Fire Girls. Now we see a strangely familiar pattern of regimentation in schools, divorcing children from nature.

Organized camping evolved from several strands of interest, but the concerns of citizens about children's freedom to play and the creation and preservation of playgrounds—both natural and built—reflect current concerns about the diminution of outdoor spontaneous play and the destruction of wild places for such play. By 2007 there were 7,000 members of the American Camping Association and 2,400 accredited camps. Many summer camps today are specialized, focusing on sports, computers, cheerleading, losing weight, or being entertained, but some have stuck to the historical emphasis on building campfires, hiking, studying plants and animals, fishing, canoeing, and learning about the wilderness—these camps are among those in need of emulation. A few operators of summer camps are returning to nature, taking children to the real wilderness, living in primitive shelters, taking long hikes, engaging with nature, bathing in cold water, cooking over open fires, and otherwise getting close to nature. Some have waiting lists, and kids' initial misgivings are being replaced with awe and wonder at being transformed by the magical qualities of wild places.

The Children's Museum Movement

This movement began with the founding of the first children's museum in Brooklyn in 1899, followed by those at the Smithsonian and in Boston, Detroit, and Indianapolis. Innovations during the 1960s resulted in interactive exhibits for children of all ages, intended for them to gain firsthand experience through sensory involvement and hands-on manipulation and problem solving. The Indianapolis children's museum is the largest in the nation. By 2008 there were more than 300 children's museums in the United States with 82 percent having opened since 1976, making them the fastest growing segment of the museum industry (Din, 1998; Association of Children's Museums, 2008).

The Strong Museum in Rochester, New York, was renovated and re-established as the National Museum of Play in 2006. This museum is a beacon for promoting the value of children's play and play environments. Between 2004 and 2006

Figure 9.3 The Children's Museum of Houston is expanding outdoors and bringing families together to play and learn: FlowWorks, Nature Center (background) and active playground equipment (left).
Source: Photograph courtesy of Cheryl McCallum.

the original Strong Museum nearly doubled its physical plant, making it the second largest children's museum in the United States, and during this period changed its name to the Strong National Museum of Play. Their holdings include one of the most comprehensive collections of dolls, toys, and other play objects in the world, and they house the National Toy Hall of Fame, which features the best and most popular toys of childhood.

> Strong is the only museum in the world devoted to play ... an exciting, hands-on, welcoming place to play, learn, and dream; a place to pretend, wonder, and explore; a place to discover the past and imagine the future; and a place to rekindle memories and make new ones. (Strong National Museum of Play website)

It is even more than this, featuring a full size, working, restored carousel, a preschool, a research library and archives, extensive interactive collections, and the Dancing Wings Butterfly Garden. In 2007 the museum hosted a joint conference of the American Association for Play/USA and the Association for the Study of Play (TASP). TASP now has its permanent headquarters there. The scholarly play resources at the museum promise to make it a gathering place for play scholars. In summer 2008 they published the first issue of a scholarly journal devoted to play—the *American Journal of Play*. Collectively, these activities and resources are expected to be very influential in promoting the resurgence of play in America.

The early interest in children's play and play environments, interactive exhibits, and hands-on experiences among museums remained alive into the twenty-first century and is expanding today. In 2007 the Association of Children's Museums had 341 member institutions in three countries, with 82 percent opening since 1976. As they form new facilities and renovate existing ones, many museums are expanding activities for children into outdoor spaces, creating traditional and adventure playgrounds and special natural habitats to enhance opportunities for physical, cognitive, and emotional development.

All of the innovative approaches of a century ago, intended to save children from debilitating conditions, are relevant to the current play deprivation—each in unique ways. What early reformers knew and later Americans forgot is that play results in learning, and play deprivation results in weak, unhealthy children. Their time tested child-saving movements continue to be promising approaches to the complex issues of child health, development, and well-being, yet are not sufficient to resolve the pressing needs of children in a postmodern world. Consequently, a widening range of organizations and agencies are reinforcing and complementing the work of traditional child-saving groups. Collectively, these reforms are gaining energy, expanding rapidly across private, public, and governmental groups and organizations and setting the stage for a child-saving movement of unprecedented proportions. The visionary work of early reformers paid dividends, and the movements they created continue to serve as models, but much more is needed to revive children's free, outdoor play and learning in nature.

Building Ecosystems for Play

This dual crisis—the diminution of outdoor play and children's estrangement from nature—is inspiring a growing number of organizations to reconsider the effects of losing touch with natural habitats and free play. Children should not be the "canaries in the coal mine," used to monitor the effects of substituting testing for recess, lawsuits for negotiation, cookies for carrots, and the Internet for playgrounds. They are not responsible for the play and nature crisis, and they have virtually no influence on the solutions, but they suffer the consequences—and ultimately pass them on. It is adults—parents, teachers, all of us—who fail when children lose their age-old rights to free play and learning and the wonders of nature. We are the weak ones—we adults who have lost touch with our children. We must attend to what they need, not just to what they want. Working collectively toward common goals, individuals and groups can overcome the ravages of high stakes testing, cyber play, and standardized schooling. They can multiply their influence and bring nature, recess, free spontaneous play, and hands-on learning back to children. A growing backlash against the forces that deny play and nature to children shows signs of becoming a child-saving movement that could dwarf the movement of a century ago. A renewed emphasis on the whole child and learning and development through play is essential to success.

Child Development Centers and Learning and Development through Play

America's best child care and child development centers have remained true to their philosophical roots in child development research and essentially untouched by high stakes testing. These centers have, as a group, the most developmentally beneficial playgrounds in America, thanks in large part to the nature of their teachers' training in child development and play. For motor or exercise play, they combine downsized motor apparatus and open space for organized games similar to those found in schools and parks. However, unlike most public schools and parks, they provide for a broad range of developmental needs on their playgrounds—language, social, cognitive, physical, aesthetic, and therapeutic. For make-believe play and constructive play, they provide sand, water, tools, construction materials, and various loose parts. For social play, they provide wheeled vehicle paths, tricycles, and other wheeled toys. For nature study and tool use, they provide planters and small garden plots for tending plants, and facilities for small animals. Art materials are available both indoors and outdoors. Storage facilities are located conveniently on the playground to house the many loose parts (Palmer, 1916; Garrison, 1926; Foster and Mattson, 1929; Frost, 1992; Greenman, 2005; Fromberg and Bergen, 2006; Frost, et al., 2008). Further, American child development centers have preserved the decades-old traditions of creating play centers in classrooms for our youngest children, understanding that play is fundamental for early learning— play is learning. The very nature of play makes it amenable to expression and benefit in many types of play environments.

Expanding the Voice of Play and Play Environments

Emerging organizations and agencies are filling the gaps between children's play needs and contemporary adult expectations by speaking out about the importance of play. Organizations formed during recent years—the Alliance for Childhood, the National Institute for Play, Playing for Keeps, the Voice of Play, KaBoom, and Boundless Playgrounds—are all committed to spreading the news that play is essential for children's health, development, and wellbeing. Their work complements that of public gardens, organized camps, children's museums, zoos, public parks, and schools. All emphasize the developmental and learning values of play and work in natural habitats, gardens, and playgrounds, and extend their interest and influence to preserving wilderness areas and the earth's ecosystem. A massive integrated effort will be required to counter play deprivation and associated factors.

The Alliance for Childhood, directed by Joan Almon, supports policies and practices that promote children's healthy development and love of learning. The Alliance is funded by grants and donations from foundations and individuals. Several of its programs support the restoration of child-initiated imaginative play. It sponsors research on child-initiated play and issues information and calls to action for educators and policy makers to support play. It sponsors a campaign to raise public consciousness about the importance of play; joins prominent child development experts in challenging the emphasis on computers in early childhood and elementary schools; and calls for a rethinking of the emphasis on high stakes testing and its potential health effects on children.

The National Institute for Play (NIFP) was founded by Stuart Brown to disseminate knowledge and implement the practices and benefits of play into public life. Guided by a Board of Directors and a council of advisors, the NIFP gathers research from scientists and practitioners, initiates projects to expand scientific information about play, and translates this emerging knowledge into programs and resources for society. Playing for Keeps is a national organization, founded by John Lee II and Edward Klugman, to improve the quality of children's lives by promoting healthy constructive play. On April 26, 2008, at the annual conference of the Association of Children's Museums (ACM), Playing for Keeps became a part of the ACM, adding even more emphasis on children's play to the work of children's museums. A central purpose of the organization is to help bridge the gap between what research has shown and what parents and others need to know about helping children achieve their full potential through play. The organization focuses on constructive play—creative, imaginative, and nonviolent—and communicates information about play to parents, educators, toy manufacturers, and others.

In early 2007 the International Playground Equipment Manufacturers' Association (IPEMA) initiated the "Voice of Play" to raise awareness about the importance of play for health and development. IPEMA's direct ties to playground equipment manufacturers make it a potential source of influence for reconsidering safety standards, reducing their scope, ensuring their clarity, developing internal consistency and one simple, universal set of clear guidelines, reacquainting children with risky play, and bringing common sense to safety standards. It can also play a prominent educational role in convincing adults about the values of outdoor play.

KaBoom, a national nonprofit organization formed in 1995, works among children in disaster areas and other contexts, and exemplifies the growing alternatives for reshaping playgrounds and demonstrating what everyday people can do. KaBoom's goal is to establish a great place to play within walking distance of every child in America. By 2008 it had led more than 1,500 playground construction projects, with assistance from community leaders and funding partners, which are expanding at the rate of about 230 per year.

Yet another self-build program, the Community Built Organization, organizes and directs community volunteers in building their own playground equipment using natural or manufactured building materials. A growing number of groups are preparing nature playgrounds, emphasizing the use of natural materials and plants.

Boundless Playgrounds is a nonprofit organization created to help communities develop playgrounds that enable children with and without disabilities to play together. The program was inspired by a couple that lost a child to spinal muscular atrophy and worked with 1,200 volunteers to develop a playground to honor that child. Boundless Playgrounds was officially formed in 1997 by parents and professionals, and by 2008 they had helped establish more than 125 playgrounds in 24 states and Canada, with dozens more in development. Statewide initiatives establish playgrounds with support from families, civic groups, government agencies, corporations, foundations, and community leaders.

Nonprofit Organizations and Coalitions

Hundreds of Young Men's Christian Association (YMCA) locations throughout the country are participating in Activate America and a related program, Pioneering Healthy Communities. In January 2008 the Associated Press and the Robert Wood Johnson Foundation announced that the Activate America program was being implemented in more than 370 YMCA locations around the country. Through this program, staff members are trained, facilities are redesigned, and activities are modified to address the health and fitness needs of communities. These programs support local groups, advocate for safe play areas, and promote the provision of walking, jogging and bike paths, and healthy food choices. The YMCA is in a unique position to help improve the lifestyles of our youngest citizens since they are the largest nonprofit provider of child care in the nation.

The Common Good Coalition, a nonpartisan organization founded by Philip Howard, is dedicated to restoring rationality and common sense to law and lawsuits affecting children's health, play, and public schools. The coalition's interests and influence go well beyond law to target obesity, fitness, restoring free play, the No Child Left Behind Act, and other issues related to education, civil justice, and the value of play. The work of these groups includes conducting polls, hosting forums, and engaging with leaders in healthcare, education, law, business, and public safety. From July 29 through July 31, 2008, Common Good hosted an Internet forum in the first of a two-part series on obesity (enter "New Talk"). The participants were national experts in play, sports and physical education, government agencies and research centers, writers, psychologists, experts in child development, health, pediatrics, foundations, coalitions, and parks and recreation, and professional organizations. The three-day discussion was arguably the most thorough examination of the obesity and fitness crisis to date.

On February 15, 2007, a news release announced the formation of Partnership for Play Every Day (PFP), a national, diverse group of public, private, and nonprofit organizations with a primary mission of ensuring that American youth have at least 60 minutes of physical activity each day. They promote this goal by raising the number of play spaces and the quality of play in settings readily accessible to children, and by increasing the number of voices supporting play. The Partnership for Play was convened by the Young Men's Christian Association (YMCA), the National Recreation and Park Association (NRPA), and the National Association for Sport and Physical Education (NASPE). In 2008 this was perhaps the largest of the contemporary organizations promoting the value of play. Its sheer scope and quality of supporters and partners place the PFP in a very strong position to influence play opportunities for American children. The PFP in 2008 was comprised of 36 national organizations, 10 corporate sponsors and a board of expert advisors including the National League of Cities, the National Park Service, Stanford University, and the U.S. Access Board. The PFP calls for and assists communities in working together to provide spaces and opportunities for children and youth to become physically active. For example, it pushes for redesigning communities and the 300,000 playgrounds at elementary schools and city parks with fitness in mind. This is especially timely, for playgrounds are one of the most active places that children use regularly.

Private Foundations

Private foundations are also contributing to the new child-saving movement. The Kaiser Family Foundation is a nonprofit foundation serving as a clearing-house of news and information on healthcare. It operates a research and communications program and disseminates information, free of charge, to policy makers, media, healthcare groups, and the public. The foundation's contributions to children's play, fitness, and health included in 2003 the first national study of media use among the youngest children—"Zero to Six: Electronic Media in the Lives of Infants, Toddlers and Preschoolers." This study was supported and extended in 2005 by a scholarly history of research brief, and these studies were complemented, in 2006, by yet another study, "Child's Play: 'Advergaming' and the Online Marketing of Food to Children." Collectively, these are major tools for scholars who study child obesity, fitness, and play while offering practical insights for other groups.

In 2007 the Robert Wood Johnson Foundation (RWJF) pledged $500 million to help reverse the obesity epidemic by 2015. This money will finance research and programs that improve access to healthy, affordable foods and increase physical activity in schools and communities. The mission of the RWJF is to improve the health and healthcare of all Americans. This is done by collecting and producing evidence about targeted health issues and distributing knowledge, ideas, and expertise. The foundation forms partnerships and collaborates with other funding groups and advocates. Childhood obesity and related fitness and physical activity comprise one of several critical health issues targeted through integrated strategies—gathering evidence, taking action, and advocacy.

The activities of the RWJF are extensive but a few examples show the comprehensive approach to one of their targets, obesity, and illustrate the potential for change. The foundation supported an evaluation of Arkansas Act 1220, which mandated a comprehensive, successful approach to attacking obesity in public schools; worked with The Food Trust advocacy organization to ensure access to healthy food in Pennsylvania; worked with the Alliance for a Healthier Generation to improve nutrition and physical activity in the nation's schools; worked with national organizations representing elected and appointed officials to educate them about increasing physical activity and healthy nutrition among children. RWJF's interest in research is exemplified by its support of a series of major reports, "F as in Fat: How Obesity Policies Are Failing in America," by the Trust for America's Health.

The connections between obesity, fitness, and play are recognized and supported through such grants as "The Power of Play." This grant supports Sports 4 Kids in their work with 32,000 students in 75 elementary and middle schools in the San Francisco Bay area to provide play areas and trained play coordinators before, during, and after school. Site coordinators are trained and assigned to schools full-time to organize play and physical activity. The program is spreading across the nation and is based on one core premise: play is the child's natural way to learn, be active, and develop. The RWJF program exemplifies successful partnerships of programs contributing to the early twenty-first century child-saving movement and illustrates the value of integrating programs to attack multifaceted problems such as the current play/fitness/health crisis.

Enter the Government

There is little doubt that legislation is needed to help resolve the play, obesity, fitness, and health crisis. Yet the United States stands virtually alone among the nations of the world in failing to ratify the United Nation's Convention on the Rights of the Child that confirms children's right to play and leisure. The passing of one bill through state and national legislation can make a greater impact on resolving such large-scale issues than a lifetime of work by a single group of reformers. Fortunately, legislators at all levels are awakening to the long-term effects of the health and fitness crisis and are drafting legislation to counter the threat. Thanks to the leadership of the governor of Arkansas, the Arkansas Center for Health Improvement, and the Arkansas legislature, state leaders passed Act 1220 in 2003, calling for measures to improve access to healthier foods, promote physical activity, and report children's Body Mass Index (BMI) to parents. At that time, about 38 percent of Arkansas children were overweight or at risk of becoming overweight. The Robert Wood Johnson Foundation report "Assessment of Childhood and Adolescent Obesity in Arkansas: Year Four (2006–7)" found that childhood obesity appears to have stabilized during the past four years, but many children were still overweight or at risk. The program appears to have been successful in curtailing childhood obesity in Arkansas, and sets an example for other state lawmakers. During the 2006–7 school year, 99 percent of Arkansas schoolchildren participated in BMI assessments.

On July 1, 2008, the Texas Education Agency (2008) reported the results of a groundbreaking physical fitness assessment of almost 2.6 million Texas public-school children in grades 3–12, using the Cooper Institute's FITNESSGRAM. This assessment includes a one-mile run, curl-ups, push-ups, shoulder stretches, trunk lift, and a skin fold test, and measures body composition, aerobic capacity, strength, endurance, and flexibility. Fitness levels declined with each passing grade level, corresponding with declining recess and physical education in upper grades. Preliminary results show that about 32 percent of third-grade girls and about 28 percent of third-grade boys achieved the "Healthy Fitness Zone" prescribed for the assessment. In seventh grade, only 21 percent of the girls and 17 percent of the boys met this achievement level, and by 12th grade only 8 percent of the girls and 9 percent of the boys met the health standard.

In 2008 Texas ranked sixth among states for obesity among children aged 10–17 with a rate of 19 percent. Dr. Kenneth Cooper, the founder of the Cooper Aerobics Center in Dallas, stated: "I hope these results shock the state into reality and into action. We must immunize children against obesity while in elementary school." Inactive children tend to remain inactive and obese into adulthood. The costs go well beyond the immediate and future health of the obese children themselves to weigh heavily on the economy. About $2.5 million in private funds paid for the Texas assessment, but Texas businesses spent about $3.3 billion in 2005 on costs related to obesity. The wake-up call resulting from this assessment is influencing state legislators to continue drafting legislation that addresses the obesity and fitness problems of schoolchildren. One bill, already passed, requires a minimum level of physical education and/or recess.

The Federal Obesity Prevention Act of 2008, influenced by the work of the Partnership for Play and sponsored by Senators Harkin, Dodd, Bingaman, Kennedy, and Mikulski, was a direct response to studies revealing the scope of obesity in America and predicting that the next generation of children may be the first to be less healthy and have shorter life spans than their parents. Senator Dodd referred to the obesity epidemic as "a medical emergency of hurricane-like proportions," needing the resources and manpower of the Federal government to combat it. The sponsors of this bill wisely proposed an integrated, comprehensive approach to curbing obesity and improving the health of children and adults, including clear roles and accountability among all Federal agencies.

The bill proposes giving grants to states to plan, implement, and assess model communities of play. The work would include identifying barriers to play and physical activity in homes, schools, community venues, child care centers and workplaces, using a Community Play Index to assess policies, programs, and environmental barriers to play. The models are to include both nutrition and play, and activity programs planned and operated by community coalitions including local agencies, parks and recreation, health departments, education agencies, city planning groups, healthcare providers, hospitals, faith based organizations, elected officials, businesses, and colleges and universities. Identifying, expanding, and improving the places to play—playgrounds, sport fields, physical activity clubs, schools providing recess, and spaces for people with disabilities—and increasing their number would be priorities. The programs would also target physicians to help families improve nutrition and physical activity, and raise awareness of the need for physical activity and proper nutrition. Such sorely needed government programs are among the promising antidotes to child obesity and related health and fitness problems for people of all ages. The U.S. Department of Agriculture proposed in April 2007 that schools be required to bring their cafeteria menus into compliance with the latest U.S. dietary guidelines. In that same month the Institute for Medicine, which advises Congress on health and science, issued new guidelines for providing healthy food in schools and other places.

The Transportation Equity Act for the twenty-first century, enacted in 1990 and reauthorized in 2008, is to physical activity what the farm bill is to nutrition—intended to get people moving while preserving and enhancing the environment. Its many features include a recreational trails program for the acquisition of easements or property for trails, and restoration and maintenance of existing trails or pathways. The funds can also be used to support public transportation, provide safe routes to school, and initiate bicycle and pedestrian projects. Urban design and transportation policies in America tend to target motorized transportation and make it easy, even necessary, to be sedentary. The looming energy crisis is coming to the aid of physical activity, and global warming is turning our attention to the preservation of natural environments where children have played over the centuries. With thought, planning, and coordination, multiple agencies and groups can simultaneously confront and deflect the perfect storm that threatens children's play, fitness, and health.

The President's Council on Physical Fitness and Sports (PCPFS) is an advisory committee of volunteers formed in 1956 to advise the president through the Secretary of Health and Human Services about fitness, physical activity, and sports. Physical activity guidelines, fitness tests, and other resources are provided for children, adults, older adults, women during pregnancy, and those with chronic medical conditions and disabilities. Campaign promises by President Obama to emphasize early childhood education were expressed in the passage of the American Recovery and Reinvestment Act in February 2009. This act provides several billion dollars for child care assistance for low-income families, Head Start, military child development, and various other early childhood programs supporting play and play environments for young children.

Confronting the Play/Fitness/Health Crisis and Restoring Outdoor Play

Should additional approaches to providing play and playgrounds be explored and expanded? Yes. Are multiple types of play environments and schoolyard habitats good for kids? Yes! Architects, naturalists, manufacturers, self-build proponents, and others are capable of designing and constructing good and bad play environments. Even children are remarkably adept at creating adventurous, exciting play environments when given time and access to materials or natural settings. Limited space, governmental and private ownership, and parental fear do not allow free roaming in the vacant lots and open wilderness once available to children. Such limitations on free, traditional play are unlikely to be reduced sufficiently to ameliorate the play-related restrictions that modern children encounter. Play environments must now provide props, natural and built, that invite and accommodate various forms of play in restricted spaces. No standard approach to environmental design meets all of children's play needs. Few adult designs reflect the depth of creativity seen when children themselves search out or develop their own play spaces in junk yards or wildscapes, and such spaces for imaginative construction play and creativity are in short supply in confined schoolyards and the other spaces available to children.

A growing twenty-first century child-saving movement comprising non-profit organizations, professional organizations, businesses, media, partnerships, communities, policy makers, and countless others is rising to counter the play/fitness/health crisis. This movement needs greater coordination, more support for approaches shown by research and experience to be effective, and legislation to address the factors—recess, physical education, playgrounds, recreation and nature areas, community redevelopment—that are needed to make physical activity a part of everyday life for both children and adults. Programs are not likely to be effective unless entire families participate and adults act as models for their children. Couch potato parents, increasingly turn to motorized wheelchairs as they age and their bodies deteriorate from lack of exercise. They tend to rear couch potato children who face the same stark future. The following proposed steps arise from this study of the evolution of play and playgrounds in America, their diminution during the past three to four decades, and the consequences of play deprivation on the fitness, health, and well-being of children.

Convincing Adults that Children Need Play at Home and Recess at School

A fundamental need underpinning all the rest is to educate American adults—parents, teachers, and others who influence children—about the value of play for children's development. They must come to know that play is an innate, biological process, characteristic of all healthy children around the world, and just as essential as the other basic needs of food, water, and shelter; that the seemingly innocuous process of free, spontaneous, outdoor play builds bodies and brains and contributes to academic success; that free, active, outdoor play every day helps assure physical fitness and is an antidote to obesity, depression, poor socialization skills, and the other consequences of play deprivation; that play is therapeutic and helps children cope with phobias, physical and mental illness, injury, natural and man-made disasters, and maintain order and stability in their lives; and that the need for play does not fade away but is required for lifelong fitness and mental and physical health.

Studies of more than 10,000 children found that children with recess had higher behavior scores in classrooms than those with little or no recess. Further, children from families with lower incomes and lower levels of education and those who attended public schools were less likely to have recess (Barros, et al., 2009). Fortunately, many child care/child development centers maintain programs that alternate various forms of indoor and outdoor play for preschool children, but, upon entry to public school, children find that time-honored recess is being devalued, shortened, and abandoned. National Recess Week, the first week in March, is a reminder that free, unstructured play time is associated with improved test scores, language, cooperation, problem solving, persistence, motivational skills, turn-taking, general development, fitness, and overall health. Preschool children benefit from a play-focused program wherein much of the day is spent in active, playful learning indoors and outdoors, and elementary-school children need an hour of physical activity every day at school, at least half of this in free, recess play, plus regular outdoor activity at home.

Countering Pills and Disabilities

The medical and health professions must rethink their approaches to health-care, focusing on prevention as well as cures for keeping people healthy. The "magic pill" of doping with medicines and drugs may make people feel better temporarily, but history shows that the limited benefits are too frequently overcome by growing reliance on or addiction to a magic elixir or surgical treatment. Adults today are the most pill-popping generation in history and they are passing on this behavior to their children. Schools have pill cabinets where children go throughout the day to take their prescribed medications for depression, hyperactivity, allergies, and a host of other diseases or assumed ones. Of all the professions with considerable power to influence nutrition and fitness, the medical profession appears to be failing to advise their clients about the shortcomings of drugs and the power of play, physical activity, and nutrition in the prevention of disease, especially obesity and its appalling health consequences.

"Pill peddlers" form a steady stream to doctors' offices, leaving samples of the latest drugs to be handed out to patients. These drugs are hawked on television and in "health" magazines and other sources, with warnings that the side effects may be worse than the disease and in fact may kill you. Yet, following months or years of inactivity and poor nutrition adversity for themselves and their children, patients choose the hoped-for quick cure. Doctors, they conclude, are perhaps the best-trained professionals and know what they are doing. Pills, they reflect, even surgery, would be preferable to eating "tasteless" food and enduring the "pain" and inconvenience of exercise. Consider, for example, the growing practice of prescribing "body sculpting" for adults and teenagers. Two ads in an August 24, 2008, daily newspaper offered the following: liposuction in three varieties—laser liposuction, smart lipo, and power-assisted liposuction—botox, cosmetic fillers, laser epilation, silicone injection therapy, photo-cancer treatment, liquid face lifts, fruit peels, bariatric surgery, and gastric bypass.

Not so visible but equally pernicious are the formidable numbers of schoolchildren and the elderly being diagnosed with or assumed to have such disorders as ADHD and depression, and taking long series of potentially dangerous drugs. Neuroscientists at the First Annual Conference of the National Institute for Play, meeting at Stanford University on October 31 and November 1, 2008, showed graphic images detailing brain aberration resulting from the use of such drugs. Certain individual differences or natural variations in children's physical activity patterns, once accepted as normal "individual differences," now enhanced by the required sedentary activity at school desks and home video screens, are seen as aberrant behavior in need of medical correction. Fortunately, the medical profession is stepping up preventive medicine and developing programs to assist people in healthy, drug- and surgery-free approaches to health and fitness, and neuroscientists are finding that activity is frequently more effective than pills. People do not outgrow their need for play, and the therapeutic options of physically and mentally challenging play and sensible nutrition are inexhaustible for all who choose to employ them. The consequences of substituting doping for sensible diet and activity reach into old age, and diseases such as Alzheimer's and Parkinson's are being connected by neuroscientists to such factors.

Turning off the Tech Toys

Another once-touted "magic bullet"—computers—is equally suspect. Nicholas Carr wrote in *Atlantic Monthly* (July 2008) a provocative essay about the computer issue, "Is Google Making Us Stupid?" He praised the power of computers as a godsend for writers, allowing them to do research in minutes that once required days in the stacks of a traditional library. However, he also pointed out: "That boon comes at a price." Such swiftly moving streams of particles chip away at memory, concentration, and contemplation. His writer friends and the present writer agree; the more we concentrate on skimming through long passages and hopping from source to source, the harder it is to concentrate on a single strand of thought or long passage. I sit here writing after on-and-off research on this book for four years, and am surrounded by two rooms containing hundreds of books and research papers, two computers stuffed with email, websites, and research documents, several desks cluttered with "stickie notes," and a bad case of eye strain from staring at a computer screen for too many hours. When I leave this cyber existence and go outside to play or work, bleary eyed, with children at a school research site, I cannot help but wonder just how countless hours of computers and TV are going to affect their brains, psyche, concentration, and fitness in the future. I saw my first TV in high school and my first computer in graduate school. These kids begin to develop high-tech proficiency in preschool. In his captivating book *The Flickering Mind*, Todd Oppenheimer (1990, pp. xiv, xx) wrote:

> America's students have become a distracted lot. Their attention span—one of the most important intellectual capacities anyone can possess—shows numerous signs of diminishing. Their ability to reason, to listen, to feel empathy, among other things, is quite literally flickering ... technology has become the ultimate innovation, the device that will let schools get closer to their academic dreams no matter what the goals may be ... The reality ... is crushingly discouraging.

Technology is simultaneously an addictive toy and a tool of unbelievable complexity and devout attraction, so prevalent that Nicholas Negroponte (1995, pp. 6–7), the founder of the MIT Media Lab, wrote that it is "being taken for granted by children in the same way adults don't think about air (until it's missing)." He predicted that people will eventually live "in digital neighborhoods in which physical space will be irrelevant and time will play a different role." Indeed, despite the evidence that technology, used in proper balance and with discretion, can be an extraordinary learning tool, its growing use as a constant companion and confidant—a virtual umbilical cord to the world—raises serious questions about whether traditional spontaneous outdoor games and forms of play will survive.

Already children are denied opportunities for hands-on manipulation and exploration of real objects, forget how to play imaginative games, fail to learn through kinesthetic experience, and rarely engage in face-to-face social play with their peers. As I write on March 2, 2009, I see a story by Kevin Cowherd in today's *Austin American Statesman*, excerpted from the *Baltimore Sun*. Looking for "ways to waste more time on the Internet," Kevin joined Facebook, the popular social networking site, to "cavort with the young" in their online playground. His child has about "577 anonymous strangers as friends," and some have thousands! This leaves the reader to marvel at such a phenomenal waste of time that could be spent in constructive activities.

Getting Children back to Nature

All the organizations and foundations discussed here can contribute to reacquainting children with the joys and brain-building experiences of playing in nature. Those of us who played in the wilderness as children naturally reflect about our freedom to roam the hills and valleys, explore the remote places, learning the ways of animals and savoring the delights of nature, and we yearn for a return to such awe-inspiring experiences. Realistically, we are not going to see parents suddenly turning their children loose, unsupervised, in such wild places, even if they were readily available. Unfortunately, they are not available for most children due to urbanization, private ownership, and remoteness from neighborhoods. In January 2008 a Texas landowner sprayed children playing in a public creek near his property with shotgun pellets. Further, thanks to sensational, repetitious reporting by the media about child abductions, injuries, and other possible calamities, parents no longer allow their children to venture far from home, in many instances even within their own neighborhoods.

Intensified awareness of the relationships between learning, health, obesity, and human well-being brought these concerns to a nationwide and, later, an

Figure 9.4 The "Land Down Under" (named by a child): wildscape created in a water retention area.
Source: Courtesy of Redeemer Lutheran School, Austin, Texas.

international audience. On April 24, 2006, Richard Louv (2005) called for a campaign to "Leave No Child Inside" and to reconnect children and nature (Charles, et al., 2008). By June 2007 the campaign had been extensively reported by the media throughout the United States and Europe, and public conscious-ness and action had attracted a diverse assortment of people who were working together on a wide range of initiatives—walkable cities, active-living by design, simple living, health, citizen science, and land trust movements.

A landmark event took place in Washington in 2008 when the "No Child Left Inside Act of 2007" was ratified by Congress (Charles, et al., 2008). This act was built from evidence provided by the Children and Nature Coalition that out-of-classroom learning is critical for children's emotional, physical, and intellectual health. Research demonstrated that the pressures for testing resulting from the "No Child Left Behind Act" were damaging to children's achievement, development, and fitness, but outdoor activity and firsthand experiences in nature can improve academic performance, self esteem, responsibility, personal health (including obesity), and an understanding of nature.

The act focused on environmental literacy for children in kindergarten through 12th grade, training for their teachers, and education to help combat climate change and preserve the environment. By 2008 more than forty state and regional campaigns and community-based, multisector collaboratives had formed or were being assembled, and bills were passed in several states to sup-port the back to nature campaign. Consistent with the trend of these initiatives, the scope broadened to include religious leaders (spiritual wonders of nature), the Sierra Club (saving the planet), and the healthcare community (the health connections). In sum, the appeal is virtually universal—and rapidly spreading. Outdoor play of any kind helps prevent obesity and related diseases, nurtures physical fitness, and improves development, learning, and overall well-being.

I live in a neighborhood of several hundred families, close to a beautiful park, natural woodland, and a playground adjacent to a clear stream flowing into a lake, but children do not go there unless accompanied by adults on special occa-sions such as community functions and family outings. In fact, they do not play outside. When they exit the school bus in mid-afternoon, they go directly into the house, rarely acknowledge greetings from any adult walking on the sidewalk, and the community reverts to its ghost-town appearance. During my twelve-year residence in the community, I have seen as many as three children playing in the yards or streets only one time, and I have never seen an unattended child in the beautifully wooded neighborhood park or wading in the creek.

However, this is not the final word on the issue. In this same city, Austin, Texas, a host of corporations, agencies, volunteers, designers, politicians, and others are cooperating in the greening and redevelopment of the 711 acre abandoned Mueller Airport site into a mixed use, urban village. This village will feature more than 140 acres of parks, greenbelts, trails, a lake, plazas, and playscapes.

The site is encircled by a "green necklace," and five miles of village paths are linked to the city's fifty mile park-and-trail system. The emphasis on greening and fitness is resulting in every home achieving high green-building ratings and being located within 600 feet of green space. These green spaces serve important ecological roles, including filtering rainwater before it re-enters watersheds. The master developer started work in 2002, and more than 380 mixed income families now live in energy efficient homes along tree-lined streets within walking distance of the expected 10,000 permanent jobs. Medical facilities, athletic facilities, playing fields, schools, plazas, a children's museum, a retail center, a children's shelter, a one million square foot town center, and a proposed rail-line station have been completed or are in progress, with much more in the planning stages. In March 2009 the city of Austin was the largest metropolitan area in the nation to achieve Community National Wildlife Habitat Certification, with 900 certified wildlife habitats throughout the city. Such innovations, intended to preserve natural resources and improve the fitness and health of residents of all ages, are springing up rapidly, exceeding 6,000 in Texas and 113,000 nationwide.

Equity for Children in Poverty

The crisis in play, fitness, and health, like other crises in the past, has inordinate effects across socioeconomic and cultural contexts. It extends beyond the mere diminution of play and play environments and encompasses past failures to provide equal opportunity to all children, especially to the poor. Indeed, the solutions extend far beyond the provision of playgrounds, parks, and recess to encompass a shift in societal values and, consequently, a changed culture of childhood. In past centuries, the problems of obesity and poor physical fitness were primarily seen among the aristocracy or upper class. The poor, even children, engaged in hard manual labor, and their food was limited but came directly from the land. Now the diets of the poor are typically carbohydrate and calorie rich, and they suffer the same fate as other children through confinement to their indoor cyber playgrounds. Consequently, the poorest communities and states with the lowest educational levels have the highest rates of obesity and poor fitness.

Extensive research literature demonstrates that family income is a consistent predictor of grades, standardized test scores, and educational attainment. The income–achievement gap is present in kindergarten and grows bigger over time. Gary Evans and Michelle Schamberg (2009), writing in the *Proceedings of the National Academy of Science*, which publishes "original research of exceptional importance," demonstrate in extensive reviews of literature and original research that "allostatic load," an index of chronic stress, grows more severe the longer children are exposed to childhood poverty, resulting in increasing levels of memory deficit in young adults. The duration of poverty in childhood is negatively associated with health and mortality in later adulthood. Imaging work with both animal and human brains shows altered neurotransmitter activity and suppression of neurogenesis (creation of neurons), and volume reduction in the hippocampus and prefrontal cortex (Evans and Schamberg, 2009). The consequences of the accelerating effects of stress from family poverty, particularly evident in school achievement, raise questions about the associated effects of high stakes testing, loss of recess, and other issues discussed in Jonathan Kozol's (1991) compelling book *Savage Inequalities.*

Jonathan Kozol's book is a searing exposé of the indignities of poverty for schoolchildren, especially in cities, and the extremes of wealth and poverty in American schools and their effects on children. Schools highest in poverty enrollment have the least time for recess (Barros, et al., 2009) and the lowest levels of fitness. Studies of the fitness levels of 2.6 million students in Texas public schools found that schools serving children with the lowest income parents have the highest obesity levels and lowest fitness scores, and those highest in parent income have the lowest obesity levels and the highest fitness scores (Texas Education Agency, 2008). This same pattern is seen in studies by the Trust for America's Health (Levy, et al., 2009). Parents with higher incomes and education levels compensate in part for lack of outdoor free play by enrolling their children in organized sports, recreational activities, and summer camps, and they are more active in the affairs of their children's schools, helping ensure their access to balanced curricula.

The first White House Conference on Children in a Democracy was called by President Franklin D. Roosevelt in 1940, when America was slowly beginning to emerge from the Great Depression, a world war was imminent, minorities were exploited, and political patronage was threatening the democratic process. The conference report (U.S. Superintendent of Documents, 1940, pp. 192–3) concluded that children from low-income homes, minorities, children living in slums, and children with disabilities were deprived of recreational areas, artistic events, toys, and playgrounds. These conditions mirror in large degree the problems of contemporary children who live in slums and barrios and others equally poor but living in isolated regions such as the Appalachians. Further, contemporary America has out-of-control political patronage, wars threatening escalation, a staggering national debt, growing poverty, and an expanding population fed by immigration. The 2003 Census Report showed a steady rise in the number of families in poverty since 1999, and data released in August 2008 revealed that a half-million more children lived in poverty in 2007 than in 2006. These data do not take into account the inflationary surge in 2008 centered on energy costs. A quarter of those living in the United States will begin their lives in urban slums, and more than half of all the children born in the world will live in urban slums during their childhood (Nabhan and Trimble, 1994, p. 11). Resolving the problems of poverty is one of the major requirements for coping with play deprivation and the changing culture of childhood.

Popular literature tells us that many kids are overindulged by hovering, "helicopter" parents, and that is true, particularly in middle and upper income families. However, hovering is not so common among poor families and single-parent families. Many are forced by circumstances of survival to underindulge their children, and the effects may be painfully visible when their children arrive at school. Children of poverty tend to attend the poorest schools, have the least experienced teachers, be denied the facilities and instructional materials of schools in high-income areas, score lowest on high stakes tests, have depleted time for recess, play, PE, and the arts, and suffer, inordinately, the crippling effects of punitive measures dealt out for low test scores and higher levels of obesity. The poor and minorities are least likely to be taken or sent regularly by their parents to special play and learning venues such as children's museums, parks and summer camps, or to have opportunities to engage in a variety of sports appropriate for their age group. Such deficiencies are exacerbated by excessive high-calorie food and poor nutrition. Every organization that supports children's play, such as foundations and nonprofit organizations, or provides play and learning spaces, such as parks, children's museums, and summer camps, can consider ways to ensure that all children, rich or poor, have many opportunities for outdoor play in both built and natural playscapes.

Coupled with the lack of play spaces and opportunities, the children of slums and barrios may spend their childhoods with little or no opportunity to play in clean dirt, swim in clear, running streams, hear and see animals in their natural habitats, feel the sensations of walking through meadows and woodlands on dewy mornings, climb trees, and explore wild places. These are the experiences that bond children to the natural world, sharpen their senses, inspire a sense of beauty, build emerging concepts of biology, geology, physics, and language. And they are critical brain-building experiences for complementing the physical, social, and cognitive skills developed in recess, free playground play, and compact nature areas in backyards, schoolyards, and neighborhood parks.

The poor suffer more than others from the brain-dead view that the only worthwhile learning is that of classrooms full of bleary-eyed children memorizing trivia for tests. We must replace the policies of the failed No Child Left Behind Act that stuffs the poor and minorities into schools labeled "low performing" and "unacceptable." Emerging movements to address the play, fitness, and health crisis of American children must not take the path of comprehensive reform for the well-to-do and half-hearted, underfunded efforts for the poor and dispossessed.

From Junk Food to Basic Nutrition

Taking action to improve physical fitness is more complex than merely getting kids active. They must also have good nutrition. A not-so-atypical scenario is Billy going home from school to an empty house, heading to the refrigerator for junk food and sugary drinks, and settling down for TV, video games, social networking, texting, or talking to friends by cellphone. He has been instructed to lock the doors and stay inside. His parents arrive home from work exhausted, carrying pizza from a pick-up window and ready for an evening in front of the TV. Sometimes they take Billy to play soccer, followed by a late evening stop at the ice cream shop. Billy has sugar pops or fruit loops for breakfast, grabs a bag of chips and a candy bar before jumping in the car (or on the bus) that takes him to school, where his lunch is fried tater tots, chili dogs, carrot sticks (that he discards), chocolate milk, and apple sauce or cake. Billy's school has eliminated recess from the curriculum in favor of preparing for standardized tests. His school is "low-performing" or "unacceptable" and under pressure to improve or be closed. This triple whammy—a diet of fat and calories, a full day of sitting in his seat, and beat-up teachers pressured for better test performance—leaves Billy with poor concentration, low energy, an expanding waistline, and a growing distaste for school.

Some schools are improving their cafeteria menus by removing sugary and empty calorie drinks from the premises while adding potentially more damaging substitutes. Nationwide some are establishing in-school coffee bars featuring sugary, caffeinated drinks such as coffee, cappuccinos, lattes, scones, and other high calorie, sugary goodies. The top seller in one such school bar is Snickers-flavored Frapp, a mix of caramel, chocolate, hazelnut syrups, milk, a powdered dairy base, and a shot of espresso—plus a topping of whipped cream and more chocolate syrup. Only one parent in this school blocked the Frapp for her child. One child said she knocks back four or five coffee flavored shakes before the final (opening) bell rings, and adds, "I hardly ever eat anything else" (Bloom, 2009).

State and national policy makers have the power to change the damaging diets in schools, and several states are active in doing this. In September 2005 the governor of California signed school nutrition bills, described as the first and best of their kind, directed at getting junk food and soda out of schools. In September 2007 the California Assembly passed a bill requiring that calories on fast food menu boards be listed, and that nutrition information be printed on chain restaurant menus. In that same year, 2007, twenty states passed menu-labeling bills. In 2008 the California legislatures took yet another forward step by passing a bill banning all trans fats in restaurants by 2011 and New York City became the largest city in the nation to require its restaurants, cafeterias, and schools to go trans fat free. Other cities and towns are following their lead. (Trans fat is a man-made fat that is more damaging for the blood vessels and heart than saturated fats.) These are examples of bills that can be passed quickly, make an immediate difference to the nutrition of thousands of schoolchildren and adults, influence food processing leaders to improve the nutritive qualities of foods, and lead parents to begin reading the ingredients of the food items they purchase.

Getting Parents Active and Emotional: Countering Fear

Efforts to make kids fit and healthy, and their environments green, will not succeed unless parents become better informed, take control of their children's lives, get positively emotional, and model the lives they seek for their children. Programs cannot replace parents, and they too benefit from the time they spend in nature and play with their children. Kids need models; they need daily talk and prompting; they need lots of time *with* parents in healthy forms of play and work; they need to be released from the shackles of excessive restrictions and overparenting on the one hand and underparenting on the other. After almost a half-century working with children and teachers in private and public schools and universities, I have seen a diminution of balance, order, and responsibility in children's lives, and the growing dismay of teachers. Many children now arrive in kindergarten unable to sit in a circle, form a line, use the bathroom appropriately, follow simple instructions, distinguish their property from that of their peers, or button their coats and tie their shoes. Others arrive with a parent in tow who is expecting to spend the day, waiting to tell the teacher how to take care of his/her overindulged child the first morning while twenty-five other five-year-olds are arriving. Teachers commonly tell me that the situation worsens each year, and they look forward to the day they can retire.

The timeless advice from parents of a bygone culture fits here: if you mess it up, clean it up; if you break it, fix it; if you want to eat, you work; it's okay to try your wings but be careful and use good sense. Thirty years ago, as the age of indulgence and self-gratification was creeping upon us, Japanese author Daisaku Ikeda (1979) spoke of the overindulged as "glass children." Even during that early period he described them as having no toughness, so weak you expect them to break, seemingly made of glass. Many are so clumsy and inexperienced they cannot handle scissors and knives. Plastic model kits have eliminated the need for tools. Today we see these same weaknesses magnified as many adults prohibit children from handling tools for fear they might injure themselves; will not let them play in the neighborhood for fear they might be abducted; will not let them play traditional games that allow contact with balls or other children for fear they might be injured or stimulate their hormones; clean their rooms for them; haul them everywhere they go; intervene for them even in minor disputes—and the list goes on. Such prohibitions, seemingly minor in themselves, tend to shape children's lives as they are repeated over and over. The effects extend well beyond the playground and become obvious when parents must accompany their children to fill out college entrance exams or job application forms.

Meaningful work, like play, can build physical, mental, and emotional fitness and health, but work is passing modern children by. Many children leaving elementary school have never learned the rudiments of using simple garden tools, felt the satisfaction and dignity of a job well done, experienced the special sensations of sweat, dirt, blisters, and sore muscles from engaging in challenging work or play. Even common chores around the house and yard, gardening with parents, special construction projects using hand tools, and work roles at school such as raking wood chips around playground equipment and helping with playground safety inspections, are all beneficial for young children. When our research workers install, inspect, and maintain school playgrounds at our major research site, we involve the children, who quickly understand the procedures and engage with passion, reaping the benefits of new knowledge and the satisfaction of making meaningful contributions. The children also plant the school gardens, donate herbs to Meals-on-Wheels, tend the habitats, and engage all the while in learning about the newfound mysteries of small animal life. Even the tasks of maintaining the classroom can become a meaningful work experience when properly conducted by teachers.

In this case, the disappearance of "real play," or play that bubbles up from the child instead of as a result of adult directives, emerges from hours watching TV and computer screens, adult instructions, fear of accidents at play, and "stranger danger." "Children have a deep-felt need to play out the stories of their lives" (Almon, 2009). Parents need to know that kidnapping and abuse at play are far less of a threat than that from family members and presumed friends of the family. And they need to know that "risky," skinned knee play is essential for mastering the challenges of built and natural play environments. We cannot go back again to times when children were reared to work for basic family needs

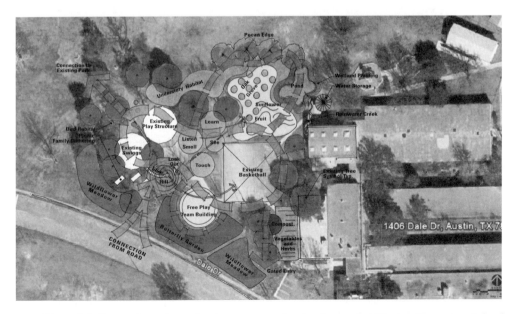

Figure 9.5 Postmodern play and nature-scape, under development at Wooten Elementary School and adjacent Wooten Park, Austin, Texas.
Source: Wooten Elementary Nature Play Garden, Design Development Drawing by TBG Partners.

and spent hours exploring wilderness playgrounds and playing traditional games, but we can teach them to make wise choices—reintroduce them to the wild places that are available and to the meaningful world of work. Joyful work carries many of the characteristics of play and they flow into the same meaningful stream. This is exemplified in various theoretical perspectives of "deep play" (Ackerman, 1999), flow (Csikszentmihalyi, 1990), self-actualization (Maslow, 1962), and "transcendental play" (Frost, 2003).

Kids need parents who say to those who spearhead destructive tech toys, cyber play, wacky testing programs, and other misguided for-profit and politically inspired plans, "We're mad as hell and we're not going to take it anymore!" They say this when they limit their children's TV time to one or two hours a day and help children select programs; they say it when they prohibit sexual and violent video games, monitor their children's cyber play, and discuss and explain the reasons to their children. They say this when they insist on a balanced school program including recess, PE, the arts, and healthy cafeteria food. Values and the ability to take control of one's life are developed early. If those responsible for children were really concerned about quality education, they would be concerned about creativity, reflection, planning, responsibility, ethics, the arts and humanities, and individual differences.

How can adult fear be managed and children allowed to return to their special, natural, and built outdoor play places? One part of the solution is seen in

Figure 9.6 Play and contemplation in natural wonderlands sharpen the senses, invigorate the mind and body, and nourish the soul.
Source: Courtesy of the Texas Parks and Wildlife Department, Chase A. Fountain, photographer.

European adventure playgrounds, where trained playworkers are available to work their magic with children and give parents a sense of safety for their children (Frost, 2008a). Reformers of the early twentieth century understood this need and established college programs to train play leaders, but these were abandoned decades ago in the United States and have not been resurrected. Now, a gradual reawakening to the need is resulting in the provision of young adults during the summer in some city park playgrounds. Sarah Lawrence College, a long-time leader in child development and early childhood education, set a badly needed example by initiating a program for training playworkers in June 2008. The program was designed for professionals and graduate students who serve as social workers, play therapists, childlife specialists in hospitals, early childhood educators, and playworkers in parks, playgrounds, and children's museums. Campus classes are complemented by the observation of children in play settings and include theory and practice in children's play—history, culture, child advocacy, development, and practice. Such training is essential for drawing attention to the importance of play and the need for playworkers, and for its influence in creating other training programs and providing trained adults. They can help gain the confidence of parents in releasing their children back to exciting outdoor play venues.

Today we must consider whether depriving children of their innate need for play and nature should be treated as child abuse, commonly defined as depriving children or imposing physical or emotional injury. The United States is the only nation that has not ratified the United Nation's Convention on the Rights of the Child, guaranteeing the child's right to play and leisure. We need to step up and join other nations in valuing and endorsing the basic right of children to engage in free, spontaneous, outdoor play in natural and built settings.

Remembering Lessons from History

This long journey through the history of children's play and play environments was marked by successive crises and disasters. Every one left its mark on children and their play, but none succeeded in cutting it off or bringing it down. Even under the most terrible conditions children played their traditional games in their traditional ways—*until now*. Colonial children played during periods of oppressive exposure to the extreme conditions of a new land; Native American children played even when they were being herded onto desolate reservations by their strange occupiers; immigrant children from Europe and American farms played when sentenced to fight for survival on the streets and in the gutters of our great cities and the sweatshops of their factories; slave children played even under the watchful eyes of those expecting only back-breaking labor and subservience. Children of the Great Depression and the Great Dust Storms played in the fields of arid farms and during the long tortuous trips in the migrant stream. All these children found their wild, outdoor places for free, active play, and they carried on their centuries-old cultural traditions through play. Now, for the first time in history, the children of entire industrialized nations, especially American children, are losing their natural outdoor grounds for play and forgetting how to engage in free, spontaneous outdoor play. The consequences are profound.

There is no "quick fix" or "magic bullet" for resolving the play, fitness, and health crisis for American children. The approaches must be multiple, coordinated, and preventive in nature. They must be expansive in scope, taking on some of the characteristics of a Marshall Plan or a Moon Shot, or the early twentieth century child-saving movement. Fortunately, many of the innovative approaches for saving children initiated by that movement have continued and are expanding during the early twenty-first century. We need to organize communities, rethink and rebuild neighborhoods so that it is easy to walk to stores, parks, playgrounds, and schools, encourage various forms of locomotion—walking, jogging, biking—and combine the necessity for physical activity with the greening of America and the protection of the planet from global warming.

Only the rare crisis stands alone, unaffected by efforts to resolve another. We must get people emotional (positive) about saving play and natural play environments for present and future generations, and call on politicians, organizations, agencies, and volunteer groups to develop national and local policies that directly or indirectly help resolve the crises affecting children. Many have started, and more are joining the evolving movement at an unprecedented rate. On March 4, 2009, Gordon Brown, Prime Minister of the U.K., addressed the U.S. Congress about the worldwide economic crisis, stating that he had never before seen a world so ready as now to "come together" to seek resolutions.

The lessons to be learned from the successes and failures in dealing with crises throughout America's history pose formidable challenges for resolving our complex, interrelated, man-made play, play environments, fitness, and health crisis. Having seen the history of the diminution of play and play environments, and the changing culture of childhood, and alert to the consequences, we must help children rediscover traditional free, creative, outdoor play and recess, and their wild, natural playscapes. The future test of our resolve is whether we "come together," as did our counterparts a century ago, to form a child-saving movement to rescue children from the forgotten streets and slums of cities, the barrios of border towns, and the ravages of life in many out-of-the-way regions of our southern mountains. We must free all children and teachers from the illogical rigors of test-based school curricula and isolated cyber playgrounds, release them to play, and learn to preserve their natural play and learning environments. Americans *are* "coming together" but we are not yet ready to dance in the end zone because we forget too easily the lessons of history.

References

ABC News. (1996). *Romania: What happened to the children?* (Television series episode). In *Turning Point*. New York: American Broadcasting Company.

Abernethy, D. and Otter, M. (1979). History of IPA: Part II. *IPA Newsletter*, 7, 3–4.

Ackerman, D. (1999). *Deep play*. New York: Random House.

Addams, J. (1909). *The spirit of youth and the city streets*. New York: Macmillan.

—— (1945). *Twenty years at Hull House with autobiographical notes*. New York: Macmillan.

Allen, Lady of Hurtwood. (1968). *Planning for play*. Cambridge, MA: MIT Press.

Almon, J. (2009). The fear of play. *Exchange Magazine*, March–April. www.childcareexchange.com/eed/issue.php?id=2202.

Alsberg, H. G. (1934). *America fights the Depression: A photographic record of the Civil Works Administration*. New York: Coward-McCann.

Alschuler, R. H. and Heinig, C. (1936). *Childhood play*. Washington, D.C.: Association for Childhood Education International.

American Society for Testing and Materials. (1993). *Standard consumer safety performance specification for playground equipment for public use*. West Conshohocken, PA: The Society.

Amrein, A. L. and Berliner, D. C. (2002). The impact of high-stakes testing on student academic performance (research report). Tempe, AZ: Arizona State University, Education Policy Studies Laboratory.

Andrews, E. L. (1998). Where a lawsuit can't get any respect. *New York Times*, March 15.

Aries, P. (1962). *Centuries of childhood*. New York: Random House.

Aristotle. (1925). *Works of Aristotle*. Oxford: The Clarendon Press.

—— (1943). *Politics*. New York: The Modern Library.

Association for Childhood Education International (ACEI). (2001). ACEI position paper on standardized testing (by Vito Perrone), http://www.acei.org/onstandard.html.

Association of Children's Museums. (2008). http:www.children'smuseums.org.

Axline, V. (1947a). Nondirective play therapy for poor readers. *Journal of Consulting Psychology*, 11, 61–9.

—— (1947b). *Play therapy: The inner dynamics of childhood*. Boston: Houghton-Mifflin.

Bailey, L. H. (1905). *The nature study idea*. New York: Doubleday.

Barros, R. M., Silver, E. J., and Stein, R. E. K. (2009). School recess and group classroom behavior. *Pediatrics*, 123(2), 431–6.

Bartoletti, S. C. (1996). *Growing up in coal country*. Boston, MA: Houghton Mifflin.

Beckwith, J. (1985). Equipment selection criteria for modern playgrounds. In J. L. Frost and S. Sunderlin (Eds.), *When children play* (pp. 209–14). Wheaton, MD: Association for Childhood Education International.

Begley, S. (1996). Your child's brain. *Newsweek*, February 29, 55–8.

Bekoff, M. and Begley, S. (2001). Social play behavior: Cooperation, fairness, trust, and the evolution of morality. *Journal of Consciousness Studies*, 8, 8–81.

Bengtsson, A. (1972). *Adventure playgrounds*. New York: Praeger.

—— (1979). History of IPA: Part III. *IPA Newsletter*, 7, 6–8.

Benjamin, J. (1974). *Grounds for play: In search of adventure*. London: Bedford Square Press.

Bloom, M. (2009). Lunchrooms latch onto coffee craze. *Austin American-Statesman*, February 19, pp. A1, A6.

Blow, S. (1908). *The songs and music of Friedrich Froebel's mother play*. New York: D. Appleton.

Brace, C. L. (1880). *The dangerous classes of New York and twenty years' work among them*. New York: Wynkoop & Hallenbeck.

Brokaw, T. (1998). *The Greatest Generation*. New York: Random House.

Brown, S. (1994, December). Animals at play. *National Geographic*, 186(6), 2–35.

—— (1997). *Discovering the intelligence of play: A new model for a new generation of children* (videotape). Available from Touch the Future, 4350 Lime Ave., Long Beach, CA 90807.

—— (1998). Play as an organizing principle. In M. Bekoff and J. Byers (Eds.). *Animal play: Evolutionary, comparative, and ecological perspectives* (pp. 243–59). Cambridge: Cambridge University Press.

Brown, S., with Vaughan, C. (2009). *Play: How it shapes the brain, opens the imagination, and invigorates the soul.* New York: Avery/Penguin.

Brownback, S. (2003). Hearing examines impact of entertainment on children's health. Washington, D.C.: Senate Subcommittee on Science, Technology, and Space. Retrieved March 15, 2004, from http://www.lionlamb.org.

Bruce, H. (1999). *Gardening for the senses: Gardening as therapy.* Winter Springs, FL: Winner Enterprises.

Bruya, L. D. and Langendorfer, S. J. (1988). *Where our children play: Elementary school playground equipment.* Reston, VA: American Alliance for Health, Physical Education, Recreation, and Dance.

Bureau of Product Safety (BPS). (1972). *Public playground equipment.* Washington, D.C.: Food and Drug Administration.

Burriss, K. G. and Boyd, B. F. (Eds.). (2005). *Outdoor learning and play: Ages 8–12.* Olney, MD: Association for Childhood Education International.

Butler, G. D. (1936). *Playgrounds: Their administration and operation.* New York: A. S. Barnes.

—— (1965). *Pioneers in public recreation.* Minneapolis, MN: Burgess.

Butwinick, E. (1974). *Petition requesting the issuance of a consumer product safety standard for public playground slides, swinging apparatus and climbing equipment.* Washington, D.C.: United States Consumer Product Safety Commission.

Callois, R. (1961). *Man, play, and games.* London: Thames & Hudson.

Carr, N. (2008, July/August). Is Google making us stupid? *Atlantic Monthly,* 301(6).

Carter, J. (2001). *An hour before daylight: Memories of a rural boyhood.* New York: Simon & Schuster.

Cavallo, D. (1981). *Muscles and morals: Organized playgrounds and urban reform, 1880–1920.* Philadelphia: University of Pennsylvania Press.

Charles, C., Louv, R., Bodner, L., and Guns, B. (2008). *Children and nature 2008: A report on the movement to reconnect children to the natural world.* Santa Fe, NM: Children and Nature Network.

Children's Aid Society. (1854). *First Annual Report.* New York.

Chudacoff, H. P. (2007). *Children at play.* New York: New York University Press.

Chugani, H. T. (1994). Development of regional brain glucose metabolism in relation to behavior and plasticity. In G. Dawson and K. W. Fischer (Eds.), *Human behavior and the developing brain.* New York: Guilford Press.

Cohen, R. (Ed.). (2002). *Dear Mrs. Roosevelt.* Chapel Hill, NC: University of North Carolina Press.

Cole-Hamilton, I., Harrop, A., and Street, C. (2002). *The value of children's play and play provision: A systematic review of the literature.* London: New Policy Institute.

Coles, R. (1970). *Uprooted children: The early life of migrant farm workers.* Pittsburgh, PA: University of Pittsburgh Press.

Colson, F. H. (1924). *Quintiliani Institutio Oratoria,* Book I. Cambridge: Cambridge University Press.

Comenius, J. A. (1910). *The great didactic of Comenius,* 2nd ed. (M. W. Keatinge, Trans.). London: Adam & Charles Black.

Committee on Accident Prevention of the American Academy of Pediatrics. (1969). *Proposed voluntary standard for children's home playground equipment.* Evanston, IL: The Academy.

Consumer Product Safety Commission (CPSC). (1973). *Proposed safety requirements for heavy-duty playground equipment regulations.* Washington, D.C.: The Commission.

—— (1981a, 1981b). *A handbook for public playground safety* (two volumes). Washington, D.C.: The Commission.

—— (2008, August). *The safety review* (cpsc.gov).

Cravens, H. (1993). *Before Head Start: The Iowa Station and America's children.* Chapel Hill, NC: University of North Carolina Press.

Crawford, R. W. (1956). A new look for Philadelphia. *Recreation,* 49(9), 322–3.

Crawford, S. (2000). *Childhood in Anglo-Saxon England.* Stroud: Sutton.

Cronin, J., Dahlin, M., Atkins, D., and Kingsbury, G. (2007). *The proficiency illusion.* Washington, D.C.: Thomas B. Fordham Institute.

Csikszentmihalyi, M. (1990). *Flow: The psychology of optimum experience.* New York: Harper & Row.

Curtis, H. S. (1914). *Play and recreation for the open country.* Boston: Ginn.

—— (1917). *The play movement and its significance.* Washington, D.C.: McGrath Publishing Co., and National Recreation and Park Association.

Daniels, B. C. (1995). *Puritans at play: Leisure and recreation in Colonial New England.* New York: St. Martin's Press.

Daniels, S. (2006). The consequences of childhood overweight and obesity. *Childhood Obesity,* 16(1), 47–68.

Darian-Smith, K. and Factor, J. (2005). *Child's play: Dorothy Howard and the folklore of Australian children.* Melbourne, Australia: Museum Victoria.

David, J. (Ed.). (1968). *Growing up Black: From slave days to the present—25 African-Americans reveal the trials and triumphs of their childhoods.* New York: Avon Books.

Davis, A. F. (1967). *Spearheads for reform: The social settlements and the progressive movement 1890–1914.* New York: Oxford University Press.

Davis, M. (1936). *The lost generation.* New York: Macmillan.

Deckelbaum, R. J. and Williams, C. L. (2001). Childhood obesity: The health issue. *Obesity Research,* 9, S239–43.

DeMause, L. (1974). *The history of childhood.* New York: Psychohistory Press.

Dennison, B., Straus, J. H., Mellits, E. D., and Charney, E. (1988). Childhood physical fitness tests: Predictor of adult physical activity levels? *Pediatrics,* 82, 3.

Dewey, J. (1896). Imagination and expression. In *John Dewey: The early works, 1882–1898.* Carbondale, IL: University of Illinois Press.

Dietz, W. (2001). The obesity epidemic in young children. *British Medical Journal,* 322: 313–14.

Dietz, W. and Gortmaker, S. L. (1985). Do we fatten our children at the television set? Obesity and television viewing in children and adolescents. *Pediatrics,* 75, 807–12.

Din, H. W. (1998). "A history of children's museums in the United States, 1899–1997: Implications for art and music education in art museums." Unpublished doctoral dissertation, Ohio State University.

Doidge, N. (2007). *The brain that changes itself: Stories of personal triumph from the frontiers of brain science.* London: Penguin.

Dorgan, E. J. (1934). *Luther Halsey Gulick: 1865–1918.* Washington, D.C.: McGrath.

Douglass, F. (1978). Narrative of the life of Frederick Douglass, an American slave. In T. L. Webber (Ed.), *Deep like the rivers: Education in the slave quarter community 1831–1865.* New York: W. W. Norton.

Dulles, F. R. (1940). *America learns to play.* New York: D. Appleton-Century.

Dupree, A. H. (1957). *Science in the Federal government: A history of policies and activities in 1940.* Cambridge, MA: Belknap Press.

Earle, A. M. (1898). *Home life in Colonial days.* New York: Macmillan (reprinted 1953).

—— (1899). *Child life in Colonial days.* New York: Macmillan.

Eastman, C. A. (1902). *Indian boyhood.* Williamstown, MS: Corner House Publishers (reprinted 1975).

Eells, E. (1986). *History of organized camping: The first 100 years.* Martinsville, IN: American Camping Association.

Egan, T. (2006). *The worst hard time.* Boston: Houghton Mifflin.

Eifermann, R. R. (1971). Social play in childhood. In R. B. Herron and B. Sutton-Smith (Eds.), *Child's play.* New York: John Wiley & Sons.

European Committee for Standardization. (1998). *European standard for playground equipment.* Brussels: The Committee.

Evans, G. W. and Schamberg, M. A. (2009). Childhood poverty, chronic stress, and adult working memory. *Proceedings of the National Academy of Science,* Early Edition (daily online), April 7, 106(14).

Ferguson, C. J. and Dettore, E. (Eds.). (2007). *To play or not to play: Is it really a question?* Olney, MD: Association for Childhood Education International.

Foster, J. C. and Mattson, M. L. (1929). *Nursery school procedure.* New York: D. Appleton.

Frederickson, W., Jr. (1959). Planning play equipment. *Recreation,* 52, 186–9.

Freedman, R. (1983). *Children of the wild west.* New York: Clarion Books.

Freud, A. (1946). *The psychoanalytical treatment of children.* London: Imago.

Freud, S. (1909). Analysis of a phobia in a five year old boy. In *The standard edition of the complete psychological works of Sigmund Freud*. London: Hogarth.

Freud, S. (1938). *The basic writings of Sigmund Freud* (A. A. Brill, Trans. and Ed.). New York: Modern Library.

Froebel, F. (1887, 1902). *Education of man* (W. N. Hailmann, Trans.). New York: Appleton (original trans. 1826).

—— (1908). *Autobiography of Friedrich Froebel*. London: Swan Sonnenschein.

—— (1909). *Pedagogics of the kindergarten*. New York: D. Appleton.

Fromberg, D. P. and Bergen, D. (2006). *Play from birth to twelve and beyond: Contexts, perspectives, and meanings*, 2nd ed.. New York: Garland Publishers.

Frost, J. L. (1975). At risk. *Childhood Education*, April–May, 51, 298–304.

—— (1986a). Children in a changing society: Frontiers of challenge. *Childhood Education*, March–April, 242–8.

—— (1986b). Children's playgrounds: Research and practice. In G. Fein and M. Rivkin (Eds.), *The young child at play: Reviews of research* (Vol. 4). Washington, D.C.: National Association for the Education of Young Children.

—— (1988). The evolution of American playgrounds. *Young Children*, 43(5), 19–28.

—— (1989). Play environments for young children in the USA: 1800–1990. *Children's Environments Quarterly*, 6(4), 17–24.

—— (1992). *Play and playscapes*. Albany, NY: Delmar.

—— (1997). Child development and playgrounds. *Parks and Recreation*. Arlington, VA: National Recreation and Park Association.

—— (2003). Bridging the gaps: Children in a changing society. *Childhood Education*, 80(1), 29–34.

—— (2004). How adults enhance or mess up children's play. *Archives of Pediatrics and Adolescent Medicine*, 158(1), 16.

—— (2005a, December). How playground regulations and standards are messing up children's play. *Today's Playground*, 5(7), 14–19.

—— (2005b. Lessons from disasters: Play, work, and the creative arts. *Childhood Education*, 82(1), 2–8.

—— (2006a). The dissolution of outdoor play: Causes and consequences, http://www.ipema.orgnews/default.aspx.

—— (2006b, March–April). Revisit the safety rules: Part II. *Today's Playground*, 6(1), 28–35.

—— (2007, Summer). The changing culture of childhood: A perfect storm. *Childhood Education*, 83(4), 225–33.

—— (2008a, August). Playworkers: An antidote for adult interference in children's play. *Playground Magazine*, 8(4), 12–15.

—— (2008b, September). Reconnecting children: The art of creative play and work. *Playground Magazine*, 8(6), 26–9.

Frost, J. L., Bowers, L. E., and Wortham, S. C. (1990). The state of American preschool playgrounds. *Journal of Physical Education, Recreation and Dance*, October, 91–6.

Frost, J. L. and Brown, S. (2008, July). The consequences of play deprivation. *Playground Magazine*, 8(3), 26–30.

Frost, J. L., Brown, P. S., Sutterby, J. A., and Thornton, C. D. (2004). *The developmental benefits of playgrounds*. Olney, MD: Association for Childhood Education International.

Frost, J. L. and Jacobs, P. (1995). Play deprivation and juvenile violence. *Dimensions*, 23(3), 13–20.

Frost, J. L., Keyburn, D., and Sutterby, J. A. (2009, in press). Notes from the land down under: Transforming sterile schoolyards into nature and play wonderlands. In J. Hoot and J. Szente, *The earth is our home: Children caring for the environment*. Wheaton, MD: Association for Childhood Education International.

Frost, J. L. and Kissinger, J. B. (1976). *The young child and the educative process*. New York: Holt, Rinehart and Winston.

Frost, J. L. and Klein, B. L. (1979). *Children's play and playgrounds*. Boston: Allyn & Bacon (reprinted 1983, Austin, TX: Playscapes International).

Frost, J. L. and Sunderlin, S. (Eds.). (1985). *When children play: Proceedings of the International Conference on Play and Play Environments*. Wheaton, MD: Association for Childhood Education International.

Frost, J. L. and Wortham, S. C. (1988). The evolution of American playgrounds. *Young Children*, 43(5), 19–28.

Frost, J. L., Wortham, S. C., and Reifel, S. (2005, 3rd ed. 2008). *Play and child development*. Upper Saddle River, NJ: Merrill Prentice Hall.

Fry, A. R. (1994). *The orphan trains*. New York: New Discovery Books.

Furedi, F. (2005). Making sense of child safety. In S. Waiton and S. Baird, *Cotton wool kids: Making sense of child safety* (pp. 4–6). Glasgow, U.K.: Generation Youth Issues.

Garrison, C. G. (1926). *Permanent play materials for young children.* New York: Charles Scribner's Sons.

Garrison, C. G., Shelly, E. D., and Dalgliesh, A. (1937). *The Horace Mann kindergarten for five-year-old children.* New York: Teachers College, Columbia University Bureau of Publications.

Gill, T. (2005). If you go down to the woods. *Ecologist.* Cited in *Exchange Every Day*, April 17, 2006, http://www.childcareexchange.com/eed/issue.php?id+1440 or http://www.theecologist.org/archive_detail.asp?content_id = 481.

Ginsberg, O. (2000). Sustainability from the children's perspective—A journey through the landscape of German children's city farms, http://www.cityfarmer.org/germancfarms.html.

Ginsburg, K. R. (2006). Clinical report: The importance of play in promoting healthy child development and maintaining strong parent–child bonds. *American Academy of Pediatrics* (enter "AAP Play" in an Internet search engine).

Golden, M. (1990). *Children and childhood in classical Athens.* Baltimore, MD: Johns Hopkins Press.

Goodenough, E. (Ed.). (2007). *Where do the children play?* Michigan Television.

—— (2008). *A place for play.* The National Institute for Play.

Gore, A. (2006). *An inconvenient truth: The planetary emergency of global warming and what we can do about it.* New York: Rodale Books.

Green, H. (2007). Exercise and healthy eating. *Exchange Every Day*, November 29.

Greene, M. L. (1911). *Among School Gardens.* New York: Russell Sage Foundation.

Greenman, J. (2005). *Caring spaces, learning places: Children's environments that work.* Redmond, WA: Exchange Press.

Groos, K. (1898). *The play of animals.* New York: D. Appleton.

—— (1901). *The play of man.* New York: D. Appleton.

Grotberg, E. (1975). *200 years of children.* Washington, D.C.: U.S. Dept. of Health, Education, and Welfare.

Grover, K. (1992). *Hard at play: Leisure in America, 1840–1940.* Amherst: University of Massachusetts Press; Rochester, NY: The Strong Museum.

Gulick, L. H. (1909, July). Popular recreation and public morality. *Annals of the American Academy of Political and Social Science*, 34, 34.

—— (1915). The social function of play. *Journal of Education*, 81, 598–9.

—— (1920). *A philosophy of play.* Washington, D.C.: McGrath.

Hale, E. E. (1908). *A New England boyhood.* New York: Grosset & Dunlap (reprinted 1927).

Hall, G. S. (1923). *Life and confessions of a psychologist.* New York: Appleton.

Hamlin, G. (1917). *A son of the middle border.* New York: Grosset & Dunlap.

Hanawalt, B. A. (1993). *Growing up in medieval London: The experience of childhood in history.* New York: Oxford University Press.

Hardy, S. (1982). *How Boston played: Sport, recreation, and community 1865-1915.* Boston, MA: Northeastern University Press.

Harris, M. J., Mitchell, F. D., and Schechter, S. J. (1984). *The homefront: America during World War II.* New York: G. P. Putnam's Sons.

Hart, R. A. (1997). *Children's participation: The theory and practice of involving young citizens in community development and environmental care.* London: Earthscan Publications and UNICEF.

Hawke, D. F. (1988). *Everyday life in early America.* New York: Harper & Row.

Healy, J. M. (1990). *Endangered minds: Why our children don't think.* New York: Simon & Schuster.

—— (1998). *Failure to connect: How computers affect our children's minds.* New York: Simon & Schuster.

Hemenway, H. D. (1909). *How to make school gardens.* New York: Doubleday.

Hetherington, C. W. (1914). The demonstration play school. *Education*, 5(2), 679–707.

Hetherington, E. M. (Ed.). (1975). *Review of child development research.* Chicago: University of Chicago Press.

Hewes, D. (Ed.). (1976). NAEYC's first half century 1926–76. *Young Children*, September, pp. 462–76.

Hill, P. S. (1923). *A conduct curriculum for the kindergarten and first grade.* New York: Charles Scribner's Sons.

—— (1942). *Kindergarten.* Washington, D.C.: Association for Childhood Education International.

Hirsh-Pasek, K. and Golinkoff, R. M. (2003). *Einstein never used flash cards.* New York: Rodale.

Hodge, C. F. (1902). *Nature study and life.* Boston and London: Ginn.

Hogan, P. (1995). *Philadelphia boyhood: Growing up in the 1930s.* Vienna, VA: Holbrook & Kellogg.

Holtzclaw, W. H. (1968). The Black man's burden. In J. David (Ed.), *Growing up Black* (pp. 106–19). New York: Avon Books.

Hoover, H. (1930). Address of President Hoover. In *White House Conference: 1930*. New York: The Century Co.

Howard, D. (1977). *Dorothy's world: Childhood in Sabine Bottom, 1902–1910*. Englewood Cliffs, NJ: Prentice-Hall.

Hug-Hellmuth, H. (1921). On the technique of child analysis. *International Journal of Child Analysis*, 2, 287.

Ikeda, D. (1979). *Glass children and other essays* (B. Watson, Trans.). Tokyo: Kodanska International.

International Kindergarten Union (IKU). (1913). *The kindergarten: Reports of the Committee of Nineteen on the theory and practice of the kindergarten*. Boston: Houghton Mifflin.

Iowa Child Welfare Research Station. (1934). *Manual of nursery school practice*. Bulletin of the State University of Iowa, Iowa City, IA: The University.

Jacobson, W. (1940). Safety versus lawsuits. *Recreation*, 34(2).

Jago, L. (1971). *Learning through experience*. London: London Adventure Playground Association.

James, W. (1890). *The principles of psychology*. New York: Henry Holt.

Johnson, G. E. (1907, 1937). *Education by play and games*. Boston: Ginn.

Johnson, S. (2004). *Mind wide open: Your brain and the neuroscience of everyday life*. New York: Scribner.

Jones, H. E. (1956). The replacement problem in child analysis. *Child Development*, 27, 237–40.

Keeler, R. (2008). *Natural playscapes*. Redmond, WA: Exchange Press.

Kellert, S. R. (2005). *Building for life: Designing and understanding the human–nature connection*. Washington, D.C.: Island Press.

Kirkpatrick, E. A. (1903). *Fundamentals of child study: A discussion of instincts and other factors in human development with its practical applications*. New York: Macmillan.

Klein, M. (1932). *The psychoanalysis of children*. London: Hogarth.

Knapp, R. F. and Hartsoe, C. E. (1979). *Play for America: The National Recreation Association 1906–1965*. Arlington, VA: National Recreation and Park Association.

Koch, K. (1908). Folk and child play: Report of the Central Committee on Folk and Child Play in Germany. *American Physical Education Review*, 13 (A. L. von der Osten, Trans.).

Kozol, J. (1991). *Savage inequalities: Children in America's schools*. New York: Harper Perennial.

Lambert, J. (1992). *Adventure playgrounds: A book for play leaders*. N.p.: Out of Order Books.

Lambert, J. and Pearson, J. (1974). *Adventure playgrounds*. Baltimore, MD: Penguin Books.

Lancy, D. F. and Tindall, A. (1976). *The anthropological study of play: Problems and prospects*. Cornwall, NY: Leisure Press.

Landreth, G. (1991, 2002). *Play therapy: The art of the relationship*. Bristol, PA: Accelerated Development.

Larcom, L. (1889). *A New England girlhood: Outlined from memory*. Williamstown, MS: Corner House Publishers (reprinted 1985).

Lawson, L. J. (2005). *City bountiful: A century of community gardening in America*. Berkeley: University of California Press.

Layard, R. and Dunn, J. (2009). *A good childhood: Searching for values in a competitive age*. London: Penguin.

Ledermann, A. and Trachsel, A. (1959). Creative playgrounds and recreation centers. *Recreation*, 20(8), 436–8.

Lee, J. (1902). *Constructive and preventive philanthropy*. New York: Macmillan.

—— (1915). A brief history of the playground movement in America. *The Playground*, 9(1), 2–11, 39–45.

—— (1920). Foreword to L. H. Gulick's *A philosophy of play*. Washington, D.C.: National Recreation and Park Association.

—— (1927). Play, the architect of man. *The Playground*, 21(9), 460–3.

—— (1929). *Play in education*. New York: Macmillan.

Lehman, H. C. and Witty, P. A. (1926). Changing attitudes toward play. *The Playground*, 20(8), 436–8.

Lenhart, A., Kahne, J., Middaugh, E., Macgill, A., Evans, C., and Vitak, J. (2008). *Teens, video games and civics: Teens' gaming experiences are diverse and include significant social interaction and civic engagement*. Pew Internet and American Life Project. Retrieved September 17, 2008, from www.pewinternet.org/PPF/r/263/report-display.asp.

Levinson, B. (1972). *Companion animals and human development*. Springfield, IL: Charles C. Thomas.

Levy, J., Vinter, S., Laurent, R. S., and Segal, L. M. (2009). *F as in fat: How obesity policies are failing in America*. Washington, D.C.: Trust for America's Health and Robert Wood Johnson Foundation.

Liebschner, J. (1992). *A child's work: Freedom and guidance in Froebel's educational theory and practice*. Cambridge: The Lutterworth Press.

Lipton, M. A. (1974). Paper presented at a National Conference on Early Intervention, May 5–8. University of North Carolina at Chapel Hill.

Lloyd, F. S. (1931). Play as a means of character education for the individual. *Recreation*, 24(11), 587–92.

Locke, J. (1902). *How to bring up your children*. London: Sampon Low, Marston & Co.

—— (1989). *Some thoughts concerning education*. Oxford: Clarendon Press.

Louv, R. (2005). *Last child in the woods: Saving our children from nature-deficit disorder* (rev. ed. 2008). Chapel Hill, NC: Aloquin Books.

—— (2008). *Last child in the woods: Saving our children from nature-deficit disorder* (rev. ed.). Chapel Hill, NC: Aloquin Books.

McConnell, W. H. (1973). *Public playground equipment*, October 15. Iowa City, IA: College of Medicine.

MacElroy, M. H. (1929*). Work and play in Colonial days*. New York: Macmillan.

McKibben, B. (1989). *The end of nature*. New York: Random House.

McLerran, A. (1991). *Roxaboxen*. New York: Lothrop, Lee & Shepard Books.

Marano, J. E. (2008). *A nation of wimps: The high cost of invasive parenting*. New York: Broadway Books.

Marcus, B. H., Williams, D. M., Dubbert, P. M., Sallis, J. F., King, A. C., Yancey, A. K., Franklin, B. A., Buchner, D., Daniels, S. R., and Claytor, R. P. (2006). Physical activity intervention studies: What we know and what we need to know. A scientific statement from the American Heart Council on Nutrition, Physical Activity, and Metabolism. *Circulation*, 114, 2739–52.

Marten, J. (2005). *Childhood and child welfare in the Progressive Era: A brief history with documents*. Boston: Bedford/St. Martin's.

Maslow, A. H. (1962). Some basic propositions of a growth and self-actualization psychology. In Association for Supervision and Curriculum Development Yearbook. *Perceiving, Behaving, Becoming: A New Focus for Education*. Washington, D.C.: Association for Supervision and Curriculum Development.

Mauldin, M. A. and Giles, J. R. (1989). *Adventure playground final evaluation report*. Houston, TX: Mauldin Consulting Services.

Mead, M. (1928). *Coming of age in Samoa*. New York: Morrow.

—— (1956). *New lives for old: Cultural transformation–Manus, 1928–1953*. New York: Morrow.

Meisels, S. J. and Atkins-Burnett, S. (2004, January). The Head Start National Reporting System: A critique. Beyond the journal—*Young Children* on the web. Retrieved from www.journal. naeyc.org/btj/200401/meisels.asp.

Mendoza, J. A., Zimmerman, F. J., and Christakis, D. A. (2007). Television viewing, computer use, obesity, and adiposity in US preschool children. *International Journal of Behavioral Nutrition and Physical Activity*, 4, 44. Retrieved July 16, 2008, from http://www.ijbnpa.org/content/4/1/44.

Mero, E. B. (Ed.). (1908). *American playgrounds*. New York: Macmillan.

Millar, S. (1954). *The psychology of play*. New York: Jason Aronson.

Miller, P. (1939). *The New England mind in the seventeenth century*. Cambridge, MA: Harvard University Press.

Mintz, S. (2004). *Huck's raft: A history of American childhood*. Cambridge, MA: Harvard University Press.

MIT News Office. (2006). MIT researchers watch brain in action. July 27. http://web.mit.edu/ newsoffice/2006/.

Mitchell, E. D. (1937). *The theory of play*. Baltimore, MD: Penguin Books.

Mitchell, E. D. and Mason, B. S. (1934). *The theory of play*. New York: A. S. Barnes.

Mokdad, A. H., Marks, J. S., Stroup, D. F., and Gerberding, J. L. (2004, March). Actual causes of death in the United States, 2000. *Journal of the American Medical Association*, 291(10), 1238.

Moore, R. C. and Wong, H. H. (1997). *Natural learning: Creating environments for rediscovering nature's way of teaching*. Berkeley, CA: MIG Communications.

Morgan, E. S. (1966). *The Puritan family: Religion and domestic relations in seventeenth-century New England*. New York: Harper & Row (original work published 1923).

Moustakas, C. E. (1953). *Children in play therapy*. New York: McGraw-Hill.

Murchison, C. (Ed.). (1931). *A handbook of child psychology*. Worcester, MA: Clark University Press.

Musselman, V. (1950). What about our playgrounds? *Recreation*, 44(4), 5.

—— (1956). Firming the foundation. *Recreation*, 49(2), 62.

Nabhan, G. P. and Trimble, S. (1994). *The geography of childhood: Why children need wild places.* Boston: Beacon Press.

NAEYC Organizational History and Archives Committee. (1976). NAEYC's first half century 1926–76. *Young Children,* September, pp. 462–76.

NAEYC Website. (2007). *History of NAEYC.* Washington, D.C.: The Association.

Nash, J. M. (1997). Fertile minds. *Time: Special Report,* February 3, pp. 48–56.

National Association for the Education of Young Children (NAEYC). (1988). *Testing of young children: Concerns and cautions.* Washington, D.C.: The Association.

National Center for Health Statistics. (2008). *Prevalence of overweight among children and adolescents: United States, 2003–2004.* Retrieved July 13, 2008, from http://www.cdc.gov/nchs/nhanes.htm.

National Coalition on Television Violence. (1985, May–June). N.C.T.V. Newsletter, 6.

National Institutes of Health, Office of Dietary Supplements. (2008). *Dietary Supplement Fact Sheet: Vitamin D.* http://ods.od.nih.gov/factsheets/vitamind.asp.

National Recreation Association (NRA). (1931). Report of Committee on Standards in Playground Apparatus (Bulletin 2170). New York: The Association.

National Recreation Association (NRA). (1954). Play sculptures for playgrounds. *Recreation,* 47(8), 500–1.

—— (1957). "Dennis the Menace" playground. *Recreation,* 50(136–7), 151.

—— (1958). Imagination visits the playground. *Recreation,* 52, 130–1.

—— (1959). Designs for play. *Recreation,* 52(4), 130–1.

—— (1960). Playgrounds in action. *Recreation,* 53, 154–5.

—— (1962). Playground equipment: Today and tomorrow. *Recreation,* 55, 187–9.

National Recreation and Park Association (NRPA). (1976). *Proposed Safety Standard for Public Playground Equipment.* Arlington, VA: Consumer Product Safety Commission.

Neergaard, L. (2007). Researchers: Kids' bones weaker; rickets reappears. *Austin American Statesman,* November 27, p. A-9.

Negroponte, N. (1995). *Being digital.* New York: Vintage.

Nichols, R. B. (1955). New concepts behind designs for modern playgrounds. *Recreation,* 48(4), 154–7.

Nichols, S. L. and Berliner, D. C. (2007). *Collateral damage: How high stakes testing corrupts America's schools.* Cambridge, MA: Harvard Education Press.

Nichols, S. L. and Berliner, D. C. (2008, March). Taking the joy out of learning. *Educational Leadership,* 65, 6.

Nichols, S. L., Glass, G. V., and Berliner, D. C. (2005). *High stakes testing and student achievement: Problems for the No Child Left Behind Act.* Tempe, AZ: Arizona State University, Education Policy Studies Laboratory.

Nicholson, M. (1971). *Adventure playgrounds.* London: National Playing Fields Association.

Ogden, C. L., Carroll, M. D., Curtin, L. R., McDowell, M. A., Tabuk, C. J., and Flegal, K. M. (2006, April 5). Prevalence of overweight and obesity in the United States, 1999–2004. *Journal of the American Medical Association,* 295(13), 1549–55.

Opie, I. (1993). *The people in the playground.* New York: Oxford University Press.

Opie, I. and Opie, P. (1969). *Children's games in street and playground.* Oxford: Clarendon Press.

Oppenheimer, T. (2003). *The flickering mind: The false promise of technology in the classroom and how learning can be saved.* New York: Random House.

Orme, N. (2001). *Medieval children.* New Haven, CT: Yale University Press.

Painter, F. V. N. (1889). *Luther on education.* Philadelphia, PA: Lutheran Publication Society.

Palmer, L. A. (1916). *Play life in the first eight years.* Boston: Ginn.

Pattnik, J. (2004/05). On behalf of their animal friends: Involving children in animal advocacy. *Childhood Education,* 81, 95–100.

Pecora, N., Murray, J. P., and Wartella, E. A. (2007). *Children and television: Fifty years of research.* Mahwah, NJ: Lawrence Erlbaum Associates.

Perry, B. D. (1996). Neurodevelopmental factors in the "cycle of violence." *Children, youth, and violence: Searching for solutions* (pp. 1–122). New York: Guilford.

Pestalozzi, J. H. (1892). *Leonard and Gertrude.* Boston: D. C. Heath.

—— (1977). *How Gertrude teaches her children.* New York: Gordon Press.

Piaget, J. (1951). *Play, dreams and imitation in childhood.* London: Routledge & Kegan Paul.

Playground Association of America (PAA). (1908). *Proceedings of the Second Annual Playground Congress and Yearbook.* New York: The Playground Association.

—— (1910). Proceedings of the third annual conference of the Playground Association: Report of the Committee on Development. *The Playground,* 4(1), 270–84.

Playground and Recreation Association of America. (1925). *The normal course in play*. New York: The Association.

Plato. (1952) *The dialogues of Plato*. Chicago: Encyclopedia Britannica Inc.

—— (2000). *Laws*. Amherst, NY: Prometheus Books.

Popham, W. J. (2002, February). Today's standardized tests are not the best way to evaluate schools or students: Right task–wrong tool. *American School Board Journal*, 21.

Quintilian. (1965). *On the early education of the citizen-orator*. New York: The Bobbs-Merrill Co.

Rainwater, C. E. (1922). *The play movement in the United States*. Washington, D.C.: McGrath.

Rajakumar, K. and Thomas, S. (2005). Reemerging nutritional rickets: A historical perspective. *Archives of Pediatrics and Adolescent Medicine*, 159, 335–41.

Rawick, G. P. (1972). *From sundown to sunup: The making of the Black community*. Westport, CT: Greenwood Publishing.

Rawls, W. (1961). *Where the red fern grows*. New York: Bantam Books.

Rheingold, H. L. (1985). The first twenty-five years of the Society for Research in Child Development. In A. B. Smuts and J. H. Hagen (Eds.), *History and research in child development* (pp. 126–40). Monographs of the Society for Research in Child Development, 50.

Riis, J. A. (1902, later ed. 1913). The *battle with the slum*. New York: Macmillan.

—— (1957). *How the other half lives*. New York: Hill & Wang (original work published 1890).

Rivkin, M. S. (1995). *The great outdoors: Restoring children's right to play outside*. Washington, D.C.: National Association for the Education of Young Children.

Robert Wood Johnson Foundation. (2007). *Recess rules: Why the undervalued playtime may be America's best investment for healthy kids and healthy schools*. Princeton, NJ: The Foundation.

Robinson, C. M. (1908). Landscape gardening for playgrounds. In Playground Association of America, *Proceedings of the Second Annual Playground Congress* (pp. 64–74). New York: The Association.

Robinson, T. N. (2000, October). The epidemic of pediatric obesity. *Western Journal of Medicine*, 173(4), 220–1.

Roblin, B. (2001). In K. Thompson and H. MacAustin (Eds.), *Children of the Depression*. Bloomington: University of Indiana Press.

Rosenberg, K. S., Johnson, C. N., and Harris, P. L. (2000). *Imagining the impossible: Magical scientific and religious thinking in children*. New York: Cambridge University Press.

Ross, J. and Gilbert, G. (1985). The national children and youth fitness study: A summary of the findings. *Journal of Health, Physical Education, Recreation and Dance*, 56, 45–60.

Rousseau, J.-J. (2001 edn). *Emile* (B. Foxley, Trans.). London: Everyman.

Rusk, R. R. (1956). *The doctrines of the great educators*. New York: Macmillan.

Rylant, C. (1982). *When I was young in the mountains*. New York: Dutton.

Salter, M. A. (1976). Preface. In D. F. Lancy and B. A. Tindall (Eds.), *The anthropological study of play: Problems and prospects* (pp. v–vii). Cornwall, NY: Leisure Press.

Sapora, A. V. and Mitchell, E. D. (1961). *The theory of play and recreation*. New York: The Ronald Press.

Sarahan, N. and Hager, R. (1980). *Where do the children play? On adventure playgrounds*. Houston, TX: The Park People, Inc.

Scanlon, K. (Ed.). (2001). Vitamin D Expert Panel Meeting. Atlanta, GA: Centers for Disease Control.

Scheuer, L. J. and Mitchell, D. (2003). Does physical activity influence academic performance? *Sportapolis*. Retrieved October 9, 2008, from http://www.sports-media.org/sportapolisnewsletter19.html.

Schorsch, A. (1979). *Images of childhood: An illustrated social history*. New York: Mayflower Books.

Schwartzman, H. B. (1978). *Transformations: The anthropology of children's play*. New York: Plenum.

Schwimmer, J. B., Pardee, P. E., Lavine, J. E., Blumkin, A. K., and Cook, S. (2008). Cardiovascular risk factors and the metabolic syndrome in pediatric nonalcoholic fatty liver disease. *Circulation*, 118, 277–83.

Sears, R. R. (1975). Your ancients revisited: A history of child development. In E. M. Hetherington (Ed.), *Review of child development research*, 5, 1–73. Chicago: University of Chicago Press.

Senge, P., Scharmer, C. O., Jaworski, J., and Flowers, B. S. (2004). *Presence: An exploration of profound change in people, organizations and society*. New York: Doubleday.

Shahar, S. (1990). In D. Wood (Ed.), *The church and childhood* (pp. 243–60). Oxford: Oxford University Press.

Shaw, R. H. and Davenport, E. C. (1956). A playground that pleases children. *Recreation*, 49(2), 62.

Siegel, A. W. and White, S. H. (1982). The child study movement: Early growth and development of the symbolized child. *Advances in Child Development and Behavior*, 17.

Singer, D. G. and Singer, J. L. (2005). *Imagination and play in the Electronic Age*. Cambridge, MA: Harvard University Press.

Singer, D. G., Singer, J. L., D'Agostino, H., and DeLong, R. (2009, Winter). Children's pastimes and play in sixteen nations: Is free play declining? *American Journal of Play*, 1(3), 283–312.

Sluckin, A. (1981). *Growing up in the playground: The social development of children.* Boston: Routledge & Kegan Paul.

Smail, W. M. (1938). *Quintilian on education*. Oxford: Oxford University Press.

Smith, A. (2005). *The brain's behind it: New knowledge about the brain and learning*. Stafford, U.K.: Educational Press.

Smuts, A. B. (1985). The National Research Council Committee on Child Development and the founding of the Society for Research in Child Development. In A. B. Smuts and J. H. Hagen (Eds.), *History and research in child development* (pp. 108–25). Monographs of the Society for Research in Child Development, 50.

Society for Neuroscience. (2000). Exercise and the brain. Retrieved October 9, 2008, from http://www.sfn.org/index.cfm?pagename+bainBriefings_exercise.

Solley, B. A. (2007, Fall). ACEI position paper: On standardized testing. *Childhood Education*, 84(1), 31–7.

Sommers, C. (2005). One nation under therapy. In S. Waiton and S. Baird (Eds.), *Cotton wool kids: Making sense of child safety* (pp. 7–8). Glasgow, U.K.: Generation Youth Issues.

Sorensen, C. T. (1968). Preface. In L. A. Hurtwood, *Planning for play*. Cambridge, MA: MIT Press.

Spargo, J. (1906). *The bitter cry of the children*. New York: Macmillan.

Spariosu, M. (1989). *Dionysus reborn: Play and the aesthetic dimension in modern philosophical and scientific discourse*. Ithaca, NY: Cornell University Press.

Spencer, C. and Blades, M. (2006). *Children and their environments: Learning, using and designing spaces*. New York: Cambridge University Press.

Stanford Prevention Research Center, Stanford University School of Medicine. (2007). *Building 'Generation Play': Addressing the crisis of inactivity among America's children*. Stanford, CA: Stanford University.

Stanley, J. (1992). *Children of the Dust Bowl: The true story of the school at Weedpatch Camp*. New York: Scholastic, Inc.

Steinbeck, J. (1939/1992). *The grapes of wrath*. New York: Penguin Press.

Stengel, R. (1985). Snapshot of a changing America. *Time*, September 12, 16–18.

Stevens, P. (Ed.). (1977). *Studies in the anthropology of play: Papers in memory of Allan Tindall*. West Point, NY: Leisure Press.

Stine, S. (1997). *Landscapes for learning: Creating outdoor environments for children and youth*. New York: John Wiley.

Stow, E. (1924). *Boys' games among the North American Indians*. New York: E. P. Dutton.

Sutton-Smith, B. (1972). *The folk games of children*. Austin, TX: University of Texas Press.

—— (1997). *The ambiguity of play*. Cambridge, MA: Harvard University Press.

Swaminathan, S. and Yelland, N. (2003). Global perspectives on educational technology. *Childhood Education*, 79(5), 258–60.

Sweeney, T. (1974, May). *Petition to the Consumer Product Safety Commission*. Cleveland Heights, OH: Coventry School PTA.

Sylwester, R. (1995). *A celebration of neurons: An educator's guide to the human brain*. Alexandria, VA: Association for Supervision and Curriculum Development.

Tai, L., Hague, M. T., McLellan, G. K., and Knight, E. J. (2006). *Designing outdoor environments for children*. New York: McGraw-Hill.

Talbot, J. and Frost, J. L. (1989). Magical playscapes. *Childhood Education*. 66(1), 11–19.

Taylor, G. (1936). *Chicago Commons through forty years*. Chicago: Chicago Commons Association.

Terkel, S. (1970). *Hard times: An oral history of the Great Depression*. New York: Random House.

Texas Education Agency. (2008). Texas tests fitness of 2.6 million students; Finds elementary students are in best shape. Retrieved July 8, 2008, from http://www.tea.state.us/comm/page1.html.

Thompson, D. and Bowers, L. (1989). *Where our children play: Community park playground equipment*. Reston, VA: American Alliance for Health, Physical Education, Recreation and Dance.

Thompson, K. and MacAustin, H. (2001). *Children of the Depression*. Bloomington: University of Indiana Press.

Tsanoff, S. V. (1897). *Educational value of the children's playgrounds*. Philadelphia, PA: Author.

Tucker, M. J. (1974). The child as beginning and end: Fifteenth and sixteenth century English childhood. In L. DeMause (Ed.), *The history of childhood* (pp. 229–57). New York: The Psychohistory Press.

Ulich, R. (1945). *History of educational thought.* New York: American Book Co.

United States Office of Education (1933a). *Bulletin of information for emergency nursery schools: Administration and program.* Bulletin Number 1. Washington, D.C.: U.S.O.E.

—— (1933b). *Bulletin of information for emergency nursery schools: Housing and equipment.* Bulletin Number 2. Washington, D.C.: U.S.O.E.

—— (1936). *Bulletin of information for emergency nursery schools: Housing and equipment.* Bulletin Number 5. Washington, D.C.: U.S.O.E.

USA Today. (2003). Head Start resists efforts to give pupils a real boost, February 10, p. 14A.

U.S. Superintendent of Documents. (1940). First White House Conference on Children in a Democracy. Washington, D.C.

Valenzuela, A. (Ed.). (2005). *Leaving children behind: "Texas-style" accountability fails Latino youth.* Albany, NY: State University of New York Press.

Van Slyck, A. A. (2006). *A manufactured wilderness: Summer camps and the shaping of American youth.* Minneapolis, MN: University of Minnesota Press.

Vogt, M. N. and Vogt, C. (1979). *Searching for home: Three families from the orphan trains.* Grand Rapids, MI: Martha Nelson Vogt & Christina Vogt.

Wald, L. D. (1915). *The house on Henry Street.* New York: Dover Publications.

Wang, Y. and Beydoun, M. A. (2007, July 12). Obesity rates continue to climb in the United States. Johns Hopkins Bloomberg School of Public Health Center for Human Nutrition. Retrieved September 17, 2008, from http://www.sciencedaily.com/releases/2007/07/070711001502.htm.

Warner, C. D. (1877). *Being a boy.* New York: Houghton Mifflin.

Warren, A. (1996). *Orphan train rider: One boy's true story.* Boston: Houghton Mifflin.

—— (2001). *We rode the orphan trains.* Boston: Houghton Mifflin.

Washington, B. T. (1968). *Growing up Black.* New York: Avon Books (cited in J. David (Ed.), 1968).

Webber, T. L. (1978). *Deep like the rivers: Education in the slave quarter community 1831–1865.* New York: W. W. Norton.

Weber, E. (1969). *The kindergarten: Its encounter with educational thought in America.* New York: Teachers College, Columbia University.

Weikart, P. S. (1987). Round the circle: Key experiences in movement for children ages three to five. Ypsilanti, MI: High Scope Press.

West, E. (1989). *Growing up with the country: Childhood on the far western frontier.* Albuquerque: University of New Mexico Press.

What entertainers are doing to your kids. (1985). *U.S. News and World Report*, October 28, pp. 46–9.

White, C. C. and Holland, M. (1969). *No quitting sense.* Austin: University of Texas Press.

Wilson, P. (2008). The cultural origins and play philosophy of playworkers: An interview with Penny Wilson. *American Journal of Play*, 1(3), 269–82.

Winston, P. (1984). Despite fitness boom, the young remain unfit. *Education Week*, October 31, 9.

Woods, R. A. (Ed.). (1970). *The city wilderness: A settlement study of residents and associates of the south end house.* New York: Garrett Press.

Wormser, R. (1994). *Growing up in the Great Depression.* New York: Atheneum.

Wortham, S. C. (2002). *Childhood: 1892–2002.* Olney, MD: Association for Childhood Education International.

Wortham, S. C. and Frost, J. L. (1990). *Playgrounds for young children: National survey and perspectives.* Reston, VA: American Alliance for Health, Physical Education, Recreation and Dance.

Wretlind-Larsson, S. (1979). History of IPA: Part I. *IPA Newsletter*, 7, 15–17.

Index